Harry R. Moody, PhD
Editor

Religion, Spirituality, and Aging: A Social Work Perspective

Religion, Spirituality, and Aging: A Social Work Perspective has been co-published simultaneously as *Journal of Gerontological Social Work*, Volume 45, Numbers 1/2 and 3 2005.

Pre-publication
REVIEWS,
COMMENTARIES,
EVALUATIONS . . .

"This work, EDITED BY AN OUT-STANDING SCHOLAR AND ACTIVIST IN THE FIELD OF GERONTOLOGY, presents an eclectic set of contributions that individually and, in some instances, collectively can inform both professionals and non-professionals interested in the realities of aging, religion, and spirituality. While some chapters emphasize social work practice, the scope of the individual entries will appeal to a broader readership with both specialized and general interests in the themes inherent in the title."

Monsignor Charles J. Fahey
Professor Emeritus
Fordham University

More Pre-publication
REVIEWS, COMMENTARIES, EVALUATIONS . . .

"**P**rofessionals serving our older populations will gain from the content of this book. Clergy from many religions will also be better able to meet the needs of their followers based on new insights into the outcomes of spiritual and religious believers and activities. This book OFFERS CUES FOR MAKING EFFECTIVE TURNS IN OUR SPIRITUAL JOURNEYS AND IMPROVING THE QUALITY OF OUR LIVES AS WE LIVE LONGER."

James E. Birren, PhD
Associate Director
UCLA Center on Aging
Emeritus Dean and
Professor of Gerontology
University of Southern California

"**E**VERY SOCIAL WORKER AND PROFESSOR OF SOCIAL WORK SHOULD READ THIS. Religion is a vital dynamic, as is spirituality in the real world of service to older adults. Harry R. Moody has done a splendid job of pulling together an absolutely first-class group of scholars from the fields of gerontology, social work, religion, and ethics to address an extremely important gap in the social work curriculum."

Stephen Garrad Post, PhD
Professor
Department of Bioethics
Case School of Medicine
Case Western Reserve University

"**F**rom the definitive opening chapter by the eminent social gerontologist David Moberg to the erudite final chapter by Eugene Bianchi, the breadth and depth of this collection of essays provide A MAJOR CONTRIBUTION TO THE UNDERSTANDING OF RELIGION, SPIRITUALITY, AGING, AND SOCIAL WORK. These essays will both inform and challenge the reader."

Dr. Melvin A. Kimble, PhD
Professor Emeritus of Pastoral Theology and Director, Center for Aging, Religion, and Spirituality
Luther Seminary
St. Paul, Minnesota
Editor of Viktor Frankl's Contribution to Spirituality and Aging

Religion, Spirituality, and Aging: A Social Work Perspective

Religion, Spirituality, and Aging: A Social Work Perspective has been co-published simultaneously as *Journal of Gerontological Social Work*, Volume 45, Numbers 1/2 and 3 2005.

Monographic Separates from the *Journal of Gerontological Social Work*™

For additional information on these and other Haworth Press titles, including descriptions, tables of contents, reviews, and prices, use the QuickSearch catalog at http://www.HaworthPress.com.

Religion, Spirituality, and Aging: A Social Work Perspective, edited by Harry R. Moody, PhD, (Vol. 45, No. 1/2 and 3, 2005). *"From the definitive opening chapter by the eminent social gerontologist David Moberg to the erudite final chapter by Eugene Bianchi, the breadth and depth of this collection of essays provide a major contribution to the understanding of religion, spirituality, aging, and social work. These essays will both inform and challenge the reader." (Dr. Melvin A. Kimble, PhD, Professor Emeritus of Pastoral Theology and Director, Center for Aging, Religion, and Spirituality, Luther Seminary, St. Paul, Minnesota; Editor of* Viktor Frankl's Contribution to Spirituality and Aging)

Group Work and Aging: Issues in Practice, Research, and Education, edited by Robert Salmon, DSW, and Roberta Graziano, DSW (Vol. 44, No. 1/2, 2004). *Although there is a considerable amount of writing on both group work and social work with the elderly, there is surprisingly little about applying this practice method to this specific age group.* Group Work and Aging: Issues in Practice, Research, and Education *fills this gap by presenting penetrating articles about a mutual aid approach to working with diverse groups of older adults with varied needs. Respected experts and gifted researchers provide case studies, practice examples, and explanation of theory to illustrate this practice method with aging adults, their families, and their caregivers. Each well-referenced chapter delivers high quality, up-to-date social group work practice strategies to prepare practitioners for the needs of the growing population of elderly in the near future.*

Gerontological Social Work in Small Towns and Rural Communities, edited by Sandra S. Butler, PhD, and Lenard W. Kaye, DSW (Vol. 41, No. 1/2 and 3/4, 2003). *Provides a range of intervention and community skills aimed precisely at the needs of rural elders.*

Older People and Their Caregivers Across the Spectrum of Care, edited by Judith L. Howe, PhD (Vol. 40, No. 1/2, 2002). *Focuses on numerous issues relating to caregiving and social work assessment for improving quality of life for the elderly.*

Advancing Gerontological Social Work Education, edited by M. Joanna Mellor, DSW, and Joann Ivry, PhD (Vol. 39, No. 1/2, 2002). *Examines the current status of geriatric/gerontological education; offers models for curriculum development within the classroom and the practice arena.*

Gerontological Social Work Practice: Issues, Challenges, and Potential, edited by Enid Opal Cox, DSW, Elizabeth S. Kelchner, MSW, ACSW, and Rosemary Chapin, PhD, MSW (Vol. 36, No. 3/4, 2001). *This book gives you an essential overview of the role, status, and potential of gerontological social work in aging societies around the world. Drawing on the expertise of leaders in the field, it identifies key policy and practice issues and suggests directions for the future. Here you'll find important perspectives on home health care, mental health, elder abuse, older workers' issues, and death and dying, as well as an examination of the policy and practice issues of utmost concern to social workers dealing with the elderly.*

Social Work Practice with the Asian American Elderly, edited by Namkee G. Choi, PhD (Vol. 36, No. 1/2, 2001). *"Encompasses the richness of diversity among Asian Americans by including articles on Vietnamese, Japanese, Chinese, Taiwanese, Asian Indian, and Korean Americans." (Nancy R. Hooyman, PhD, MSW, Professor and Dean Emeritus, University of Washington School of Social Work, Seattle)*

Grandparents as Carers of Children with Disabilities: Facing the Challenges, edited by Philip McCallion, PhD, ACSW, and Matthew Janicki, PhD (Vol. 33, No. 3, 2000). *Here is the first comprehensive consideration of the unique needs and experiences of grandparents caring for children with developmental disabilities. The vital information found here will assist practitioners, administrators, and policymakers to include the needs of this special population in the planning and delivery of services, and it will help grandparents in this situation to better care for themselves as well as for the children in their charge.*

Latino Elders and the Twenty-First Century: Issues and Challenges for Culturally Competent Research and Practice, edited by Melvin Delgado, PhD (Vol. 30, No. 1/2, 1998). *Explores the challenges that gerontological social work will encounter as it attempts to meet the needs of the growing number of Latino elders utilizing culturally competent principles.*

Dignity and Old Age, edited by Rose Dobrof, DSW, and Harry R. Moody, PhD (Vol. 29, No. 2/3, 1998). *"Challenges us to uphold the right to age with dignity, which is embedded in the heart and soul of every man and woman." (H. James Towey, President, Commission on Aging with Dignity, Tallahassee, FL)*

Intergenerational Approaches in Aging: Implications for Education, Policy and Practice, edited by Kevin Brabazon, MPA, and Robert Disch, MA (Vol. 28, No. 1/2/3, 1997). *"Provides a wealth of concrete examples of areas in which intergenerational perspectives and knowledge are needed." (Robert C. Atchley, PhD, Director, Scribbs Gerontology Center, Miami University)*

Social Work Response to the White House Conference on Aging: From Issues to Actions, edited by Constance Corley Saltz, PhD, LCSW (Vol. 27, No. 3, 1997). *"Provides a framework for the discussion of issues relevant to social work values and practice, including productive aging, quality of life, the psychological needs of older persons, and family issues." (Jordan I. Kosberg, PhD, Professor and PhD Program Coordinator, School of Social Work, Florida International University, North Miami, FL)*

Special Aging Populations and Systems Linkages, edited by M. Joanna Mellor, DSW (Vol. 25, No. 1/2, 1996). *"An invaluable tool for anyone working with older persons with special needs." (Irene Gutheil, DSW, Associate Professor, Graduate School of Social Service, Fordham University)*

New Developments in Home Care Services for the Elderly: Innovations in Policy, Program, and Practice, edited by Lenard W. Kaye, DSW (Vol. 24, No. 3/4, 1995). *"An excellent compilation. . . . Especially pertinent to the functions of administrators, supervisors, and case managers in home care. . . . Highly recommended for every home care agency and a must for administrators and middle managers." (Geriatric Nursing Book Review)*

Geriatric Social Work Education, edited by M. Joanna Mellor, DSW, and Renee Solomon, DSW (Vol. 18, No. 3/4, 1992). *"Serves as a foundation upon which educators and fieldwork instructors can build courses that incorporate more aging content." (SciTech Book News)*

Vision and Aging: Issues in Social Work Practice, edited by Nancy D. Weber, MSW (Vol. 17, No. 3/4, 1992). *"For those involved in vision rehabilitation programs, the book provides practical information and should stimulate readers to revise their present programs of care." (Journal of Vision Rehabilitation)*

Health Care of the Aged: Needs, Policies, and Services, edited by Abraham Monk, PhD (Vol. 15, No. 3/4, 1990). *"The chapters reflect firsthand experience and are competent and informative. Readers . . . will find the book rewarding and useful. The text is timely, appropriate, and well-presented." (Health & Social Work)*

Twenty-Five Years of the Life Review: Theoretical and Practical Considerations, edited by Robert Disch, MA (Vol. 12, No. 3/4, 1989). *This practical and thought-provoking book examines the history and concept of the life review.*

Gerontological Social Work: International Perspectives, edited by Merl C. Hokenstad, Jr., PhD, and Katherine A. Kendall, PhD (Vol. 12, No. 1/2, 1988). *"Makes a very useful contribution in examining the changing role of the social work profession in serving the elderly." (Journal of the International Federation on Ageing)*

Gerontological Social Work Practice with Families: A Guide to Practice Issues and Service Delivery, edited by Rose Dobrof, DSW (Vol. 10, No. 1/2, 1987). *An in-depth examination of the importance of family relationships within the context of social work practice with the elderly.*

Ethnicity and Gerontological Social Work, edited by Rose Dobrof, DSW (Vol. 9, No. 4, 1987). *"Addresses the issues of ethnicity with great sensitivity. Most of the topics addressed here are rarely addressed in other literature." (Dr. Milada Disman, Department of Behavioral Science, University of Toronto)*

Religion, Spirituality, and Aging:
A Social Work Perspective

Harry R. Moody, PhD
Editor

Religion, Spirituality, and Aging: A Social Work Perspective has been co-published simultaneously as *Journal of Gerontological Social Work*, Volume 45, Numbers 1/2 and 3 2005.

The Haworth Social Work Practice Press
An Imprint of The Haworth Press, Inc.

New York • London • Victoria (AU)
www.HaworthPress.com

Published by

The Haworth Social Work Practice Press, 10 Alice Street, Binghamton, NY 13904-1580 USA

The Haworth Social Work Practice Press is an imprint of The Haworth Press, Inc., 10 Alice Street, Binghamton, NY 13904-1580 USA.

Religion, Spirituality, and Aging: A Social Work Perspective has been co-published simultaneously as *Journal of Gerontological Social Work,* Volume 45, Numbers 1/2 and 3 2005.

The development, preparation, and publication of this work has been undertaken with great care. However, the publisher, employees, editors, and agents of The Haworth Press and all imprints of The Haworth Press, Inc., including The Haworth Medical Press® and Pharmaceutical Products Press®, are not responsible for any errors contained herein or for consequences that may ensue from use of materials or information contained in this work. Opinions expressed by the author(s) are not necessarily those of The Haworth Press, Inc. With regard to case studies, identities and circumstances of individuals discussed herein have been changed to protect confidentiality. Any resemblance to actual persons, living or dead, is entirely coincidental.

Cover design by Kerry E. Mack

Library of Congress Catalog-in-Publication Data

Religion, spirituality, and aging: a social work perspective/Harry R. Moody, editor.
    p. cm.
    "Co-published simultaneously as Journal of gerontological social work, volume 45, numbers 1/2 and 3 2005"–T. p. verso.
    Includes bibliographical references and index.
    ISBN-10: 0-7890-2498-5 (hard cover: alk. paper)
    ISBN-13: 978-0-7890-2498-5 (hard cover: alk. paper)
    ISBN-10: 0-7890-2499-3 (soft cover: alk. paper)
    ISBN-13: 978-0-7890-2499-2 (soft cover: alk. paper)
1. Older Christians–Religious life. 2. Aging–Religious aspects–Christianity. 3. Older people–Services for. I. Moody, Harry R.
BV4580.R46 2005
259´.3–dc22
                                         2005008218

Indexing, Abstracting & Website/Internet Coverage

This section provides you with a list of major indexing & abstracting services and other tools for bibliographic access. That is to say, each service began covering this periodical during the year noted in the right column. Most Websites which are listed below have indicated that they will either post, disseminate, compile, archive, cite or alert their own Website users with research-based content from this work. (This list is as current as the copyright date of this publication.)

Abstracting, Website/Indexing Coverage . . . . Year When Coverage Began

- *Abstracts in Social Gerontology: Current Literature on Aging* **1989**
- *Academic Abstracts/CD-ROM* **1993**
- *Academic Search: database of 2,000 selected academic serials, updated monthly: EBSCO Publishing* **1995**
- *Academic Search Elite (EBSCO)* **1995**
- *Academic Search Premier (EBSCO) <http://www.epnet.com/ academic/acasearchprem.asp>* **1993**
- *AgeInfo CD-Rom <http://www.cpa.org.uk>* **1995**
- *AgeLine Database <http://research.aarp.org/ageline>* **1978**
- *Alzheimer's Disease Education & Referral Center (ADEAR)* **1994**
- *Applied Social Sciences Index & Abstracts (ASSIA) (Online: ASSI via Data-Star) (CDRom: ASSIA Plus) <http://www.csa.com>* **1987**
- *Behavioral Medicine Abstracts (Annals of Behavioral Medicine)* . . . **1992**
- *Biosciences Information Service of Biological Abstracts (BIOSIS), a centralized source of life science information <http://www.biosis.org>* **1993**
- *Business Source Corporate: coverage of nearly 3,350 quality magazines and journals; designed to meet the diverse information needs of corporations; EBSCO Publishing <http://www.epnet.com/ corporate/bsourcecorp.asp>* **1993**

(continued)

(continued)

(continued)

Special Bibliographic Notes related to special journal issues
(separates) and indexing/abstracting:

- indexing/abstracting services in this list will also cover material in any "separate" that is co-published simultaneously with Haworth's special thematic journal issue or DocuSerial. Indexing/abstracting usually covers material at the article/chapter level.
- monographic co-editions are intended for either non-subscribers or libraries which intend to purchase a second copy for their circulating collections.
- monographic co-editions are reported to all jobbers/wholesalers/approval plans. The source journal is listed as the "series" to assist the prevention of duplicate purchasing in the same manner utilized for books-in-series.
- to facilitate user/access services all indexing/abstracting services are encouraged to utilize the co-indexing entry note indicated at the bottom of the first page of each article/chapter/contribution.
- this is intended to assist a library user of any reference tool (whether print, electronic, online, or CD-ROM) to locate the monographic version if the library has purchased this version but not a subscription to the source journal.
- individual articles/chapters in any Haworth publication are also available through the Haworth Document Delivery Service (HDDS).

Religion, Spirituality, and Aging: A Social Work Perspective

CONTENTS

ABOUT THE EDITOR

Harry R. Moody, PhD, is currently Director of Academic Affairs for AARP in Washington, DC. He also serves as Senior Associate with the International Longevity Center-USA and Senior Fellow Civic Ventures.

Dr. Moody is the author of over 100 scholarly articles, as well as a number of books including: *Abundance of Life: Human Development Policies for an Aging Society* (Columbia University Press, 1988); *Ethics in an Aging Society* (Johns Hopkins University Press, 1992); and *Aging: Concepts and Controversies,* a gerontology textbook now in its 5th edition. His most recent book, *The Five Stages of the Soul,* was published by Doubleday Anchor Books (1997) and has been translated into seven languages worldwide.

Moody is a graduate of Yale and holds a PhD in philosophy from Columbia University. From 1999 to 2001 he served as National Program Director of the Robert Wood Johnson Foundation's Faith in Action Program and, from 1992 to 1999, was Executive Director of the Brookdale Center at Hunter College.

About the Contributors

Rabbi Richard F. Address, DMin, is Director, Department of Jewish Family Concerns, Union for Reform Judaism, 633 3rd Avenue, New York, NY 10017.

Stephanie C. Boddie, PhD, is affiliated with Washington University.

Mark Brennan, PhD, is affiliated with Lighthouse International, New York, NY.

Ram A. Cnaan, PhD, is affiliated with the University of Pennsylvania.

Amy Cohen, MFA, is affiliated with Nassau Community College.

Susan A. Eisenhandler, PhD, is Assistant Professor of Sociology, Department of Sociology, University of Connecticut, 99 East Main Street, Waterbury, CT 06702.

Jennifer J. Kang, MPS, is affiliated with the University of Pennsylvania.

Denise King, MSW, is a doctoral candidate at the School of Social Work, University of Maryland.

Terry L. Koenig, PhD, is affiliated with the School of Social Work, University of Buffalo, State University of New York, 685 Baldy Hall, Buffalo, NY 14260-1050.

Sarah B. Laditka, PhD, is Associate Professor and MHA Program Director, Department of Health Services Policy and Management, Arnold School of Public Health, University of South Carolina.

David O. Moberg, PhD, is Sociology Professor Emeritus, Marquette University, 7120 West Dove Court, Milwaukee, WI 53223-2766.

Carmen L. Morano, PhD, LCSW-C, is affiliated with the School of Social Work, University of Maryland, 525 West Redwood Street, Baltimore, MD 21201.

Vicki Murdock, PhD, is Assistant Professor of Social Work, University of Wyoming/Casper Center, 125 College Drive, Casper, WY 82601.

Holly Nelson-Becker, PhD, LCSW, is affiliated with the University of Kansas, 1545 Lilac Lane, Lawrence, KS 66044.

Leonie Nowitz, MSW, is affiliated with the Center for Lifelong Growth, 400 Central Park West, New York, NY 10025.

Marty Richards, MSW, is Affiliate Assistant Professor of Social Work, University of Washington, School of Social Work, 693 Blue Sky Drive, Port Townsend, WA 98368- 9055.

Dwight Roth, MSW, is affiliated with the Sociology Department, Hesston College, Box 3000, Hesston, KS 67062.

Henry C. Simmons, PhD, is Professor of Religion and Aging, Union-PSCE, 3401 Brook Road, Richmond, VA 23227.

John-Raphael Staude, PhD, is Adjunct Professor of History and Psychology, Osher Institute for Lifelong Learning, San Diego State University, 4634 Pavlov Avenue, San Diego, CA 92122.

Foreword

The publication of this volume is a particularly joyful occasion for Joanna Mellor and me for at least three reasons. First, is the subject. As Dr. Moody points out in his introduction to the volume, the history of the profession of social work and the attitudes of social workers toward religion is one of ebbs and flows. Yet one reality which social workers, regardless of their own religious beliefs, non/beliefs, questions and uncertainties, in their practice with older people and their families, must take into account is the centrality of religion and houses of worship in the lives of many of those with whom we work.

Parenthetically, during World War II, it was claimed that "there were no atheists in the foxholes." This turned out not to be entirely true, of course, and similarly the claim that religion becomes increasingly important as people grow older turns out to be not entirely accurate. This having been noted, it is clear that for many older people, the house of worship is an important *place* and *institution* in their lives, and for some, going to the church or mosque or synagogue is a social, as well as spiritual activity. And for some of these folk, religion and religious observances are part of their aging, not life long patterns of behavior. So the subject is one that merits the attention of social workers.

Second reason for our pride: we believe that this is one of the best volumes that we have ever published, and we urge, dear readers and subscribers, that you share your copy with your colleagues, and, if possible, urge them to purchase their own copies. The critical questions in this domain are all addressed in this volume, and the writing is erudite, well reasoned, well organized–all of the elements you want in your professional reading.

[Haworth co-indexing entry note]: "Foreword." Dobrof, Rose. Co-published simultaneously in *Journal of Gerontological Social Work* (The Haworth Social Work Practice Press, an imprint of The Haworth Press, Inc.) Vol. 45, No. 1/2, 2005, pp. xxiii-xxiv ; and: *Religion, Spirituality, and Aging: A Social Work Perspective* (ed: Harry R. Moody) The Haworth Social Work Practice Press, an imprint of The Haworth Press, Inc., 2005, pp. xvii-xviii. Single or multiple copies of this article are available for a fee from The Haworth Document Delivery Service [1-800-HAWORTH, 9:00 a.m. - 5:00 p.m. (EST). E-mail address: docdelivery@haworthpress.com].

xvii

And third, Rick, Joanna, and I were across-the-hall colleagues, when Joanna was Executive Director of the Hunter/Brookdale and Sinai Geriatric Education Center; and Rick was variously Director, Acting Director, and Deputy Director of Hunter/Brookdale; and I was usually the Director. Rick, the PhD in Medieval Philosophy; Joanna, the English-born Social Worker, and I, the Social Worker born and bred in Colorado, traveled different paths to Brookdale, and the differences among us added to the zest with which we discussed matters of great moment. "Those were the days"–wonderful days for all three of us, I think, and so Joanna and I take great personal, as well as professional, joy in presenting this volume to you.

Rose Dobrof

Introduction:
Knowledge, Practice, and Hope

Harry R. Moody, PhD

In his masterwork, the *Critique of Pure Reason*, the great philosopher Immanuel Kant concluded that all of philosophy, speculative as well as practical, could be summed up in three questions: "What can I know? What ought I to do? What may I hope?" (Kant, 2003). These three questions define the domains of theory of knowledge (epistemology), ethics, and religion. In this collection of articles we may usefully proceed by organizing the contributions as a range of answers to Kant's three questions, addressed now to the subject of religion, spirituality, and aging.

WHAT DO WE KNOW ABOUT RELIGION AND AGING?

The first question (What can we know?) has its response in the first section of articles which report on empirical research on the role of religion and spirituality in the lives of older people. David Moberg's opening article is a summary of a lifetime's research and meditation on religion and aging (Piedmont and Moberg, 2004; Moberg, 2001). To begin with, Moberg acknowledges the difficulty of making a clear definition or boundary between "religion" and "spirituality." These two key terms have a complex semantic history. A witty comment on that history was summed up by a cover article in "Mother Jones" magazine a

[Haworth co-indexing entry note]: "Introduction: Knowledge, Practice, and Hope." Moody, Harry R. Co-published simultaneously in *Journal of Gerontological Social Work* (The Haworth Social Work Practice Press, an imprint of The Haworth Press, Inc.) Vol. 45, No. 1/2, 2005, pp. 1-10 ; and: *Religion, Spirituality, and Aging: A Social Work Perspective* (ed: Harry R. Moody) The Haworth Social Work Practice Press, an imprint of The Haworth Press, Inc., 2005, pp. 1-10. Single or multiple copies of this article are available for a fee from The Haworth Document Delivery Service [1-800-HAWORTH, 9:00 a.m. - 5:00 p.m. (EST). E-mail address: docdelivery@haworthpress.com].

Available online at http://www.haworthpress.com/web/JGSW
doi:10.1300/J083v45n01_01

1

few years ago which proclaimed that "Spirituality is the new religion." In a more serious vein, Henry Simmons in his article in this collection serves to clarify the recent history of terminology about spirituality while at the same time helping us to understand attitudinal differences among cohorts who have experienced changes in the meaning of religion over the life-course (Simmons and Wilson, 2001).

Along with other great researchers, David Moberg draws our attention not only to trends in the field but also to questions still unresolved. Research to date seems to support the common-sense observation that inclination to spiritual matters increases with advancing age and that religious affiliation and practice has benefits for health and well-being. But, if true, these findings prompt a further question: why should these empirical connections hold true? Is religion itself a kind of "intervention" that can itself bring forth good things? Or is there something else that brings the benefits? These are vital questions to ask at a time when technical rationality (e.g., health sciences) tends to assimilate all human activity to a model of instrumental reason. As Habermas has argued, the assimilation of our cognitive interests to a single, restricted model of reason may have unwelcome consequences (Habermas, 1972). For example, what do we gain, and what do we lose, as we begin to "measure" spirituality and deploy it as one more technique to improve the welfare of elders?

These questions, still unresolved, are of the utmost importance to social work, which has its own history of attitudes toward religion. On the one hand, social workers, whatever their own beliefs, have long recognized that religion plays a role as a coping mechanism in the lives of older people, and this coping role is what Holly Nelson-Becker emphasizes in her article. On the other hand, organized social work in the 20th century tried to distance itself from its own origins as form of religious charity in favor of a becoming scientific and professional enterprise. It is only recently that social work has come to a more favorable view of religion (Cnaan et al., 1999). It is entirely understandable, then, that social workers would be willing to accommodate religion to the degree that religion itself can be seen as a kind of tool, a set of coping strategies. Prayer and meditation, acts of altruism, and study of scripture all can be seen as interventions or mechanisms: that is, can be appropriated for the instrumental purpose of technique and management. Yet, there remains a gap between this scientific language and the language of the life-world of respondents themselves, as reported by Nelson-Becker in her empirical study. What do we make of the fact that our detached, objective formulation of the role of religion seems so distant from how older people themselves understand their own life of faith?

One way of approaching this question is furnished by the work of Susan Eisenhandler, who understands religion in complex phenomenological terms (Thomas and Eisenhandler, 1994; Eisenhandler, 2003). In the qualitative research reported in this collection, Eisenhandler's respondents were drawn from both long-term care facilities and community settings, and she also interviewed people who acted as formal leaders representing religious activities: the social system that could strengthen coping strategies identified by Nelson-Becker.

Eisenhandler points to a paradox in thinking about religion, spirituality and aging. In recent years, the social scientific study of religion related to age has become more accepted and acknowledged in importance for coping with the stresses of life (Levin and Koenig, 2004). Yet, that acknowledgment seems remote from any appreciation of a genuine faith dimension on the part of many scientific researchers. Moreover, the language of Eisenhandler's respondents themselves makes clear that it is difficult to separate religion from the social milieu in which faith itself appears as "the finding thing" which weaves together fragments of life in old age. If we cannot easily separate out, or measure, or demarcate the religious dimension of lives, then how can we convert religion, or the more favored idea of spirituality, into an "instrument" or "intervention" for social work practice?

Practitioners may find these questions from research frustrating. They may reasonably ask, "What has religion done for me lately or done for my clients?" The article by Morano and King shows that whatever benefit religion may or may not have for helping with the stress of caregiving, that benefit will vary depending on ethnicity and cohort–a message of importance for those who think about religion as an "intervention." Religion, of course, is certainly *not* an intervention that can be "prescribed" but is typically part of a social network or institutional practice. This point is brought home by the research reported in the article by Cnaan, Boddie, and Kang. Their point is, quite simply, "Look to congregations." Cnaan and his co-authors begin with the empirical observation that religion enhances the quality of life of older people and sustains the social networks that are essential for mutual care. Whatever our personal opinions about organized religion, it is in congregational life, above all, that we are likely to find institutions that support those social networks.

Yet, Cnaan and his co-authors also found that congregations vary tremendously in their actual contribution to quality of life for their older parishioners. In the congregational sample they studied in Philadelphia, nearly half of all churches or synagogues do not provide any formal social service for elders, despite the well-known fact that large and growing proportions of congregations are older than age 65. The researchers also confirmed what informed observers of American religious life would readily acknowledge: namely, serving older adults is not a top priority for most congregations, despite the demographic imperative. So again, we confront a contradiction. From all that qualitative researchers have learned, religion continues to play a large and complex role in the lives of older people. From what social scientists have learned, religion can be a powerful coping mechanism and contributor to quality of life. But from what Cnaan, Boddie, and Kang report, the potential for congregational support remains unfulfilled. Congregations represent an underutilized resource which could greatly benefit from the skills and perspective of professional social work.

Is the answer, then, simply to "Send in the social workers" or "Bring more social services into congregational life?" Not quite, and, once again, we begin with Kant's first question: What can we know? Research gives a reality-check to any enthusiasm about the role of faith-based institutions in providing services. On the one hand, as Cnaan and others have argued, congregations offer an "invisible caring hand" in providing social welfare to those in need (Cnaan and Boddie, 2002). On the other hand, recent research suggests that congregations in practice offer only very limited services with fleeting contact. Chaves argues that there is there is no great untapped reserve of resources in congregations for faith-based services, because most of them are small: 60% with fewer than 100 active members (Chaves, 2004). These facts may be unwelcome. But, as Senator Daniel Moynihan once observed, people are entitled to their own opinions; they're not entitled to their own facts. The facts show that, from a policy perspective, there are serious limits to what congregations can do.

Pondering the limits prompts another question. What do we really know about how social workers go about using religion or spirituality as an intervention with older clients? Here we touch the heart of the matter and Vicki Murdock has conducted an important empirical study of this question, reported in detail in her article. Murdock's random sample of nearly 300 gerontological social workers reveals that social workers tend to think favorably about religion and spirituality as part of a holistic response to the needs of their diverse clientele. That's the good news. The bad news is that a huge proportion (70%) admitted they had only minimal preparation for dealing with religion or spirituality. Moreover, less than a quarter of respondents reported satisfaction with what educational preparation they had been given. If we want to "Send in the social workers" to help respond to the spiritual challenge of old age, then we'd better start preparing them differently in the future.

WHAT OUGHT WE TO DO?

Kant's second question, What ought we to do? is the central question of ethics and the touchstone for "best practices." It is interesting to note that Murdock found that ethical concerns, not personal religious beliefs, are decisive in shaping whether social workers actually make use of spiritual interventions with their clients. In the second part of this collection, we focus on matters of practice and ethics in thinking about standards and normative guidelines for religion and spirituality in gerontological social work.

Terry Koenig's article reports on a qualitative study of the ways that caregivers draw on religion and spirituality in coping with ethical dilemmas. These dilemmas are so difficult because whichever we choose–say, in favoring safety or autonomy–the result may be a situation in which there is guilt. We confront the enduring question: "Did I make the right choice?" Contemporary bioethics prefers to address these ethical dilemmas in terms of rules and principles: e.g., autonomy, beneficence, justice, and so on (Moody, 1992). But in practice, there is no algorithm or decision-procedure that tells us what to do when principles conflict with one another. We face what Kierkegaard would call an existential choice. What Koenig's respondents report confirms the power of spiritual dimension at these moments of ethical decision-making. In this account, religion becomes not so much a coping strategy as a way of illuminating the choices that make us human.

There is no organizational setting where these "everyday" ethical dilemmas are more common than in long-term care facilities (Kane and Caplan, 1990). We might assume, then, that religion and spirituality would be widely accepted as an approach to coping with the challenges of life in nursing homes. But we would be wrong, as Marty Richards points out in her article. Just as congregations, despite their large numbers of older people, have often failed to take aging seriously, so long-term care facilities, even when they have religious origins, have neglected religion and spirituality. Their neglect sometimes takes the ironic form of recognition: for example, "Oh, we have clergy who come to take care of those spiritual concerns." Yet, Marty Richards reminds us of a point we have seen over and over again: it is difficult to isolate the religious dimension of life from the total social context in which people live. Richards argues that social work, with its aspiration to becoming "scientific," has "lost its way" in responding to the religious and spiritual dimensions of later life. The way back is not remote from the best practice of social work in any setting. The way back, Richards argues, involves listening in the deepest way to life stories, the search for meaning, on the part of elders in long-term care settings. The way back means that we must come to grips with the human cry for hope, which is Kant's third question.

It turns out that we cannot easily separate the ethical from the religious questions in gerontological social work, and this theme is taken up by Leonie Nowitz in the setting of practice with community-dwelling elders. Nowitz is specifically concerned with the role of the geriatric care manager. Where a nursing home may separate out bureaucratic roles (clergy, social work, etc.), the care manager in a home setting is involved with negotiating all the details of daily living with family members. Religion is a central part of this picture. Nowitz insists that care managers can help families and elders best when social workers acknowledge the spiritual dimensions of caregiving itself. The demand here is to be fully present to suffering and the search for meaning, which is a challenge for the professional as much as it is for the family or the one receiving care. The practice of listening is at the heart of all "best practices" in our professional work with older people (Ram Dass, 2001).

The practice of listening is so important that it suggests a need to find creative interventions that can help staff become better listeners. Mark Brennan, Sarah Laditka, and Amy Cohen report on an innovative project that permitted the art of listening to become a systemic practice in the milieu of a long-term care facility. The "Postcards to God" project gave permission to institutionalized elders to find their own words that might express their search for meaning and effort to communicate with a Divine Power.

Along these same lines, Rabbi Richard Address describes a variety of new rituals that could have the power to endow the later years with deeper meaning. But Address's wish to re-imagine "sacred aging" comes up against a question: will religious institutions be willing to experiment with new forms and practices? Congregations, no more than long-term care facilities, have been willing to initiate the kind of "culture change" that Dwight Roth describes in his discussion of the Eden Alternative and its utopian critique of conventional long-term care (Thomas, 1996; Thomas, 2004). Roth finds hope not just in a new model of care but in educating a new generation of students who can practice the art of listening grounded in deeper appreciation of the life stories of older people.

The best practices described by Brennan and coauthors, as well as Address and Roth, help remind us of what might be in the world of gerontological social work. They underscore the importance of hope as we face the challenges of daily professional work in a challenging field.

WHAT MAY WE HOPE?

A persistent theme in all the articles in this collection is that elders are not a foreign species but, simply, "our future selves." In the concluding section the authors turn their gaze not on clients or institutions but on themselves and on their own experience of time and aging. John Raphael Staude writes of autobiography as a spiritual practice, evoking a theme that reaches back to St. Augustine's *Confessions* and comes alive for gerontologists in the phenomenon of reminiscence and life-review (Berman, 1994; Kenyon and Randall, 1997; Sherman, 2000). Staude wants us to see autobiography not so much as a literary genre as a form of consciousness in which we all grapple with a spiritual journey through time. He considers specific practices that can be helpful to gerontological social workers but he links those practices to deep appreciation for the humanities. The article on "Dreams for the Second Half of Life" moves along similar lines, but emphasizes the way in which our unconscious life can also express a spiritual search. Social workers who have been taught to think of dreams in classic psychoanalytic terms may want to widen their perspective and consider dreams in light of the search for meaning in later life. They need look no further than the Bible: "Your young shall see visions and your old ones shall dream dreams" (Joel 2:28, Acts 2:17).

There is much attention these days to ideas of "successful aging" and "vital aging" and other affirmative images to later life. Most of these ideals are drawn from a secular orientation that prizes health, activity, productive engagement, and other attributes of so-called positive aging. Rabbi Samuel Seicol's article introduces a spiritual approach to our image of positive aging, reminding us, in the spirit of Viktor Frankl, that it is our own response to life that shapes whether our experience is "positive" or not. Seicol draws on his years of pastoral experience in long-term care to give a deeper appreciation of the shadows as well as the light in old age.

The article by Wayne Ewing returns us to the issue of caregiving and dementia, but now understood as part of the author's own spiritual journey, part of the "dark night of the soul" in which religion or spirituality is viewed less as a form of coping and more as a plunge into the deepest mysteries of love and death. And where shall we find guides for this journey? Surely the great spiritual masters of the past, like St. John of the Cross, have much to tell us (May, 2004). But Richard Griffin also invokes the life of a contemporary guide, Henri Nouwen, whose book on aging remains a classic rich with lessons for life (Nouwen and Gaffney, 1976). Along with the authors in this concluding section of our collection, Nouwen insisted that each of us must come to grips with our own aging. Only by looking inward can we help frail elders in need; but, conversely, if we truly allow the older person to enter into our own life, then our understanding can be transformed and we will see with new eyes. We become no longer an external observer but instead "Methusaleh's Echo" (Bouklas, 1997).

Eugene Bianchi's essay on "Elder Wisdom" is a fitting conclusion to this collection, in part because Bianchi, like the opening contributor David Moberg, is himself an elder, a professor emeritus who has spent many years meditating on the meaning of religion and age (Bianchi, 1984). I am grateful to all our contributors, but, as editor of this collection, I am particularly grateful for the opening and concluding articles from distinguished emeriti in the field. I can only echo the words of Shakespeare in the last lines of King Lear: "Those who are oldest shall have borne the most. We that are young shall never live so long or see so much." At the same time, we cannot forget that King Lear is the prototype of the old fool, not the Wise Old Man. In his daughter Goneril's words, "He hath ever but slenderly known himself." Her words are a cautionary reminder that there is no guarantee that age by itself will bring wisdom or deliver us from illusions about ourselves, about religion, or about the world (Luke, 1987).

Eugene Bianchi's contribution sums up themes explored by other authors in this collection, a reminder that elders are, once again, our future selves. What Bianchi offers is a kind of empirical interview study, but one that seeks to capture the voice of a lifelong search for meaning (Bianchi, 1994). In his view, the wisdom of age begins to blur all boundaries–between religion and spirituality, between self and world, between losses and gains. Perhaps the message is that whether in youth or age, it is not the arriving but the journey itself which counts, the ceaseless exploration of a Divine Reality which transcends whatever mere words can capture. As usual, the poets have said it best, as T.S. Eliot did in the concluding lines of his great poem about religion, spirituality and aging, *The Four Quartets*: "We shall not cease exploring and the end of all exploring will be to arrive where we started, and know the place for the first time."

REFERENCES

Berman, Harry J. (1994). *Interpreting the aging self: Personal journals in later life.* Springer.

Bianchi, E. (1984). *Aging as a spiritual journey.* New York: Crossroad.

Bianchi, E. (1994). *Elder wisdom: Crafting your own elderhood.* Crossroad.

Bouklas, G. (1997). *Psychotherapy with the elderly: Becoming Methuselah's echo.* Jason Aronson.

Chaves, M. (2004). *Congregations in America.* Harvard University Press.

Cnaan, R., and Boddie, S. C. (2002). *The invisible caring hand: American congregations and the provision of welfare.* New York University Press.

Cnaan, R., Wineburg, R. J., and Boddie, S. C. (1999). *The newer deal.* Columbia University Press

Eisenhandler, S. A. (2003). *Keeping the faith in late life.* Springer.

Habermas, J. (1972). *Knowledge and human interests* (trans. Jeremy J. Shapiro). Beacon Press.

Kane, R. A., and Caplan, A. L. (Eds.) (1990). *Everyday ethics: Resolving dilemmas in nursing home life.* Springer.

Kant, I. (2003). *Critique of pure reason* (Norman Kemp Smith, translator). Palgrave Macmillan, 2nd Rev. edition.

Kenyon, G., and Randall, W. (1997). *Restorying our lives: Personal growth through autobiographical reflection.* Praeger.

Levin, J., and Koenig, H. (2004). *Faith, medicine, and science: A festschrift in honor of Dr. David B. Larson.* The Haworth Pastoral Press.

Luke, H. (1987). *Old Age.* Parabola Books.

May, G. (2004). *The dark night of the soul: A psychiatrist explores the connection between darkness and spiritual growth.* Harper, San Francisco.

Moberg, D. O. (2001). *Aging and spirituality: Spiritual dimensions of aging theory, research, practice, and policy.* The Haworth Pastoral Press.

Moody, H. R. (1992). *Ethics in an aging society.* Johns Hopkins University Press.

Nouwen, H. J. M., and Gaffney, W. J. (1976). *Aging: The fulfillment of life.* Image Books.

Piedmont, R. L., and Moberg, D. O. (2004). *Research in the social scientific study of religion.* Brill Academic Publishers.

Ram D. (2001). *Still here: Embracing aging, changing, dying.* Riverhead Books.

Sherman, E. (2000). *The Autobiographical Consciousness of Aging.* Kearney, NE: Morris.

Simmons, H., and Wilson, J. (2001). *Soulful aging: Ministry through the stages of adulthood.* Smyth & Helwys Publishing.

Thomas, L. E., and Eisenhandler (Eds.) (1994). *Aging and the religious dimension.* Auburn House.

Thomas, W. H. (1996). *Life worth living: How someone you love can still enjoy life in a nursing home–The eden alternative in action.* Acton, MA: VanderWyk & Burnham.

Thomas, W. H. (2004). *What are old people for? How elders will save the world.* Acton, MA: VanderWyk & Burnham.

RESEARCH

Research in Spirituality, Religion, and Aging

David O. Moberg, PhD

SUMMARY. Research on the concept of "spirituality" demonstrates its overlap with "religion," so for many purposes they need to be considered together as "spirituality/religion." Investigations of age differences point to the likelihood that spirituality tends to increase during later adulthood. It has important positive relationships with various measures of life satisfaction, psychosocial well-being, and both physical and mental health. It benefits therapy for recovery from illness and is a source of meaning and purpose in life. Spiritual interventions help to relieve psychological distress and death anxiety, as well as the stresses of caregiving. Because of its therapeutic value, prayer is an important resource for

This paper is an updated version of a manuscript prepared as the basis for the author's 15-minute oral presentation in a plenary session of the ICIHS Research Conference on Integrating Research on Spirituality and Health and Well-Being into Service Delivery, National Institutes of Health, Bethesda, MD, April 1-3, 2003.

[Haworth co-indexing entry note]: "Research in Spirituality, Religion, and Aging." Moberg, David O. Co-published simultaneously in *Journal of Gerontological Social Work* (The Haworth Social Work Practice Press, an imprint of The Haworth Press, Inc.) Vol. 45, No. 1/2, 2005, pp. 11-40 ; and: *Religion, Spirituality, and Aging: A Social Work Perspective* (ed: Harry R. Moody) The Haworth Social Work Practice Press, an imprint of The Haworth Press, Inc., 2005, pp. 11-40. Single or multiple copies of this article are available for a fee from The Haworth Document Delivery Service [1-800-HAWORTH, 9:00 a.m. - 5:00 p.m. (EST). E-mail address: docdelivery@haworthpress.com].

11

coping with problems experienced during the life course. The Spiritual Well-Being Scale and many other instruments have been developed to measure spirituality and related concepts. As in all other domains of research on people, they all have limits and must be applied with caution for both technical and ethical reasons. Nevertheless, applications of the research findings, which overwhelmingly demonstrate the importance of spirituality to human well-being, already are improving the effectiveness of clinical work and social services in all of the health and human service professions. As scientific knowledge of spirituality expands, so does awareness of the need for further research, including the refinement of methodological procedures, expansion to new topics, and extension to international cultures and diverse religions. The outlook for research on spirituality and the consequent practical applications to benefit humanity is very promising. *[Article copies available for a fee from The Haworth Document Delivery Service: 1-800-HAWORTH. E-mail address: <docdelivery@haworthpress.com> Website: <http://www.HaworthPress. com>* © *2005 by The Haworth Press, Inc. All rights reserved.]*

KEYWORDS. Spirituality, religion, aging, well-being, prayer, interventions, ethics

The study of spirituality and religion was generally neglected in the medical, social, and behavioral sciences until recently. The "lack of enthusiasm on the part of epidemiologists for investigating the health effects of religion" (Levin & Vanderpool, 1987, p. 598; see also Larson, Sherrill, & Lyons, 1994; Weaver et al., 1998) was evident in all research disciplines except for a small minority of social and behavioral scientists who considered it important, many of whom benefited from the moral support of the Society for the Scientific Study of Religion, the Religious Research Association, and sections on religion in their professional associations.

Despite the general disdain for studying religion and spirituality in relationship to health and illness, evidence about their relevance was gradually built up through scattered findings of studies that included one or more religious variable, even though the results were often buried in statistical tables and not discussed in the accompanying research papers (McFadden & Levin, 1996, pp. 151-152). As these findings were compiled in meta-analytical articles and books (e.g., Levin & Vanderpool, 1987; Koenig, Smiley, & Gonzales, 1988; Levin & Vanderpool,

1991; Koenig, 1995; Koenig, McCullough, & Larson, 2001), the consistency of findings that linked religion and health strongly suggested the empirical, clinical, and theoretical significance of spirituality and religion and eventually influenced their inclusion in training for the medical, nursing, psychotherapy, and social work professions (e.g., Bergin & Richards, 1997; Bullis, 1996; Canda, 1998).

During the latter part of the twentieth century, the early heritage of studying religion in disciplines like psychology and sociology was revived and extended (see, e.g., Demerath, Silverman, & Lehman, 2000). Some persons in other scientific disciplines also began asking questions related to spirituality, and they joined philosophers and theologians to ask questions like *Whatever happened to the soul?* (Brown, Murphy, & Malony, 1998).

Some of the research included attention to spirituality and aging. Only a brief survey of its highlights is possible in the confines of this paper. My attention will focus upon conceptual issues, typical research, the relevance of the research to applications in clinical and social services, precautions for both clinical applications and research investigations of spirituality, and directions for future research.

THE CONCEPT OF SPIRITUALITY

It is very difficult to define *spirituality*. David Aldridge (2002, pp. 25-54), professor of qualitative research in the medical faculty at the University of Witten-Herdecke, has summarized nine definitions of spirituality that emphasize *meaning and unity* as the essence of spirituality, eight that interpret it as a dimension of persons that *transcends* self or any experience at hand, three that focus upon it as *a motivating force or belief in a power* apart from a person's own existence, three that link it with *breath and its activities*, and four emerging from postmodern interpretations as something *non-observable and metaempirical*. There is no universally accepted definition, but we clearly are moving toward a universal consensus that there is a "something" about people that we can call "the human spirit" and therefore a reality that we can label as *spirituality*.

That the essence of humanity is spiritual reflects teachings in the Judeo-Christian Bible: People–male and female (Genesis 1:27)–were created in the image of God. Jesus described God as spirit (John 4:24). It follows that *spirit* (often interchangeable with *soul* in the Bible) is the whole person, the totality of one's being. We are spirit, and we possess a body and a mind.

Spirituality encompasses everything that pertains to our spirits. It is an aspect of all that we are, have, and do (Moberg, 2002b). For the very reason that the core of human nature is spirit, we cannot get away from it to examine it as if we were completely separate from it, nor can we study it scientifically with full objectivity. To use the words of psychologist Daniel Helminiak (1996, p. 272), "simply to be human is already to be spiritual. So underlying all expressions of spirituality is a core that is universal, a core that is simply human."

This is consistent with recent interpretations of research on children by the former director of the Religious Experience Research Center in Oxford, England, David Hay (reported by Lacombe, 2000), who concluded that everyone has a human predisposition of spirituality that can be nurtured or starved but never dies. However, both verbal usage and operational research definitions reflect the cultural values (Wheeler, Ampadu, & Wangari, 2002), philosophical assumptions, and theological positions of their users. Group differences in the meanings attributed to both spirituality and religion contribute to disagreements about their definition and operationalization.

Every definition focuses upon only variously selected aspects of the totality it represents, so there are countless implicit definitions of spirituality in literary and religious allusions, scholarly treatises, clinical applications, and general discourse. Every operational definition used in scientific research and in evaluative scales to "measure" spirituality reflects only small portions of the overarching reality; they all select fragments of the whole and therefore are not necessarily equivalent.

The overlap of spirituality with religion is especially significant to the definitional issue. *Religiosity* (religiousness) most often refers to commitment to a religious faith like Judaism and Islam, holding the personal beliefs (as in the Deity) that one's faith advocates, and participating in the rituals and other activities associated with that faith. *Spirituality* has a more experiential and existential focus upon an individual's internalized faith, values, and beliefs and their influence upon daily behavior, although the behavior is not its primary focus. There is far more research under the rubric of "religion" than of "spirituality," partly because it is more easily observed by others, but also because spirituality has been accepted as a researchable subject only recently.

Studies by Zinnbauer et al. (1997), Zinnbauer, Pargament, and Scott (1999), and Zinnbauer and Pargament (2002) have demonstrated that spirituality overlaps significantly with religiousness in both the everyday parlance of American people and the understandings of professional people like nurses and clergy. Most people consider themselves to be both religious and spiritual, although spirituality means different things to different people. Research consistently shows that between two-thirds and three-fourths of Americans consider themselves to be both spiritual and religious, with about half of the remainder saying they are "spiritual only" and the others split between "religious only" and neither (Marler & Hadaway, 2002). There is therefore a growing consensus in sociology and psychology that the study of spirituality and of religiousness should be pursued together (Moberg, 2001, pp. 12-13; see Hill et al., in press).

RESEARCH FINDINGS

The following summary of research relevant to spirituality, aging, and health is selective and representative of the research to date. I shall sketch some of the findings that deal with age differences, religion and well-being, spiritual needs, prayer, and research instruments to investigate spirituality.

Age Differences

Since 1939 or earlier, survey research and public opinion polls have consistently found senior adults (past 65) to be highest on measures of religion and spirituality, with only an occasional exception of reduced attendance at religious services among the oldest old, higher proportions of whom have problems of mobility. This once was used to support the now discredited versions of secularization theory that predicted lower religiousness with each generation, for decade after decade the pattern is so consistent that it cannot be attributed to only a cohort explanation. The persistently higher levels of religiousness among the oldest generation are more likely a product of the deepening of spiritual interests and concern during the later years, although differential survival may also contribute to it, for people who are more religious and spiritual live longer than others (Moberg, 1997; see Hummer et al., 1999).

Among the leading "secrets" people past age 85 gave Hogstel and Kashka (1989) for good health and long life are faith in God and Christian living. Brennan and Missinne (1980) found that senior adults tended to retain earlier beliefs in God and the afterlife, but considerably higher proportions prayed or meditated regularly and considered themselves to be "a religious person" "now" than had "always" done so. Retrospective responses of 176 people in a senior apartment retirement facility in Omaha, Nebraska, to the statement, "I have become more religious as I have aged," produced similar results. Half (50.6%) strongly or somewhat agreed, while only one-sixth (17.6%) strongly or somewhat disagreed, and under one-third (30.7%) neither agreed nor disagreed (Wotherspoon, 2000, p. 78).

Among the 1,188 women in the Search Institute survey of Lutheran Church–Missouri Synod, significant differences were evident between the young (18-34), young middle aged (35-49), older middle aged (50-64), and senior (65+) women. On almost every measure of religion and spirituality, the older respondents scored significantly higher than those who were younger, a finding that is typical in studies of American Christians (Moberg, 1999).

A rare longitudinal study followed the same persons, born in 1920/21 or 1928/29, over several decades. While the overall levels of spirituality were relatively low, they all, irrespective of gender and cohort, showed a significant increase in spirituality from late middle age (mid-50s to late 60s) to their older adulthood (late 60s to mid-70s). This supports the conclusion that there is a general tendency for individuals to become more interested in spiritual interests and practices as they grow older. Earlier in life the patterns of change were much more varied. Women turned toward increased spirituality earlier and at a faster rate than the men (Wink & Dillon, 2002). Of course, there are a variety of patterns of religious transitions during the life course. For some people there is a high degree of stability (no change), but for others religiosity may increase, decrease, or show a curvilinear trajectory (Ingersoll-Dayton, Krause, & Morgan, 2002).

Religion and Well-Being

The earliest research on what we now call spirituality was done under the label of religion or religiosity. Survey research with 219 subjects, for example, found that the positive association of church membership with personal adjustment in old age, observed in several studies, was not attributable to the membership per se but to the religious activities and beliefs that are more characteristic of members than of non-members (Moberg, 1951).

The 1971 White House Conference on Aging popularized the concept of "spiritual well-being," the label given its section on religion (see Moberg, 1971). The National Interfaith Coalition on Aging formed as one of its by-products struggled with interfaith and interdenominational differences, eventually arriving at a one-sentence "working-with" definition: "Spiritual well-being is the affirmation of life in a relationship with God, self, community, and environment that nurtures and celebrates wholeness" (NICA, 1975). That definition has been useful in many pastoral and clinical contexts, but it is not easily operationalized for research purposes.

Subsequent studies by many researchers, mostly with young and middle-aged subjects, have rather consistently revealed that life satisfaction, well-being, and similar concepts, with few exceptions, are associated with higher levels of religiousness and most of all with intrinsic rather than extrinsic religion (Moberg, 1995; McFadden, 1995). One of the few exceptions is a study of elderly Jewish women residing in old age homes in Israel who defined themselves as not religious (33.9%), traditional (31.5%), orthodox (28.9%), or ultra orthodox (5.6%). Their religiousness, measured on a six-item scale of beliefs, was not correlated with subjective well-being (Iecovich, 2001).

Witter et al. (1985) found that the positive relationship between religion and subjective well-being was stronger among the older than the younger samples in 28 studies of the subject, a finding confirmed by Ellison (1991), whose research showed that people with stronger religious faith have higher life satisfaction and happiness than others. In research by Koenig, Kvale, and Ferrel (1988), only health accounted for more of the explained variance in morale among people past age 75 than did religious behaviors and attitudes. Such relationships are possibly even stronger among African Americans (Nye, 1992-1993; Ortega, Crutchfield, & Rushing, 1983; Coke, 1991). Older adults whose sense of meaning in life is derived from religion tend to have higher levels of self-esteem, life satisfaction, and optimism than others, and that relationship is stronger among African Americans than White persons (Krause, 2003; see also Krause, 2002).

Spiritual Needs and Coping

Religion and spirituality are among the most significant means for coping with the crises and problems of living and dying (Pargament, 1997; Kaye & Raghavan, 2002). In-depth interviews of older adults in nursing homes and independent living in Australia revealed six categories of spiritual need that provide a basis for assessing opportunities for spiritual growth. These were helping people clarify their centers of ultimate meanings, respond to those meanings through religious and spiritual actions and symbols, find and reframe memories and experiences linked with final meanings, transcend their losses and suffering, establish intimacy with God and others, and find hope (MacKinlay, 2001). That research also contributed to MacKinlay's (in press; see also Fleming, in press) conclusion that pastoral interventions that focus upon issues of meaning can greatly improve the quality of life for both populations and relieve much of the distress of people with depression or dementia.

Among hospitalized medically ill elderly men, the use of religious means of coping was inversely associated with depression (Koenig et al., 1992). A similar association of better psychological health among elderly people with high levels of religious activities and beliefs was noted by Morse and Wisocki (1987).

As part of the Massachusetts Elder Health Project, Chang, Noonan, and Tennstedt (1998) explored the relationship between religious/ spiritual coping and psychological distress among 127 informal caregivers to community-residing disabled elders. Although they used only a single item to measure religious/spiritual coping, they found that the three-fourths who agreed that it was used at least to some extent to handle their caregiving experience had better relationships with the care recipients, lower levels of depression, and less role submersion (intrapsychic strain) than the others, so they recommended incorporating aspects of the "faith factor" into caregiving research. In their comparison of demographically matched Black and White mothers of adults who have developmental disabilities, Miltiades and Pruchno (2002) found that religious coping was a positive source of satisfaction, but the Black mothers had higher levels of religious coping and caregiving satisfaction, but also higher caregiving burdens because of their poorer health, so they were in greater need of the services of churches and other faith-based organizations.

A study by McFadden and Hanusa (1998) found that meaningful connections of nursing assistants with elderly long-term clients were facilitated by stimulating their recognition of the ways they experience spirituality.

Missinne's (2000) survey of 78 people aged 60 an older in the Omaha area discovered that nearly two-thirds (63%) felt their lives had a definite purpose and meaning, while only 5% felt they had little meaning, and the other 32% were indecisive. Those aged 78 to 95 had higher Purpose in Life scores than younger respondents. The values from which they derived the most meaning were family, spiritual needs, good health, helping others, and self-reliance. Surprisingly, 30% reported that illness and suffering were positive experiences for them, and another 25% said they were neutral, so one must make the best of it.

Religiousness is negatively associated with fear of death (Cicirelli, 2002). Several studies by Thorson and Powell (2000) found negative correlations between death anxiety and intrinsic religious motivation, between age and death anxiety, and between age and depression (see also Thorson, 1991). The Duke longitudinal study on aging similarly found that lack of a fear of death was associated with frequent Bible reading, belief in a future life, and religious conceptions of death. Widowed persons who had a deep religious faith adapted with emotional stability. Happiness, feeling useful, and personal adjustment were correlated with religious activity and attitudes (Palmore et al., 1985, p. 457).

Prayer and Health

McCullough's (1995) review of research on relationships between prayer and various measures of health summarizes the findings of 35 studies. Eight that examined linkages with measures of subjective well-being found that both the frequency of prayer and the presence of religious and mystical experience during prayer predicted well-being, although some of the associations may have been due to confounding variables like religious commitment and sociodemographic characteristics. About eighteen studies were of prayer as a resource for coping–coping with chronic pain, other medical problems, and such life stressors as surgery and death of a spouse. Although most studies found positive relationships, some had mixed results, possibly partly because of design flaws. Of four that investigated relationships between prayer and psychiatric symptoms, again revealing predominantly helpful effects, only one used rigorous methodology. It compared the results of students using relaxation training with those emphasizing devotional meditation and prayer and a no-treatment control group. The six weeks of biweekly sessions resulted in increased muscular tension in the relaxation group but the lowest levels of anger and anxiety among the devotional group (Carlson et al., 1988).

Three studies of prayer for the recovery of ill persons were poorly designed and had equivocal results, but Byrd's (1988) research on the effects of intercessory prayer on patients admitted to the coronary care unit of San Francisco General Hospital for acute coronary distress during a nine-month period was a carefully designed double-blind clinical trial. The 192 patients, each randomly assigned to receive daily prayers from three to seven "born again" Catholic and Protestant Christians outside the hospital, were similar to a control group upon admission. However, the experimental prayed-for group had significantly better outcomes on six of the 26 health variables measured upon admission and at release from the hospital than those not prayed for, and they also had better overall symptom severity scores. There was no attempt to control for praying by the patients themselves, nor by their relatives, friends, clergy, church groups, and others that undoubtedly occurred for many patients outside of the research design, but the random selection for the treatment and control group presumably held that variable constant.

In another study, 524 of 990 patients admitted to the coronary care unit of St. Luke's Hospital in Kansas City were randomly assigned to a control group and 466 to a group prayed for separately by five to seventy-five volunteers from a variety of Christian traditions. Neither the patients nor their physicians were aware of the study. Intercessors were given only first names and asked to pray daily for speedy recovery for four weeks. Those prayed for did 11% better ($p > .04$) on 35 medical measurements than the control group (Harris et al., 1999).

A similar study involved 196 coronary artery bypass surgery graft patients at the University of Michigan Medical Center. The patients who themselves prayed privately had better psychological outcomes a year after the surgery than those who did not. Because important coexisting factors were controlled, the possibility that the effect of praying resulted merely from better affective conditions at the outset was ruled out (Ai et al., 1998; see Ai et al., 2000). Additional research by Ai et al. (2002) found that during the health crisis of cardiac care, private prayer, but neither general religiosity nor the types of prayers used, predicted optimism and healthier affect, so these relationships are complex.

Prayer in a daily program for mentally impaired Jewish elders was found to have significant therapeutic value (Abramowitz, 1993). Among Catholic, Jewish, and Protestant mentally ill or impaired patients who had been religiously active in the past, the use of familiar religious rituals, symbols, and worship patterns has significant therapeutic value (Ellor, Stettner, & Spath, 1987). A pilot study on the therapeutic use of Rossiter-Thornton's (2000) "prayer wheel" that uses eight components of prayer activity (apparently prayer with meditation) suggests that is a promising and inexpensive non-denominational intervention, at least for the treatment of anxiety and depression (Rajagopal et al., 2002).

Susan Melia's (2001) interviews, along with those of Susan McFadden, found that women aged 65 to 98 have more time and space for prayer than younger women. With aging, their prayers had changed, mainly toward becoming more simple, spontaneous, intimate, meaningful, personal, flexible, and open with God as a valued companion. They had many ways of praying (devotions, meditation, liturgical practices, spiritual readings, walks in nature, intercession, solitary, or with others). The life of many was one of prayer and relationship, with prayer as a constant activity. Praying structured their days and served as a source of connection with others as well as with God. Baesler's (2002) research comparing young with middle-aged adults also found differences in the types of prayers between the age groups.

Tan (1996, pp. 371-375) has summarized aspects of the use of prayer in psychotherapy. It includes talking with God, but also other ways of focusing attention upon or experiencing relationships with the Divine. He recommends that such prayers include confession, thanksgiving, and praise or worship of God, that they comprise not only petitions for one's own healing and intercession for others, but also that they not be used simply as a technique for anxiety reduction or desensitization. He identifies seven steps of inner healing prayer (for healing memories) and warns of the complications of exorcism, i.e., prayer for deliverance from evil spirits or from demon possession. Tan warns, too, that there are times when prayer ought not be used in psychotherapy, even with religiously committed clients.

Research Instruments

The most widely used instrument for both research and clinical evaluations of spirituality is the Spiritual Well-Being Scale constructed by Paloutzian and Ellison (1982, 1991). It consists of twenty questions. Ten on the "vertical dimension" comprise a Religious Well-Being sub-scale. Its items pertain to perceptions of being loved by and experiencing a fulfilling relationship with God. The other ten are on the "horizontal dimension," comprising an Existential Well-Being sub-scale that measures one's sense of purpose, direction, satisfaction in life, and adjustments to one's self and community. The SWB Scale has been validated, standardized, and used in hundreds of studies with very diverse samples. By 2003 there had been over 700 requests for its use (Paloutzian, 2003). Almost invariably its scores have been significantly and positively correlated with other measures of health and well-being (Bufford, Paloutzian, & Ellison, 1991; Ledbetter, Smith, Fischer, &

Vosler-Hunter, 1991; Ledbetter, Smith, Vosler-Hunter, & Fischer, 1991). It is an excellent tool for general populations, although it has a ceiling effect, so it does not discriminate degrees of differences within groups of religious people in which most members have high levels of well-being. Besides research, it is being used for clinical counseling and for evaluating the effectiveness of programs of patient care by comparing its measures before, during, and after treatment (Paloutzian, 2003).

Wotherspoon (2000) conducted one of the few research projects using the SWB Scale to study aging people. There were 176 responses from residents of a senior-apartment retirement facility in Omaha (only 29 were men). Women scored significantly higher than men on the Religious Well-Being subscale, and religious well-being was more important to them than existential well-being. The SWB scores and both subscale scores were significantly correlated with self-assessed ratings of health and of religiosity.

Numerous additional scales to measure various aspects of religiousness and spirituality have been constructed (see Hill & Hood, 1999; MacDonald, LeClair, Holland, Alter, & Friedman, 1994; MacDonald, Friedman, & Kuentzel, 1999; MacDonald, Kuentzel, & Friedman, 1999). Many carry the word "spiritual" in their titles, and others include both spiritual and religious components. To survey them and their findings is far beyond the scope of this paper, except to note that their operating definitions of spirituality diverge quite widely. Nevertheless, spirituality is such a broad and diffused concept, connected as it is with the totality of personhood, that they all may indeed reflect components or aspects of its hundreds, if not thousands, of potential indicators.

RELEVANCE OF THE RESEARCH TO CLINICAL AND SOCIAL SERVICES

There are "heaps" of anecdotal, clinical, historical, and theological evidence on the importance of spirituality and religious faith to health and well-being. We have seen that social and behavioral research findings also preponderantly support that conclusion. The relatively few exceptions can be traced to limitations of the methods used, operational definitions of spirituality or other variables, deficiencies of research techniques and procedures, unique characteristics of the populations studied, and similar issues. Each "outlier" that deviates from the general pattern deserves in-depth investigation, of course, as also does each oversimplified conclusion that accompanies it.

Simply reporting research findings, however, is not likely by itself to bring about many changes in professional interventions and social policy. Demonstrations of how to apply the findings of basic research and theory about spirituality are needed, and these ideally should have multiple components. (Possible methodological models include Pillemer, Suitor, and Wethington, 2003; Farkas et al., 2003.) The professional approach may involve an *implicit* integration of spirituality with clinical practice in which the therapist does not initiate discussion of spiritual issues, nor openly, directly, or systematically use spiritual resources like prayer, Scripture or other sacred texts, referral to religious groups or personnel, or other religious practices, as is done in the *explicit* approach that is especially useful for religiously committed clients (Tan, 1996).

Some research has demonstrated the wisdom of giving overt attention to spiritual concerns in therapy and social services. Among them, the study of prayer at the University of Michigan Medical Center (mentioned above) concluded that bringing a spiritual dimension into health care for elderly adults "will help accomplish better functioning of . . . patients, and it may also contribute to substantial reduction in health care costs" (Ai et al., 1998, p. 599).

Eck's (2002) survey of the uses of spiritual interventions in psychotherapy identifies appropriate ethical, cultural, and professional practice contexts for their evaluation and use in addressing disordered cognitions, behaviors, and relationships.

Numerous suggestions on how to be spiritually sensitive in psychotherapy are woven into Gary Moon's (2002) interview with David G. Benner, who is described as "a pillar and a pioneer in the modern integration movement" (p. 64). In it Moon proposes additional but different training from that of the past, along with a new specialty, "applied soulologist" (p. 70).

A recent book on *Aging and Spirituality* (Moberg, 2001) includes several chapters on professional applications of current knowledge, each with references to additional resources on their respective subjects: Health care (Soerens, 2001), hospices (Angeli, 2001), counseling (Driscoll-Lamberg, 2001), social work (Watkins, 2001), chaplaincies (Friberg, 2001), and public policy (Stein, 2001). These and a rapidly growing body of other resources demonstrate that spirituality can be explicitly incorporated into nonsectarian professional work with clients in any of the human services.

Assessing the spirituality of clients may begin casually, but the process deserves to become more systematic. Fortunately, many steps toward such assessments already have been taken by professional people (Ellor, 2003). Whenever spiritual issues emerge as a part of the diagnostic process, appropriate interventions or referrals ought to be provided or brought to the attention of those who need them. Examples of this approach include:

- The thoroughly documented study by Richards and Bergin (1997) of the basic need for and methods of incorporating spirituality in professional counseling.
- The inclusion of spiritual care in nursing (Catterall et al., 1998; Ross, 1997; Reed, 1991).
- The tangible suggestions of Lipson, Dibble, and Minarik (1996) on how to recognize and act in accord with the religious and spiritual orientations, rituals, and practices of specific ethnic and religious groups encountered in nursing practice.
- The increasing attention to spirituality in social work practice (Bullis, 1996; Canda, 1998; Canda & Fuman, 1999) and geriatric counseling (Thibault, 2003).
- The deepening desire to give explicit attention to spiritual needs in professional and lay pastoral ministries (VandeCreek, 1999; Knox, 2002; MacKinlay & Ellor, in press).
- Sulmasy's (2002) biopsychosocial-spiritual model for the care of patients at the end of life.

In addition, service providers are increasingly aware that religious communities are important resources for promoting the well-being of people through their role in the prevention of problems, healing of emotions, cognitions, and behaviors, and empowerment for social action in groups that feel oppressed or distressed (Maton & Wells, 1995). While many religious congregations can be faulted for "not doing enough to serve aging people," they in fact already are doing a great deal.

> The emotional calm produced by prayer and meditation, the pleasure of attending worship, the concerned responses of clergy, the social support offered by a caring community, the opportunities for intergenerational contact, and the encouragement of health-related behaviors may all be factors contributing to the well-being of older

persons. Additionally, religion offers individuals . . . a fundamental sense of the meaningfulness of life . . . (McFadden, 1995, p. 171)

As recognition of the importance of spirituality and of healing the whole person is diffused throughout all the health and helping professions, the local parish or congregation may become even more of a "primary health place" (Struve, 2001). Expansion of the parish nurse movement on the one hand and the stresses on financing the health care system on the other also may contribute to change in that direction.

Clinical applications of research findings, properly analyzed and implemented, can in themselves constitute trials of alternative approaches in efforts to discover the most appropriate procedural applications and to test hypotheses about them.

Precautions

Like most research on human beings, none of the findings on spirituality and well-being are absolutely conclusive or definitive, even though the piling up of consistent evidence for more than half a century strongly suggests that spirituality is indeed an important component of total wellness. Because all dimensions of humanity–body, mind, and soul or spirit–are interrelated, whatever aids the wellness or causes the illness of one domain influences all of the others. But how to implement genuinely holistic services is a major challenge for all human service occupations. Every profession is limited, so therapeutic specialties that separate parts of the body from each other, the body from the mind, or the spirit from both as in pastoral care, therefore are necessary. Yet all practitioners should recognize that their clients are whole persons, so other domains of life besides those covered by their own profession may greatly affect their own effectiveness. It may be humanly impossible ever to be completely holistic, but if that is a targeted goal, cooperative efforts may move closer and closer to it.

In light of the increasingly rich trove of research findings about spirituality, numerous hypotheses about its significant protective mechanisms, its role in therapy, and its importance to the holistic well-being of people can be formulated. Although the evidence that appropriate applications in all human services enhance the well-being of individuals and society already is strong, numerous possibilities are not yet firmly supported by appropriate research. There are several reasons for caution about generalizations in both research and clinical applications.

One danger is that recognizing the tentativeness of all research dealing with humanity may prevent human service professionals from applying any research findings. Waiting for definitive answers will never bring any action at all. *Every intervention represents an act of faith and hope* that is based upon a trove of evidence from previous knowledge and experience. While we are doing "the best we can," we also are testing, modifying, and expanding that treasure trove. Even under the best of current knowledge, we walk humbly by faith and with only blurred or cloudy sight.

Another complication is that we sometimes jump too quickly from research findings to premature applications. Levin (1996) has summarized several types of misinterpretations of epidemiological research findings that have resulted from fundamental confusion over definitions, misunderstanding the nature of disease, and failure to recognize research limitations. They include the conclusion that religious involvement promotes healing (the research reveals a preventive factor, but has not studied its therapeutic efficacy for curing diseases), that religious people do not get sick (only that they have a lower incidence of certain diseases and conditions), that spirituality is a protective factor (only religious involvement has been studied, not spirituality as commonly conceived), that prayer heals (it needs much more research), that religion is the most important factor in health (the correlates are moderate, and religious faith and practice do not overcome influences like nutrition, good genes, smoking cessation, and other protective factors), that there is empirical evidence of a supernatural influence on health (the supernatural is outside of or beyond nature, and science can investigate only observable natural phenomena), and that other factors like social support explain away the association between health and religion (indirect and confounding associations do occur, but they elucidate pathways and mechanisms by which religion benefits health without necessarily eliminating the associations). "Therefore the general effects of religious indicators on morbidity rates and health outcomes are no more an artifact of confounding than are the epidemiologic effects of other psychosocial factors, such as social support or bereavement" (p. 857).

Service providers need to be aware of the diversity of conceptions, definitions, and possible applications of findings about spirituality. Not all spiritualities and religions, nor all denominations and sects within any specific religion, are equivalent to all others, and the same applies to spiritual interventions, some of which may do more harm than good (Oates, 1970). Even those that are predominantly beneficial for most people in a majority of circumstances may have negative consequences for a few, especially if they are improperly introduced. In addition, some persons in every professional and lay or amateur context occasionally deviate from their professed ideals, sometimes even to the extremes of hypocritically living behind a false front or of criminal abuse (Benyei, 1998; Moberg, 1987; see Gruber, 1995).

Some critics refuse to believe the findings of research. A few engage in card-stacking evidences and allegations to discredit it, but others have honest doubts. Their arguments should be respected and the data on all sides of disagreements checked in order to determine the extent to which the conclusions should be accepted, rejected, or held in abeyance. (For an excellent example of a pertinent critique, see Weaver, Flannelly, and Stone, 2002.) Analyzing effectiveness to identify the best methods and techniques for serving people's spiritual needs is a challenging future task. So is identifying relationships between the diverse aspects and components of spirituality and holistic well-being.

Ethics

Ethical values pose another set of problems. Service providers are tempted to jump to conclusions prematurely, as in the tendency to stereotype persons, thereby to assign them to a particular set of interventions, and then to respond to each person as if every individual in the same category has identical needs, limitations, abilities, interests, beliefs, and responses. (Assuming that characteristics of a population as a whole apply to every person within it or that every unit or part of an agency or program has the same features as those characterizing the whole is sometimes labeled "the ecological fallacy"; see Moberg 1983).

Numerous ethical issues are involved in complex questions about the constitutionality of using religious interventions in public agencies and the religious liberty issues related to recommending spiritual therapy, especially for persons who may not be eager for it (see Golden & Sonneborn, 1998). The need for balancing the non-establishment of religion and religious liberty provisions in our federal and state constitutions poses continual problems that are only partly solved by focusing upon spirituality instead of religion. Too often this issue has resulted in the complete exclusion of religious and spiritual considerations from what ought to be holistic services to clients of the social service and health professions. Eck (2002, p. 268) has estimated on the basis of various sets of evidence that "somewhere between fifty and ninety percent of the clients that are seen in therapy have a spiritual or religious orientation that is important to them. . . . [S]uch a significant part of a client's orientation to life should be a part of the growth [that] therapy is trying to facilitate."

Another significant dilemma with respect to spirituality, health, and holistic well-being is that the more we learn about the positive and negative consequences of various types of spirituality, the more we may be tempted to impose the wholesome types upon clients in violation of their freedom. An imposed spirituality, whatever its religious connections, is not truly the same as one that develops naturally out of people's autonomous choices in the regular course of life.

At the same time, if research and professional practice reveal that some forms of spirituality or religiosity produce consequences harmful to persons or to society at large, that knowledge ought not be withheld from constituents. But will warnings about harmful spiritual and religious practices constitute a violation of religious liberty, or is advising about them equivalent to giving advice about diets, tobacco, recreational drugs, exercise, and other health-related habits? Is it ever professionally acceptable to suggest that a client consider changing her participation in a religious/spiritual group to another that differs from the one into which she was born? Is "evangelism" (sharing good news) always a violation of both political correctness and religious liberty? If it is, are we entrapping people into their forefathers' religion and thus denying them the exercise of religious liberty? If it is ethical to encourage people to exercise their own free choice to adopt a wellness-inducing spirituality, under what conditions is that option offered under such strong social pressure that it becomes unethical?

NEEDS FOR FUTURE RESEARCH

Research on spirituality still is in its infancy, and work explicitly on spirituality and aging is even more limited, for most investigations to date are not age-specific. All conceivable aspects of spirituality and its relationship to other areas of holistic well-being are potential targets for research and clinical testing. Every topic that has been mentioned raises additional questions, even though they all suggest a predominantly positive relationship between well-being and spirituality/religiousness.

One of the most inviting topics for study is caregiving during the last stage of life, for when death beckons, people with negative attitudes toward religious and spiritual interventions offer little opposition to prayers, clergy visits, and other spiritual therapies. "At the end of life, the only healing possible may be spiritual. A biopsychosocial-spiritual model of health care is necessary to accommodate such an approach" (Sulmasy, 2000, pp. 31-32). Sulmasy (p. 32), e.g., has outlined a nine-point research agenda for investigating the role of spirituality in the care of patients nearing death. He calls for multi-pronged research that recognizes all dimensions of each human person and provides a foundation for genuinely treating patients holistically. Koenig (2002) similarly provides perceptive insights for further study of religion and spirituality at the end of life that are based on evidence from research and clinical experience.

McCullough's (1995) survey of the studies of prayer and health indicates that "the empirical investigation of intercessory prayer has been plagued with methodological flaws . . . [and the research] is relatively primitive" (p. 20). He raises numerous questions for further investigation, points to methods by which that complex subject can be investigated, and contributes to ways in which theory and research can promote healthy views of prayer among spiritual seekers and committed Christians. This suggests the need for improvements in the quality of the methods used in research on spiritual, aging, and well-being, a challenge Ai and associates (2002) are confronting.

Research Methodology

Methodological issues deserve painstaking attention, whatever their professional or academic frame of reference, institutional context, or precise topic of investigation. All of the qualitative and quantitative methods of social gerontology (Reker, 1995; Weiland, 1995), the experimental and survey techniques of the behavioral sciences, and the clinical and epidemiological procedures of the health sciences can play an important role in expanding our understanding of spirituality.

Added to problems of measurement that apply to all human sciences and health professions are many special issues pertaining to the investigation of spirituality and relevant clinical applications (see Levin, 1994). All indicators used to assess and measure spirituality are merely reflectors, consequences, or accompaniments of spiritual health and illness, not the complex phenomenon itself. The results reflect a broad range of definitions and interpretations of spirituality and related concepts, all of which are subject to misinterpretation, biases, imperfect measurement, reduction of ineffable and sublime realities to mundane empirical and temporal concepts, and the assumption that feelings of spiritual wellness constitute spiritual health even when a spiritual illness or cancerous growth is actually present. The same indicators may be used as reflections of more than one phenomenon. For instance, typical measurements of belief in an afterlife are entangled with measures of religion and both reflect social desirability, so research on their relationships is easily contaminated (Falkenhain & Handal, 2003).

The evaluative criteria behind the scales and indicators used to identify or measure concepts like religious orientation, well-being, and mental health affect the findings of relationships between them (Ventis, 1995). For example, the lack of a relationship between religiousness and subjective well-being among elderly Israeli women (Iecovich, 2001) undoubtedly relates to both differences between Judaism and Christianity and a unique operational definition of religiousness.

At this undeveloped stage of our clinical, scientific, and scholarly understanding of spirituality, the attempt to use "universally applicable" scales for evaluation and measurement may satisfy no one. "Generic instruments . . . are based upon evaluative criteria and infused with indicators for evaluation or measurement that come from one or a few ideologies–ideologies so implicit, subtle, and held so unconsciously that their value base often is unacknowledged by researchers, clinicians, and educators" (Moberg, 2002a, p. 55). Whenever we limit our work on spirituality to the use of generic measures intended to apply to everybody, we are reducing the likelihood of finding unique differences not only among people who belong to different religions, but also among their various subcultural minorities. Glossing over uniquenesses can contribute to the oppression of minorities whose normative commitments or cultural practices cause low scores that make them victims of disrespect, prejudice, and discrimination.

It therefore is wise to construct or adapt research instruments and assessment tools to fit each religious and ideological group. Only after comparing the results of numerous particular studies will we be properly prepared to develop measures of spirituality that are equally valid and reliable for use in any and all groups of people. "But even if the search is ultimately in vain, it will serendipitously yield vastly increased understanding of the spiritual nature of humanity and of the means by which to enhance spiritual well-being" (Moberg, 2002a, p. 58).

Triangulation

Viewing spirituality and health from numerous perspectives will enlighten us far more than seeing them from one angle alone. (For findings related to physical and mental health, see especially Koenig, McCullough, and Larson, 2001.) In both clinical and research applications, there is a need for intra- and inter-disciplinary meta-analytical studies that pull together the findings of diverse investigations. Some of these may compare and contrast the wide-ranging uses of the concept of "spirituality" itself, relating scientific research definitions to those in the humanities, including literature, history, music, and especially comparative religions and theological studies. (Needed are in-depth comparisons and analyses of the operational definitions incorporated into the indexes, interviews, case studies, assessment techniques, and scales of religiosity and spirituality that are used in social and behavioral science research with those implicit in the applied professions and human services, as in the clinical tests and interview questions used in medical, counseling, psychiatric, psychological, social work, and pastoral care professions, as well as in the theological and humanistic studies) (see Fosarelli, 2002; MacKinlay, Ellor, & Pickard, 2001; Kimble & McFadden, 2003; McFadden, Brennan, & Patrick, 2003; Lawler & Younger, 2002). Such comparisons could considerably increase our understanding of spirituality, its manifestations and correlates in all domains of the body, mind, and spirit, and the professional and everyday ways by which it enhances holistic wellness and averts detriments.

The eight hypothesized pathways (and there likely are many more) by which dimensions of religious involvement influence well-being and health (Levin, 1996, pp. 858-859) deserve the triangulation of multidisciplinary investigations on diverse types of people at all ages, heeding the basic guidelines for research and evaluation summarized by Moberg (2001).

Most of the research on spirituality and aging to date has been done in the social and cultural context of Euro-Americans with Christian ancestry and traditions, so a majority of the measures of spirituality that have been developed are implicitly linked to that background. This is not surprising, given the history of the USA and the dominance of Christianity in its population, especially among those in late life. However, the increasing dominance of secular norms in the public square and escalating pluralism in American society, including the growing influence of New Age philosophies and Eastern religions, challenge the hegemony of Judeo-Christian values. The concepts of religious experience and spirituality in Buddhism, Hinduism, Islam, Zoroastrianism, and other religions, are considerably different (see Hood, 1995), but even within Christianity there is a broad range of perspectives on spirituality, and minorities like African Americans sometimes feel exploited when the uniqueness of their complex models of religiosity is ignored or demeaned (Chatters & Taylor, 1994; Wallace, 2003).

Basic philosophical, ideological, and theological differences, both within each major world religion and between them, are at the heart of the various evaluations and measurements. There undoubtedly are healthful and pathological elements common to all; acknowledging them can help to reconcile alienated people groups and help people develop wholesome spirituality in their everyday lives, gleaning its existential and practical benefits for every human circumstance and venture.

CONCLUSIONS

Value judgments pervade every component of research and practice related to spirituality and aging. Every clinical assessment and evaluation, as well as every scientific measure, of spirituality, is based upon worldviews and philosophical/theological values that establish the criteria by which to explicitly or implicitly judge and appraise positive and negative spirituality, spiritual wellness and illness, spiritual development and retrogression, mature and immature spirituality, even true and false spirituality.

Once the components of "positive spirituality" (Crowther et al., 2002) are satisfactorily identified, therapists and clinicians will be tempted to "prescribe" them, even as they now recommend physical and mental medicine and therapy while warning against harmful "snake medicine" and "folk cures." But spirituality deals so much with personal choice and other transcendent issues of the existential being itself that we may never know all of its components. There very likely are significant differences between individuals who adopt spiritual or religious behaviors out of a desire to obtain the typical accompaniments of faith and those who do so out of an intrinsic personal faith without regard to "rewards," the latter receiving its fruits, but the former not.

Eventually some prescribed therapies may prove harmful, while others that are proscribed may be recognized as aspects of positive spirituality. Research on the spirituality-health connection is in its earliest stages; spiritual interventions should be patient-centered rather than caregiver-focused, and they should be offered only with permission, respect, and sensitivity (p. 619). As knowledge of the importance of spirituality to well-being in late life increases, evidence-based therapies are expanding, sometimes in the shadow of complicated paradoxes (O'Connor, 2002).

What I indicated a generation ago in my evaluation of the need for sociological investigations of the spiritual nature of humanity still applies in all disciplines and professions:

The immediate practical problem related to this subject . . . is to convince religiously unbelieving sociologists [and others] that they should leave the door open to the possibility that man [i.e., every human being] has a spiritual dimension of ultimate commitment or concern even in modern secularistic societies. . . . [T]he situation pertinent to science and man's spiritual nature is not a battle between "pure science" and "religious bias." Rather it is in every instance a case of *science plus biases* versus *science plus different biases.* (Moberg, 1967, p. 33)

As whole persons, people deserve to be recognized and dealt with holistically as body, mind, and spirit in every domain and all stages of life.

REFERENCES

Abramowitz, L. (1993). Prayer as therapy among the frail Jewish elderly. *Journal of Gerontological Social Work*, 19 (3/4), 69-73.

Ai, A. L., Dunkle, R. E., Peterson, C., & Bolling, S. F. (1998). The role of private prayer in psychological recovery among midlife and aged patients following cardiac surgery. *The Gerontologist*, 38 (5), 591-601.

Ai, A. L., Dunkle, R. E., Peterson, C., & Bolling, S. F. (2000). Spiritual well-being, private prayer, and adjustment of older cardiac patients. In J. A. Thorson (Ed.), *Perspectives on spiritual well-being and aging* (pp. 98-119). Springfield, IL: Charles C Thomas Publisher.

Ai, A. L., Peterson, C., Bolling, S. F., & Koenig, H. (2002). Private prayer and optimism in middle-aged and older patients awaiting cardiac surgery. *The Gerontologist*, 42(1), 70-81.

Aldridge, D. (2000). *Spirituality, healing, and medicine: Return to silence.* London & Philadelphia: Jessica Kingsley Publishers.

Angeli, E. A. G. (2001). Spiritual care in hospice settings. In D. O. Moberg (Ed.), *Aging & spirituality*, pp. 113-124. Binghamton, NY: The Haworth Press, Inc.

Baesler, E. J. (2002). Prayer and relationship with God II: Replication and extension of the relational prayer model. *Review of Religious Research*, 44(1), 58-67.

Benyei, C. R. (1998). *Understanding clergy misconduct in religious systems.* Binghamton, NY: The Haworth Pastoral Press.

Bergin, A., & Richards, P. S. (1997). *A spiritual strategy for counseling and psychotherapy.* Washington, DC: American Psychological Association.

Blasi, A. J. (1999). *Organized religion and seniors' mental health.* Lanham, MD: University Press of America.

Brennan, C. L., & Missinne, L. E. (1980). Personal and institutionalized religiosity of the elderly. In J. A. Thorson & T. C. Cook Jr. (Eds.), *Spiritual well-being of the elderly* (pp. 92-99). Springfield, IL: Charles C Thomas Publisher.

Brown, W. S., Murphy, N., & Malony, H. N. (1998). *Whatever happened to the soul? Scientific and theological portraits of human nature.* Minneapolis, MN: Fortress Press.

Bufford, R. K., Paloutzian, R. F., & Ellison, C. W. (1991). Norms for the Spiritual Well-Being Scale. *Journal of Psychology & Theology,* 19, 56-70.

Bullis, R. K. (1996). *Spirituality in social work practice.* Philadelphia: Taylor and Francis.

Byrd, R. C. (1988). The therapeutic effects of intercessory prayer in a coronary care unit. *Southern Medical Journal,* 81, 826-829.

Canda, E. R. (1998). *Spirituality in social work: New directions.* Binghamton, NY: The Haworth Press, Inc.

Canda, E. R., & Fuman, L. B. (1999). *Spiritual diversity in social work practice: The heart of helping.* New York: Free Press.

Carlson, C. R., Bacaseta, P. E., & Simanton, D. A. (1988). A controlled evaluation of devotional meditation and progressive relaxation. *Journal of Psychology & Theology,* 16, 362-368.

Catterall, R. A., Cox, M., Greet, B., Sankey, J., & Griffiths, G. (1998). Spiritual care: The assessment and audit of spiritual care. *International Journal of Palliative Nursing,* 4 (4), 162-168.

Chang, B-H., Noonan, A. E., & Tennstedt, S. L. (1998). The role of religion/spirituality in coping with caregiving for disabled elders. *The Gerontologist,* 38 (4), 463-470.

Chatters, L. M., & Taylor, R. J. (1994). Religious involvement among older African-Americans. In Levin, J. S. (Ed.), *Religion in aging and health* (pp. 196-230). Thousand Oaks, CA: Sage Publications.

Cicirelli, V. G. (2002). Fear of death in older adults: Predictions from terror management theory. *Journal of Gerontology: Psychological Sciences,* 57B(4), P358-P366.

Coke, M. M. (1991). *Correlates of life satisfaction among the African-American elderly.* New York: Garland Publishing.

Connelly, R., & Light, K. (2003). Exploring the "new" frontier of spirituality in health care: Identifying the dangers. *Journal of Religion & Health,* 42(1), 35-46.

Crowther, M. R., Parker, M. W., Achenbaum, W. A., Larimore, W. L., & Koenig, H. G. (2002). Rowe and Kahn's model of successful aging revisited: Positive spirituality–The forgotten factor. *The Gerontologist,* 42 (5), 613-620.

Demerath, N. J. III, Silverman, W., & Lehman, E. C. Jr. (2000). Moving forward by looking back: A half-century of the SSSR, RRA, and social scientific research on religion (Special issue: 50th anniversary of SSSR). *Journal for the Scientific Study of Religion,* 39 (4), 393-557.

Dillon, M., Wink, P., & Fay, K. (2003). Is spirituality detrimental to generativity? *Journal for the Scientific Study of Religion,* 42(3), 427-442.

Driscoll-Lamberg, A. (2001). Integrating spirituality in counseling with older adults. In D. O. Moberg (Ed.), *Aging & spirituality,* pp. 125-132. Binghamton, NY: The Haworth Press, Inc.

Eck, B. E. (2002). An exploration of the therapeutic use of spiritual disciplines in clinical practice. *Journal of Psychology & Christianity,* 21 (3), 266-280.

Ellison, C. G. (1991). Religious involvement and subjective well-being. *Journal of Health & Social Behavior,* 32, 80-99.

Ellor, J. W. (2003). The role of spiritual assessment in counseling older adults. In M. A. Kimble & S. H. McFadden (Eds.), *Aging, spirituality, and religion: A handbook,* Vol. 2 (pp. 286-298). Minneapolis, MN: Fortress Press.

Ellor, J. W., Stettner, J., & Spath, H. (1987). Ministry with the confused elderly. *Journal of Religion & Aging,* 4 (2), 21-33.

Falkenhain, M., & Handal, P. J. (2003). Religion, death attitudes, and belief in afterlife in the elderly: Untangling the relationships. *Journal of Religion & Health,* 42(1), 67-76.

Farkas, M., Jette, A. M., Tennstedt, S., Haley, S. M., & Quinn, V. (2003). Knowledge dissemination and utilization in gerontology: An organizing framework. *The Gerontologist,* 43 (special issue 1), 47-56.

Fleming, R. (in press). Depression and spirituality in Australian aged care homes. In E. MacKinlay (Ed.), *Mental health and spirituality in later life.* Binghamton, NY: The Haworth Press, Inc.

Fosarelli, P. (2002). Fearfully wonderfully made: The interconnectedness of body-mind-spirit. *Journal of Religion & Health,* 41(3), 207-229.

Friberg, N. (2001). The role of the chaplain in spiritual care. In D. O. Moberg (Ed.), *Aging & spirituality,* pp. 177-190. Binghamton, NY: The Haworth Press, Inc.

Garces-Foley, K. (2003). Buddhism, hospice, and the American way of dying. *Review of Religious Research,* 44(4), 341-353.

Golden, R. L., & Sonneborn, S. (1998). Ethics in clinical practice with older adults: Recognizing biases and respecting boundaries. *Generations,* 22 (3), 82-86.

Harris, W. S., Gowda, M., Kolb, J. W., Strychacz, C. P., Vacek, J. L., Jones, P. G., Forker, A., O'Keefe, J. H., & McCallister, B. D. (1999). A randomized, controlled trial of the effects of remote, intercessory prayer on outcomes in patients admitted to the coronary care unit. *Archives of Internal Medicine,* 159 (19), 2273-2278.

Helminiak, D. A. (1996). *The human core of spirituality: Mind as psyche and spirit.* Albany: State University of New York Press.

Hill, P. C., & Hood, R. W. Jr. (Eds.) (1999). *Measures of religiosity.* Birmingham, AL: Religious Education Press.

Hill, P. C., Pargament, K. I., Hood, R. W. Jr., McCullough, M. E., Swyers, J. P., Larson, D. B. et al. (in press). Conceptualizing religion and spirituality: Points of commonality, points of departure. *Journal for the Theory of Social Behavior.*

Hogstel, M. O., & Kashka, M. (1989). Staying healthy after age 85. *Geriatric Nursing,* 10 (1), 16-18.

Hood, R. W. Jr. (Ed.) (1995). *Handbook of religious experience.* Birmingham, AL: Religious Education Press.

Hummer, R. A., Rogers, R. G., Nam, C. B., & Ellison, C. G. (1999). Religious involvement and U. S. adult mortality. *Demography,* 36 (2), 273-285.

Iecovich, E. (2001). Religiousness and subjective well-being among Jewish female residents of old age homes in Israel. *Journal of Religious Gerontology,* 13 (1), 31-44.

Ingersoll-Dayton, B., Krause, N., & Morgan, D. (2002). Religious trajectories and transitions over the life course. *International Journal on Aging & Human Development,* 55(1), 51-70.

Kaye, J., & Raghavan, S. K. (2002). Spirituality in disability and illness. *Journal of Religion & Health,* 41(3), 231-242.

Kimble, M. A., & McFadden, S. H. (2003). *Aging, spirituality, and religion: A Handbook, Volume 2*. Minneapolis, MN: Augsburg Fortress.

Knox, I. S. (2002). *Older people and the church*. London: T & T Clark.

Koenig, H. G. (1995). *Research on religion and aging: An annotated bibliography*. Westport, CT: Greenwood Press.

Koenig, H. G. (2002). A commentary: The role of religion and spirituality at the end of life. *The Gerontologist*, 42 (Special Issue III), 20-23.

Koenig, H. G., Cohen, H. J., Blazer, D. G., Pieper, C., Meador, K. G., Shelp, F., Goli, V., & DiPasquale, R. (1992). Religious coping and depression among elderly, hospitalized medically ill men. *American Journal of Psychiatry*, 149, 1693-1700.

Koenig, H. G., McCullough, M. E., & Larson, D. B. (2001). *Handbook of religion and health*. New York: Oxford University Press.

Koenig, H. G., Smiley, M., & Gonzales, J. A. P. (1988). *Religion, health, and aging: A review and theoretical integration*. Westport, CT: Greenwood Press.

Krause, N. (2002). Church-based social support and health in old age: Exploring variations by race. *Journal of Gerontology: Social Sciences*, 57B(6), S332-S347.

Krause, N. (2003). Religious meaning and subjective well-being in late life. *Journal of Gerontology: Social Sciences*, 58B(3), S160-S170.

Lacombe, M. (2000). First impressions: Evidence of a hard-wired spirituality, an interview with David Hay. *Science & Spirit*, 11(3), 20-21, 41.

Larson, D. B., Sherrill, K. A., & Lyons, J. S. (1994). Neglect and misuse of the R word: Systematic reviews of religious measures in health, mental health, and aging. In J. S. Levin (Ed.), *Religion in aging and health: Theoretical foundations and methodological frontiers* (pp. 178-195). Thousand Oaks, CA: Sage Publications.

Lawler, K. A., & Younger, J. W. (2002). Theobiology: An analysis of spirituality, cardiovascular responses, stress, mood, and physical health. *Journal of Religion & Health*, 41(4), 347-362.

Ledbetter, M. F., Smith, L. A., Fischer, J. D., & Vosler-Hunter, W. L. (1991). An evaluation of the construct validity of the Spiritual Well-Being Scale: A factor-analytic approach. *Journal of Psychology & Theology*, 19, 94-103.

Ledbetter, M. F., Smith, L. A., Vosler-Hunter, W. L., & Fischer, J. D. (1991). An evaluation of the research and clinical usefulness of the Spiritual Well-Being Scale. *Journal of Psychology & Theology*, 19, 49-55.

Levin, J. S. (Ed.) (1994). *Religion in aging and health: Theoretical foundations and methodological frontiers*. Thousand Oaks, CA: Sage Publications.

Levin, J. S. (1996). How religion influences morbidity and health: Reflections on natural history, salutogenesis and host resistance. *Social Science and Medicine*, 43 (5), 849-864.

Levin, J. S., & Vanderpool, H. Y. (1987). Is frequent religious attendance really conducive to better health? Toward an epidemiology of religion. *Social Science and Medicine*, 24 (7), 589-600.

Levin, J. S., & Vanderpool, H. Y. (1991). Religious factors in physical health and the prevention of illness. In *Religion and prevention in mental health: Conceptual and empirical foundations*. Binghamton, NY: The Haworth Press, Inc. (*Prevention in Human Services*, Vol. 9, No. 2), pp. 41-64.

Lipson, J. G., Dibble, S. L., & Minarik, P. A. (1996). *Culture and nursing care*. San Francisco: UCSF Nursing Press.

MacDonald, D. A., Friedman, H. L., & Kuentzel, J. G. (1999). A survey of measures of spiritual and transpersonal constructs: Part One–Research update. *Journal of Transpersonal Psychology*, 31 (2), 137-154.

MacDonald, D. A., Kuentzel, J. G., & Friedman, H. L. (1999). A survey of measures of spiritual and transpersonal constructs: Part Two–Additional Instruments. *Journal of Transpersonal Psychology*, 31 (2), 155-177.

MacDonald, D. A., LeClair, L., Holland, C. J., Alter, A., & Friedman, H. L. (1995). A survey of measures of transpersonal constructs. *Journal of Transpersonal Psychology*, 27 (2), 171-235.

MacKinlay, E. (2001). The spiritual dimension of caring: Applying a model for spiritual tasks of ageing. In E. MacKinlay, J. W. Ellor & S. Pickard (Eds.), *Aging, spirituality, and pastoral care: A multi-national perspective* (pp. 151-166). [Co-published as *Journal of Religious Gerontology*, 12 (3/4]. Binghamton, NY: The Haworth Press, Inc.

MacKinlay, E. (Ed.) (in press). *Mental health and spirituality in later life*. Binghamton, NY: The Haworth Press, Inc.

MacKinlay, E. (in press). Mental health and spirituality in later life: Pastoral approaches. In E. MacKinlay (Ed.), *Mental health and spirituality in later life*. Binghamton, NY: The Haworth Press, Inc.

MacKinlay, E., Ellor, J. W., & Pickard, S. (Eds.) (2001). *Aging, spirituality, and pastoral care: A multi-national perspective*. [Co-published as *Journal of Religious Gerontology*, 12 (3/4)]. Binghamton, NY: The Haworth Press, Inc.

Marler, P. L., & Hadaway, C. K. (2002). "Being religious" or "being spiritual" in America: A zero-sum proposition? *Journal for the Scientific Study of Religion*, 41 (2), 289-300.

Maton, K. I., & Wells, E. A. (1995). Religion as a community resource for well-being: Prevention, healing, and empowerment pathways. *Journal of Social Issues*, 51 (2), 177-193.

McCullough, M. E. (1995). Prayer and health: Conceptual issues, research review, and research agenda. *Journal of Psychology & Theology*, 23(1), 15-29.

McFadden, S. H. (1995). Religion and well-being in aging persons in an aging society. *Journal of Social Issues*, 51 (2), 161-175.

McFadden, S. H., Brennan, M., & Patrick, J. H. (Eds.) (2003). *New directions in the study of late life religiousness and spirituality*. [Co-published as *Journal of Religious Gerontology*, 14 (1), 2002 and (3/4), 2003]. Binghamton, NY: The Haworth Press, Inc.

McFadden, S. H., & Hanusa, M. (1998). Nourishing the spirit in long term care: Perspectives of residents and nursing assistants on sources of meaning in residents' lives. *Journal of Religious Gerontology*, 10 (4), 9-26.

McFadden, S. H., & Levin, J. S. (1996). Religion, emotions, and health. In C. Magai & S. H. McFadden (Eds.), *Handbook of emotion, adult development, and aging* (Chap. 19, pp. 349-365). San Diego, CA: Academic Press.

Melia, S. P. (2001). Older women find that prayer matures along with them. *Aging & Spirituality*, 13 (1), 1, 7.

Miltiades, H. B., & Pruchno, R. (2002). The effect of religious coping on caregiving appraisals of mothers of adults with developmental disabilities. *The Gerontologist*, 42(1), 82-91.

Missinne, L. E. (2000). The meaning of life in old age. In J. A. Thorson (Ed.), *Perspectives on spiritual well-being and aging* (pp. 126-133). Springfield, IL: Charles C Thomas Publisher.

Moberg, D. O. (1951). *Religion and personal adjustment in old age*. PhD dissertation, University of Minnesota (*Dissertation Abstracts*, 12, 341-342, 1952).

Moberg, D. O. (1967). The encounter of scientific and religious values pertinent to man's [i.e., humanity's] spiritual nature. *Sociological Analysis*, 28 (1), 22-33.

Moberg, D. O. (1983). The ecological fallacy: Concerns for program planners. *Generations*, 8 (1), 12-14.

Moberg, D. O. (1995). Applications of research methods. In M. A. Kimble, S. H. McFadden, J. W. Ellor, & J. J. Seeber (Eds.), *Aging, spirituality, and religion: A handbook* (pp. 541-557). Minneapolis, MN: Fortress Press.

Moberg, D. O. (1997). Religion and aging. In K. F. Ferraro (Ed.), *Gerontology: Perspectives and issues* (pp. 193-220). New York: Springer Publishing Co.

Moberg, D. O. (1999). *Woman of God: An assessment of the spirituality of women in the Lutheran Church–Missouri Synod*. St. Louis, MO: Lutheran Women's Missionary League.

Moberg, D. O. (Ed.) (2001). *Aging & spirituality: Spiritual dimensions of aging theory, research, practice, and policy*. Binghamton, NY: The Haworth Press, Inc.

Moberg, D. O. (2002a). Assessing and measuring spirituality: Confronting dilemmas of universal and particular evaluative criteria. *Journal of Adult Development*, 9 (1), 47-60.

Moberg, D. O. (2002b). Religion and spirituality. *Social Compass*, 49 (1), 133-138.

Moon, G. W. (2002). A personal journey to spiritually sensitive psychotherapy: An interview with David G. Benner. *Journal of Psychology & Christianity*, 21 (1), 64-71.

Morse, C. K., & Wisocki, P. A. (1987). Importance of religiosity to elderly adjustment. *Journal of Religion & Aging*, 4 (1), 15-26.

NICA (1975). *Spiritual well-being*. Athens, GA: National Interfaith Coalition on Aging.

Nye, W. P. (1992-1993). Amazing grace: Religion and identity among elderly black individuals. *International Journal of Aging & Human Development*, 36 (2), 103-114.

Oates, W. E. (1970). *When religion gets sick*. Philadelphia: The Westminster Press.

O'Connor, T. St. J. (2002). Is evidence-based spiritual care an oxymoron? *Journal of Religion & Health*, 41(3), 253-262.

Ortega, S. T., Crutchfield, R. D., & Rushing, W. A. (1983). Race differences in elderly personal well-being: Friendship, family, and church. *Research on Aging*, 5 (1), 101-118.

Palmore, E. B., Busse, E. W., Maddox, G. L., Nowlin, J. B., & Siegler, I. C. (Eds.) (1985). *Normal Aging: 3. Reports from the Duke longitudinal studies, 1975-1984*. Durham, NC: Duke University Press.

Paloutzian, R. F. (2003). A time-tested tool: The SWB Scale in nursing research. *Journal of Christian Nursing*, 19(3), 16-19.

Paloutzian, R. F., & Ellison, C. W. (1982). Loneliness, spiritual well-being, and quality of life. In L. A. Peplau & D. Perlman (Eds.), *Loneliness: A sourcebook of current theory, research, and therapy* (pp. 224-237). New York: Wiley Interscience.

Paloutzian, R. F., & Ellison, C. W. (1991). *Manual for the Spiritual Well-being Scale.* Nyack, NY: Life Advance, Inc.

Pargament, K. I. (1997). *The psychology of religion and coping.* New York: The Guilford Press.

Parker, M. W., Bellis, J. M., Bishop, P., Harper, M., Allman, R. M., Moore, C., & Thompson, P. (2002). A multidisciplinary model of health promotion incorporating spirituality into a successful aging intervention with African American and White elderly groups. *The Gerontologist,* 42(3), 406-415.

Pillemer, K., Suitor, J. J., & Wethington, E. (2003). Integrating theory, basic research, and intervention: Two case studies from caregiving research. *The Gerontologist,* 43 (special issue 1), 19-28.

Rajagopal, D., Mackenzie, E., Bailey, C., & Lavizzo-Mourey, R. (2002). The effectiveness of a spiritually-based intervention to alleviate subsyndromal anxiety and minor depression among older adults. *Journal of Religion & Health,* 41(2), 153-166.

Reed, P. G. (1991). Spirituality and mental health in older adults: Extant knowledge for nursing. *Family and Community Health,* 14 (2), 14-25.

Reker, G. T. (1995). Quantitative and qualitative methods. In M. A. Kimble, S. H. McFadden, J. W. Ellor, & J. J. Seeber (Eds.), *Aging, spirituality, and religion: A handbook* (pp. 568-588). Minneapolis, MN: Fortress Press.

Richards, P. S., & Bergin, A. E. (1997). *A spiritual strategy for counseling and psychotherapy.* Washington, DC: American Psychological Association.

Ross, L. (1997). The nurse's role in assessing and responding to patients' spiritual needs. *International Journal of Palliative Nursing,* 3 (1), 37-42.

Rossiter-Thornton, J. F. (2000). Prayer in psychotherapy. *Alternative Therapies,* 6(1), 125-128.

Soerens, A. E. (2001). Spiritual care by primary health care providers. In D. O. Moberg (ed.), *Aging & spirituality,* pp. 101-111. Binghamton, NY: The Haworth Press, Inc.

Stein, S. S. (2001). Toward better care: Connecting spirituality to the long-term needs of elders. In D. O. Moberg (Ed.), *Aging & spirituality,* pp. 193-209. Binghamton, NY: The Haworth Press, Inc.

Struve, J. K. (2001). The future of the church as a primary health place. *Journal of Religious Gerontology,* 13 (2), 17-24.

Sulmasy, D. P. (2002). A biopsychosocial-spiritual model for the care of patients at the end of life. *The Gerontologist,* 42 (special issue 3), 24-33.

Tan, S-Y. (1996). Religion in clinical practice: Implicit and explicit integration. In E. Shafranske (Ed.), *Religion and the clinical practice of psychology,* pp. 365-387. Washington, DC: American Psychological Association.

Thibault, J. M. (2003). Spiritual counseling of persons with dementia. In M. A. Kimble & S. H. McFadden (Eds.), *Aging, spirituality, and religion: A handbook, Vol. 2* (pp. 23-32). Minneapolis, MN: Fortress Press.

Thorson, J. A. (1991). Afterlife constructs, death anxiety, and life reviewing: The importance of religion as a moderating variable. *Journal of Psychology & Theology,* 19 (3), 278-284.

Thorson, J. A., & Powell, F. C. (2000). Developmental aspects of death anxiety and religion. In J. A. Thorson (Ed.), *Perspectives on spiritual well-being and aging* (pp. 142-158). Springfield, IL: Charles C Thomas Publisher.

Ventis, W. L. (1995). The relationships between religion and mental health. *Journal of Social Issues*, 51 (2), 33-48.

Wallace, R. M. (2003). The theological view of aging that permeates the African American experience. In M. A. Kimble & S. H. McFadden (Eds.), *Aging, spirituality, and religion: A handbook, Vol. 2* (pp. 330-344). Minneapolis, MN: Fortress Press.

Watkins, D. R. (2001). Spirituality in social work practice with older persons. In D. O. Moberg (Ed.), *Aging & spirituality*, pp. 133-146. Binghamton, NY: The Haworth Press, Inc.

Weaver, A. J., Flannelly, K. J., & Stone, H. W. (2002). Research on religion and health: The need for a balanced and constructive critique (guest editorial). *Journal of Pastoral Care & Counseling*, 56 (2), 213-219.

Weaver, A. J., Kline, A. E., Samford, J. A., Lucas, L. A., Larson, D. B., & Gorsuch, R. L. (1998). Is religion taboo in psychology? A systematic analysis of research on religion in seven major American Psychological Association journals: 1991-1994. *Journal of Psychology & Christianity*, 17 (3), 220-232.

Weiland, S. (1995). Interpretive social science and spirituality. In M. A. Kimble, S. H. McFadden, J. W. Ellor, & J. J. Seeber (Eds.), *Aging, spirituality, and religion: A handbook* (pp. 589-611). Minneapolis, MN: Fortress Press.

Wheeler, E. A., Ampadu, L. M., & Wangari, E. (2002). Lifespan development revisited: African-centered spirituality throughout the life cycle. *Journal of Adult Development*, 9 (1), 71-78.

Wink, P., & Dillon, M. (2002). Spiritual development across the adult life course: Findings from a longitudinal study. *Journal of Adult Development*, 9 (1).

Witter, R. A., Stock, W. A., Okun, M. A., & Haring, M. J. (1985). Religion and subjective well-being in adulthood: A quantitative synthesis. *Review of Religious Research*, 26, 332-342.

Wotherspoon, C. M. (2000). The relationship between spiritual well-being and health in later life. In J. A. Thorson (Ed.), *Perspectives on spiritual well-being and aging* (pp. 69-83). Springfield, IL: Charles C Thomas Publisher.

Zinnbauer, B. J., & Pargament, K. I. (2002). Capturing the meanings of religiousness and spirituality: One way down from a definitional Tower of Babel. *Research in the Social Scientific Study of Religion*, 13, 23-54.

Zinnbauer, B. J., Pargament, K. I., Cole, B., Rye, M. S., Butter, E. M., Belavich, T. G., Hipp, K. M., Scott, A. B., & Kadar, J. L. (1997). Religion and spirituality: Unfuzzying the fuzzy. *Journal for the Scientific Study of Religion*, 36(4), 549-564.

Zinnbauer, B. J., Pargament, K. I., & Scott, A. B. (1999). The emerging meanings of religiousness and spirituality: Problems and prospects. *Journal of Personality*, 67(6), 889-919.

Religion, Spirituality, and Aging for "The Aging" Themselves

Henry C. Simmons, PhD

SUMMARY. This article explores some likely characteristics of the particular and specific experiences of the relationship between religion and spirituality for cohorts born before 1935 by attending to three main points: (1) the word "spirituality" came into common usage in the 1960s, well after people born before 1935; (2) for some in cohorts born before 1935, "spirituality" had negative connotations; (3) a definition of "spirituality" is possible that can express the experience of older adults and, at the same time, sharpen our current understanding of the term to include cognitive, experiential, and volitional elements. *[Article copies available for a fee from The Haworth Document Delivery Service: 1-800-HAWORTH. E-mail address: <docdelivery@haworthpress.com> Website: <http://www. HaworthPress.com> © 2005 by The Haworth Press, Inc. All rights reserved.]*

KEYWORDS. Religion, spirituality, cohort, cognition, experience, volition

The cohorts referred to in "religion, spirituality, and *aging*" have their own particular and specific experiences of the interrelatedness of religion and spirituality.[1] This relationship deserves to be explored, lest

---

[Haworth co-indexing entry note]: "Religion, Spirituality, and Aging for 'The Aging' Themselves." Simmons, Henry, C. Co-published simultaneously in *Journal of Gerontological Social Work* (The Haworth Social Work Practice Press, an imprint of The Haworth Press, Inc.) Vol. 45, No. 1/2, 2005, pp. 41-49; and: *Religion, Spirituality, and Aging: A Social Work Perspective* (ed: Harry R. Moody) The Haworth Social Work Practice Press, an imprint of The Haworth Press, Inc., 2005, pp. 41-49. Single or multiple copies of this article are available for a fee from The Haworth Document Delivery Service [1-800-HAWORTH, 9:00 a.m. - 5:00 p.m. (EST). E-mail address: docdelivery@haworthpress.com].

Available online at http://www.haworthpress.com/web/JGSW
© 2005 by The Haworth Press, Inc. All rights reserved.
doi:10.1300/J083v45n01_03

a reader from a later cohort read back into the experience of these older adults more recent and narrower understandings of the relationship between religion and spirituality. Note I use the term "cohorts" (plural). Once, I mentioned to my mother (born 1906) that my wife's mother (born 1896) was comfortable living alone because she didn't mind if she died alone. To which my mother replied, "That may be OK for people of her generation. Their faith is like a stone wall. For people of my generation, the wall has started to crumble."

This brief article explores some likely characteristics of the particular and specific experiences of the relationship between religion and spirituality for cohorts born before 1935[2] by attending to three main points: (1) the word "spirituality" came into common usage in the 1960s, well after people born before 1935 had developed a clear sense of their religious tradition and had, perhaps, come to faith; (2) for some in these cohorts, "spirituality" had negative connotations; (3) a definition of "spirituality" is possible that can express the experience of older adults and, at the same time, sharpen our current understanding of the term.

GROWING UP AS A CHILD OF THE CHURCH[3]

Religion, like language, is a cultural acquisition. "Strictly speaking nothing is 'natural' in a child because the cultural universe to which he [sic] comes helps to form and define his [sic] behavior. Nor is the child simply a void. The idea of God does not grow up in his [sic] mind by spontaneous generation."[4] In an era when religion was nurtured and reinforced by family devotions, Sunday observance, and weekly worship, a child in a church-going household would find the religious practices of his or her church quite "natural." Likewise, this child, while recognizing certain commonalities between the church he or she attended and the churches attended by friends of other denominations, would know himself or herself to belong to a specific church of a specific denomination–St. Mark's Lutheran or Central Methodist, for example.

Elizabeth Tisdell recounts her experience of seeing the interactive play *Late Nite Catechism* with her 80-year-old father. She says, "The participatory audience was the 'class,' and instantly it seemed as though we had entered a time machine that brought us back to 1963, as Sister (she had no 'last name'), dressed in full habit, taught us 'the facts' of the Catholicism of our youth."[5] Tisdell goes on to say, "I agree with the director of the play: Catholics, especially those of northern and middle European descent who attended Catholic school, do share *a common cultural bond* whether we are one of those 'lapsed ones' or not" (11).

While this "common cultural bond" may be most clear for Catholics with certain experiences, it is my contention that similar common cultural bonds bind others to the denomination of their childhood, whether or not in adulthood they have changed denominations or stopped attending church altogether. I base this on three studies. The first is my own engagement through years of interviewing people born in the teens and twenties who agreed to participate in the project of helping me understand their world so that I could more effectively prepare religious education curricula to meet their needs.[6] The second is the dissertation project of Janet Ramsey referred to in her book with Rosemary Blieszner,[7] about which we spoke on several occasions. Ramsey interviewed in depth a group of women (Roman Catholics) in Blue Ridge, Virginia and another group (Lutherans) in Wilster, in northwestern Germany. One of her findings was that the religious faith that her respondents gave as the reason for being able to cope was expressed in terms that reflected the roots and life-experiences of these women in their churches. "A Mighty Fortress is Our God" did not have the same stirring, supportive resonances for the Roman Catholics as it did for the Lutherans. Finally I note the study from Hartford Seminary, *Faith Communities Today*. One of the conclusions on denomination identity reads: "It should be no surprise that these denominationally strong congregations are heavily populated with 'cradle' members.' A full two thirds of congregations in the strongest identity category reported that more than 40 percent of their adherents were lifelong members of the denomination."[8]

FROM RELIGION TO FAITH

This does not, of course, address the issue of faith, only that of religion as a cultural acquisition. As a person grew to a more self-conscious understanding of his or her world and began to take responsibility for choices, there may have been periods of doubt, times of revolt, moments of psychological atheism that ended in a personal appropriation of the tradition–a leap of faith, an embrace of the Divine, a surrender to God's power and mercy. In some denominations this would have been a personal surrender to God, in others it would have happened more publicly. Whatever the case, and however much the externals of the practice of religion remained the same, these now-older adults encountered the Mystery and were to one degree or another transformed. They moved from "doubt to the certainty of faith, from insecurity to trust, from the consciousness of being a sinner to the attaining of salvation with the gift of grace."[9]

In interviews, I ask how they described a person who was deeply invested in faithful participation in the church. They stumble around for words, and I ask, "Well, would you have said that this person was devout? Or pious? Or spiritual?" Here they are certain–none of the above. They knew who these persons were: "Mrs. Price who had the Great Dane and took care of the flowers," or "My youth leader," or "Mrs. Theresa, who smiled at us and hugged us so warmly after church even when we had been noisy and restless." Some may have even said that a certain person was a "good Catholic" or a "good Methodist," but there was no word or phrase like "deeply spiritual" or "with real spirituality" that comes to mind.

GROWING UP BEFORE "SPIRITUALITY" WAS PART OF THE LANGUAGE

And that is, of course, because the word "spirituality" did not come into common usage in the United States until after the mid-1960s. In his magisterial article, "Toward Defining Spirituality," Walter Principe notes: "But whereas Robert's dictionary [*Dictionnaire . . . de la langue française*] recognized in 1964 the newer general meaning of *spiritualité* and its application to a particular person or group, no English dictionary has been found that gives anything more than 'the quality or condition of being spiritual; attachment to or regard for things of the spirit as opposed to material and worldly interest.' "[10]

It is likely that some preachers of the earlier decades of the 20th century had taken pains to make clear what the Apostle Paul had meant by contrasting 'spirit'–namely what was ordered, led, or influenced by the Spirit of God, with 'flesh'–everything in a person (including mind, will, or heart) that is opposed to this influence of the God's Spirit.[11] Nevertheless, this would have given little opening to the understanding of "spirituality" that would become so widespread in the later decades of the 20th century.

Widespread, certainly; but also very imprecise and often with the vaguely mystical, ineffable overtones that are difficult to pin down, in part because they have been influenced by Eastern mysticism (which is far from my experience), in part because they seem to separate spirituality from the whole of life. I will return to this later as I come to a definition of "spirituality" that connects and resonates deeply with what at least some members of pre-1935 cohorts lived intuitively.

THE "SPIRITUALITY OF THE CHURCH"

But first, a word about ways in which "spirituality" is a negative term. "First, there is a population of Christians in every denomination, oftentimes 'cradle members,' who are not attracted to religious brico-lage–where pieces of theology and piety are chosen by the individual from what can be quite different religious traditions and perspectives are pasted together in a unique configuration pleasing to the spiritual seeker making the choices."[12] Some of "the aging" find this kind of spirituality little to their liking.

Secondly, for some Presbyterians in the Southern United States, their first introduction of the phrase "the spirituality of the Church" was thoroughly negative. Ernest Trice (E. T.) Thompson–a distinguished historian–delivered a convocation address to the combined student bodies of Union Theological Seminary (where he taught) and the Presbyterian School of Christian Education in 1961, which he titled "The Spirituality of the Church." He began, "Presbyterian roots run far back into the past, into the great Reformation of the 16th century and beyond. We are concerned here, however, only with Presbyterianism in what is now the Southern United States, and more particularly with what became its 'distinctive doctrine'–the spirituality of the church."[13]

Thompson traces the history of the denomination's self-understanding and concludes, "For 75 years, three-fourths of our history as a denomination, from 1861, that is, to approximately 1935, the generally accepted view of the Presbyterian Church in the United States was that its mission was limited to evangelism and to the fostering of an individual or family morality" (40). This is the "distinctive doctrine" or the "spirituality of the church." He continues,

> During this period the church had little or nothing to say about the social, racial, economic, national, and international problems that were peculiar to our region, or that we in the South faced with the rest of the nation–nothing about worsening race relations, nothing about the Jim Crow laws, which are comparatively recent, for example; nothing about worsening industrial relations [. . .] nothing about the responsibility of Christian men [sic] to apply the principles of Christian love and justice to all the relationships of life. (41)

It is little wonder that, to this day, for some older Southern Presbyterians the word "spirituality" is deeply negative. However, this very negative feeling about the word "spirituality" will actually strengthen the definition of "spirituality" to which I now turn.

"SPIRITUALITY" DEFINED

It would be presumptuous and simply wrong to imagine that there were none in the pre-1935 cohorts who, to use our current language, had a "deep and vibrant spirituality"–whether they themselves would use that term or not. What we need, then, is a definition and description of "spirituality" that will honor their lives. At the same time, we must recognize, as Studs Terkel puts it, "For so many there's a recurring refrain, 'I'm not religious, I'm spiritual,' as though they sought separation from the institution, yet, as individuals, truly believed."[14] And so our definition and description of "spirituality" must also honor their lives.

I turn again to Walter Principe who notes three levels that the word spirituality must encompass: the real or existential level–the lived experience; the "formulation of a teaching about the lived reality, often under the influence of some outstanding spiritual person" (136); and, finally, the total context of a person's theological and religious attitudes, as well as the context of "psychological, sociological, philosophical, linguistic, and other influences [that] also must be considered because in some way each fashions the person's or the tradition's spiritual ideal and response to that ideal" (138).

Working backwards from the third level, we see that "spirituality" can be a demanding field for scholarly study to the extent that spirituality refers to some public/private entity, not merely the inner life of one individual. At the second level we understand the force of great spiritual leaders (e.g., Francis of Assisi, John Calvin, Mother Theresa, Martin Luther King, Jr., Ram Dass), whose way of life, writings, and example become a pattern for others. But it is at the first level, lived experience, that we find the most useful working definition of spirituality: "the way in which a person understands and lives within his or her historical context that aspect of his or her religion, philosophy or ethic that is viewed as the loftiest, the noblest, the most to lead to the fullness of the ideal or perfection being sought."[15]

A simpler version of this might read: *Spirituality is the way a person understands and lives, in historical context, a chosen ideal to which that person commits, in sensitivity to the realm of the spirit.* In a religious context I would shorten the definition by referring to "a chosen religious ideal." The root of the word religious is *religare*–"to tie fast." Thus, "a chosen ideal to which that person commits" or "to which that person ties himself or herself fast" carries much of the same meaning without using the word "religious."

This definition has a cognitive dimension ("understands"), an experiential dimension ("lives"), a volitional dimension ("chosen"), a dimension of intensity ("to which that person commits"), a historical dimension ("in historical context"–both personal and social history), and an explicitly spiritual dimension ("in sensitivity to the realm of the spirit"). Any definition of spirituality that neglects even one of these dimensions is inadequate because it does not account for the whole of a life lived. In this definition, spirituality is akin to a deliberately chosen lifestyle undertaken in sensitivity to the realm of the spirit.

This definition implicitly distinguishes between spirituality and mysticism. We are told by individuals who claim *mystical experiences* that "something more than just relative, contingent, here-and-now is at stake. Here things, sounds, nature–the world in its profoundest sense–opens up and reveals an ultimate reality, the 'secret,' the 'mystery,' the 'light' of reality, the cosmic foundation, the Absolute (God, Brahma, dharma, emptiness, nirvana)."[16] It seems unlikely that more than a handful of the aging of whom I speak will have been engaged in mystical experiences as described above. "True enough, the life of prophetic religion [Judaism, Christianity, Islam] includes experiences of receiving a 'call' or a revelation from God; but they come less often, they have essentially less to do with ecstatic raptures, and in any event they do not abolish the subject/object split."[17]

The explicitly spiritual dimension ("in sensitivity to the realm of the spirit") is open enough to account for a specifically religious meaning ("God's Spirit," the "Holy Spirit") that will be important to people deeply rooted in organized religion, or for whom God's Spirit is a real and present reality. It is also open to another, more colloquial, understanding of spirit, as in "What a great spirit she has." This latter points to the way that the demands of everyday life leave us choices about how we will respond. Karl Rahner, a Roman Catholic theologian of the 20th century, captures the importance of real-life choices in these common happenings:

> When a person experiences laughter or tears, bears responsibility, stands by the truth, breaks through the egoism in his or her life with other people; when someone hopes against hope, faces the shallowness and stupidity of the daily rush and bustle with humor

and patience, refusing to become embittered; where someone learns to be silent and in this inner silence lets the heart's evil die rather than spread outwards; in a word, wherever someone lives as he or she would like to live, combating egoism and the continual temptation to inner despair.[18]

Rahner concludes these words with "there is the event of grace." But it does not dramatically alter his meaning to change this to "there is sensitivity to the realm of the spirit."

APPLICATION OF THIS UNDERSTANDING OF SPIRITUALITY

Clearly, many older adults have "lived and understood, in historical context, a chosen religious ideal, in sensitivity to the realm of the spirit/Spirit." As foreign as the word "spirituality" might seem to them (or have seemed to them), it does, in this definition, apply and resonate deeply. At the same time, many people of other ages and cohorts, who use the word "spirituality" to refer to something like "an awareness and honoring of wholeness and the interconnectedness of all things through the mystery"[19] can also understand that this broader definition of spirituality fits them . . . and challenges them. If spirituality is "the way a person understands and lives, in historical context, a chosen ideal to which that person commits, in sensitivity to the realm of the spirit," there is no possibility of cordoning off the "spiritual" from real and everyday choices, lifestyles, and commitments.

Those born before 1935 are–at least some of them, sometimes–great inspirations to those who are privileged to interact with them. They have indeed "fought the good fight." They "cope with life stresses, including those most typical of the later years, such as health problems, the death of loved ones, or retirement-related changes."[20] They are people who have in the past and continue to, in Rahner's words, "experience laughter and tears, bear responsibility, stand by the truth, face the shallowness and stupidity of the daily rush and bustle with humor and patience, and lived as they would like to live combating egoism and the continual temptation to inner despair."

They are unlikely to put to all this the word "spirituality." They are more likely to remember the church in which they grew up, the good and bad times of their lives, the tumultuous times through which they lived, their children's lives, and the role the church and other church members played in their lives. They are likely to pray, and will be consoled, perhaps, by familiar prayers, psalms, and hymns. They have their own particular and specific experiences of the interrelatedness of religion and what we are calling "spirituality." We can honor that, while ourselves seeking the truest ideal to which we can commit ourselves in our own historical contexts, in sensitivity to the realm of the spirit.

NOTES

1. Recent studies include *Journal of Religious Gerontology*, 14/4, 2003. These studies are both empirical and analytical, and point the reader to a wide range of other studies.

2. The choice of 1935 is fairly arbitrary although it coincides with the beginning of Social Security.

3. Because it is what I know first-hand, I speak here of Christian denominations, not other religions or faiths.

4. Antoine Vergote (1969). *The Religious Man: A psychological study of religious attitudes*. Trans. Marie-Bernard Said. Dublin, Gill, and Macmillan, p. 274.

5. Elizabeth J. Tisdell (2003). *Exploring Spirituality and Culture in Adult and Higher Education*. San Francisco: Jossey-Bass, p. 9.

6. Cf.: Henry C. Simmons (Winter, 1993), "Discovering the Public/Private World: A Research Note.' In *Journal of Psychology & Theology*, 21(4), pp. 319-322.

7. Janet L. Ramsey and Rosemary Blieszner, *Spiritual Resiliency in Older Women: Models of strength for challenges through the life span*. Thousand Oaks, CA: Sage, 1999, p. 11.

8. Scott Thumma, "Denominational Identity and Church Vitality." *<http:fact. hartsem.edu/topfinding/topicalfindings.htm>* (27 October 2003).

9. Hans Küng et al. (1986, 1993). *Christianity and World Religions: Paths of dialogue with Islam, Hinduism, and Buddhism*. Maryknoll, NY: Orbis books, p. 177.

10. Walter Principe (Spring 1983). "Toward Defining Spirituality." In *SR*, 12/2, pp. 127-141.

11. Principe, 130.

12. Joseph Coalter (undated). "One Mapping of the American Religious Context." Ms., pp. 21, 20.

13. Ernest Trice Thompson (1961). "The Spirituality of the Church: A distinctive doctrine of the Presbyterian Church in the United States." Richmond, VA: John Knox Press, p. 7.

14. Studs Terkel (2002). *Will the Circle Be Unbroken: Reflections on death, rebirth, and hunger for a faith*. New York: Ballentine Books, p. xix.

15. Principe, 136.

16. Küng, 171, 170.

17. Küng, 177.

18. Reference unknown–I typed these words out on a 4x6 file-card 30 years ago, without noting where they were from.

19. Tisdell, 28.

20. Ramsey & Blieszner, 10.

Religion and Coping in Older Adults:
A Social Work Perspective

Holly Nelson-Becker, PhD, LCSW

SUMMARY. Religion is an important coping resource for many older adults. This paper briefly describes social work's religious roots, makes a distinction between religion and spirituality for older adults, and presents empirical data showing how older adults employ religious strategies to cope with life challenge. The study reports on religious coping in an available sample of 79 European American and African American older adults residing in urban community dwellings. Implications suggest how social workers and others may support religious coping. *[Article copies available for a fee from The Haworth Document Delivery Service: 1-800-HAWORTH. E-mail address: <docdelivery@haworthpress.com> Website: <http://www. HaworthPress.com> © 2005 by The Haworth Press, Inc. All rights reserved.]*

KEYWORDS. Religion, older adults, religious coping, social work

American society has become increasingly ethnically diverse over the last century as immigration reforms have altered ethnic and racial

---

The author gratefully acknowledges the assistance of the Council for Jewish Elderly, Chicago, IL and the University of Chicago School of Social Service Administration for the dissertation grant supporting this research.

[Haworth co-indexing entry note]: "Religion and Coping in Older Adults: A Social Work Perspective." Nelson-Becker, Holly. Co-published simultaneously in *Journal of Gerontological Social Work* (The Haworth Social Work Practice Press, an imprint of The Haworth Press, Inc.) Vol. 45, No. 1/2, 2005, pp. 51-67; and: *Religion, Spirituality, and Aging: A Social Work Perspective* (ed: Harry R. Moody) The Haworth Social Work Practice Press, an imprint of The Haworth Press, Inc., 2005, pp. 51-67. Single or multiple copies of this article are available for a fee from The Haworth Document Delivery Service [1-800-HAWORTH, 9:00 a.m. - 5:00 p.m. (EST). E-mail address: docdelivery@haworthpress.com].

Available online at http://www.haworthpress.com/web/JGSW
doi:10.1300/J083v45n01_04   *51*

composition. Concomitant with ethnic diversity has come cultural and religious diversity. Major theistic and cosmological world religions such as Judaism, Christianity, Islam, Hinduism, and Buddhism are now strongly represented among individuals professing affiliation with a religious tradition. Though significant numbers of US residents may not be formally connected with a religious tradition, older adults particularly have been raised in a religiously grounded culture.

Religious values and traditions, unlike spiritual values, have often been transmitted through families (Wulff, 1997), so for many people, even where religious expressions and affiliations may be dissimilar, religion may be a family-based phenomenon. For some groups who have been historically marginalized, including women and African Americans, religion has served as a vehicle for empowerment and connection. For a few, religion itself–beliefs, rituals, and practices–has been a source of oppression. Whether promoting positive or negative effects (see Spilka, 1986), religion is a force in our current cultural context.

Religion may provide answers to existential questions, social support, purpose, spiritual guidance, and other resources. Thus, social work interventions that successfully and respectfully treat individuals who define themselves as religious and or/spiritual should continue to be developed and empirically tested. This article will briefly describe the history of social work related to religion, the distinctions between the terms religion and spirituality, the importance of research on religious interventions especially for older adults, an empirical example of ways older adults employ religious strategies to manage life challenge, and suggest implications for practice.

HISTORICAL TRENDS

From the late 19th century to the first two decades of the 20th century, the development of social work was primarily influenced by sectarian institutions and ideologies related to charity and community service (Bullis, 1996; Canda, 1997; Loewenberg, 1988; Marty, 1980; Neibuhr, 1932). The Charity Organization Society promoted by Mary Richmond, the Settlement House movement for immigrants advanced by Jane Addams, and Jewish communal services were all influential to the foundation of social work. Addams envisioned Hull House in Chicago as "a cathedral of humanity capacious enough to house a fellowship of common purpose" (Addams, 1981, p. 71), one example of the intermingling between religious action and social work thought of the era.

From the 1920s to through the 1970s, social work began to distance itself from religious roots in order to gain acceptance as a profession in competition with other emerging professions (Canda, 1997; Loewenberg, 1988). Religion was not viewed as "scientific" and social work was struggling to define itself through use of scientific and quasi-scientific interventions for social problems. Concerns with separation of church and state were also paramount as social work was increasingly being administered by governmental organizations.

In the late 70s historical theologian Martin Marty and others began to call social work to return to its religious roots in new ways by providing attention to spirituality as an aspect of human behavior and one component of a holistic understanding that included biological, psychological, social aspects (Derezotes, 1995; Joseph, 1988; Marty, 1980). This resurgence was paralleled by general social trends in the culture, including the rise of religiously conservative politics and New Age movements. In sociological terms with important nuances for social work, religious space is being reconstructed (Roof, 1993), especially as it incorporates a concern with individual and communal spiritual pursuits.

DEFINITIONS OF RELIGION AND SPIRITUALITY

Because the focus of this article concerns religious coping, it is important to discuss distinctions between the terms religion and spirituality. Outside the social work profession, religion is often considered an all-inclusive domain (Browning, 1991; Canda, 1999). In religious studies departments and divinity schools, spirituality usually references particular Christian beliefs and practices.

By contrast, in social work religion takes on this narrower perspective and spirituality is the all-inclusive domain. Spirituality for social work is associated with the human quest for meaning (Canda, 1997). It is viewed as a process of integrating all aspects of the person: the wholeness of what it is to be human, the search to build meaningful relationships with others, and the ground of existence whether that is understood theistically, nontheistically, or in any other way (Canda, 1999). Spirituality is the irreducible essence of a person. Religion, however, refers to the beliefs, experiences, practices, and ethical values associated with a particular faith tradition. Religion is thus circumscribed.

Older adults recognize the term religion and associate particular meaning with it that may include spiritual aspects. Nonetheless, many find it difficult to identify particular significance in the term spirituality.

It is not their word of choice and the meaning is elusive (Nelson-Becker, 2003). Thus, religious coping is the expression that best captures the full range of coping related to religious practices of older adults.

STRESS AND RELIGIOUS COPING

The stress and coping paradigm has been a valuable framework for understanding late-life adaptation (Kahana et al., 1999). Older adults face normative challenges in the form of bereavement, health problems, and relationship difficulties that highlight lack of congruence between person and environment. A critical life events approach to measuring stress identifies the event as a discrete change in a person's environment that is externally confirmable and requires a response (Billings & Moos, 1981; Jones & Kinman, 2001). A life event may be defined as unexpected, falling outside the parameters of everyday experience unlike daily hassles and uplifts (Lazarus & Folkman, 1989). Life events can subsume crises such as diagnosis of cancer or unanticipated death of a spouse. By contrast, chronic conditions may include stressors that are always present but not appraised as consistently difficult. A caregiving relationship in which an older adult provides care to an even older relative and experiences the vacillating benefits/costs is one example of a chronic stressor. Stress is the perceived outcome of an imbalance where the care receiver may require more than the care provider can easily give.

Response to Life Challenge

These life challenges motivate an active or passive behavioral reaction (Gottlieb, 1997; Snyder, 2001; Zeidner & Endler, 1996). Kahana et al. (1995) emphasize that life events and chronic conditions provide contexts of mutual interpretation among actors that may or may not result in appraisal of stress overload. In other words, such factors as the presence of social support may moderate the stressor. Stress requires a response to either alter the nature of the situation or one's response to it (Lazarus & Folkman, 1984). The former is referred to as problem-focused coping and the latter as emotion-focused coping. Problem-focused coping or instrumental coping is thus oriented toward an action stance. The goal is to ameliorate the underlying problem by solving it or minimizing its effects. By contrast, emotion-focused coping consists of cognitive restructuring to reduce emotional distress, not to change or eliminate the problem.

Religious Coping Studies

Propst Ostrom, Watkins, Dean, and Mashburn (1992) looked at the efficacy of religious and nonreligious cognitive-behavioral therapy for treating depression in religious clients and found religious imagery and forms of prayer to be important resources in psychotherapy. Koenig (1998) authored 99 articles on studies related to the correlation of religion with mental and physical health, generally finding religion to be a predictor of positive mental health and recovery from illness. Pargament (1997) considered how religious coping and ritual affects the outcomes of negative life events, finding either positive or nonsignificant effects. In managing life challenge, there is evidence that religious behaviors offer one important type of support.

The current cohorts of older adults tend to be more religiously oriented than younger cohorts because of period effects (Roof, 1998). Consequently, at this time religious resources hold promise as useful strategies some older adults may choose for managing problems. A study recently conducted by the author addressed this issue by focusing on religious and spiritual problem-solving strategies in a low income minority older adult population. This population was urban and community dwelling, a relatively healthy group.

METHOD

An available sample of 79 older adults age 58 to 92 who resided in four northern and southern locations in a major Midwest metropolitan city was developed by inviting individuals to participate through recruitment meetings and in housing lobbies. This was done after receiving IRB approval from university and community social service organizations as well as approval from apartment managers. A small monetary incentive was provided on completion of the interview.

The median age of participants was 78. Forty-seven percent of northern respondents were European American and predominantly Jewish while 53% of southern respondents were African American. Sixty-two percent earned less than $10,000 per year; an additional 30% earned less than $15,000. The median educational level was twelve years. Most of the sample (84%) was female. Fewer men survive to older ages as confirmed by the census data of the high-rise apartments where respondents dwelt. Thirty percent attended church or synagogue regularly, though in an older sample, some older adults who would attend do not because of health and transportation barriers. Thirty-four percent described themselves as nonattending. The two groups, European American and African American, did not differ significantly in demographic characteristics.

The interview protocol began with a question inviting respondents to identify the three primary life challenges they had encountered looking back across their lives retrospectively. In terms of normal memory functioning, this represents some bias as elders are more likely to recall early life events and recent ones. After identifying salient problems they had faced, these elders were asked to identify the ways they responded to determine if religious or spiritual resources were specified. Study participants then answered direct questions about the personal importance of religion in their lives and how they specifically applied religion and spirituality in managing life challenges. Respondents completed a Spiritual Strategies Scale developed for the study (Nelson-Becker, 1999), the Life Satisfaction Index (Neugarten, Havighurst, & Tobin, 1962), and the Geriatric Depression Scale (Yesavage, Brink, Rose, & Leirer, 1983).

RESULTS AND DISCUSSION

Life challenges were organized into four general categories in order of greatest frequency: personal events/processes (death of a loved one, health issues, marital issues, family relationships); societal events/processes (World War II, the Great Depression, emigration, discrimination); negative environmental life events (idiosyncratic circumstances); and personal traits/chronic problems (for example, alcoholism and bipolar illness). The only category differing significantly between the two groups was societal events/processes: only European Americans (EA) identified challenges here, even though problems of discrimination were detailed in the context of narrative responses in the African American (AA) group.

Responses to life problems consisted of (in order of greatest frequency) social resources (job, friends, family, community activities), religious resources (prayer, church community, Bible, or sacred text, faith), personal resources (depended on self, became strong, did things for others, maintained commitment, fulfilled a role) and idiosyncratic responses (trusting physicians, looking to the future, crying, coping poorly).

Religious resources were more likely to be cited by the AA group (81% versus 8%). But when specifically asked about frequency of using religion and spirituality to solve problems, responses were somewhat moderated across groups: 43% of EAs apply religious problem solving "Always" or "Often," 24% "Sometimes," and 32% "Never." Ninety-five percent of African-American respondents apply religious problem solving "Always" or "Often."

How do older adults operationalize religious problem solving? Qualitative responses to the open-ended question, "How do you use religion in your own life to solve life challenge/problems/difficulties?" focused on functional properties. See Table 1, "Religious Problem Solving." In the voice of respondents, the vault from concept to practice was visualized.

Prayer

> The first thing is prayer. People pray for me, I pray for me, and I pray for others. It's the only way to go in life. If you don't have God in your life, it's rough. I don't see how people manage. (# 78, AA female)

A primary means of handling problems cited by 43 percent of this sample was prayer. Even though prayer was an active response one engages for both oneself and for others, this participant also acknowledged membership in a community where people include her in their prayer.

Prayer was associated with maintaining a positive attitude and with belief. "I pray and have lots of faith and I think positively. I try to keep a positive attitude, be a positive thinker" (#1, AA female). Prayer was also linked to hope in a favorable outcome, though the exact nature of that anticipated outcome may or may not be clear. "He might not come when you want him, but he's on time. It won't happen the way you expect. Yes, it solved my pain" (#3, AA female).

Prayer is described as a discipline, "I believe in practicing the presence of God. That is, I just talk to Him. I acknowledge Him in all things I want to do or am going to do–and He answers. I have my daily prayer time" (#27, AA female). A similar integration with other daily life routines as well as a commitment to keeping faith is affirmed below.

TABLE 1. Religious Problem Solving

Item	Frequency	% of Sample
Praying* (4)	34	43
Living a good, moral life* (1)	11	14
Reading and using scripture* (2)	5	6
Helping others, getting involved in community* (9)	5	6
Meditating* (3)	5	6
Seeking help from religious leaders, listening, sharing ideas* (2)	4	5
Thinking positively, reframing* (2)	4	5
Keeping faith, believing in God, turning it over to God* (2)	4	5
Guidance, comparing problem to Christ's teaching* (2)	2	3
Feeling better after church attendance, rituals	2	3
Don't use religion to solve problems	2	3
Religion stabilizes my life, is protective	2	3
"God helps those who help themselves."	1	1
Listening to religious TV	1	1
Never use religion	3	4
Total	85	**

Note. *This item was also identified in response to the question, "How do you use spirituality in your own life to solve problems?" The number in parentheses is the number of responses.

**The sum of frequencies is greater than 79 as respondents listed strategies that they considered of equal value. The total percent is greater than 100 using 79 as N.

At 12:00 on Wednesday, I go down in prayer. When I pray and ask the Lord to lead and guide me in the way I should go, it seems as though it's a great relief. I just depend on Him to lead me the way He thinks that I should go. Religion helps me in a lot of ways. When I feel that I'm depressed about things, it just seems that I think about how the Lord is able and He rules the world. I feel like He can move mountains. When I get that feeling, it helps. (#20, AA female)

When she refocused the context of her immediate problem to take a larger perspective, she found herself less encumbered by it. This is an example of emotion-focused coping detailed by Lazarus and Folkman (1984).

Prayer was often described as a way of being in the world, though at times it was directed toward an explicit purpose. An EA female illustrated, "When I'm sick, I say, 'Oh God, don't make me be a burden to my family. Make me well enough so I can take care of myself' " (#53). She did not engage in prayer regularly, but the fear of being dependent motivated her to pray for a return to health. This next EA female portrayed a vivid example of prayer during crisis.

> I use short prayer bursts. When I needed a job very very badly and I only had a week to find one because of another problem, I made a list from the Tribune. I got there and this was the last place on my list. It was 4:30 in the afternoon. I went into a drugstore in this building to call upstairs and see if the job was still available. I walked in to this telephone booth and I was screaming at God. Other people could hear me, I'm sure. I said, 'I've got to have this. Where are you? Why aren't you listening to me?' I went upstairs and I got the job. Fortunately I wasn't swearing at the time. (#76)

This narrative story placed prayer in the foreground as an approach matched to need. Although playful in tone, it encapsulated the idea of partnership or collaboration. This respondent needed a job and felt she was doing all she could to gain one. This was prayer with a sense of urgency and immediacy.

Religion as Moral Compass

Fourteen percent of the sample reported that religion provided a moral guide, a set of standards for interaction with others.

> I believe religion helps you to determine basically what is fair and right. I feel like I can really tell between right and wrong. I can follow this and it is my feeling that I will not hurt myself or other people. (#17, AA female)

Possession of a particular set of values influenced by religious tenets was both explicit and implicit. "I try to do what's right. Do unto others as you wish others to do unto you. And love them. Love my neighbors" (#11, AA male). Words from texts held sacred thus filtered into ordinary living. Similarly, an AA female reprised this theme as follows.

I do it in terms of the Golden Rule. I really and firmly believe that this is the way you have to live. I consider that kind of religious. And I do believe in helping my brother as much as I can and in sharing as much as I can. (#32)

A measure for building right relations with others is a central principle for many faiths. A 72-year-old EA male who successfully battled cancer gave his conviction about handling interpersonal relations:

I don't think of myself as a religious person but compared to others, I am. Trying to set an example of being nice, especially courtesy and manners, gives me direction. It gives me a conscience. Do not steal that cookie from the bakery tray that's open on the top of the case. (#70)

The latter respondent distanced himself somewhat from formal religious association, but then appraised himself as operating out of religious context. In addition, he implied that religious tenets support broad community norms of what it means to live in a civil society. A sense of direction and a conscience kept him from violating those norms of behavior.

Scripture or Sacred Text

While the answers to solving life challenges were not always easily apparent, scripture could be a source of help (six percent of respondents).

I don't go to church but I do read the Bible and I have read Christ's Sermon on the Mount and the Beatitudes. Every time I come up against a problem, I try to ask 'What is Christ's teaching on that?' That's how I try to live my life. I said try. I don't always succeed. (#18, EA male)

This individual used the Bible as a resource, trying to find instruction he could apply. Application of religious (usually Biblical) instruction was one part of a three-part approach to problem solving according to the next individual. "I use religion to solve problems by meditating, talking to God, and looking in the Bible for a scripture that will fit the problem or condition" (#6, AA female).

Another use of sacred text included a search for specific passages that might apply to a problem. This could be a first step that would lead to either an emotion-focused or problem-focused approach to managing a stressful situation.

> I solve problems through using the scriptures in the Bible–not to beseech God. Whatever it is will happen and He knows. Be thankful and the good will come to us. We are still in school. He knows all about it and it will work out for the best. We need to adjust the mind to accept the will of God. (#2, AA female)

Sacred text never assumed a central role for this next study participant. Because she believed it is significant to the community, she volunteered embarrassment that it was not equally significant to her.

> Well, when they have holidays like they are having now [Rosh Hashana], they read the Bible. You get a little bit of education that way. I know I do. It never stuck with me for some reason. I'm ashamed to say it, but it didn't. (#43, EA female)

Thus, while scripture was a resource accessed by some study participants in private ways, others assessed it as having public but not personal value. Many older adults were familiar with sacred passages from childhood experiences, but did not read them in their homes.

Altruism

Older adults found that when they refocused their energy towards helping others, their own problems often become less oppressive. This application was identified by six percent of respondents. A blind EA female respondent crocheted dolls for a hospital. This task diverted her from thinking about her loss and instead affirmed her ability and skill. Another AA female respondent discussed a listening stance she used with others, a skill that helped her build relationships.

> I'm a person that you can be friends with. You can even trust me if you care. If you feel like you want to cry on my shoulders you can cry on my shoulders and I will give you the most comforting words that I can give you about God and things will come right eventually. (#19)

One AA female took an active role in shepherding her community.

I go out of my way to help someone if they need help, especially children. Sometimes I just be going along the street and I'll see children arguing and I come up to them in my own way and I{knocks lightly} touch them and say, 'Think. Don't do that. That's not right.' I have approached people like that. (#14)

Altruism alone may not be linked to a religious faith or philosophy. It can also be an outcome or expression of other life views. However, some older adults who espouse religious coping do participate in activities where the receipt of tangible benefit goes to others.

Meditation

Meditation is a religious strategy cited by six percent. One 87-year-old AA female minister enlightens, "I meditate. When I get through meditating, I pray. When I get through praying, somehow the decision comes that I am to do. I accept it as God speaking to me. He comes through ideas, hunches, thoughts, impressions" (#9). Another reported, "I meditate every day. I listen to religious programs on television. I meditate sometimes for half an hour at a time" (#13, AA female). Meditation is an important way of finding peace and relieving stress for those who practice it, but this action, too, was only used by some individuals.

Help-Seeking

While older adults provided help to friends and relatives, they acknowledged that they also needed someone with whom to discuss their own problems (5%).

When I have a problem–sometimes I can go to a pastor, an elder in the church, besides the Lord. We can't live by ourselves. I can be here and just pray to the Lord and everything, but if I can go to someone and tell them and talk and get some counseling from them that would help. Certain ones you can confide in. (#25, AA female)

An EA female added, "Sometimes you need help. You can always go to a rabbi. I don't think he solves the problem, but he can help you" (#48). Acknowledging a problem one can't handle means to also admit one has deficits, so this behavioral response may not be given often in a research study. It seems to suggest that those who mentioned this were comfortable with their decision.

Summary of Religious Coping

Religious problem-solving tasks were identified by study participants rather than being checked off a list of items. As Table 1 depicts, prayer was the primary strategy respondents identify as a religious problem solving mechanism (43% of the sample). This is consistent with other studies that highlight prayer as a primary form of coping in older adults (Koenig, 1998; Pargament, 1997). Limitations of the study included lack of a random sample to eliminate bias, a small sample size that limited generalizability, a cross-sectional study that failed to consider cohort difference or changes in religious behaviors across time, and restrictions of self-report.

IMPLICATIONS FOR PRACTICE

From this investigation, it is clear that many older adults find that public and private religious strategies help them manage finitude, loneliness, questions of life purpose and meaning, physical limitations and pain, and other losses associated with aging. Religious strategies appear for some individuals to moderate life difficulties, both chronic conditions and critical events.

Family Roles

It may be difficult for younger family members who have a different relationship to religion from their parents to understand the depth of connection many elders experience. Religious rituals and hymns played in a nursing home context are often some of the few activities to engage advanced-stage Alzheimer's clients. Family members need to recognize that even where specific beliefs differ, there is renewal and validation in belonging to a community with shared beliefs and re-experiencing familiar religious rituals and symbols. An important role for family who may share different religious or nonreligious beliefs is to facilitate the continuing involvement of parents in the religious community of their choice and to listen to their religious and spiritual concerns. Social workers can help families address religious differences.

Community Roles

Community residents can support collaborative relationships and partnerships with faith-based organizations who serve older adult needs. Traditionally, churches and synagogues have been active in providing services to the elderly, such as transportation, meaningful activities, or adult daycare. Faith-based institutions help fill gaps in community service provision by providing services directly or indirectly through hosting other programs. They may offer marital enrichment programs, drug and alcohol education, and shelters for the homeless. An important role for the community is to assist in providing information and referral services that include faith-based organizations as providers of care. Community members may be also act as cultural brokers, leaders who assist practitioners in understanding nuances of culturally diverse religions and world beliefs. Social workers, too, may act as referral agents to engage older adults with these community resources.

Service Provider Roles

An important role for providers of service is to acknowledge behavioral dimensions of religious preference and to recognize the needs an individual encounters on multiple levels. Most nursing care facilities for example now invite ministers and rabbis to conduct nondenominational religious services. Providers of care need to be especially sensitive to helping older adults act congruently with their desires to follow prescribed rituals, such as assisting Jews or Muslims to keep dietary regulations when they are no longer able to shop for themselves. Volunteers, too, may operate out of altruistic and religiously based values. They will be more easily retained when they are permitted the freedom to act congruently with their beliefs while understanding the importance of respecting religious values that are different from their own. Social workers can be involved in ensuring that diverse religious preferences are honored.

Social Work Roles

An important task for social workers is to assess a client's religious background and level of interest in use of religious resources. Individuals vary greatly in their interest in maintaining religious behavior, but if the question is not asked, older adults especially tend not to address this domain, perhaps thinking this outside the parameters of a social work practitioner's interest or role. However, social workers should be prepared to bridge the gap between social sciences and religion by exploring all dimensions of human experience (Ellor, Netting, & Thibault, 1999; Pargament, 1997).

Social workers need to develop comfort in hearing and skill in discussing client images of God or a divine power. They also need to be able to discern dysfunctional applications of and/or interpretations of religion by clients who, for example, express feelings of religious and/or spiritual guilt for failing to achieve perfection. Sometimes individuals have been wounded by religious institutions or by specific messages of intolerance. Social workers should be prepared to hear these concerns, but also build networks of clergy they may call on for their own understanding or client referral. A further task for social work practitioners is to seek continuing education on religious and spiritual issues so that they are prepared to enter a common dialogue with clients. It is important that religious and spiritual concerns not remain privileged conversations.

While religion and spirituality function in different ways for clients, they provide important means of healing for some individuals. In their role as purveyors of mental health, social workers need to become competent in integrating religious resources as potential mechanisms for change or for support. Social workers who work with older adults need to understand multiple expressions of religious coping.

REFERENCES

Addams, J. (1910). *Twenty years at Hull House.* New York: MacMillan.

Allport, G.W., & Ross, J. M. (1967). Personal religious orientation and prejudice. *Journal of Personality & Social Psychology, 5,* 432-443.

Billings, A.G., & Moos, R. H. (1981). The role of coping responses and social resources in attenuating the impact of stressful life events. *Journal of Behavioral Medicine, 4,* 139-157.

Browning, D.S. (1991). *A fundamental practical theology: Descriptive and strategic proposals.* Minneapolis: Fortress Press.

Bullis, R.K. (1996). *Spirituality in social work practice.* Washington, DC: Taylor & Francis.

Canda, E.R. (1997). Spirituality. In R.L. Edwards (Ed.), *Encyclopedia of social work, 19th edition supplement.* Washington, DC: NASW Press.

Canda, E.R., & Furman, L.D. (1999). *Spiritual diversity in social work practice: The heart of helping.* New York: Free Press.

Derezotes, D. (1995). Spirituality and religiosity: Neglected factors in social work practice. *Arete, 20*(1), 1-15.

Ellor, J.W. Netting, F.E., & Thibault, J.M. (1999). *Religious and spiritual aspects of human service practice.* Columbia, SC: University of South Carolina Press.

Gottlieb, B.H. (1997). *Coping with chronic stress.* New York: Plenum Press.

Jones, F., & Kinman, G. (2001). Approaches to studying stress. In F. Jones & J. Bright (Eds.), *Stress: Myth, theory, and research* (pp. 17-45). New York: Prentice Hall.

Joseph, M.V. (1988). Religion and social work practice. *Social Casework, 69,* 443-452.

Kahana, E., Kahana, B., Kercher, K., King, C., Lovegreen, L., & Chirayath, H. (1999). Evaluating a model of successful aging for urban African American and White elderly. In M.L. Wylke & A.B. Ford (Eds.), *Serving minority elders in the 21st century* (pp. 287-322). New York: Springer.

Kahana, E., Redmond, C., Hill, G., Kercher, K., Kahana, B., Johnson, J.R., & Young, R.F. (1995). The effects of stress, vulnerability, and appraisals on the psychological wellbeing of the elderly. *Research on Aging, 17*(4), 459-489.

Koenig, H.G. (1998). *Handbook of religion and mental health.* San Diego: Academic Press.

Lazarus, R.S., & Folkman, S. (1984). *Stress, appraisal, and coping.* New York: Springer Publishing Co.

Lowenberg, F.M. (1988). *Religion and social work practice in contemporary American society.* New York: Columbia University Press.

Marty, M.E. (1980). Social Service: Godly and Godless. *Social Service Review, 54*(4), 463-481.

Neihbuhr, R. (1932). *The contribution of religion to social work.* New York: Columbia University Press.

Nelson-Becker, H.B. (1999). Religious and spiritual problem solving in older adults: Mechanisms for managing life challenge (Doctoral Dissertation, The University of Chicago). *Dissertation Abstracts International, 60-08,* 253 pp.

Nelson-Becker, H. (2003). Practical Philosophies: Interpretations of Religion and Spirituality by African American and Jewish Elders. *Journal of Religious Gerontology, 14*(2/3), 85-99.

Neugarten, G.L, Havighurst, R. J., & Tobin, S.S. (1961). The measurement of life satisfaction. *Journal of Gerontology, 16,* 134-143.

Pargament, K.I. (1997). *The psychology of religion for coping.* New York: Guilford Press.

Propst, L.R., Ostrom, R., Watkins, P., Dean, T., & Mashburn, D. (1992). Comparative efficacy of religious and non-religious cognitive-behavioral therapy for the treatment of clinical depression in religious individuals. *Journal of Consulting & Clinical Psychology, 60,* 94-103.

Roof, W.C. (1993). *A generation of seekers: The spiritual journeys of the baby boom generation.* San Francisco: Harper.

Roof, W.C. (1998). Modernity, the religious, and the spiritual. In W.C. Roof (Ed.), *The annals of the American academy of political and social science, 558* (pp. 211-224). Philadelphia: Sage.

Snyder, C.R. (2001). *Coping with stress: Effective people and processes.* Oxford: University Press.

Spilka, B. (1986). Spiritual issues: Do they belong in psychological practice? Yes–but! *Psychotherapy in Private Practice, 4*(4), 93-100.

Wulff, D.M. (1997). *Psychology of religion.* New York: John Wiley & Sons.

Yesavage, J.A., Brink, T.L, Rose, T.L., & Leirer, V.O. (1983). Development and validation of a geriatric depression screening scale: A preliminary report. *Journal of Psychiatric Research, 17,* 37-49.

Zeidner, M., & Endler, N.S. (Eds.) (1996). *Handbook of coping.* New York: John Wiley & Sons, Inc.

Religiosity as a Mediator
of Caregiver Well-Being:
Does Ethnicity Make a Difference?

Carmen L. Morano, PhD, LCSW-C
Denise King, MSW

SUMMARY. This study used an adaptation of the stress and appraisal model to examine the mediating effects of religiosity on caregiving strain and gain with an ethnically diverse sample of 384 Alzheimer's Disease (AD) caregivers. While the regression analysis indicated that religiosity did not mediate the stress of providing care for the entire sample, there were significant differences in the use of religiosity depending on the ethnicity (African American, Hispanic, and White non-Hispanic) of the caregiver, as well as significant differences between the three cohorts in the levels of caregiving strain (depression) and gain (self-acceptance). Implications for the use of religiosity as a protective factor for AD caregivers are discussed. *[Article copies available for a fee from The Haworth Document Delivery Service: 1-800-HAWORTH. E-mail address: <docdelivery@haworthpress.com> Website: <http://www.HaworthPress.com> © 2005 by The Haworth Press, Inc. All rights reserved.]*

KEYWORDS. Alzheimer's Disease caregiving, religiosity and spirituality, African American and Hispanic caregivers

[Haworth co-indexing entry note]: "Religiosity as a Mediator of Caregiver Well-Being: Does Ethnicity Make a Difference?" Morano, Carmen L., and Denise King. Co-published simultaneously in *Journal of Gerontological Social Work* (The Haworth Social Work Practice Press, an imprint of The Haworth Press, Inc.) Vol. 45, No. 1/2, 2005, pp. 69-84; and: *Religion, Spirituality, and Aging: A Social Work Perspective* (ed: Harry R. Moody) The Haworth Social Work Practice Press, an imprint of The Haworth Press, Inc., 2005, pp. 69-84. Single or multiple copies of this article are available for a fee from The Haworth Document Delivery Service [1-800-HAWORTH, 9:00 a.m. - 5:00 p.m. (EST). E-mail address: docdelivery@haworthpress.com].

INTRODUCTION

By the year 2010, the number of persons diagnosed with Alzheimer's Disease (AD) is expected to grow from its current level of 4 million to more than 10 million (Alzheimer's Association, 2000). Likewise, the numbers of those who provide informal care to diagnosed with AD is expected to grow along a similar trajectory. Certainly, given the overwhelming evidence indicating that caregivers experience an increased risk for physical, emotional, and financial consequences as a result of their caregiving role (Biegel & Schulz, 1999; Schulz et al., 1995), it is understandable that one of the most written about topics in the gerontological literature is AD caregiving. However, with the projected increase in the number of elders from diverse ethnic backgrounds, it is important that social work research continues to develop a greater understanding of those protective factors that can mediate the strain of providing care with more diverse samples of caregivers.

Religiosity is one specific protective factor that has been found to help mediate or impact both the perception of, and reaction to, care-giving stress (Picot, Debanne, Namazi, & Wykle, 1997; Chadiha & Fisher, 2002). And while there is a growing body of research that is exploring the role of religiosity, with minority or ethnic caregivers, the vast majority of research has examined protective factors other than religiosity, with White, non-ethnic samples (Dilworth-Anderson, Williams, & Gibson, 2002).

There is also a noticeable absence of research that has focused on positive outcomes or what has been termed "caregiving gain" (Kramer, 1997). The focus of much of the early research has consistently focused on predicting those factors which are associated with negative outcomes (depression, anxiety, etc.) and not on positive outcomes (life satisfaction, self-acceptance, personal gain, etc.). Subsequently, the interventions grounded on this early research focus on reducing negative outcomes rather than having a strength-based empowerment focus, thereby increasing the likelihood of positive outcomes. Determining which factors might help to mediate the stress of providing care on both positive and negative outcomes will have implications for the person being cared for, the caregiver, and ultimately, the larger system of community-based and institutional care (Dunkin & Anderson-Hanley, 1998). Following a brief review of the caregiving literature, this study will use an adaptation of the stress and appraisal models of Lazarus and Folkman (1984) and Pearlin, Mullan, Semple, and Skaff (1990) to examine the mediating effects of religiosity on caregiving strain and gain with a sample of African American, Hispanic, and White non-Hispanic AD caregivers.

LITERATURE REVIEW

Caregiver Strain. Caregiver strain or burden has become an all encompassing term that refers to the myriad of negative consequences of caring for an adult with a disabling condition (Dunkin & Anderson-Hanley, 1998; Hunt, 2003). Emotional, physical and psychological distress; loss of time from work and personal lives; and financial drain (Biegel & Schulz, 1999; Dilworth-Anderson & Gibson, 1999; Hunt, 2003; Mitrani & Czaja, 2000) are all examples of the negative consequences experienced by caregivers. And while it is clearly evident that caregivers are more distressed or impaired as a result of their caregiving responsibilities than non-caregivers (Biegel & Schulz, Schulz et al., 1995), the impact of providing care on more diverse or mixed samples of caregivers is much less clear.

Of the many negative consequences, depression remains one of the most often studied outcomes (Schulz et al., 1995). Toseland and Smith (2001) caution that as caregivers adjust to the combination of cognitive and behavioral symptoms and physical impairments of care recipients, depression poses the greatest risk. Bane (2003) also asserts that those providing care to persons with AD report three times as many emotional stress symptoms as the general population. In addition to the noted consequences to the caregiver, caregiving strain has also been found to have serious consequences for the care recipient. For example, physical, and emotional abuse (Fulmer & Paveza, 1998), as well as institutionalization (Aneshensel, Pearlin, & Schuler, 1993), of the impaired person is all associated with increased levels of caregiving strain. Thus, understanding what factors can mediate or reduce the emotional strain of providing care can have implications for social work practice with the caregiver, the person diagnosed with AD, as well as for other professionals in health care practice and policy.

Caregiver Gain. In contrast to the well-documented negative outcomes of caregiving, research on the benefits and possible positive impacts of providing care remain quite sparse (Kramer, 1997). There is evidence to suggest that gains resulting from the caregiver role are conceptually distinct from the well documented negative impacts of it (Rapp & Chao, 2000).

Certainly from a strengths or empowerment perspective it is important to acknowledge that caregiver gain can be assessed not only as the absence of negative outcomes, but also as "the presence of feelings of satisfaction, personal growth and the idea that caregiving can provide enhancement and enrichment of the caregiver's life" (Dunkin & Anderson-Hanley, 1998, p. S54).

Within the literature related to caregiver gain, the terms caregiver uplifts, satisfaction, gratifications, finding meaning through caregiving, and benefits have been used in reference to the positive attributes derived from caregiving (Rapp & Chao, 2000). Hunt (2003) identified and defined five different positive conceptualizations of the construct of caregiving as follows: (1) *caregiver satisfaction*–the result of caregiving experiences that give life a positive flavor; (2) *uplifts of caregiving*–[daily] events that make one feel good, joyful, or glad, or satisfied; (3) *caregiver esteem*–the confidence or satisfaction caregivers feel as a direct result of caregiving; (4) *gain in the caregiving experience*–any positive return to the caregiver as a result of the caregiving experience; and (5) *finding or making meaning*–assessing positive aspects of and ways to find [higher levels of] meaning through caregiving (pp. 29-30).

Finding meaning and reward in the caregiving situation has been shown to be associated with reduced perceptions of burden and stress and with better health outcomes (Toseland & Smith, 2001). Caregiving has also been associated with feeling useful, needed, and engaged in a meaningful role that really makes a difference in the life of the care recipient; a sense of accomplishment and competence in managing complex caregiving tasks; and having the opportunity to express feelings of empathy, intimacy and love to the care recipient (Toseland & Smith, 2001). Other valued aspects of caregiving include strong family relationships, increased family loyalty and fulfilling family obligations, experiencing the care recipient's love and appreciation, maintaining a positive relationship with care recipient, seeing a good response to your efforts, and fulfilling wedding vows (Bane, 2003; Biegel & Schulz, 1999; Mayo Clinic, 2002). Therefore, this study will use a measure of self-acceptance to capture feelings of satisfaction about their caregiving role.

Religion as a Mediator of Caregiving Strain. As was previously mentioned, there is growing evidence that a number of factors that have been found to intervene or mediate the perceived strain of providing care. Positive appraisal of caregiving (Lawton et al., 1989) or the type of coping skills use by the caregiver (Fingerman et al., 1996) have all been found to mediate the strain of providing care, although the evidence to date is less than conclusive, and at times even contradictory. For example, while problem-focused coping has been found to mediate caregiving strain in White caregivers (Wright et al., 1991), Morano (2003) found Hispanic caregivers used a more emotion-focused approach, and were faring significantly better (less depressed and more life satisfaction) than White caregivers.

In other studies, African Americans were are more likely to use religious coping to help eliminate or reduce the negatives impacts of providing care (Picot, 1997; Chadiha & Fisher, 2002). Dilworth-Anderson et al. (2002) assert that African Americans tend to cope with the difficulties of caregiving using prayer, faith in God, and religion. In fact, they are more likely to include God as "part of their informal support to the same extent as family, friends, and neighbors" (p. 263). Picot et al. (1997) submit that higher levels of religiosity were reported for caregivers who were African Americans, females and older persons. Moreover, Picot's team implied that race was significantly related to perceived rewards, with African Americans reporting higher levels of reward than their Caucasian counterparts. They also surmised that the relationship between race and perceived rewards was mediated by comfort from religion and prayer.

Given this brief review of the literature, it appears that very few studies have examined the role of religiosity as a mediator of caregiving strain and gain, with a culturally diverse sample of caregivers (i.e., African American, Hispanic, and White non-Hispanic). Thus, the aims of this study are to examine the mediating effects of religiosity on caregiving strain (depression) and caregiving gain (self-acceptance) with this diverse sample of AD caregivers and to examine the role of religiosity as a coping mechanism among the three cohorts of AD caregivers.

Conceptual Model

Pearlin et al. (1990) describe caregiving stress as a process comprised of interrelated conditions to which those providing care are exposed over time. In the stress process, the caregiver's background, personal characteristics, access to and use of resources, the level and magnitude of the care recipient's needs (primary stressors) and accompanying or additional demands on the caregiver (secondary stressors) all culminate in a number of consequences for the caregiver. Accordingly, based on the stress and coping model, the extent to which caregivers demonstrate resiliency in caregiving is influenced by their ability to appraise stressful situations and draw upon available resources to cope with their individual situations.

The stress, appraisal and coping framework of Lazarus and Folkman (1984) and Pearlin et al. (1990) also indicate that the impact of caregiving is mediated by a variety of intervening factors/variables. The appraisal of burden and satisfaction (Lawton et al., 1991; Morano, 2003), the type of coping skills (Fingerman et al., 1996) and religiosity have all been studied as potential mediators of caregiving stress (Chadiha & Fisher, 2002; Dilworth-Anderson et al., 2002; Janevic & Connell, 2001; Picot, 1997). In the current study, the researchers sought to better understand the mediating processes involved in dementia caregiving with positive and negative outcomes. Specifically the focus of this study is to examine the relationship of religion as a mediator of stress on depression and self-acceptance. This study will also investigate whether the three cohorts of caregivers differed in their use of religion as a coping resource. Thus this study will test the following hypotheses:

H1: Religion will mediate the effects of problematic behavior such that as religiosity increases, depression will decrease.

H2: Religion will mediate the effects of problematic behavior such that as religiosity increases, self-acceptance will increase.

H3: The role of religion as a coping resource will vary among the three cohorts of caregivers.

METHOD

Sample

A combined convenience and purposive sample of 343 African American, Hispanic, and non-Hispanic White caregivers was studied to test the research hypothesis. While the majority of participants (approximately 67 percent) came from caregiver support groups, the researchers were required to use a variety of methods to attract sufficient numbers of African American and Hispanic caregivers to the study. Specifically, a snowball method was used to reach both African American and Hispanic caregivers. Referrals to the study were also made by community based social workers, and physicians. After explaining the purpose of the research study, those who chose to participate completed an anonymous questionnaire. Completing the questionnaire took approximately 30 minutes.

Measures

Contextual Variables. Caregiver's gender, age, income and years of education are frequently used as contextual variables in the caregiving literature. Age and gender of the caregiver were both self-reported by the caregiver. Because this study was specifically focused on co-residing familial caregivers, a measure to determine household monthly income was used. Income was measured with an eight-point scale ranging from 1 = less than $500 per month to 8 = more than $2,400 per month. The monthly income of all members residing in the household including the care recipient was added together to form a total household monthly income measure.

Stressor Variable. AD does not follow a predictable path in which each year of caregiving represents more caregiving demands. Difficult behaviors of the person with AD can occur at any time during the illness; therefore, to capture an accurate measure of the primary stress related to providing care, the Problematic Behaviors Scale (Pearlin et al., 1990) was used. Frequency of 14 problematic behaviors, such as keeping the caregiver awake or repeatedly asking questions, were reported on a four-point scale that ranging from 4 = five or more days to 1 = no days (Pearlin et al.). This scale demonstrated good reliability with this sample (alpha = .83).

Religiosity. A five item version of a scale developed by Chatters, Levin, and Taylor (1992) was use to measure Religiosity and Spirituality. The scale contained items that inquired as to the use of religion (2 items) and spirituality (2 items) and 1 global item that inquired to the role of religion specifically as a coping resource for providing care. The measure inquired about attendance in religious services as well as how the caregivers perceived the role of religion and spirituality as a source of comfort in their caregiving role. The measure used in the study demonstrated sufficient internal reliability with a reported alpha of .89.

Outcomes. The short form of the Center for Epidemiological Studies Depression Scale (CES-D) (Shrout & Yager, 1991) was used to measure depression. The short-form CES-D has been proven to be a reliable measure of depression with a reported alpha in earlier research of .73 (Chang, Noonan, & Tennstedt, 1998), while not placing unnecessary burden on respondents. With this sample the alpha was .67, indicating sufficient reliability.

Self-acceptance was measured by the short form of a measure developed by Ryff and Keys (1995) that inquired as to what degree providing care impacted how the caregivers saw themselves. Scores on this scale ranged from a low of 3 to a high of 18 with higher scores being associated with a greater sense of self-acceptance.

Analysis

Analyses conducted with ordinary least squares (OLS) multiple regression analysis implemented by the SPSS General Linear Model procedure was used to answer the first two research hypotheses. A one-way ANOVA was also completed using the SPSS software to determine if the categorical variable ethnicity explained differences in the degree of religiosity.

The use of a regression analysis is an appropriate statistical analysis given that the dependent variables are continuous and there are multiple predictor variables (Koeske & Koeske, 1993). To demonstrate that a variable has a "true" mediating effect it is necessary to carry out a maximum of three regression analyses. In the first step of the regression the contextual variables were entered as a block, in the second step the independent/predictor (problematic behavior) was entered, and in the third and final step the hypothesized mediator, religiosity was entered. Hierarchical regression analyses for the hypothesized mediating variable were completed separately for each of the outcome variables.

FINDINGS

Sample Characteristics

A total of 348 AD caregivers completed the research protocol. The details of caregiver demographic information can be found in Table 1. The racial mix for the sample consisted of 147 (42%) Caucasian, 113 (33%) Hispanic, and 88 (25%) African American. Consistent with the caregiving literature, the caregivers were primarily women (75%) caring equally for either a spouse (47.7%) or a parent (47.7%) with a mean age of approximately 79 years. Caregiver ages ranged from 17 to 94 years, with a mean age of 62.2 years. The White caregivers were significantly older (67.6) than either the Hispanic (58.7) or African American (57.7) caregivers. A mean income of more than $2,400 per month was reported for the entire sample.

The mean level of education for the sample was approximately 13 years; however, when considering education by ethnicity, the mean was slightly higher for the African Americans in this sample than for either

TABLE 1. Characteristics of AD Caregivers

Variable	Total N = 348	African American n = 88 25%	Hispanic n = 113 32%	White n = 147 42%
Caregiver age *Mean(SD)*	62.2(15)	57.7(14)	58.7(14)	67.6(13)
Patient age *Mean(SD)*	78.7(15)	77.6(14)	77.6(9)	80.1(7)
Gender N(%) Female Male	260(75%) 88(25)	73(83%) 15(17%)	80(71%) 33 (29)	107(73) 40(27)
Education *Mean(SD)*	13.1(3)	13.8(3)	12.8(3)	13.0(3)
Monthly income *Mean(SD)*	9.2(5)	12.1(7)	7.2(4)	9.0(4)
Problematic behavior *Mean(SD)*	28.1(9)	27.7(10)	28.3(8)	28.1(9)
Religiosity total *Mean(SD)*	15.0(5)	17.7(4)	16.8(3)	12.0(5)
Depression *Mean(SD)*	9.5(3)	8.6(3)	9.2(3)	10.2(3)
Self-acceptance *Mean(SD)*	13.0(3)	13.3(4)	13.7(3)	12.3(3)

the Hispanics or White caregivers. This finding was inconsistent with the caregiving literature in which both Hispanics and African Americans are typically described as less educated than their non-Hispanic counterparts.

In addition to there being a significant difference in the caregivers perceived religiosity/spirituality (this will be discussed further in the next section) the data indicated additional differences on the two outcome measures among the three cohorts of caregivers. The White caregivers reported the highest levels of depression ($p < .001$) and lowest level of self-acceptance ($p < .05$) among the three cohorts. There was no significant difference in either depression or self-acceptance between the Hispanic and African American caregivers.

RESULTS

H1: Religion will mediate the effects of problematic behavior such that as religiosity increases, depression will decrease.

The total variance accounted for by the regression equation for depression was approximately 18% ($R^2 = .179$; $F = 3.827$, $p < .05$). Three coefficients were statistically significant on the last step of the regression. Caregiver age was significant ($\beta = .158$, $p = .003$). Older caregivers experienced higher rates of depression than younger caregivers. Second, income status was significant ($\beta = -.151$, $p = .004$) with individuals who had less income reporting higher rates of depression than individuals who had a higher income. Lastly, problematic behavior of the care recipient was also significant ($\beta = .330$, $p < .0001$) with greater problematic behaviors resulting in higher levels of depression. Although increased religiosity appeared to contribute to decreased depression, it was not found to mediate the effects of problematic behavior on depression when it was introduced in the final step of the regression. Table 2 provides the variance accounted for and the standardized coefficients from the final step of the regression model. All statistical assumptions for this analysis were adequately met. Thus, it was concluded that the data did not confirm the research hypothesis.

H2: Religion will mediate the effects of problematic behavior such that as religiosity increases, self-acceptance will increase.

The total variance accounted for by the regression equation for self acceptance was approximately 10% ($R^2 = .090$, $F = 11.16$, $p < .001$). The same entry of the variables was used for this model. Table 2 provides the variance accounted for and standardized coefficients from the final step of the regression model. Three coefficients were statistically significant in the last step of the regression. Caregiver age was significant ($\beta = -.118$, $p = .032$) with older caregivers experiencing lower rates of self-acceptance than younger caregivers. Problematic behaviors exhibited by the care recipient was also significant ($\beta = -.184$, $p = .001$) with caregivers who were caring for someone who exhibited more problematic behaviors having lower levels of self-acceptance. Religiosity was also significant ($\beta = .184$, $p = .001$) on the last step of the regression, and as was predicted, when religiosity increased, self-acceptance increased, thus this hypothesis was partially supported by the data. However, because religiosity did not reduce the impact of problematic behaviors on self-acceptance, it could not be said that religiosity mediated the strain of providing care on self-acceptance.

H3: The role of religion as a coping resource will vary by race and ethnicity.

TABLE 2. Regression Analysis of AD Caregiver Stressor Variable and Hypothesized Mediators

Dependent Variable	Predictors and Mediators	R^2	Standardized β	t
Depression				
	Caregiver age	.069	.158	3.026*
	Patient age	.069	.035	.696
	Income	.069	−.151	−2.877*
	Caregiver education	.069	.001	.029
	Problematic behaviors	.172	.330	6.641**
	Religiosity	.179	−.097	−1.956*
Self-acceptance				
	Caregiver age	.034	−.118	−2.152*
	Patient age	.034	−.052	−.972
	Income	.034	.086	1.560
	Caregiver education	.034	−.021	−.385
	Problematic behaviors	.062	−.184	−3.514**
	Religiosity	.090	.174	3.341**

* = $p < .05$, ** = $p < .001$

A one-way analysis of variance (ANOVA) was used to determine if religiosity varied among the three cohorts of caregivers. The data indicated that there was significant variance in the measure of religiosity among the three groups, African American caregivers reported the highest level of religiosity with a mean score of approximately 18, followed by Hispanics (17), then White non-Hispanics (12) ($F = 67.19$; $p < .001$). The overall model was significant; therefore, it was concluded that the data did support this hypothesis.

DISCUSSION

While the hypothesis that religion would mediate the effect of problematic behavior on depression was not statistically significant, there was an indication that the role of religiosity was substantively associated with depression. Those reporting with higher levels of religiosity did report significantly lower levels of depression. The regression coefficients indicated a positive effect for religiosity, and perhaps a larger sample, a more sensitive instrument measuring religiosity, or an assessment of religiosity with more specific characteristics of religiosity would yield different results. Picot et al. (1997) had suggested that rather than mediating the effects of stress, religion served as a deterrent of stress by "raising the threshold at which the caregiver perceives stress" (p. 91). Such an assessment takes into account the caregivers' level of religiosity prior to entering the caregiving experience, which was not a consideration for the current study.

Religiosity was found to be a partial-mediator of problematic behavior on the caregivers perceived self-acceptance. Unfortunately, since the impact of problematic behavior was not reduced to non-significance (Baron & Kenny, 1984), it could not be said that religiosity fully mediated the strain of problematic behavior. Again however, the data did indicate that religion did in fact have a significant impact on perceived self-acceptance. As the level of religiosity increased so too did the caregivers' perception of self-acceptance. This does indicate that incorporating some form of religious support could serve as a protective factor, especially with ethnically diverse caregivers.

Significant differences in the level of religiosity, as well as in the level of depression and self-acceptance, were found among the three cohorts of caregivers. Confirming some of the earlier research in this area (Picot et al., 1997; Chadiha & Fisher, 2002), this study also found the African American caregivers reported the highest level of religiosity and self-acceptance, as well as the lowest levels of depression. And while the Hispanic caregivers reported slightly lower religiosity than the African American caregivers, they were still significantly higher than the White non-Hispanic caregivers. Additionally, both the African American and Hispanic caregivers reported both lower levels of depression and greater levels of self-acceptance than the White caregivers. While the role of religiosity was not found to significantly mediate caregiving strain, the overall the findings of this study indicate that religiosity is an important protective factor. Lastly, of the three cohorts, the White non-Hispanic AD caregivers appeared to be faring less well than either of the other two cohorts.

LIMITATIONS

Although 97% of the caregivers attending the support groups agreed to participate in the study, the self-selection of participants in any research limits the external validity, as they might not be representative of those caregivers not motivated to seek help (Connell & Gibson, 1997). In addition to some of the limitations present in most, if not all, quasi-experimental research, this study is limited by two obvious factors. First, the use of a convenience/purposive sample of caregivers from AD caregiver support groups limits the ability to generalize any of the findings from this study to other AD caregiving populations. Although use of support groups and day care centers is a common and accepted practice in the literature, gathering data from these traditional locations can not be generalized to the larger caregiving population. Future research, particularly qualitative research, is needed to better understand how these variables might predict both caregiving strain and gain.

IMPLICATIONS FOR SOCIAL WORK PRACTICE

The findings of this study indicate that there is still much to be learned about the role of religiosity as a mediator of caregiving strain and gain. Given the strengths-based practice of social work, it is important that developing a greater understanding of those factors that contribute to positive outcomes is equally important and warrants further study. For example, interventions with a focus on building or developing skills to increase positive outcomes might be more effective and efficient than those that interventions that focus primarily on reducing the negative outcomes.

The significant difference found in the level of religiosity among the three cohorts also has implications for social work practice. Exploring how religiosity impacts not only the response to providing care, but the caregivers' perception of positive, as well as negative outcomes, will help in the development of more culturally sensitive intervention strategies. The findings of this study appear to indicate that a faith-based location to conduct an intervention would appear to be more appropriate for ethnic caregivers than it might be for White caregivers.

Lastly, although this study did not find religiosity to be as important for the White caregivers, the implications of these findings should not imply that religiosity and spirituality are not important to non-ethnic caregivers. At the minimum the findings of this study indicate a need for further research in this area. Perhaps a more sensitive measure of religiosity, or a larger sample would have produced different results. Certainly given the positive relationship of religiosity both on depression and self-acceptance, it would appear that social work practitioners must develop the skills to assess the role of religiosity and spirituality of all clients. Perhaps more importantly, schools of social work must do a better job of preparing future social work practitioners to understand how to assess the role of religiosity and spirituality in the lives of all clients.

REFERENCES

Alzheimer's Association. (2000). *Fact Sheet*. Chicago: The Alzheimer's Association.

Aneshensel, C . S., Pearlin, L. I., & Schuler, R. H. (1993). Stress, role captivity, and the cessation of caregiving. *Journal of Health & Social Behavior, 34*, 54-70.

Bane, S.D. (undated). Caregivers: Rewards and stressors. Retrieved October 20, 2003 from *http://iml.umkc.edu/casww/rewdstrs.htm*.

Baron, R. M., & Kenny, D. A. (1986). The moderator-mediator variable distinction in social psychological research: Conceptual, strategic, and statistical considerations. *Journal of Personality & Social Psychology, 51*, 1173-1182.

Biegel, D. E., & Schulz, R. (1999). Caregiving and caregiver interventions in aging and mental illness. *Family Relations, 48*(4), 345-355.

Chadiha, L. A., & Fisher, R. H. (2003). Contributing factors to African American women caregivers' mental well-being. Retrieved October 20, 2003 from http// www.rcgd.isr.umich.edu/prba/perspectives/springsummer2002/chadiha.pdf.

Chang, B. L. (1999). Cognitive-behavioral intervention for homebound caregivers of persons with dementia. *Nursing Research, 48*(3), 173-182.

Chang, B. H., Noonan., A. E., & Tennstedt, S. L. (1998). The role of religion/spirituality in coping with caregivers for the disabled elders. *The Gerontologist, 38*(4), 463-470.

Chatters, L. M., Levin, J. S., & Taylor, R. J. (1992). Antecedents and dimensions of religious involvement among older Black Americans. *Journal of Gerontology: Social Sciences, 47*, S269-S278.

Cox, C., & Monk, A. (1993). Hispanic culture and family care of Alzheimer's patient. *Health and Social Work, 18*, 92-101.

Daly, A., & Jennings, J. (1994). Effective coping strategies of african americans. *Social Work, 40*(2), 240-249.

Damron-Rodriguez, J., Wallace, S., & Kington, R. (1994). Service utilization and minority elderly: Appropriateness, accessibility, and acceptability. *Gerontology & Geriatrics Education, 15*(1), 45-63.

Dilworth-Anderson, P., & Gibson, B. E. (1999). Ethnic minority perspectives on dementia, family caregiving, and interventions. *Generations*, 40-45.

Dilworth-Anderson, P., & Williams, S. W. (1999). The context of experiencing emotional distress among family caregivers to elderly African Americans. *Family Relations, 48*(4), 391-397.

Dilworth-Anderson, P., Williams, I. C., & Gibson, B. E. (2002). Issues of race, ethnicity, and culture in caregiving research: A 20 year review (1980-2000). *The Gerontologist, 42*(2), 237-272.

Dunkin, J. J., & Anderson-Hanley, C. (1998). Dementia caregiver burden: A review of the literature and guidelines for assessment and intervention. *Neurology, 51*(1), 1-15.

Fingerman, K. L., Gallagher-Thompson, D., Lovett, S., & Rose, J. (1996). Internal resourcefulness, task demands, coping, and dysphoric affect among caregivers of the frail elderly. *International Aging and Human Development, 42,* 229-248.

Fulmer, T., & Paveza, G. (1998). Neglect in the elderly patient. *Geriatric Nursing, 33,* 457-465.

Goodman, C. R., Zarit, S. H., & Steiner, V. L. (1997). Personal orientation as a predictor of caregiver strain. *Aging and Mental Health, 1*(2), 149-158.

Haley, W. E. (1997). The family caregiver's role in Alzheimer's disease. *Neurology, 48*(5), 25S-29S.

Harwood, D. G., Baker, W. W., Cantillon, M., Lowenstein, D. A., Owenby, R., & Duara, R. (1998). Depressive symptomology in first degree family caregivers of Alzheimer's disease patients: A cross-ethnic comparison, *Alzheimer's Disease and Associated Disorders, 12,* 340-346.

Hunt, C. K. (2003). Concepts in Caregiver Research. *Journal of Nursing Scholarship, 35*(1), 27-32.

Janevic, M. R., & Connell, C. M. (2001). Racial, ethnic, and cultural differences in the dementia caregiving experience. *The Gerontologist, 41*(3), 334-347.

Knight, B. G., & McCallum, T. J. (1998). Heart rate reactivity and depression in African American and white dementia caregivers: Reporting bias or positive coping. *Aging and Mental Health, 2*(3), 212-222.

Koeske, G. F., & Koeske, R. D. (1993). A preliminary test of a stress-outcome model for reconceptualizing the burnout phenomenon. *Journal of Social Service Research, 17*(3/4), 107-128.

Kramer, B. J. (1997). Gain in the caregiving experience: Where are we? What next? *Gerontologist, 37,* 218-232.

Lawton, M. P., Moss, M., Kleban, M. H., Glicksman, A., & Rovine, M. (1991). A Two-factor model of caregiving appraisal and psychological well-being. *Journal of Gerontology: Psychological Sciences, 46*(4), 181-189.

Lawton, M. P., Kleban, M. H., Moss, M., Rovine, M., & Glicksman, A. (1989). Measuring caregiving appraisal. *Journal of Gerontology, 44*(3), P61-P71.

Lazarus, R. S., & Folkman, S. (1984). Stress, appraisal, and coping. New York: Springer Publishing.

Mayo Clinic (2002). Alzheimer's caregiving: Balancing your need with those of your loved one. Retrieved October 20, 2003 from http://www.cnn.com/HEALTH/AZ/00013.html.

Mitrani, V. B., & Czaja, S. J. (2000). Family-based therapy for dementia caregivers: Clinical observations. *Aging & Mental Health, 4*(3), 200-210.

Morano, C. (2003). Appraisal and coping: Moderators or mediators of stress in Alzheimer's disease caregivers? *Social Work Research, 27,* 116-128.

Pearlin, L. I., Mullan, J. T., Semple, S. J., & Skaff, M. M. (1990). Caregiving and the stress process: An overview of concepts and their measures. *The Gerontologist,* 583-593.

Picot, S. J., Debanne, S. M., Namazi, K. H., & Wykle, M. L. (1997). Religiosity and perceived rewards of black and white caregivers. *The Gerontologist, 37*(1), 89-101.

Rapp, S. R., & Chao, D. (2000). Appraisals of strain and of gain: Effects on psychological well-being of caregivers of dementia patients. *Aging and Mental Health, 4*(2), 142-148.

Ryff, C. D., & Keyes, C. L. M. (1995). The structure of psychological well-being revisited. *Journal of Personality & Social Psychology, 69*, 719-727.

Schulz, R., O'Brien, A. T., Bookwala, J., & Fleissner, K. (1995). Psychiatric and physical morbidity effects of dementia caregiving: Prevalence, correlates, and causes. *Gerontologist, 35*, 771-791.

Tennstedt, S. (1999, March 29). Family caregiving in an aging society. Retrieved March 6, 2002 from *http://aoa.gov/caregivers/FamCare.html*.

Toseland, R. W., & Smith, T. (2001). Supporting caregivers through education and training. Administration on Aging, National Family Caregiver Support Program, Washington, DC. Retrieved October 27, 2003 from *www.aoa.gov/aoacarenet/ EdandTrng-Toseland.html*.

United States Bureau of the Census (2000). National Projections

Wallhagen, M. I. (1993). Perceived control and adaptation in elder caregivers: Development of an explanatory model. *International Journal of Aging & Human Development, 36*, 219-237.

Wright, S. D., Lund, D. A., Caserta, M. S., & Pratt, C. (1991). Coping and caregiver well-being: The impact of maladaptive strategies. *Journal of Gerontological Social Work, 17*, 75-91.

Wright, L., Hickey, J., Buckwalter, K., Hendrix, S., & Kelechi, T. (1999). Emotional and physical health of spouse caregivers of persons with Alzheimer's disease and stroke. *Journal of Advanced Nursing, 30*(3), 552-564.

"Religion Is the Finding Thing":
An Evolving Spirituality in Late Life

Susan A. Eisenhandler, PhD

SUMMARY. This paper discusses some important dimensions of faith
and of the social contexts surrounding faith that are illustrative of continuity and growth in spirituality in the lives of older adults. Examples of
an evolving spirituality emerge in the analysis of a recent qualitative research study that probed the nature of religious experience among
thirty-one community-dwelling elders and fifteen elders residing in
long-term care facilities. Face-to-face interviews with these forty-six
older adults and with seven people who directed or assisted with formal
and informal programs of faith comprise the empirical base for this paper. The seven people, I refer to them mnemonically as faithreps,
worked in various ways in the long-term care settings to provide programs involving faith to older adults. The faithreps came from a range of
educational and religious backgrounds and are not accurately or handily
categorized.

An evolving spirituality is shaped by the older person's links to the
structural and the socio-relational contexts that have been created
through interaction in the past as well as through interaction in the present. Moreover, the interaction of older adults and faithreps encourages

---

Grateful acknowledgement for partial support of transcription services is tendered
to the University of Connecticut Research Foundation and the Consortium for Gerontological Education.

[Haworth co-indexing entry note]: "'Religion Is the Finding Thing': An Evolving Spirituality in Late
Life." Eisenhandler, Susan A. Co-published simultaneously in *Journal of Gerontological Social Work* (The
Haworth Social Work Practice Press, an imprint of The Haworth Press, Inc.) Vol. 45, No. 1/2, 2005, pp.
85-103; and: *Religion, Spirituality, and Aging: A Social Work Perspective* (ed: Harry R. Moody) The
Haworth Social Work Practice Press, an imprint of The Haworth Press, Inc., 2005, pp. 85-103. Single or multiple copies of this article are available for a fee from The Haworth Document Delivery Service
[1-800-HAWORTH, 9:00 a.m. - 5:00 p.m. (EST). E-mail address: docdelivery@haworthpress.com].

Available online at http://www.haworthpress.com/web/JGSW
doi:10.1300/J083v45n01_06

spiritual growth because as social actors engaged with one another over a sustained period of time in an institutional setting, questions and dialogue about life and its meaning are regularly evoked. The social interactions that foster spiritual evolution may be an admixture of the secular and the sacred. Such socio-relational contexts were once part of the naturalistic settings of daily life among the old, but now must emerge through the efforts and planning of others. The salience of faith among present cohorts of older adults sensitizes us to the necessity of devoting more consideration to optimal ways of strengthening and building contexts that are conducive to the evolution of spirituality. *[Article copies available for a fee from The Haworth Document Delivery Service: 1-800-HAWORTH. E-mail address: <docdelivery@haworthpress.com> Website: <http://www.HaworthPress. com> © 2005 by The Haworth Press, Inc. All rights reserved.]*

KEYWORDS. Religion in late life, religion and spirituality in old age, identity in late life, religion and identity among older adults, the social value of faith, religion in everyday life of the old

INTRODUCTION:
SOCIAL MILIEUS OR CONTEXTS
FOR RELIGION AND SPIRITUALITY

Much has changed in the past decade with respect to the study of religion and late life. The discussion of faith in old age and in social life has moved to the front of gerontological and social analysis as evidenced in these few works among many other important contributions (Atchley, 1999; Koenig, 1998; Putnam, 2000; Roof, 1999; Wuthnow, 1998, 2003). Though religion is still not considered central to the understanding of late life or life at any age by the vast majority of social scientists, there has been much work dedicated to examining the instrumental functions of belief in the sacred or in patterns of observing faith, and to the adjunctive, measurable, and generally salutary role that participation in religion has in the lives of older adults. In turning away from characterizations of religion, spirituality, and faith as tangential elements, there has been an elevation for all three to the status of variables that ought to be included in a wide variety of research on late life and aging, and that is rightly perceived to be a sign of progress.

Nonetheless, this movement to the front if not the center stage of research in social gerontology, has been accompanied by a reduction of interest in faith in and of itself. Faith is treated in tandem with other co-variants and while considered important it is eclipsed as an area of study in its own right and with regard to its humanistic content (Cole, 2002). Religion has in a sense been converted into an ancillary if necessary component of study, which is much better than neglecting or dismissing it, but full acknowledgment of a distinctive and important role in ordinary social relations and human behavior remains to be formulated. Some of this interest is also, as Sorokin (1956) noted decades ago, characteristic of the episodic swings, the "fads and foibles," of scholarly and cultural concerns about appropriate areas of study in the social sciences. How faith will be reckoned in post-modern or post-structural perspectives on social identity in late life (e.g., Gilleard and Higgs, 2000) does not appear certain or clear.

Simultaneous with the emergence of an enlarged vision of religion's instrumental role in aging and old age, is the effluent scholarship of what may be called the literature of maturation. This research and writing has added to the basic vocabulary of religion and adult development by pointing to related dimensions such as spirituality, faith, gero-transcendence, transpersonal awareness, wisdom. This anarchy and proliferation of theoretical concepts and attempts to measure them is the expected and useful result of pushing across intellectual boundaries to examine old age and religion. Without doubt the welter of terms is a kind of rudimentary language that will be refined by lively debate and further study. Closing discussion and debate prematurely may truncate both the lexicon and understanding of faith, mind, spirit, and age. As to measurement, scales that have face validity and statistical reliability have been the goal of several researchers and are extant if not yet successful in setting a universal standard for the field.

I allude to the profusion of ways that scholars and researchers approach the topic both to highlight the dramatic change in emphasis that has occurred and to suggest that religion or faith, and spirituality, may not be experienced or embodied as distinctive dimensions either in social life or in individual experience. Thus, I often use the terms as if they were interchangeable, though I have written earlier (1994) and others have as well (e.g., Fowler, 1981, among them) that the distinguishing feature may be the level of generality associated with religion (institutional/organizational and concrete/material) and spirituality (personal/ individual and abstract/ephemeral). In a similar though not identical fashion, Vaillant (2002) distinguishes between religiosity and spirituality in case studies and interviews he analyzes. I have found (2003) that most older adults do not think of themselves in terms of spirituality and do not include that word in the language they use to describe and explain what faith is and how they observe or practice their respective faith. Nevertheless at an analytical level, spirituality is a qualitatively different offshoot of religion and faith although it too is strongly tied to lived experience. This may be what Merton (1958: 27) meant when he insisted that "spiritual life is not mental life." "[It] is first of all a *life*" (Merton, 1958:46, emphasis Merton's). The two, religion and spirituality, are distinctive as concepts but fused and virtually inseparable in the social lives we live.

The task of refining analytic terms and theoretical constructs has not mitigated the press or reality of deculturation–a process of stripping meaning and presence from the old (Gutmann, 1987). Nor has it expanded the availability of places and occasions for the systematic examination of questions about old age and the meaning of life by elders. Butler's (1963) cornerstone essay on life review posited the value of reflecting on life's meaning, a social task often linked to religion as frequently as it is associated with adult development, psychiatry, or psychology. Traditionally religions and religious programs have raised questions of meaning and have articulated frameworks for understanding life and its purpose. When the cultural contribution of religion or faith was woven more carefully into American social structure, the socio-cultural pockets of interaction it provided gave people of all ages ample settings and occasions for thinking about the purpose of life. In the absence of such contexts, some, for example, Gutmann (1987), have suggested the need to create places or "developmental milieus" where older adults can work with these questions about life's meaning and value. Religion and participation in programs linked to faith and spirituality are social niches that may also be developmental milieus. Elsewhere (1994), I have argued that secular, small groups may stimulate the person's capacity to understand the value of his or her life and the ups and downs of old age itself. Such engagement with others in activities that ask for creativity and innovation, even as a response if not as an initiative from older adults, provides them with compelling and real reasons to "choose life" (Deuteronomy 30:19). Complementary ideas have been discussed by Atchley (1999) and Wuthnow (2003). Indeed, one of Wuthnow's recent themes is that artistic engagement and its creative impact extends beyond the participants in religious worship to the structure and viability of the organization itself.

The remainder of this paper details and analyzes some of the experiences older adults recounted as participants in programs related to religion in the course of moving through their daily lives. In a microcosm, and as a way of heightening awareness rather than of testing hypotheses, evidence of an evolving spirituality, or of possessing greater perspective on the sacred in their present circumstances, is disclosed. This growth of spirit is not restricted exclusively to those in long-term care facilities. However, examples drawn from that domain are provided in the hope that faithreps, gerontological social workers, and others may gain a deeper appreciation for the benefits that accrue from nurturing these or similar milieus within nursing homes. Community-dwelling elders in this study were mobile (most had driver's licenses and vehicles) and consequently were more adept at maintaining the face-to-face ties with others in their respective congregations and religious groups. Elders living in long-term care facilities did not have this mobility or freedom to sustain contact and involvement with the worlds outside the facility. Consequently they were dependent upon others to meet these particular needs.

METHODOLOGY AND SAMPLE

All of the older adults interviewed in the study constitute what is ordinarily known in social science as a purposive or theoretical sample. Older people were approached about their willingness to participate in the study because they had been nominated as people who were likely to be receptive and open to talking about their family backgrounds, life events, and religious experiences. In addition, as I solicited names of prospective participants, I kept an eye on two social characteristics that have some influence on the experience of faith and ideas about it, namely, sex and residential status. There was also a deliberate attempt on my part to include non-white elders among those to be interviewed, just as there was an attempt to insure that economically privileged as well as less-privileged elders were included in the study. Within these parameters, a purposive sample emerged. Once nominations had been received, I proceeded to call people to schedule interviews, or in the case of the 15 long-term care participants, I contacted institutional liaisons and then arranged interviews with older adults. More extensive discussion of methodology and research design is found in the book based on this study, *Keeping the Faith in Late Life* (2003).[1]

SUSTAINED FAITH AND AN EVOLVING SPIRITUALITY ALONG TRADITIONAL PATHS

At 74, James continues his lifelong pattern of worship by attending congregational religious services as often as they are offered in his current home, Chelsea Court, a large long-term care facility. He also prays in his own words every day–morning and evening. Prayer is his communication with the divine, however, it is equally important as a way to bring others into the communication in a special way via remembrance. He tells me, ". . . I used to pray with the, you know, words we were taught. But I think I'm more individual now because I've got so many people to pray for and they got [chuckles] all my nephews are married, and they've got about five kids apiece, my great nieces and nephews, you know. And you've got to include them, you've got to. So it takes me a half an hour to pray, for crying out loud . . . I take them . . . and I pray for each one as an individual. I get closer that way when I pray as an individual. If I say the rosary or something–I mean, I will say the rosary, but to me that was fine when I wasn't here, when I was away from this place, Chelsea Court. But now I feel I'm equipped to pray the way I want to pray. And that's what this has done for me here because it's always available. I mean, you can always go to church [mass is regularly held in the long-term care facility's chapel] and pray. You can always talk to somebody [God] that way." The provision of on-site routinely scheduled worship has provided James with the freedom to develop special prayers for family members, a new dimension of spirituality for him. He is also sustained by the traditional practice of attending formal worship.

Another facet of an evolving spirituality is discerned in the casual, but significant talks James has with two staff members of the facility. This informal group of three takes up inquiry about books–secular and religious–that each one has read or is reading and they talk with one another about larger issues that flow from the books. When he compared his reading today with earlier years, James described the time spent on reading as much more than before. He reads the Bible as well as other books, chiefly biography and religion. He enjoys talking about his understanding and interpretation with two staff members who are also members of the religious order that originally supervised the facility. These "chats" are periodic but unstructured. They also are the source of suggestions for further reading. The group's discussions about issues such as the role of women in the church, and other changes in Roman Catholicism, are termed helpful by James since they are informed by the greater authority and expertise of two people well-versed in theology and doctrinal matters. And yet he notes that they all enjoy the biographies of religious and civil leaders because the human side of great people is revealed. He has found reading to be an activity that takes him a bit further in understanding God and life.

James and his friends "laugh" about some of the predicaments the authors highlight in the life stories. The humor leavens his day and is something spontaneous that kindles his interest in ideas and matters that are larger than everyday comings and goings at the nursing home. It is a stark and welcome contrast to the treatment he describes as characteristic of his female co-residents, "I'm a sex object, when I go down for dinner," he admits with something of a twinkle in his eye. The staff members treat his thoughts about religion and reading seriously, and in so doing acknowledge him as a person, not merely an available male. James likes these discussions and genuinely appreciates being addressed as a "fully thinking" adult. Though he still misses his late wife, he is not looking for companionship based on ordinary "table talk." Indeed, his status as an available male poses a dilemma and nagging question for him–do the women residents respond to him as a unique person or do they simply express interest in him because he is one of the few functional men in the facility? James's engagement with traditional observances of faith has evolved into an new offshoot or spiritual path–that of reading and discussion. The fact that he anticipates this interaction reinforces an orientation to the future and a positive disposition to the problematic dimensions of daily life in a nursing home. In a constricted social environment, he has found a way to grow socially and spiritually.

DEVOTIONAL GROUPS AND AN EVOLVING SPIRITUALITY ALONG TRADITIONAL PATHS

Several other long-term care residents described the positive and novel value of somewhat larger groups that meet regularly in most of the long-term care facilities. An accurate way to refer such groups is to use the phrase, devotional groups. The devotional groups that people looked forward to varied in terms of structure, format, frequency of meeting, official denominational status, and the nature of the leadership provided by the faithrep as well as by the faithrep's formal education in religion. Perhaps because of this crazy quilt or non-standardized pattern to the devotional offerings across the nursing homes, older people were able to find relevance and meaning in their involvement with the devotional activities. The range and diversity of devotional groups as well as the commitment of faithreps was noted in compelling comments by older adults and was observed firsthand by me in the participant observations conducted with three devotional groups. The content and activity of devotional groups ranged from recitation of the rosary, to weekly gatherings where older adults participated in reading and responsive discussion, to those programs that offered a short, daily affirmation and opportunity for each person to give voice to matters that were important to them. The key element shared among the devotional groups was the face-to-face interaction of participants. Gathering people together for talk about matters of spirit, soul, and daily life, heightened the impact the experience had for older participants. The difficulties members (group leaders and older residents) faced in order to arrive at the appointed place and time for the devotional group made this seemingly easily arranged activity a saga of its own and a testament to perseverance of all members. Surmounting issues of sharing space with competing groups in the same facility, managing to get people with various assistive technology to the group itself, were acts of commitment from everyone involved and made the devotional group and the message and lesson of religion a great pleasure and comfort to all.

Even when the group was dyadic, or one on one, the chance to connect on a religious and spiritual level was much appreciated. As Patrick, 86, recounted, "When I've got the book there [he points to a Bible] and I pray–I've got two other booklets over there," he was able to find some peace in facing his death. He sometimes used a rosary for his own prayer, but was more likely to say the rosary weekly as part of a small group. "Some days there's only myself and her [a pastoral care team member who visits the nursing home]. And I said to her, 'You shouldn't have to come up here just for one.' She says, 'I'll come up here if there's just one. I love to say the rosary and you say it with me.' Some of the people don't answer the prayers, you know. But I answer them all."

Through interaction with others, all participants in the devotional groups–the faithreps who organized and directed religious and devotional programs and the older adults themselves–become visible to one another socially and spiritually. This observation about visibility is reminiscent of Myerhoff's findings. The senior center in Venice, CA and the walkways and benches around it became the places or social contexts where regular interaction with respect to secular matters and those regarding Judaism sustained individuals in their identities and permitted exploration of novel aspects of self. Similarly older adults and faithreps in my study were sustained in faith through interaction and some evolved in spiritual dimensions as the result of engaging with religiosity in slightly different ways than they were accustomed to based on earlier experiences.

The faithreps spoke about the impact on their own sense of faith and spirituality by noting that their work with older adults posed challenges that they had not typically encountered in age-integrated religious programs. The faithreps I interviewed were not speaking of issues related to death and dying so much as they were observing the intensive openings that rather prosaic moments of devotional groups presented to individuals and to the groups as a whole. One faithrep put it this way. "The stretching we do here when we talk about the message of the day, pray together, and repeat the daily affirmation [a religious passage that the group leader presented to each member of the group] reminds everyone of God's love and presence for each person even here [nursing home] where it's often a trial to remember the day and date." Faithreps work in the interstices of everything else that envelops older adults in nursing homes. The occasions for interaction that largely improvise on traditional religious rituals are sources of spiritual growth for them and for the older adults they serve. Indeed, both the older adults and the faithreps recognize that a substantial feature of spiritual life and growth is in this coming together. Moreover, one faithrep who was employed full-time to oversee religious and spiritual activities, observed that a program she would like to introduce to the facility would involve participation by a range of staff members at the nursing home.

As small as the devotional programs were, they remained largely separate from other daily activities in nursing homes. That, as two of the faithreps observed, was problematical for everyone. The programs were perceived to be defined or treated as a "side" activity. Yet the ability to organize the programs and offer them on a routine basis posed sufficiently complex challenges for the faithreps and called them to work with a variety of other staff to insure that the programs were offered regularly. However, ideas about including staff and friends or family of the residents in the programs were held in abeyance or consigned to the future. As one of the two faithreps with full-time employment status said, "if I could offer this (devotional group) or open it to staff, I can only imagine the good effect it would have on all of us." In the crunch of organizing, coordinating, and leading the devotional programs, even a professional (religiously educated) staff member was hard-pressed to include others.

The diverse devotional groups were discussed enthusiastically by older residents and staff. Some of the elders noted that this new kind of religious commitment did not call upon their former, formal religious and spiritual roles; that is, roles that had been based on active financial contribution and consistent levels of participation in churches, congregations, or synagogues. What was now required of them in the devotional groups was a more difficult role–the role of continuing God's work within a smaller circle of life where the material dimensions were no longer as useful ways to measure or to understand one's place in life. It is in this sense that a statement from one of Buber's many essays on Hasidism resonates. "Genuine religious movements do not offer man the solution of the world mystery but equip him to live from the strength of the mystery; they do not instruct him about the nature of God, but show him the path on which he can meet God." (Buber, 2002: 64) An evolving spirituality in late life will vary across religious denominations nor will such growth solve the mysteries of life, many of which will remain, but an evolving spirituality reminds people of the known paths as well as the new paths that are open to them in late life. The delightful mosaic of devotional programs sprouting in some nursing homes gives an inkling about the possibility of new paths.

AN EVOLVING SPIRITUALITY AMONG COMMUNITY-DWELLING ELDERS DRAWS UPON READING AND PRAYER

Books, prayer books, core sacred texts as well as devotional pamphlets and brochures of all sorts were read by many in the study, generally on specific occasions, but in some instances, devotional literature was a daily mainstay for many older adults in the study. However, there was an important distinction drawn between the activity and nature of interaction involved with reading and the activity and interaction involved in praying. As one of the oldest members of the sample said after describing her prayer practice, "I don't know anything special I do. I read my Bible. I used to start, I don't know how many times I've read the Bible through. I've got marks in the Bible every time I read it, so when I know a chapter, I mark it. And then I'll get through and then I'll go back and maybe start with Genesis and read through again. Genesis or Matthew or songs. I don't know. I don't pick out anything special. I just read. And every time I read it, I won't say every time, but many times I read it I think, 'I didn't see that before.'"

Wanda, 83, prays regularly. "Well, I know I have to keep going and when I say my prayers I pray just for strength [chuckles]. Just to get through it [life every day]–just for strength." Others agreed that praying was a source of strength; they were fortified intangibly but in a manner that helped them to work through difficult situations. Prayer stimulated the flow of physical energy and psychological balance necessary to keep doing what needed to be done in their lives. Accordingly, the act of praying may be treated analytically as a conversation that encourages active coping. Prayer is an interaction that permits recognition of difficult issues posed in late life and it is a long-familiar activity which simultaneously acknowledges the challenges confronted and offers reasons for the person to keep moving through the day. Prayer becomes a trunkline for communication with the divine and engages people with spirituality in ways that are novel as well as traditional. The dialogical features of prayer sustain the social and spiritual construction of the person's self and identity. Many older people reported that they "prayed over" an issue or an event, and that this interaction helped them despite their frank recognition that not all prayers were answered based on the person's expectations. Reading was equally important as a religious and spiritual interaction, but its yield is more aptly termed intellectual. Reading sacred or religious texts is an activity conducive to religious and spiritual growth but along a different axis. When reading is discussed with others (as was the case with James and others), the impact on growth was more visible if not more profound.

Lest contrasting experiences be overlooked in this analysis, it was the case that several people in the study neither prayed nor attended or regularly observed religious or spiritual practices. Residential status was not the discriminating factor as non-religious elders were found in the community and in long-term care; however, it was more difficult to participate in formal, communal worship within long-term care facilities even in facilities that offered on-site services. The alteration in participation was echoed in the remarks of several long-term care residents but is summed up aptly by Rebecca, an interviewee from Gubrium's study of nursing home residents. "'When I came here, that [daily formal religious participation] all stopped and so I'm kind of lost when I think of religion. Now I've let it all slip by. There was nothing I could do about it.'" (Gubrium, 1993: 29) The phrase slipping by captures the tenor and tempo of loosening the formerly meaningful ties to collective or communal worship. It is a quiet phenomenon that effaces the imprint of behaviors which once were salient. Were it possible for nursing homes to broaden their scope by doing more in the way of meeting daily religious

and spiritual interests (and given the large tasks they've already been assigned by society to meet physical needs, it may be unfair to expect
them to add on yet another dimension of life), there might be a reduction
in the slipping by of formal and collective participation in religious services for current cohorts of the elderly.

Nonetheless, the informal dimensions of religion such as prayer sustain and create meaning and provide purpose and activity in life. Having
a voice and using it to pray is an extremely important aspect of self and
identity in late life. As Pauline, 87, observed "It seems as though God
gives us words to say. They just come to me. I don't have no certain time
to pray. I pray when I get up in the morning, when I go to bed at night.
No special time. And I think about–like, during the day, to myself, God
is good . . . God don't fail. And if you believe that He don't fail, it does
you good." In the high rise apartment building where she makes her
home, there is a distinctive place-marker on her door. A neighbor and
friend made and painted a wooden angel with accompanying words,
"Shh . . . Talking with God," to grace Pauline's doorway.[2,3]

NON-TRADITIONAL, EVOLVING SPIRITUALITY: "FINDING NEW WAYS TO PUT AN AWARENESS OF GOD INTO WORDS" AND INTO LATE LIFE

Anne is a searcher, ahead of her time and cohort, at least with respect
to the kinds of searches people have taken in order to reach a heightened
awareness or "transpersonal" bond with others (Moody & Carroll,
1997). Anne was the one person I spoke with in the study who described
a lifelong journey and spiritual search peppered with vicissitudes that
had brought her during the last few years to a point of understanding
that seems characteristic of Joan Erikson's concept of gero-transcendence (Achenbaum & Modell, 1999). At the time of our interview she
was 77 and living in Chelsea Court's "independent" living unit. She had
a number of serious health problems, most of them had been resolved
through surgery and successful though long-term recuperation. These
health problems moved her into long-term care. Anne spoke at length of
the spiritual journey that had threaded through her life–from her days in
high school through cross-country moves, a divorce, and the uncertainties of raising children on her own at a time when one held a pariah status for doing so.

Anne had reached a level of oneness with others some years ago
when she actively sought out different religions and different traditions

in order to move to a faith that understood that the dilemmas of divorce did not cast one's spirituality into a void. Her extensive contact with other religious traditions as well as the education she obtained brought her almost full circle to her religious identification today. But as she stated emphatically, it was not the "religion itself that was important, it was the realization that after all, we were one." This hard won spiritual understanding continues to evolve now that she resides in a long-term care setting suffused by the religion that had excluded her and her children many years ago. She follows her present religion in this facility, but also uses the dedicated religious spaces found within the buildings for daily meditation sessions. She is also one of the most conscientious participants in collective worship: she attends formal services offered in the nursing home 2 or 3 times a week. She reads widely about a range of religions and intends to take classes at a nearby college now that her physical health and strength have been recovered. In terms of Joan Erikson's original formulation of gero-transcendence (Achenbaum & Modell, 1999) and in terms of the cosmic consciousness suggested by recent objective measures (e.g., Tornstam, 1999), Anne's search exemplified a road not taken by most others in the study.

Another person whose life reflects an evolving, non-traditional spirituality is Jack, 85. I literally bumped into him a year after our interview as he was entering and I was exiting a local health food restaurant and store. He is among the most fashionably dressed elders–always a dapper and stylish wardrobe–denim and sweatshirts have not found their way into his closet. Yet he is also someone who talked extensively about the now absent meaning found in traditional forms of faith and in his regular participation in formal worship. Jack is increasingly drawn to a different level of understanding of his life and of human life. He commented extensively on the latest findings from physics and astronomy–findings about the universe and what those findings reveal about our purpose as human beings. He explicitly acknowledged that this was not the kind of talk that would endear him to the majority of his local congregation, nor is it the kind of talk he would think of expressing to them or to most others. He noted how his growing awareness of the limitations inherent in conventional understandings of faith and the very definition of God had sparked new ways of thinking about spirituality and consciousness. Like the majority of those I talked with, his was and is a deeply rooted engagement with faith, but the fundamental concerns he has had since his wife's death several years ago have taken him in a new and much different direction–one he appreciates and is exploring with a wide-range of reading–but one that is at a different level than weekly worship.

His was an erudite and thoughtful search that was prompting him to move even further along the transpersonal dimension of being at one with others. In one sense this is an extension of concerns he has had for most of his mid to late life. For example, Jack has long been a major and anonymous donor to several area school scholarships and has supported other community charities without a nameplate to honor his generosity. The gero-transcendence here is one of increasing depth and doing even more with respect to supporting others at the same time that his thinking and reading have lead him to perceptions of the permeable and gossamer boundaries between science and faith. During the formal interview he showed me the more "socially oriented" book he had just begun reading, it was none other than *Bowling Alone*.

These intimations of spirituality and gero-transcendence were reflected in remarks from Ed. At 60 he was the youngest member of the study and a recent widower. To keep spiritual beliefs alive and to keep himself going he often walked in woods and enjoyed public trails and parks. "Nature, swamps, ducks. You sit back and wonder how everything began. It's hard to start someplace, like, the ducks or the animals, where did they come from? Where'd it start from?" To be engaged this way, is indicative of a way of relating to the world without seeing every interaction as instrumental or contingent upon a material gain and it requires an orientation to the intrinsic worth of a material setting (in this case, nature) and the capacity to make it part of a way of living. It is a way of seeing the sacred in the natural world, an evolution of self by gaining a more transcendent perspective.

People created ways of drawing upon inchoate understandings of themselves and their beliefs in order to spark incipient aspects of spirituality in late life. Gwen, who had relatively little formal schooling (8th grade), found her gift in poetry and acquired a new perspective on self and the value of her life. She had lived in a subsidized housing project with her husband for the past 12 years, having moved there after spending virtually all her married life in a two-family home in a neighboring city. She had surmounted serious health problems that left her "in the dumps, depressed" and had found a means of expression through the language and rhythm of words. In fact, she began to write short greetings and letters of affection, sympathy, and love for others who came to her. Gradually people pressed her to take some money for doing this service and eventually she did. As her confidence grew she submitted work locally and became a published poet. No, not in the parlance of our day, "a world class poet," but a working one nevertheless. This accomplishment and tangible sign of acceptance in a wider circle of people unknown to her made the dream of having her poetry published even sweeter and was tied to her belief that divine plans are not foreclosed by a person's age or health.

Others found their dreams realized in activities that are often dismissed as passive and unimportant–reading, walking, teaching prayers to grand-nieces and grand-nephews, working on church newsletters. Carol, 79, found a way to fulfill her dream of being helpful to others and to expand upon her religiously linked belief in service . A cancer survivor, widow (3 years) and long-term nursing home resident who did not drive, she read once a week during the school year to an elementary class. She and the children took great pleasure from spending 35-36 hours over the course of a school year sharing books and stories. Consistent support over a decade from nursing home staff and administrators, assured Carol of transportation to and from the reading program, and gave her the opportunity to establish and develop a way of relating to younger people that consolidated values that were both religious and spiritual. In a similar vein, Jean, 72, unmarried but with several great nieces and nephews nearby, has been able to teach them how to say their prayers and is a principal force in their religious socialization. In recent years she took each in turn for unremunerated child care and discovered that guiding and teaching them, passing on her faith, was one of the best experiences of her life. An evolving spirituality may lead older adults into many areas of participation and interaction that enlarge a religious and social perspective.

CONCLUSION

These quiet paths, the traditional and non-traditional ones, disclose some of unpretentious activities–those of lifelong interest, others newly taken up in late life–connected with religious dimensions of identity. These activities presented only the intrinsic value of the activity itself as a benefit to older adults, but all created a sense of having a life worth living and inspired older adults to move purposively through each day and to evolve in faith and spirit. Huston Smith (2001: 253) recently alluded to Sufis and their perspective on faith and daily life. "Sufis respect their ecstatics, referring to them affectionately as spiritual drunkards who hang out in God's tavern; but they hold in higher regard those who can see God everywhere while they are sober–which is to say, *see God everywhere in daily life*. [italics mine] This requires considerable reflective talent . . . " Without disputing the amount of reflective talent required to "see God everywhere in daily life," Smith captures a religious perspective that resonates cross-culturally in Marie's remark that "religion is the finding thing." Religion and spirituality orient older adults to themselves by moving them beyond narrow concerns to an enlarged sense and others and life as a whole. Thus, programs and milieus that sustain a religious ethic or spiritual awareness may be powerful forces in transforming the experience of old age and in fostering renewal and growth. Following Kierkegaard's admonition, older adults and faithreps in this study do not make for eternity "an end where the end is not" (1962: 236). "The possibility of the good," is alive and is perceived by elders to be part of faith and daily life that keeps most of them, but not every one, from despair. Religion and an evolving spirituality are the finding things–they establish or at least point to new ways of understanding life, and for the faithreps who are working to open those paths by directing programs for older adults, there are opportunities for taking in a deeper awareness of life as it unfolds in interaction.

NOTES

1. A few general characteristics of the sample are outlined here. Research interviews and related field work such as observations were completed during the year of August 24, 1999 to August 25, 2000. Overall, 46 people, 60 years old and older, with an actual age range of 36 years, from 60 to 96, were interviewed. In addition to interviews with the elderly, six formal observations of group interaction were completed and seven interviews with people connected to spiritual and religious programs for the elderly were conducted. As a thumbnail description there were: 31 women, 15 men; 6 non-whites (about 13% of the total); 31 were community-dwelling residents and 15 resided in long-term care settings.

The mean age for community-dwelling men was 80, for women it was 76. For men and women combined, the mean age was 77 with a mode at 74 and a median of 78. The age range in the community-dwelling sample was 60-93. The mean age for men residing in long-term care settings was 77, for women it was 86. For men and women combined, the mean age was 83 and the mode and median ages were 79. The age range was 73-96.

With respect to marital status in the total group, 18 were widowed, 17 were married (among the 17 in the married category are 10 people or 5 couples who are married), 8 were single (had never married), and 3 were divorced or separated. In the community-dwelling sample, 18 people lived with others and 13 lived alone. In the long-term care sample, 5 people lived alone; that is, they had private rooms at the time of the interview, and 10 shared a room with one other person, that is, they had roommates. Everyone interviewed for the study had a clear religious identification which for the most part stemmed from an ascriptive status of their parents and from childhood socialization. In the sample as a whole there were 21 Roman Catholics, 18 Protestants, and 7 Jews. Religious identification does not automatically translate into membership in an actual congregation or regular, active participation in formal worship. The total number of active participants in religious services was 34. Overall, 15 Roman Catholics, 15 Protestants and 4 Jews were active participants in formal worship.

2. There are many definitions of prayer, some of these are described in my recent book. After writing the book I read a re-issue of Abraham Heschel's work, *The Prophets*, and found this general definition of prayer. I find it captures the elements of transcendent concern and the manner of communicating with God that is central to most definitions of prayer that older adults conveyed in their interviews with me.

"Prayer, too, is an act consisting of a moment of decision or turning, and of a moment of direction. For to be engaged in prayer and to be away from prayer are two different states of living and thinking. . . . To be able to pray, one must alter the course of consciousness, one must go through moments of disengagement, one must enter another course of thinking, and must face a different direction."

The course one must take in order to arrive at prayer is on the way to God. For the focus of prayer is not the self. . . . When we analyze the consciousness of a supplicant, we discover that it is not concentrated upon his own interests, but on something beyond the self. . . . Thus in beseeching Him for bread, there is one instant, at least, in which the mind is directed neither to one's hunger nor to food, but to his mercy. This instant is prayer" (Heschel: 2001/1962, 564).

3. To a large extent, much of what is presented here bespeaks a continuity of cultural folkways surrounding religion, particularly its role in bringing solace and inspiration to people. The two quotations below provide a characteristic sense of what people understood as the core of religion. The remarks are meant to remind readers of the powerful way that faith was woven into culture and society. With respect to those adults born before WWII (1939), solace and moral guidance were, for the most part, taken for granted and absorbed seamlessly in the process of growing up. Thusm, religious engagement and folkways of faith became part of what I call bedrock socialization for pre-WWII cohorts. Social change after WWII fractured that bedrock for younger cohorts and generations.

In an interview drawn from a compilation by the Federal Writer's Project (1975: 234-235) during the Great Depression in the U.S., one working-man reminds us of the prevailing view of faith back then. "You know, when you're blue and down at the mouth and don't see any use anyhow, a good sermon just lifts you up. . . . if you're poor all your life, then you get a high place in the Kingdom. Just do the best you know how and the Lord will take care of you either here or hereafter. It sure is a comfort."

Another interviewee from the project, Andrew Jonas, was one of fifteen children. He cared for his elderly, infirm mother, and remarked "Some of the Burns Chapel brothers come for me and Ma on Sundays, so we can get to church. I sure love goin' to meetin's. Looks like there's a heap of comfort in religion, and I shore believe in prayer. I aim to make out just the best I can, and put my trust in the Lord" (p. 355).

These comments are glimmers of the predominant place religion held in people's lives.

REFERENCES

Achenbaum, W. A., & Modell, S. M. (1999). Joan and Erik Erikson and Sarah and Abraham: Parallel awakenings in the long shadow of wisdom and faith. In L. E. Thomas & S. A. Eisenhandler (Eds.), *Religion, belief, and spirituality in late life.* (pp. 13-32). New York: Springer.

Atchley, R. C. (1999). *Continuity and adaptation in aging: Creating positive experiences.* Baltimore: Johns Hopkins.

Buber, M. (2002). Spirit and body of the Hasidic movement. In A.D. Biemann (Ed.), *The Martin Buber reader.* (pp. 63-71). New York: Palgrave Macmillan (essay originally published in 1935).

Butler, R. (1963). The life review: An interpretation of reminiscence in the aged. *Psychiatry,* 26, 65-76.

Cole, T. R. (2002). On the possibilities of spirituality and religious humanism in gerontology or reflections of one aging American cultural historian. In L. Andersson (Ed.), *Cultural gerontology* (pp. 25-44). Westport, CT: Greenwood.

Eisenhandler, S. A. (2003). *Keeping the faith in late life.* New York: Springer.

Eisenhandler, S. A. (1994). A social milieu for spirituality in the lives of older adults. In L. E. Thomas & S. A. Eisenhandler (Eds.), *Aging and the religious dimension* (pp. 133-145). Westport, CT: Auburn.

Federal Writers' Project. (1975). *These are our lives.* New York: W. W. Norton. (original work published in 1939).

Fowler, J. W. (1981). *Stages of faith: The psychology of human development and the quest for meaning.* San Francisco: Harper and Row.

Gilleard, C., & Higgs, P. (2000). *Cultures of ageing.* Harlow, England: Pearson Education Limited.

Gubrium, J. F. (1993). *Speaking of life: Horizons of meaning for nursing home residents.* New York: Aldine de Gruyter.

Heschel, A. J. (2001). *The prophets.* New York: Harper-Collins Publishers (originally published in 1962).

Kierkegaard, S. (1962). *Works of love.* (H. Hong & E. Hong, Trans.) New York: Harper and Row (original work published in 1847).

Koenig, H. (1998). *Handbook of religion and mental health.* New York: Academic Press.

Merton, T. (1958). *Thoughts in solitude.* New York: Farrar, Straus, and Giroux.

Moody, H. R., & Carroll, D. (1997). *The five stages of the soul.* New York: Anchor.

Myerhoff, B. (1980). *Number our days.* New York: Touchstone.

Putnam, R. D. (2000). *Bowling alone: The collapse and revival of American community.* New York: Simon and Schuster.

Roof, W. C. (1999). *Spiritual marketplace: Baby-boomers and the remaking of American religion.* Princeton, NJ: Princeton University Press.

Smith, H. (2001). *Why religion matters: The fate of the human spirit in an age of disbelief.* San Francisco: Harper-San Francisco.

Sorokin, P. A. (1956). *Fads and foibles in modern sociology and related sciences.* Chicago: H. Regnery Company.

Tornstam, L. (1999). Late-life transcendence: A new developmental perspective on aging. In L. E. Thomas & S. A. Eisenhandler (Eds.), *Religion, belief, and spirituality in late life* (pp. 178-202). New York: Springer.

Vaillant, G. E. (2002). *Aging well: Surprising guideposts to a happier life from the landmark Harvard study of adult development.* Boston: Little, Brown, and Company.

Wuthnow, R. (2003). *All in sync: How music and art are revitalizing American religion.* Berkeley: University of California Press.

Wuthnow, R. (1998). *After heaven: Spirituality in America since the 1950s.* Berkeley: University of California Press.

Religious Congregations as Social Services Providers for Older Adults

Ram A. Cnaan, PhD
Stephanie C. Boddie, PhD
Jennifer J. Kang, MPS

SUMMARY. A large proportion of older adults are affiliated with congregations. The literature suggests that, in general, religious participation among the older adults enhances their quality of life and provides a network of social care. In this article, we explored the relevant literature on organized religion and social support for older adults. Based on a census study of congregations in Philadelphia (N = 1,393), we documented the following: (1) the number of congregations serving older adults, (2) the types of services provided, and (3) the number of beneficiaries. The study also identified the organizational factors that predict the provision of congregation-based services for older adults. The findings suggest that serving older adults is not a top priority for most congregations. Most senior programs are small and often informal. Approximately half (48%) of the congregations do not provide a formal social service. However, those congregations that are more likely to serve older adults have larger budgets, more members over 65-years-old, and a moderate political orientation. We recommend that congrega-

[Haworth co-indexing entry note]: "Religious Congregations as Social Services Providers for Older Adults." Cnaan, Ram A., Stephanie C. Boddie, and Jennifer J. Kang. Co-published simultaneously in *Journal of Gerontological Social Work* (The Haworth Social Work Practice Press, an imprint of The Haworth Press, Inc.) Vol. 45, No. 1/2, 2005, pp. 105-130; and: *Religion, Spirituality, and Aging: A Social Work Perspective* (ed: Harry R. Moody) The Haworth Social Work Practice Press, an imprint of The Haworth Press, Inc., 2005, pp. 105-130. Single or multiple copies of this article are available for a fee from The Haworth Document Delivery Service [1-800-HAWORTH, 9:00 a.m. - 5:00 p.m. (EST). E-mail address: docdelivery@haworthpress. com].

tions, social service providers, and older adults explore ways to maximize this underutilized resource of congregational services to meet the needs of the increasing number of older adults. *[Article copies available for a fee from The Haworth Document Delivery Service: 1-800-HAWORTH. E-mail address: <docdelivery@haworthpress.com> Website: <http://www. HaworthPress.com> © 2005 by The Haworth Press, Inc. All rights reserved.]*

KEYWORDS. Faith-based social services, congregations, elderly, spirituality, community care, social support

INTRODUCTION

When one considers aging in the United States and participation in religious organizations, two facts are rarely disputed. First, the most common choice for social engagement by older adults is participation in an organized religion. Second, many religious communities are composed of a high percentage of older adults as religion becomes more and more meaningful in the later years of aging. In the United States, adults over age 65 regard religion as "very important" at a 70 percent rate, and this increases to 79 percent for adults ages 65 to 74 as compared to adults ages 50 to 64 with rates of 67 percent and younger adults, ages 18 to 29, who rate religion as "very important" at only a 46 percent rate (Gallup & Lindsay, 1999). A similar trend exists among minority elders (Jackson, Antonucci, & Gibson, 1990). Data from the National Survey of Black Americans reveal a higher average of all types of religious interest among older Blacks when compared to older adults of other races and younger Blacks (Chatters & Taylor, 1989; Levin & Taylor, 1993, 1997; Taylor & Chatters, 1991). High rates of religiosity are also reported among elderly Latinos; however, their overall rates of religiosity were lower than rates for Blacks and Whites (Markides & Martin, 1983). Furthermore, among persons over 65 years of age, 64 percent watch religious programs on television (PRRC, 1987); 52 percent attend religious services regularly (PRRC, 1994); 43 percent read the Bible at least once a week; and 24 percent pray three times a day or more (PRRC, 1987). These indicators are reported to be higher than those for younger age groups.

The literature suggests that, in general, religious participation among the older adults enhances their quality of life. Religion helps make sense of the process of aging, loss of physical strength, and increased morbidity (Kermis, 1986). Current popular media emphasize youthfulness and physical health, and places little value on growing old. Religious traditions provide counter-cultural messages valuing long life and emphasizing the positive side of aging as well as calling upon young people to honor their elders. Judaism, Christianity, and Islam value the person not according to their productivity and youthful appearance but rather elevate the virtues of wisdom, experience, and openness to spiritual growth and fulfillment that accompany aging (Knapp, 1981; Moody, 1990).

The importance of religion for people's health and mental health as well as quality of life is well documented (Koenig, McCullough, & Larson, 2001). Indeed, Hadaway and Roof (1978) found that adults with high levels of religious commitment felt significantly more satisfied with their lives than persons with lower levels of commitment. Interviews with 90 elderly Blacks in Philadelphia disclosed a significant relation between feelings of well-being and the perception of support from local congregations (Walls & Zarit, 1991). Felton and Berry (1992) found that among the elderly, groups such as churches and senior centers are integral parts of their social support systems whereas younger generations tend to include individuals (people) only. Religiosity has also been found to buffer the stress of caregiving for caregivers, who with less depression and effects of stress can relate better to the elderly (Chang, Noonan, & Tennstedt, 1998). The social supports available through church attendance and the individuals' reliance on or faith in a power greater than themselves are important mitigating factors. Blacks were more likely than whites to reap the health-related benefits of religion.

The literature suggests that elderly with religious commitment exhibit healthier mental and physical states. Alexander and Duff (1992) found that religious elderly are less likely to abuse alcohol than non-religious elderly. Furthermore, Strawbridge, Cohen, Shema, and Kaplan (1997) found that those who frequently attended (weekly or more) a place of worship had significantly lower mortality rates than those who were less frequent attenders. Overall, as Ayele, Mulligan, Gheorghiu, and Reyes-Ortiz (1999) found, religion is strongly correlated with life satisfaction among the elderly. Siegel and Kuykendall (1990) reported that people who lost a spouse and were congregational members reported significantly less depression than those who were not members of a congregation. Studies have also shown that religion can allay the fears of death among adults in congregations (Kahoe & Dunn, 1976).

Idler and Kasl (1997), based on a 12-year longitudinal study, studied the effect of religious participation on functioning in a large, prospective, representative sample of elderly. They found that attendance at services is a strong predictor of better functioning, even when intermediate changes in functioning such as disability are included, and that disability has minimal effects on subsequent attendance.

Interestingly, Barusch (1999) asked elderly respondents what aspects of religion are helpful and affirming. The dominant key answers focused on gratitude. Elderly respondents viewed God as the source of all that is good and reported being grateful for life, good fortune, help in times of hardship, and material goods. Krause (2002) provided empirical support for the following model: Older adults who attend church often feel their congregations are more cohesive, older adults in highly cohesive congregations receive more spiritual and emotional support from their fellow parishioners, older respondents who receive more church-based support have a more personal relationship with God, older adults who feel more closely connected with God are more optimistic, and older adults who are more optimistic enjoy better health.

There is little doubt that most religions have a positive outlook of the aging process, that elderly people find religion to be helpful, and that the elderly are more religious than other age groups. Older people particularly affirm the importance of services provided by religious organizations. What is less studied is the extent to which religious communities in the United States make themselves instrumental in serving older people. In this study we focus exclusively on the direct services that places of worship in Philadelphia provide their members and neighboring elderly. We are not focusing on the meaning that older adults make of their congregational affiliation nor are we studying the incidental social ties formed in many congregations. Our interest focuses on local religious congregations as social service providers. The questions that we are interested in answering are the following: How many congregations provide social services to older adults, what are these services and how often are they provided? How many older adults are being served? And, which congregations tend to provide more social services for older adults?

To answer these questions, we draw data from a census of 1,393 congregations in Philadelphia documenting a range of congregation-based services. We also explain the ways we studied services for the elderly. This is followed by findings and a conclusion and implications section. The paper concludes by suggesting that congregations, social service providers, and the elderly can use local religious congregations to better meet the needs of the elderly and improve their quality of life. While many elderly find religion meaningful and attend places of worships regularly, these places of worship can be more efficiently tapped to meet the various needs of older adults in urban areas.

CONGREGATIONS AS SOCIAL SERVICE PROVIDERS

The U.S. Census Bureau estimated that by July 2003, 12.6 percent of the total population will be over age 65, and by 2025, 18.5 percent of the total population will be over age 65 (U.S. Bureau of the Census, 2000). This is a significant increase from 1900 when only about 4 percent of the United States' total population was over age 65 (U.S. Administration on Aging, 2000). With this rapid graying of America, the demand for older adult services and supports is expected to increase. When considering this demand side of older adult services, Tirrito and Spencer-Amado (2000) found that older adults expected and desired social services from their congregations. Seventy percent of the respondents reported that if church-based services were offered, they would use them. In addition, women were found to be more likely to use congregational social services than men. Tirrito and Spencer-Amado also found that older adults wished for a variety of congregational social services: support groups, meals, transportation, nursing services, availability of social workers, help with medications, housing, help with housing repairs, friendly visitors, companions, legal advice, family support groups, recreational activities, volunteer work, help to find paid work, educational programs, inter-generational programs, help with abusive family members, help with family members with mental illness, developmental disabilities, or alcoholism, and help with elderly parents. More than half (55%) of the respondents wanted programs relating to emotional health. Respondents also identified barriers that prevented them from attending services: steps (11%), poor lighting (2%), and transportation (12%).

The services supplied by religious communities to older adults are quite similar to the set of services listed above: counseling, meal provision, home repair assistance, transportation, visitation, recreation, and education. In addition, congregations provide medical care through parish nurse programs, health education, health screening, and holistic health centers in many cities (Djupe & Westberg, 1995). Tobin, Ellor, and Anderson-Ray (1986) found four key categories of care for older adults provided by religious institutions. These four categories are: (1) provision of religious programs (e.g., worship, education); (2) hosting of social service activities (e.g., meals programs or health screening); (3) provision of pastoral care services; and (4) provision of direct social services. The last one was less common even where the need was evident and no public programs were available to meet the need. More frequently, congregations serve as a social hub where older adults can meet other older adults or even younger people, finding social contacts that reduce loneliness and isolation. Johnson and Mullins (1989) concluded that "greater involvement in the social aspects of religion was significantly related to less loneliness more consistently than involvement in the various family and friendship relations" (p. 110).

Samuel and Sanders (1991) found that the key areas in which churches were involved were being providers of socialization and being providers of informal social support. They surveyed 343 ministers of major denominations in North Dakota to identify church services and activities designed for older adults. Respondents indicated that most church activities and supports were not developed specifically for older adults, and many stated that they did not wish to "segregate" their elderly members in this manner. The programs most commonly reported were elderly social events (42%) and senior clubs (36%). Only five percent of the churches had parish nurses. Indeed, Samuel and Sanders found that transportation, meals on wheels, services for the homebound, assistance with shopping, yard work, and home repairs were offered to older adult members by many congregations. Yet, informal support was much more prevalent and included being there at a time of crisis (85%) or being available as a friend (87.5%). A total of 18.2 percent of the churches worked with the community "to a great extent" to meet the needs of older adults in the churches or in the community, and 51.4 percent networked with community groups "to some extent." In many churches, older adults are encouraged to volunteer and provide leadership for church affairs. In most churches, older adults assisted with worship services, telephone ministry, Sunday school teaching, and the church library. In addition, Netting (1995) found that religious organizations sponsor a wide variety of housing options for older persons.

Sheehan, Wilson, and Marella (1988) studied 212 churches and synagogues in a Northeastern state and found that visitation programs for homebound and hospitalized older persons were the most frequent form of service offered. These visits to older adults who are homebound can promote close relationships, ease loneliness, monitor an elder's condition, and strengthen the connection between the homebound and the community. Similarly, Knapp (2001) studied 753 Churches of Christ congregations and found that the program offered most often to older adults was visitation to shut-ins. In a seven-city study of 251 congregations, Cnaan and his colleagues found that 11.6% congregations sponsored exercise programs for older adults, 17.1% sponsored organized tours, and 25.5% sponsored recreational programs (Boddie, 1999). Congregations in this study also reported providing communal on-site meals (14.7%), meals on wheels (4.8%), health care (13.1%), and home visitation (29.1%). While many congregations provided the formal programs listed above, many more congregations provided services informally. Uhlman and Steinke (1984) found that more than half the people in nursing homes would like to have pastoral visits while only a quarter receive them. Blasi, Husaini, and Drumwright (1998) found that clergy's role with older adults is often referral. When an older person comes with a mental health problem that the authors described as being distressed, most clergy (50%) refer them to mental health professionals. Among the remaining pastors, half provided counseling, prayers, and other services while the rest felt that the problems were not serious enough to require either counseling or professional referral. In the Black Church Giver Project, individuals receiving informal support from church members exhibited significantly higher levels of formal service use from community agencies than respondents not receiving support from church members (Pickard, Chadiha, Morrow-Howell, & Proctor, 2003).

In the field of health care and education, congregations are often hailed as important partners. However, it is not clear if these studies were conducted by medical or medically-oriented researchers who seek strengths in congregations or that congregations actually focus on health care and education for older adults. Djupe and Westberg (1995) raise the growing concerns both clergy and congregations have for health and wholeness. They present three programs that attempt to provide a holistic approach to health:

1. Holistic Health Centers: A family practice doctor's office is located in the church, supported by medical staff "concerned about physical health as well as relationships to God, self, family, and others" (328);
2. Parish Nurse Program: A parish nurse who serves to provide personal health counseling, makes referrals for the congregation and community, coordinates volunteers and support groups, and interprets the relationship between health and faith;

3. Congregational Health Services: This group provides programs that address the physical, emotional, and spiritual needs of older adults and are organized by the congregation's staff or cadre of volunteers.

Davis and colleagues (1994) report a Los Angeles based project of 24 churches providing cancer education and screening sessions. Similarly, Ford and colleagues (1996) used congregations to train African-Americans to provide education about asthma and its treatment. The logic behind these projects is that the congregation is essential for many people's lives and that through congregations people will be accessible, available for various types of supports, and will listen to and influenced by the clergy (McRae, Carey, & Anderson-Scott, 1998; Ransdell, 1995). Not all such collaborations are successful. Filinson (1988) documented how a mental health center trained and used church volunteers from an interfaith coalition to provide services to people with Alzheimer's disease. The project was only marginally successful. Caregivers preferred education, information, and emotional support while they avoided giving tangible, instrumental assistance. Furthermore, rather than referring people to the program, most congregations tended to handle service requests in house.

Congregational services fill a much needed gap in social services for ethnic groups. Choi and Tirrito (1999) studied a sample of Southeastern Korean-American churches and their older Korean members. They found that Korean churches are a valuable social service resource for Korean elders and can serve as a model for the provision of social services by other congregations. Similarly, Song (1998) found that Korean churches contributed to the life satisfaction for 150 Korean persons over 55-years-old. For this group, churches served religious and spiritual functions as well as social, cultural, and psychological functions. Participation in church enabled Korean elders to cope with discrimination caused by racism and ageism and to experience a more dignified life.

Not all researchers found churches to actively address the needs of older adults. For example, Tirrito and Euster (1994) reported that in spite of the noted involvement of older adults with religion and their congregation, the churches in their study offered few older adult ministries. These researchers asked adult respondents what services their churches provided for them. The responses included the following: visitation for the sick and homebound, bingo games, group healing services, support groups, senior adult choirs, trips, and even a senior prom.

Forty percent of the studied congregations had no special program for older adults.

In addition, not all older adults report their personal experiences in congregations to be positive (Krause, Chatters, Metzger, & Morgan, 2000). Krause and his colleagues documented that negative interactions were prevalent and a significant source of distress for older adults. Conflict arose with fellow parishioners, including problems associated with gossiping, being let down by others, the formation of cliques, troublesome nonverbal messages, and unresolved conflict. Problems also arose with clergy who were perceived to have become removed from their congregations and were too concerned with material possessions, or failed to adequately prepare prayers for church services.

Little is known about the organizational factors that explain congregational involvement in older adult service provision. It is unknown whether congregations' factors such as political ideology, theological ideology, size, interest of pastor, annual budgets, and staff size may explain congregational involvement in helping older adults.

One of the few studies that attempted to understand which congregations are more involved with serving older adults was conducted in Philadelphia by Morrison (1991). He found that in Black churches in Philadelphia, denominational (liberals) and size (large) differences explained levels of services to the elderly. Morrison also found that regardless of the above findings, it is clear that the clergy sets the tone, and his or her knowledge and interest in the topic are key in church involvement. Doka (1987) revealed a significant relationship only between the proportion of older adults within a congregation and the pastor's interest in both the development of specialized ministries to older adults and structural modifications of the church building. However, these intentions are often not translated to action. Doka also found no significant differences between the proportion of older adults within a congregation and the actual programs and services designed for the elderly.

Adams and Stark (1988) studied which congregations in rural North Carolina are more likely to serve the elderly. They found that most churches provided a wide variety of services, primarily informally, to older adults. They also found that socially conservative churches provided fewer services than socially liberal ones; however, the degree of theological fundamentalism was not an important predictor of failure to provide services. Finally, Knapp (2001) found that the percentage of the congregants over age 65 had little influence on the congregation's elder-friendliness. Of greater importance was the amount of money budgeted for senior adult ministry, as well as the size of the congregation and whether an organized effort to minister to senior members was established. Similarly, Looney and Haber (2001) concluded that the churches with more resources are the best ones to approach for launching new older adult exercise programs.

From the literature, we can gather that social services available to older adults are largely informal, visitation to the homebound, and opportunities that provide socialization. Congregations that tend to be involved are those who are socially liberal, have larger budgets, have larger proportion of older adults in their membership, and have the interest of clergy in providing such social services. These conclusions are not widely supported and more rigorous studying is needed. More importantly, the extent to which congregations meet the needs of older adults and the scope of such involvement remains unclear.

To advance research in this area, we will focus on the following questions: (1) How many congregations provide social services of all kinds to older adults and what types of services are provided? (2) How many older adults are being served and how often are these services provided? (3) Are there significant differences between congregations that tend to provide more or less social services for older adults?

METHODS

Sampling

The term *congregation*, as used here, includes all organized faith-based groups, whether church, synagogue, mosque, temple, ashram, or other. To develop a working list of congregations, we merged two data files: the City of Philadelphia Property Tax list and the Yellow Pages list of congregations. In order to identify the unlisted congregations, we applied three methods. First, we requested lists from every denomination and interfaith organization in the region. Second, in every interview, we asked clergy members or key-informants to identify congregations with which they collaborate along with their telephone numbers and addresses. We also enlisted the assistance of our advisory board, which is composed of religious leaders throughout the city. Finally, our research interviewers traveled block-by-block through neighborhoods to identify possibly unlisted storefront churches and other congregations not on our master file. This combination of the approaches brought us closer to a complete master list. In all, we interviewed 1,393 of the

2,120 known congregations (65.7%). Data were collected between 1999 and 2002.

Instruments

We used three research instruments. These instruments were developed and piloted. The first part of the interview (the General Form) gathered background information about the congregation, its history, membership, financial information, staff, governing structure, and relations with the wider community. The second part (the Inventory of Programs) compiled information about the congregation's social services. The interviewers covered 215 areas of possible social and community involvement, with numerous follow-up questions concerning the formal or informal nature of the program, where it was provided, and so on. We asked respondents to identify those services that had been offered in the past twelve months and to omit any that were no longer available. We used a 12-month time frame to ensure that seasonal programs such as summer camps and heating assistance would be included. One part of the second instrument was devoted to programs for older adults and included 14 areas of involvement ranging from visiting the sick to on-site health care programs for older adults. In addition, interviewees were asked to add other programs serving older adults not included in our instrument.

The third part of the interview (the Specific Program Form) was used to gather information about the most important social programs provided by the congregation, up to a maximum of five programs. With regard to these five programs, the interviewee was asked detailed questions about the program's history, legal status, staffing, who benefits, how many times a week/month/year it was offered, cost to the congregation, and much more. Among the list of potential beneficiaries were the elderly. Due to the length of interviewing time, congregations with more than five social programs were asked to choose only the five "most representative of their work." We asked respondents to start with those programs that have budgets and paid staff.

Data Collection

We spent 3-10 hours in each of the 1,393 congregations we studied. Many of the questions were close-ended but others were open-ended.

The responses were verified with documentation provided by the congregations. A face-to-face interview was selected not only to increase the response rate but also to assist interviewees by providing a context for questions, to probe when necessary, and to make use of additional information that can be observed while visiting the congregation.

The interviews and collection of congregation documents were performed by a group of (20-30) well-trained interviewers. All interviewers received both a lengthy orientation and weekly group in-service training. Each interviewer was also given a training manual that documents the information outlined above with specifications and clarification for the survey instruments. The interviewers were closely supervised and observed for the first three interviews and provided with feedback after each session. This training and supervision was to ensure that interviewers were familiar with the survey instrument, understood the intent of questions, learned to phrase questions properly, recorded responses accurately and completely, learned to probe interviewees for more complete responses, and addressed issues of confidentiality. Interviewers were also trained to understand religious customs and language of the particular congregation being interviewed.

Measurements

With regards to services for the elderly, as noted above, in the second instrument, we applied a list of 14 programs specifically related to the elderly. Interviewees noted if their congregation provides such a program, if it is a formal program, if it is carried out alone by the congregation on their properties, or if it is done as support of someone else's effort. The list of these programs appears on the right column of Table 1.

In the third instrument, we asked if older adults are among the beneficiaries and if they are the only beneficiaries. For example, a senior ministry is earmarked specifically for the elderly, but a community concert is open and available to older adults but to other age groups as well.

Questions regarding the percent of older people in the congregation and the congregational characteristics were taken from the first instrument. The interviewee was asked factual questions about the congregation such as budget size, membership composition, history of the congregation, and the clergy.

TABLE 1. Senior-Oriented Programs Provided by Philadelphia Congregations (N = 1,393)

Program type	Informal	Formal–Onsite	Formal–Offsite	Offered by others–Onsite	Assisting others	Total involved
Intergenerational programs	17.4%	10.8%	.6%	.5%	2.7%	32.0%
Grandparents programs	13.2%	4.1%	.6%	.3%	2.5%	20.7%
Loss of spouse–Support groups	25.9%	3.0%	.4%	.1%	4.2%	33.6%
Day care (older persons)	2.9%	1.7%	.4%	.2%	4.7%	9.9%
Communal (onsite) meals	4.9%	9.3%	.6%	.5%	3.2%	18.5%
Meals on wheels	4.5%	4.4%	.2%	.5%	7.5%	17.1%
Recreational programs	6.7%	15.4%	1.2%	.6%	2.9%	26.8%
Visitation–buddy system	25.4%	17.9%	.2%	3.9%	2.2%	49.6%
Organized tours	8.5%	10.3%	.6%	2.7%	1.9%	24.0%
Financial planning	9.8%	3.3%	.7%	.3%	1.8%	15.9%
Foster grandparents	3.8%	.9%	.2%	.4%	2.2%	7.5%
Transportation	29.3%	10.3%	.4%	1.7%	1.7%	43.4%
Health care	7.3%	4.7%	1.0%	.4%	3.6%	17.0%
Exercise	3.2%	4.6%	.6%	.1%	2.1%	10.6%

FINDINGS

Older Adults and the Congregations

Before we turn to the actual services provided by local religious congregations for older adults in Philadelphia, we would like to draw attention to some important statistics. According to the 2000 U.S. Bureau of Census data, there are approximately 1,517,500 people living in Philadelphia. Of them, 47 percent (713,225) are active congregation attenders (attending at least monthly) (Cnaan & Boddie, 2001). Philadelphia has the highest proportion of people 65 years and over of the 10 largest U.S. cities, at 213,722 persons (14.11% of the total city population)

(U.S. Bureau of Census, 2000). We found that about one quarter of the members of congregations in Philadelphia are people 65 years of age or older (25.7%). This percentage is somewhat similar to what Farnsley (2003) found for Indianapolis. Based on a study of more than 400 churches in Indianapolis, Farnsley reports that "Overall, 29 percent of the members are over 55 years of age." In 223 congregations (16%), it was reported that more than half or more of the congregants are elderly. In some cases these were large congregations with more than a thousand elderly members.

Stating these findings differently, in Philadelphia, about 183,299 older adults are reported to attend congregations regularly. This number implies that four out of five older adults in Philadelphia attend a place of worship regularly. Given that the numbers are taken from different sources and they are larger than the 52% who attend religious services regularly (see PRRC, 1994), this estimate may be viewed with suspicion. Yet, it is clear that a large percent of older adults attend congregations regularly.

A large number of the congregations reported some problem with accessibility. In fact more than half (53.5%) reported some form of accessibility problem ranging from narrow stairs to inaccessible bathrooms. In many of these congregations, while the parish hall is accessible, the higher floors where social and educational programs are located are inaccessible for people with physical disabilities.

One other important point to view is that congregations are often composed of one ethnic group. In fact, as we showed elsewhere (Cnaan & Boddie, 2001), nine out of ten congregations reported that 75 percent or more of their members belong to one racial or ethnic group. The majority were Black congregations (54.9%) and White congregations (26.2%). This sample also included distinctly Hispanic congregations (5.3%) and Asian-American congregations (3.5%).

Areas of Social Service Involvement

To understand the social and community involvement of local religious congregations in Philadelphia, we asked the interviewees the extent to which they were involved in 215 social programs, which fell under different social service areas. Our instrument included 14 areas of social services involvement that were primarily related to older adults. As shown in Table 1, all of the 14 areas are provided by some of the city congregations. Five programs areas are formally offered on-site by more than ten percent of the city congregations. These programs are:

intergenerational programs, recreational programs, visitation, organized tours, and transportation. In addition, communal meals are offered through more than ten percent of the congregations (10.4%) but in some cases it is offered off-site and in other by an outside provider on the congregational premises. The fact that at least ten percent of the congregations provide these programs needs to be translated into over two hundreds points of service delivery throughout the city. These programs are also provided informally by many other congregations. In many cases the distinction between a formal and informal program was difficult to discern. In this study, informal programs are those provided on an as needed basis rather than on-going services with designated volunteers and staff. We found that in addition to the above five programs, a quarter of the congregations provide informal programs such as loss of spouse support groups (25.9%) and more than one in ten provide informal grandparents programs (13.2%).

The right column of Table 1 provides the total percentage of congregations involved in any level of helping older adults. Taking this total percentage and deducting it from 100 will provide the percent of congregations totally not involved in any area of serving older adults. Two-thirds (68%) of the congregations are not at all involved in intergenerational programs. "Foster grandparents" was the program reported to be offered the least by Philadelphia local religious congregations (92.5%), followed by exercise programs (89.4%). Clearly the most commonly offered programs were visitation (not offered by 50.4% of the congregations) and transportation (not offered by 56.6% of the congregations).

In addition to the provided list, we asked the congregations if they have additional programs catering specifically to older adults. Among the many examples were: special holiday celebrations and dances such as those offered during Thanksgiving, providing a room (home) for older adults, tutorial and ESL classes, translation services, a telephone network to connect with those that miss the weekly religious services, financial and legal assistance, adoption of a nursing home, visiting nurse, crafts group, senior retreat, meetings in members' home on a rotating basis, senior seminars, linking seniors with community programs (referrals), shoveling snow from older adults' houses, employment opportunities for the aged, Wheelchair Aerobics, and Rocking Chair Aerobics, and programs for singles. Many of these programs were reported by more than one congregation and indicate that older adults have a range of needs that congregations can address. For example, seven congregations reported craft groups, six congregations reported holiday celebrations, and three congregations reported single programs. Additionally, six congregations reported to have special apartments for older adults that are rented below the market cost.

Another way of looking at the congregations' involvement in providing services to older adults is to assess how many congregations provide at least one service and how many provide more than one service. In this analysis, we included an involvement of only formal involvement and excluded all the "no" and "informal" responses. Thus, we found that a little under half of the congregations (48%) provide not even one formal program directly related to older adults. About one in five congregations (17.8%) provide only one program and exactly one in ten (10%) provide two programs. Half a percent of all studied congregations reported that they provide all 14 studied areas of social services involvement to older adults. In all, only 52% of congregations provide at least one formal program to older adults.

Specific Programs

After tallying the social service areas that the congregation is involved in, we asked the interviewee to discuss up to five programs in detail. While only nine out of ten congregations provided at least one program to any needy groups of people, we received information from 4,261 different social programs offered by the studied congregations. A small number of these programs were designated only for older adults (such as senior clubs) or open to older adults (such a community theater or a community concert). Overall, one in five programs (933 programs, 21.9%) was open to older adults. However, when we looked at the programs geared to serve only older adults this percentage dropped significantly to 6.5 percent (276 programs). These 276 programs were reported by 260 different congregations. Fourteen congregations reported two programs and one congregation reported three programs designated only for seniors. These programs included senior clubs, health promotion for older adults, visitation for the sick and shut in, exercise programs, organized tours (often to Atlantic City), coffee houses, communal meals, arts and crafts, legal advising, adopting a nursing home, and volunteer opportunities.

Put differently, only 18.7 percent of Philadelphia congregations provided a senior-designated program of any kind. Furthermore, the mean replacement value of these programs, per month, is $936. To put these two statistics in perspective, one-third of the programs offered by local religious congregations are specifically designated to serve children (33.7%). Additionally, the mean replacement value of congregational programs that are not senior-designated, per month is $1,636. These discrepancies are occurring while, on average, 25.7 percent of the members of the congregations are 65 years of age and older while only 23.5 percent are younger than 18 years.

On average, a program designated for older adults served 26.6 of the congregation's older adults and 33.1 older adults that are not members of the congregation. As such, senior-only programs were modest and, combined, served 59.7 individuals. Programs open to older adults were larger in size and served, on average, 57.4 congregational members and 90.7 community residents who are not members of the congregation, for a total of 148.1 individuals.

Congregations that Serve Older Adults

The next interesting question is which congregations tend to be involved in providing social services for older adults. We looked at congregations that reported involvement in any program for older adults (52%) and compare them to congregations that reported not to provide any program for older adults (48%). The variables we thought of as relevant and plausible explanatory ones are listed in Table 2. Our selection of explanatory variables was based upon a similar analysis performed by Cnaan and his colleagues (2002) and the literature review. We also added percentage of members that are over 65. As shown in Table 2, almost every explanatory variable is significantly associated with the provision of at least one social program for older adults. The three exceptions are the percent of adult members who are single, membership growth in the past three years, and whether the budget is balanced or not. However, the remaining 12 explanatory variables may be confounded and need to be studied conjointly.

In order to assess the relative importance of these 12 explanatory variables we performed a multiple logistic regression with the dependent variable being provision of at least one social program for older adults. In the regression, only three variables remained significant: larger annual operating budget (over $100K), larger percentage of members who are over 65 years of age, and moderate political orientation. While the first two variables are somewhat expected, the last one is more difficult to explain.

IMPLICATIONS AND CONCLUSIONS

It is well established that in the United States, where religion is highly practiced and where half of the population regularly attend places of wor-

TABLE 2. Bivariate Associations of Involvement in Serving the Elderly (N = 1,393)

Variable	Statistical method and result
Percent of members 65 years or older	t-test (congregations with more elderly do more) t = 5.1, p < .001
Change in age [Membership got younger, stayed the same, got older (past 3 years)]	Chi-square (got older do more) χ^2 = 6.6, d.f. = 2, p < .05
Percent of adult members who are single	t-test t = .3 N.S.
Number of active attenders (size of membership)	t-test (larger congregations do more) t = 7.4, p < .001
Membership growth (past 3 years)	Chi-square χ^2 = .6; N.S.
Percent of Black members	t-test (non-Black congregations do more) t = 2.8, p < .01
Number of paid clergy	Chi-square (congregations with more clergy do more) χ^2 = 96.3, d.f. = 3, p < .001
Number of paid staff	t-test (congregations with more staff do more) t = 9.0, p < .001
Annual operating budget	Chi-square (richer congregations do more) χ^2 = 141.9, d.f. = 12, p < .001
Fiscal status (surplus; balanced; deficit)	Chi-square χ^2 = .38, d.f. = 2 N.S.
Income of members (% of households with an annual income of $75,000+)	t-test (richer member congregations do more) t = 4.1, p < .001
Age of congregation	t-test (older congregations do more) t = 6.9, p < .001
Conservative vs. liberal political ideology	Chi-square (conservative and liberals do less; moderate do more) χ^2 = 12.5, d.f. = 2, p < .01
Fundamentalist vs. liberal theological ideology	Chi-square (liberals do more) χ^2 = 12.5, d.f. = 2, p < .01
Percent of members living within a mile radius from the congregation	t-test (congregations with more local residents do more) t = 3.1, p < .01

ship, older adults are most affiliated with organized religion. We found that the great majority of the older adults in Philadelphia attend congregations regularly. It is, thus, reasonable to expect that many older adults bring their developing needs to their congregations. Fountain (1986) found that alienation is both removed by congregation attendance and stated as a barrier to not attending. That is, attenders are likely to be less alienated and congregational participation is helpful to reduce alienation. This link calls upon community practitioners who work with older adults to offer them a means to become congregational members, if so wished. Thus, seniors who show interest in organized religion should be encouraged to attend and be provided with appropriate transportation assistance if needed.

Mcfadden (1995) noted that social service agencies need to be aware that many older persons turn to their congregations when challenged by health problems, household maintenance difficulties, economic difficulties, and loss of social support. Indeed, we found that congregations offered a range of informal and formal service to meet these needs. While the elderly may not be a high priority for many congregations, these congregations serve them in many ways. Among older adults, congregations are an accepted part of the social support systems, and as such, access to congregations should be offered to any interested older adults (Felton & Berry, 1992). Professionals in the community should also be aware of the social and instrumental support provided to older adults through religious congregations and the power that these groups and their religious leaders have for impacting the quality of life of older adults. Often the role served by congregations is unappreciated by non-religious professionals who do not understand how older adults participate in their congregations and how they perceive this participation as fulfilling socially and spiritually. People working with older adults should increase their understanding of the search for meaning and faith development of older adults. Better understanding of the role of religion in old age and familiarity with the world of congregations may enable social workers and other professionals to suggest and encourage new senior ministries that reflect the needs of older adults in the community.

Our first set of findings also suggests that, in Philadelphia, the majority of older adults are regular attenders of local religious congregations and that these congregations are divided by ethnic lines. As Moberg (1984) noted, "The most segregated hour of the week may still be 11:00 a.m. Sunday, the customary Protestant worship hour, but most of it is by the minorities' choice" (p. 451). This segregated nature of congregations, however, has special implications for services for older adults. As such, Korean elders can be found in Korean churches and Albanian elders in Albanian churches. It makes outreach efforts to older adults both for educational and service provision more focused and handy. First, congregations seem like the right place for practitioners to look for older adults, and second, and more importantly, interventions can be culturally sensitive, as older adults of a certain ethnic group tend to join the same congregation or set of congregations. We also found that many congregations are not handicap accessible. Our findings that more than half of the congregations reported accessibility concerns are quite alarming. This may pose a special burden on older adults as, with age, the frequency of illness, injuries, and disabilities increases. Thus, congregations need to examine their practices and procedures to assess how senior-friendly they are. Given that places of worship are exempted from the provisions of the American with Disabilities Act, the motivation for improving accessibility should come from within (Meyer, 2001). As Tirrito and Spencer-Amado (2000) noted, most old adults would like to see these barriers removed.

Our findings suggest that, in Philadelphia, half the congregations do not provide even one program designated directly to older adults and only a handful of congregational programs are senior-only programs. The existing programs are often poorly funded and attract a small number of older adults. These findings mirror other findings such as those of Tirrito and Euster (1994). It seems that although older adults is the largest group in many congregations, the focus is not on them but on the younger generations. Many attempts are reported of trying to attract children and their families as a means to keep the congregation vital and to assure future cohorts of members. While this is a legitimate concern for most congregations and almost every clergy will attest to it, the senior members are often neglected and are expected to form their own programs. Given their large participation, older adults can be viewed as underserved.

The findings suggest that elder-friendly congregations exist. These programs represent the potential to develop unique programs to meet the needs of older adults. Some are quite innovative and attentive to the changing needs of older adults. In this respect, congregations should follow Moberg's (1991) advice suggesting that "Every church needs to study its own community to determine the specific needs of its older people, and to identify the services that are already available to them, and to discern which are feasible but lacking" (p. 191).

Visiting the shut-ins was found to be an important function carried out by many congregations. This is in line with findings by other scholars. However, more than half of the congregations that are involved in this activity do so informally. When an older adult member of the congregation is absent for more than one week, there is often a mechanism to forward the person's name to the clergy or an assistant and a visit or inquiry will be made to find out if a crisis occurred and if the congregation can be of help. Many congregations also post the names of the sick and homebound in their weekly bulletin and encourage members to pray and visit these members. Other congregations participate in Stephen ministries or other lay leaders programs that provide pastoral care to members. Expanding these practices to form a reliable system for contacting the many frail older adults in the community would contribute a vital service. Social workers and other professionals can support the development of such networks of care. Systematizing this arrangement will provide many urban older adults with a free monitoring and a built in checking to see that they are functioning.

The key gatekeepers and policy makers in congregations are the clergy. Professionals should reach out to clergy and provide them with knowledge required to understand the needs of older adults and how to organize programs to meet their needs. As Tirrito and Euster (1993) showed, most clergy lack gerontological training and, even more worrying is the fact that less than a quarter of them think that such training is needed. Similarly, Samuel and Sanders (1991) found in North Dakota that only one-fourth of the ministers had taken a course on aging as part of their training. Yet, many clergy enter the ministry after theological seminaries or upon a higher call unprepared to understand and meet the needs of their older adult members (Kimble, 1995). As such, theological seminaries should instruct future clergy cohorts about issues of aging and care for older adults.

Clergy working with older adults should assist them to identify how they can participate in their congregation by acknowledging their wisdom and expertise. Clergy should make sure that neither older adults nor other congregants equate aging with loss of human value. Celebrating the assets of old age will make older adults feel better and will better integrate them into the congregation. When the congregation discusses social minister/social action, clergy should suggest and support activities and services for older adults even if these are less attractive and will not recruit young families. Clergy should have an open door policy and be aware of the needs of older adults. Finally, they should encourage relationships among older adults and with others, particularly across the generations.

Some congregations adopted a nursing home and organized social and spiritual services on an on-going basis. However, with the aging of the population, it is expected that more and more people will enter nursing homes and other long-term care facilities, both public and private. These settings should seek out collaboration with local religious congregations to meet the spiritual needs of the resident elderly along with their physical, psychological, and social needs. Chaplaincy services are important but can be enhanced and enriched through working with congregations. Congregants can adopt individual residents and offer spiritual and personal support. Reading and counseling in addition to worship opportunities can have great impact on the quality of life of these elderly individuals (Ellor, Stettner, & Spath, 1987; Richards, 1990; Richards & Seicol, 1991).

Congregations with large budgets and large membership, and those with high numbers of older adult members, are more often engaged in providing social services to older adults. We also found that congregations with a moderate political orientation tended to provide more programs to older adults. This is different than what was found by other researchers who found liberal congregations to be more engaged than conservative/fundamental congregations. We are unclear as to the importance of this finding and it may be Philadelphia-related. It clearly calls for future research.

Two issues do not go unnoticed. First, many seniors attend religious congregations and find them relevant. Second, as Tirrito and Spencer-Amado (2000) found, many clergy lack knowledge and interest in working with older adults. Consequently, numerous publications were developed and disseminated advising congregations how to work with older adults and how to best serve them (Ellor, McGilliard, & Schroeder, 1994; Knutson, 1999; Koenig & Weaver, 1997; Stenson & Hunt, 1992). Hence, it is not necessarily lack of sources that prevents clergy from leading their congregations into serving older adults. The imbalance between the participation of older adults and their low priority in the congregational totem-poll ought to be changed and clergy should be enlightened in this respect. We hope that our findings and article will assist.

REFERENCES

Adams, R. G., & Stark, B. J. (1988). Church conservatism and services for the elderly. *Journal of Religion & Aging, 4* (3-4), 69-85.

Alexander, F., & Duff, R. W. (1992). Religion and drinking in the retirement community. *Journal of Religious Gerontology, 8,* 11-19.

Ayele, H., Mulligan, T., Gheorghiu, S., & Reyes-Ortiz, C. (1999). Religious activity improves life satisfaction for some physicians and older patients. *Journal of the American Geriatrics Society, 47,* 453-455.

Barusch, A. S. (1999). Religion, adversity, and age: Religious experiences of low-income elderly women. *Journal of Sociology & Social Welfare, 26* (1), 125-142.

Blasi, A., Husaini, B. A., & Drumwright, D. A. (1998). Seniors' mental health and pastoral practices in African American churches: An exploratory study in a southern city. *Review of Religious Research, 40,* 168-177.

Boddie, S. C. (Winter 1999/2000). Aging and health: Reconsidering how religious participation matters. *Institute on Aging University of Pennsylvania newsletter,* (9), 1, 8.

Chang, B. H., Noonan, A. E., & Tennstedt, S. L. (1998). The role of religion/spirituality in coping with caregiving for disabled elders. *The Gerontologist, 38,* 463-470.

Chatters, L. M., & Taylor, R. J. (1989). Age differences in religious participation among black adults. *Journal of Gerontology: Social Sciences, 44,* S183-189.

Choi, G., & Tirrito, T. (1999). The Korean church as a social service provider for older adults. *Arete, 23* (2), 69-83.

Cnaan, R. A., & Boddie, S. C. (2001). Philadelphia census of congregations and their involvement in social service delivery. *Social Service Review, 75,* 559-589.

Cnaan, R. A., Boddie, S. C., Handy, F., Yancey, G., & Schneider, R. (2002). *The invisible caring hand: American congregations and the provision of welfare.* New York: New York University Press.

Davis, D. T., Bustamante, A., Brown, C. P., Wolde-Psadik, G., Savage, E. W., Cheng, X., & Howland, L. (1994). The urban church and cancer control: A source of social influence in minority communities. *Public Health Reports, 109,* 500-506.

Djupe, A. M., & Westberg, G. (1995). Health and wholeness: Congregation-based health programs. In M. A. Kimble, S. H. McFadden, J. W. Ellor, & J. J. Seeber (Eds.), *Aging, spirituality, and religion: A handbook* (pp. 325-334). Minneapolis, MN: Fortress.

Doka, K. J. (1985-1986). The church and the elderly: The impact of changing age strata on congregations. *International Journal of Aging & Human Development, 22,* 291-300.

Ellor, J. W., McGilliard, J. L., & Schroeder, P. E. (1994). *Let days speak, and many years teach wisdom: A congregational leaders' manual: Guiding your congregation in the age of aging.* Washington, DC: National Interfaith Coalition on Aging, National Council on the Aging.

Ellor, J. W., Stettner, J., & Spath, H. (1987). Ministry with the confused elderly. *Journal of Religion & Aging, 4* (2), 21-33.

Farnsley, II. A. E. (2003). *Rising expectations: Urban congregations, welfare reform, and civic life.* Bloomington, IN: Indiana University Press.

Felton, B. J., & Berry, C. (1992). Groups as social network members: Overlooked sources of social support. *American Journal of Community Psychology, 20,* 253-261.

Filinson, R. (1988). A model for church-based services for frail and elderly persons and their families. *The Gerontologist, 28,* 483-486.

Ford, M. E., Edwards, G., Rodriguez, J. L., Gibson, R. C., & Tilley, B. C. (1996). An empowerment-centered, church-based asthma education program for African American adults. *Health and Social Work, 21,* 70-75.

Fountain, D. E . (1986). How to assimilate the elderly into your parish: The effects of alienation on church attendance. *Journal of Religion & Aging, 2* (3), 45-55.

Gallup, G. J., & Lindsay, D. M. (1999). *Surveying the religious landscape: Trends in U.S. beliefs.* Harrisburg, PA: Morehouse.

Hadaway, C. K., & Roof, W. C. (1978). Religious commitment and the quality of life in American society. *Review of Religious Research, 19*, 295-307.

Idler, E. L., & Kasl, S. V. (1997). Religion among disabled and nondisabled persons II: Attendance at religious services as a predictor of the course of disability. *Journals of Gerontology Series B: Psychological Sciences and Social Sciences, 52*, S306-S316.

Johnson, D. P., & Mullins, L. C. (1989). Religiosity and loneliness among the elderly. *Journal of Applied Gerontology, 8*, 110-131.

Kermis, M. D. (1986). *Mental health in late life: The adaptive process.* Boston: Jones and Bartlett.

Kimble, M. (1995). Pastoral care. In M. A. Kimble, S. H. McFadden, J. W. Ellor, & J. J. Seeber (Eds.), *Aging spirituality, and religion: A handbook* (pp. 325-334). Minneapolis, MN: Fortress.

Knapp, K. R. (1981). Respect for age in Christianity. In C. LeFevre & P. LeFevre (Eds.), *Aging and the human spirit* (pp. 21-33). Chicago, IL: Exploration Press.

Knapp, J. L. (2001). Impact of congregation-related variables on programs for senior adult members. *Journal of Applied Gerontology, 20*, 24-38.

Knutson, L. D. (1999) *Understanding the senior adult: A tool for holistic ministry.* Bethesda, MD: Alban Institute.

Koenig, H. G., & Weaver, A. J. (1997). *Counseling troubled older adults: A handbook for pastors and religious caregivers.* Nashville, TN: Abingdon.

Koenig, H. G., McCullough, M. E., & Larson, D. B. (2001). *Handbook of religion and health.* New York: Oxford University Press.

Krause, N. (2002). Church-based social support and health in old age: Exploring variations by race. *Journals of Gerontology: Series B: Psychological Sciences and Social Sciences, 57B*, S332-S347.

Krause, N., Chatters, L. M., Meltzer, T., & Morgan, D. L. (2000). Negative interaction in the church: Insights from focus groups with older adults. *Review of Religious Research, 41*, 510-533.

Levin, J. S., & Taylor, R. J. (1993). Gender and age differences in religiosity among Black Americans. *The Gerontologist, 33*, 16-23.

Levin, J. S., & Taylor, R. J. (1997). Age differences in patterns and correlates of the frequency of prayer. *The Gerontologist, 37*, 75-88.

Looney, C., & Haber, D. (2001). Interest in hosting an exercise program for older adults at African-American churches. *Journal of Religious Gerontology, 13*, 19-29.

Markides, K. S., & Martin, H. W. (1983). *Older Mexican Americans.* Austin, TX: Center for Mexican American Studies.

Mcfadden, S. H. (1995). Religion and well-being in aging persons in an aging society. *Journal of Social Issues, 51*, 161-175.

McRae, M. B., Carey, P. M., & Anderson-Scott, R. (1998). Black churches as therapeutic systems: A group process perspective. *Health Education & Behavior, 25*, 778-789.

Meyer, C. (2001). The Americans with Disabilities Act: A primer for land title agents and underwriters. Downloaded from the Internet on October 9, 2003, from: *http://www.baldwinhaspel.com/artpub/cm4/ada/a-ada.html*.

Moberg, D. O. (1984). *The church as a social institution* (2nd ed.). Grand Rapids, MI: Baker Book House.

Moberg, D. O. (1991). Preparing for the graying of the church. *Review and Expositor, 88,* 179-192.

Moody, H. R. (1990). The Islamic vision of aging and death. *Generations, 14,* 15-18.

Morrison, J. D. (1991). Black church as a support system for black elderly. *Journal of Gerontological Social Work, 17* (1/2), 105-120.

Netting, F. E. (1995), Congregation sponsored housing for older adults. In M. A. Kimble, S. H. McFadden, J. W. Ellor, & J. J. Seeber (Eds.), *Aging, spirituality, and religion: A handbook* (pp. 335-349). Minneapolis, MN: Fortress.

Pickard, J., Chadiha, L., Morrow-Howell, N., & Proctor, E. (2003). Support from Members and Formal Service Use. *Poster session presented at Integrating on Spirituality and Health Conference,* Washington, DC.

Princeton Religion Research Center (1985). *Religion in America.* Princeton, NJ: The Gallup Poll.

Princeton Religion Research Center (1987). *Religion in America.* Princeton, NJ: The Gallup Poll.

Princeton Religion Research Center (1994). Importance of religion climbing again. *Emerging Trends, 16,* 1-4.

Ransdell, L. B. (1995). Church-based health promotion: An untapped resource for women 65 and older. *American Journal of Health Promotion, 9,* 333-336.

Richards, M. (Fall 1990). Meeting the spiritual needs of the cognitively impaired. *Generations, XIV* (4), 63-64.

Richards, M., & Seicol, S. (1991). Challenge of maintaining spiritual connectedness for persons institutionalized with dementia. *Journal of Religious Gerontology, 7* (3), 27-40.

Samuel, M., & Sanders, G. F. (1991). The role of churches in the supports and contributions of elderly persons. *Activities, Adaptation & Aging, 16* (2), 67-79.

Sheehan, N. W., Wilson, R., & Marella, L. M. (1988). The role of the church in providing services for the aging. *The Journal of Applied Gerontology, 7,* 231-241.

Siegel, J. M., & Kuykendall, D. H. (1990). Loss, widowhood and psychological distress among the elderly. *Journal of Consulting & Clinical Psychology, 48,* 519-524.

Song, Y. I. (1998). Life satisfaction of the Korean American elderly. In Y. I. Song and A. Moon (Eds.), *Korean American women: From tradition to modern feminism.* Praeger Publishers (pp. 193-205).

Stenson, J., & Hunt, G. B. (1992) *Linking your congregation with services for older adults.* Alexandria, VA: Catholic Charities USA.

Strawbridge, W. J., Cohen, R. D., Shema, S. J., & Kaplan, G. A. (1997). Frequent attendance at religious services and morality over 28 years. *American Journal of Public Health, 87,* 957-961

Taylor, R. J., & Chatters, L. M. (1991). Nonorganizational religious participation among elderly black adults. *Journal of Gerontology: Social Sciences, 46,* S103-111.

Tirrito, T., & Euster, G. L. (1994, February). Religious leaders: What do they need to know about planning for elderly church members? Paper presented at the Association for Gerontology in Higher Education, Cleveland, OH.

Tirrito, T., & Spencer-Amado, J. (2000). Older adults' willingness to use social services in places of worship. *Journal of Religious Gerontology, 11* (2), 29-42.

Tobin, S. S., Ellor, J. W., & Anderson-Ray, S. M. (1986). *Enabling the elderly: Religious institutions within the community service system.* Albany, NY: State University of New York Press.

Uhlman, J., & Steinke, P. D. (1984). Pastoral visitation to the institutionalized aged: Delivering more than a lick and a promise. *Pastoral Psychology, 32,* 231-238.

Walls, C. T., & Zarit, S. H. (1991). Informal support from black churches and the well-being of elderly blacks. *The Gerontologist, 31,* 490-495.

Guided by Ethics:
Religion and Spirituality
in Gerontological Social Work Practice

Vicki Murdock, PhD

SUMMARY. This random national survey anonymously explored 299 gerontological social workers' attitudes about spirituality and the use of spiritual interventions in practice. Respondents support the inclusion of religion and spirituality in education and practice as a diversity component, as part of holistic assessment, and as a fundamental aspect of human life. Nearly 70% of respondents report little or no preparation on spiritual issues during their schooling and only 24.5% report satisfaction with their educational preparation on this topic. While respondents' personal spirituality correlates positively and weakly with the use of spiritual interventions, it is ethical attitudes toward spiritual interventions that predict the use of spiritual interventions by gerontological social workers. *[Article copies available for a fee from The Haworth Document Delivery Service: 1-800-HAWORTH. E-mail address: <docdelivery@haworthpress.com> Website: <http://www.HaworthPress.com> © 2005 by The Haworth Press, Inc. All rights reserved.]*

KEYWORDS. Religion, spirituality, gerontology, ethics, diversity

[Haworth co-indexing entry note]: "Guided by Ethics: Religion and Spirituality in Gerontological Social Work Practice." Murdock, Vicki. Co-published simultaneously in *Journal of Gerontological Social Work* (The Haworth Social Work Practice Press, an imprint of The Haworth Press, Inc.) Vol. 45, No. 1/2, 2005, pp. 131-154; and: *Religion, Spirituality, and Aging: A Social Work Perspective* (ed: Harry R. Moody) The Haworth Social Work Practice Press, an imprint of The Haworth Press, Inc., 2005, pp. 131-154. Single or multiple copies of this article are available for a fee from The Haworth Document Delivery Service [1-800-HAWORTH, 9:00 a.m. - 5:00 p.m. (EST). E-mail address: docdelivery@haworthpress.com].

The unique focus of social work as a profession is its person-in-environment perspective, which provides a holistic, ecological assessment and intervention framework for practice (Hutchison, 1999). Yet, the profession of social work, like the health and social science professions, has emphasized the physical and psychological dimensions in the recent past, to the neglect, or even outright rejection, of the spiritual dimension (Canda, 1997; Loewenberg, 1988; Sherwood, 2000; Weisman, 1997). Researchers have now recognized this neglect, and are taking steps to investigate the appropriate role of the spiritual dimension in social work assessment and practice (Bullis, 1993, 1996; Canda, 1988; Derezotes, 1995; Sheridan, Bullis, Adcock, Berlin, & Miller, 1992; Sheridan, Wilmer, & Atcheson, 1994).

The study of older adults and the aging process has also been "running to catch up," as life expectancy grows from 46 years in 1900 to 77 years today, and projected to continue its advance in the years ahead (Hillier & Barrow, 1999). While spirituality is an important factor for inclusion in assessment and intervention planning at every age in the lifespan, it becomes particularly relevant as adults in their middle and older years look both forward and back in their lives. This research study explored social work practice aspects of that intersection of aging and spirituality.

DEFINITIONS

Definitions given here for spirituality and religion come from this study's research instrument (Sheridan, 2000) and are the only definition of terms given to the survey participants in the study. Spirituality is defined as "the search for meaning, purpose, and connection with self, others, the universe, and ultimate reality, however one understands it. This [search] may or may not be expressed through religious forms or institutions" (Sheridan, 2000, p. 20). Religion is defined as "an organized, structured set of beliefs and practices shared by a community related to spirituality" (Sheridan, 2000, p. 20).

Two additional terms are also defined here to further clarify the study. Personal spirituality refers to those attitudes that underlie, beliefs that support, and behaviors that express a person's search for meaning, purpose, and an integrative connection between self, others, the universe and ultimate reality. Spiritual interventions are those appropriate assessment and intervention practice behaviors that employ informed sensitivity to the client's personal spiritual beliefs and practices.

The terms "spiritual" and "spirituality" will be used to convey the larger concept of the search for meaning and connectedness, within which all religions and many individual beliefs fall. The research also assumes that the spiritual search for meaning and connectedness is a basic dimension of every human being (Otto, 1917; Hutchison, 1999). However, while every person has a spiritual dimension, not every person chooses to identify with religion as such. Thus, the phrase "religious or spiritual" in the research instrument was to be construed as inclusive of any spiritual (meaning-seeking) belief or practice.

THEORETICAL FRAMEWORK ON AGING, SPIRITUALITY, AND PROFESSIONAL COMPETENCE

Aging Theories that Address Spirituality

The literature from the professions of social work, gerontology, psychology, psychiatry, theology/pastoral care, nursing, counseling, and medicine cites the importance of spirituality in the lives of older persons (Ai, 2000; Blazer, 1991; Foley, 2000; Scovell, 1996; Stolley & Koenig, 1997; Tirrito & Spencer-Amado, 2000). Because aging inevitably brings each person closer to their own mortality, the issues of purpose and meaning in life are often highlighted in the older adult's thoughts and feelings (Koenig, 1994; Moberg, 2001). As each person ages, then, the spiritual questions of life, death and the meaning of life may be welcomed, pondered, ignored, or even denied. Theory and research are beginning to recognize the connection between these elements of spirituality and aging.

Moberg (2001) points out that "spirituality and religion have generally been ignored in theories of aging," although some theories of aging address or imply spirituality as an important component of older adulthood (p. 34). Phenomenological theories of aging support the lived experience of the person, and continuity theory suggests that the individual for whom spirituality has been an important life force will theoretically find this force valuable in later life as well (Atchley, 1977). Symbolic interactionism, useful as a gerontological theory for framing the concept of the symbolic nature of interpersonal relationships, can serve as positive and negative theory relative to spirituality/religiosity, depending upon whether the symbolic interaction is supportive and open, or ageist and stereotypical (Moberg, 2001). Furthermore, the stage theories of human development, while initially focusing on earlier adulthood, have expanded to include middle and old age (Erikson & Erikson, 1986; Vaillant, 1995). These theories highlight spirituality in the stages of generativity and integrity of the self. Crisis and grief/loss theories offer a normalizing framework for the older adults' experiences of suffering and sorrow. Finally, Pargament's (1997) theory of coping and Butler's (1963) life review/reminiscence model are two examples of practice theories that imply inclusion of spirituality as the older adult examines coping skills developed over the lifespan and the purpose and meaning of living.

This research uses an ecological framework that encompasses many of these concepts. The older adult lives, continues, copes, interacts with others, and experiences stages and changes and losses. An ecological perspective represents the holistic, systemic, and interactional approach many social workers are taught in school and use in their work (Germain & Gitterman, 1980).

Aging and Spirituality as Diversity Components

Mandates for the respectful inclusion of spirituality across the life span appear in the educational policy of the Council on Social Work Education (CSWE), which calls for addressing spiritual development across the lifespan without discrimination and with knowledge and skill (2001). The National Association of Social Workers' (NASW) 2001 *Standards for Cultural Competence* include recognition of and respect for client religious and spiritual diversity of beliefs and values in practice and policy. The CSWE/Strengthening Aging and Gerontological Education for Social Work (SAGE-SW) *Gerontological Social Work Competencies* (2000) mandate respect for the older adult's spiritual beliefs and call for gathering spiritual information in assessment and addressing spiritual needs. NASW *Bereavement Practice Guidelines* (2003) call for offering spiritual help and support and respecting religious rituals.

Another framework, then, applicable in social work theory and practice and mandated by CSWE and NASW, is cultural diversity, in which the client or client system's culture, ethnicity, age, gender, class, sexual orientation, and spiritual/religious beliefs and values are respected and considered in the practice process (CSWE, 2001; NASW, 2001). The research study presented here uses the ecological framework that incorporates the diversity perspective to view the broad, interdisciplinary, personal and social issues of aging and spirituality in social work practice as the "unit" of study.

Professional Competence

A final key issue in exploring the intersection of aging, spirituality and social work practice is the attitudes, beliefs, and behaviors of the individual social work professional on the topic of spirituality. The profession of social work has historically trained the student and the worker to address "development of the professional self," that is, competence developed through self-exploration, self-awareness, and the seeking of needed knowledge and skills (Reynolds, 1942/1985; Towle, 1954/1971). Sheridan et al. (1992) emphasize the importance of "continually examin[ing] one's views on diversity of culture, socioeconomic class, race, ethnicity, gender, and sexual orientation" (p. 200). The literature underscores the need to teach students how to identify, use and appropriately expand their personal and professional boundaries, particularly in the area of spiritual beliefs, which are often thought of as personal and private. Again, Sheridan et al. (1992) suggest that "self knowledge should involve an ongoing process and reflection on one's personal beliefs, values, and attitudes concerning the religious or spiritual dimension of human existence" and that this "is a relevant process for all social workers, whether they adhere to a particular faith, have a secular philosophy, or consider themselves antireligious" (p. 200). Canda (1988) also recommends that "social workers develop a self-understanding regarding existential issues and spiritual growth" and "examine their beliefs, motivations, values, and activities and consider the impact of these factors upon the client's spirituality" (p. 245).

Self-efficacy theory (Bandura, 1997) suggests that spirituality, as a theoretical and practical element of helping in the classroom and field, in continuing education workshops, and on the job, will only be appropriately assimilated and used by the few who feel strongly on a personal level about its value, and who engage in the self-exploration required to attain a balanced professional position. This appears to be the current situation in social work and other helping professions where spirituality is neglected in professional training and therefore in practice, unless the topic surfaces often in the professionals' daily work, allowing for on-the-job training to take place.

This research study takes the position that spirituality is much like other areas into which social workers delve in attempting to improve the human condition: social workers may not ultimately be the professional who intervenes on a given topic, but generalist social workers are often the "front line" persons who can and must assess, plan, treat, or refer

(Kaplan & Dziegielewski, 1999; Mattison, Jayaratne, & Croxton, 2000). This position rests squarely on the premise that social workers are the professionals who provide holistic assessment and oversee a treatment plan or case management plan that is inclusive of all vital aspects of the individual client or client system (Hutchison, 1999).

EMPIRICAL STUDIES ON SPIRITUALITY

Social Work Students and Faculty

Although empirical studies on aspects of spirituality in social work are still scarce in the literature, studies on social work students, faculty, and practitioners published in the 1990s and into the 21st century begin to paint an exploratory picture of where the profession stands now and where it may be heading. Recent social work students consider spiritual and religious issues to be important elements for understanding and working with the whole client or client system and want more training in theory and skills on this topic (Cascio, 1999; Kaplan & Dziegiel- ewski, 1999; Rizer & McColley, 1996; Sheridan, 1999). Students in Cascio's study "routinely deal with religion and spirituality in their field experiences" (1999, p. 142); students in the Kaplan and Dziegielewski study want "a sense of both comfort and competence in addressing the spiritual and religious needs of the clients they will serve" (1999, p. 38).

A majority of faculty supports the importance and inclusion of spiri- tual/religious material electively or infused into the curriculum but also expresses concern over how to present this material (Derezotes, 1995; Dudley & Helfgott, 1990; Sheridan et al., 1994). Many faculty members acknowledge their own limited training on religious and spiritual issues and express preference for including the topic as part of a larger empha- sis on cultural diversity (Derezotes, 1995; Dudley & Helfgott, 1990; Sheridan et al., 1994). Most students and faculty agree on the impor- tance of self-awareness as critical to appropriate social work practice (Cascio, 1999; Derezotes, 1995; Kaplan & Dziegielewski, 1999).

Social Work Practitioners

Survey results of social work practitioners focus on two major topics for consideration. Practitioners clearly felt their education had not provided adequate training in religious and spiritual issues in their schooling and they agreed with students and faculty that self-awareness is a key factor for appropriate practice (Bullis, 1993; Derezotes, 1995; Mattison et al., 2000; Sheridan & Bullis, 1991; Sheridan et al., 1992). Seventy-nine percent (79%) of practitioners in Sheridan et al.'s 1992 study responded that "religious or spiritual issues were never or rarely addressed during the course of their graduate education" (p. 190). Results of several studies of social work practitioners indicate that higher levels of personal spirituality correlated with greater use of spiritual interventions, indicating that professionals may develop their own policy about using spiritual interventions in practice, based on their own beliefs and personal or professional values, when professional training is absent or limited (Bullis, 1993; Derezotes, 1995; Mattison et al., 2000). Limitations of these empirical studies include the potential for regional differences in opinion, as some studies surveyed social workers in only one state (Bullis, 1993; Cascio, 1999; Derezotes, 1995; Sheridan et al., 1992). The lack of standardized instruments and clear definitions also limit the reliability of results (Rubin & Babbie, 1997).

The Ethics of Addressing Spiritual Issues in Social Work Practice

While there has been some discussion in the literature about using professional ethics to decide if and when to use spiritual interventions in practice (Bullis, 1993; Canda, 1989; Loewenberg, 1988; Spencer, 1961), empirical studies that included questions about ethical decision- making on spirituality are few. Jaffe (1961) found that practitioners believed referral to trained spiritual personnel was ethical and that knowing major religious systems was appropriate. Dudley and Helfgott (1990), in surveying social work faculty, noted that some respondents felt that it would be unethical to consider religious or spiritual issues in the classroom, as doing so may go against the values of social work. Bullis studied how professional ethics related to the decision to use spiritual interventions in practice (1993). His study of 112 practitioners, using a survey instrument similar to the one used in this research study, found statistically significant, weak correlations between personal ideology and intervention use, participation in a spiritual group and intervention use, and number of hours of graduate theological training and intervention use (Bullis, 1993).

Studies from Related Disciplines

Studies from related disciplines of medicine, psychology, and counseling speak to the need for more training around religion and spirituality, and the distinctions to be made between one's personal beliefs and the ability to assess and intervene professionally when a client's beliefs differ from one's own (Bergin & Jensen, 1990; Maugans & Wadland, 1991; Olive, 1995; Shafranske & Malony, 1990). Studies reported in the medical literature indicated that patients *want* their healthcare professional to address spiritual concerns with them, and often expect the professional to initiate this conversation (Maugans & Wadland, 1991; Oyama & Koenig, 1998).

METHODOLOGY

This research study employed a cross-sectional survey design that asked a random national sample of gerontological social workers anonymously about their practice, their attitudes toward personal and professional spiritual issues, and their use of spiritual interventions in their practice. The sample of gerontological social workers was created by combining two national gerontological social work registries. A pilot study prior to the full survey assessed the appropriateness and reliability of the survey instrument and the demographic/personal information questions. From a final sample of 2,828 names, 828 participants were randomly selected and a survey and cover letter were mailed to them; the return rate was 34.5% (N = 299). The instrument was an exploratory one developed by Sheridan, the "Role of Religion and Spirituality in Social Work Practice" Scale (2000), with minor revisions for this study made to reflect the gerontological focus. Reliability and validity are published for the first two pages of the scale, with the remaining three pages of survey questions not having published reliability or validity figures (Sheridan, 2000). Previous reliability for the 2-page attitude scale averaged 0.83; reliability results for this study are 0.85 (Quattelbaum, 2002; Sheridan, 2000). Validity is supported by the correlation of the general attitude and ethical attitude scales (r = 0.554, p < 0.001).

The instrument asked about attitudes, beliefs, and behaviors about spirituality in practice, as well as demographic information. Space was available for written comments, which were themed for their contribution to the understanding of attitudes, beliefs, and behaviors of the participants in their work with or on behalf of older adults.

RESULTS

Personal and professional characteristics are given in table form (Tables 1-3) for the sample, since these provide context for the correlational and regression results that follow. The sample (N = 299) reflects the typical current social work practitioner population for the United States: predominantly female, White, Christian, mid-range in age, working in rural to urban settings in 42 states and Washington, DC. The participants reported their involvement in private and communal spiritual activity, as seen in Table 2. Respondents reported a variety of affiliation activity levels and communal and private spiritual activity levels.

Regarding their professional lives, the participants responded about the settings of their practice and their educational background (Table 3). Participants were predominantly MSWs (Masters of Social Work), but the results also reflect the variety of degrees currently accepted in gerontological work, from Bachelor's degrees in social work and related fields, to the PhD in social work and related fields and the DSW (Doctor of Social Work). A great majority of these social workers had provided personal caregiving to an older person (83.7%, n = 247). Only 16.6% (n = 48) reported currently working in a religious setting.

In questions about their educational preparation on religious and spiritual issues, 69.8% of participants reported little or no training re-

TABLE 1. Personal Characteristics

Gender	Female 85.5% (n = 254)	Male 14.5% (n = 43)			
Age in years	Mean (s.d.) 52.85 (11.11)	Range 23-81			
Ethnicity	Caucasian 89.9% (n = 266)	African American 4.4% (n = 13)	Asian American 2.4% (n = 7)	Latino(a) 1.4% (n = 4)	Other 1.7% (n = 5)
Region of residence	Northeast 42.0% (n = 121)	South 22.6% (n = 65)	Midwest 20.5% (n = 59)	West 14.9% (n = 43)	

Note: Ns in tables may differ depending on missing data

TABLE 2. Personal Spiritual Activity

Spiritual Affiliation	Christian 65.2% (n = 195)	Jewish 19.1% (n = 57)	Muslim 0.3% (n = 1)	Other 1.7% (n = 5)
Affiliation Activity Level	Regular/some 37.8% (n = 112)	Limited 29.4% (n = 87)	High/Active 21.3% (n = 63)	Uninvolved 11.5% (n = 34)
Communal Spiritual Activity	1x/week 27.9% (n = 83)	2-3x/month 14.1% (n = 42)	Not at all 13.1% (n = 39)	
Private Spiritual Activity	Daily 39.3% (n = 116)	2-3x/week 26.8% (n = 79)	Not at all 9.5% (n = 28)	

TABLE 3. Professional and Work Setting Characteristics

Highest degree	MSW 78.8% (n = 231)	PhD or DSW 9.9% (n = 37)	Bachelors (BSW, BA, BS) 7.8% (n = 23)	Other Masters 3.4% (n = 10)
Gerontology specialization in school	Yes 51.0% (n = 149)	No 49.0% (n = 143)		
Years of practice	In Social Work: Mean 21.26 (s.d. 10.04); range 1-52	In Gerontology: Mean 16.30 (s.d. 8.21); range 0-40		
Direct/Indirect service	Direct service to older adults 63.1% (n = 171)	Indirect service to older adults 36.9% (n = 100)		
Setting location	Urban 39.1% (n = 113)	Mix 30.1% (n = 87)	Suburban 20.8% (n = 60)	Rural 10.0% (n = 29)
Work settings	Long term care 16.2% (n = 47)	Case management 12.7% (n = 37)	Education 11.3% (n = 33)	Hospital 8.9% (n = 26) and Private practice 8.9% (n = 26)

ceived on religious/spiritual topics, with 38.4% reporting being very or somewhat dissatisfied with the amount of training received, 36.7% (n = 108) reporting a neutral sense of satisfaction, and 24.8% (n = 73) being somewhat or very satisfied with the amount (Table 4). Responding to a question about post-graduate preparation on spirituality, 170 respondents of the 299 (58.6%) sought additional preparation on religious/ spiritual issues in continuing education venues.

TABLE 4. Educational Preparation on Spiritual Issues

Preparation in school on spirituality (N = 294)	Never or rarely 69.8% (n = 205)	Sometimes 24.8% (n = 73)	Often 5.4% (n = 16)
Satisfaction with amount of prepara-tion (N = 294)	Very or somewhat dissatisfied 38.4% (n = 113)	Neutral 36.7% (n = 108)	Somewhat or very satisfied 24.8% (n = 73)
Attendance at contin-uing education work-shops on topic (N = 290)	Yes 58.6% (n = 170)	No 41.4% (n = 120)	

The following three tables (Tables 5-7) show results of the three survey question sets regarding (1) their attitudes about spirituality in practice, (2) their sense of which spiritual interventions are ethical/unethical (or appropriate/inappropriate) to use with clients, and (3) their use of specific interventions in practice. The highest percentages of agreement were with the belief that spirituality is fundamental, that it is important to have knowledge of different faiths, that spirituality is within the scope of social work practice, and that knowledge of the client's beliefs is important for effective social work practice. Highest percentages of disagreement were found with recommending religious texts, sharing one's own beliefs, using religious language, and praying with the client. These results support the mandates of CSWE *Educational Policies* (2001), CSWE/SAGE-SW *Gerontological Competencies* (2001), and NASW *Cultural Competencies* (2001).

Participants in this study agreed that it is appropriate to gather spiritual information, to refer as needed, to help clients reflect on losses, and to help clients consider their spiritual support system; these appropriate interventions were also those used most often by the respondents. Those spiritual interventions considered inappropriate by the highest percentage of respondents included participating in clients' rituals, touching the client for "healing" purposes, assessing dreams, and recommending forgiveness; these same interventions were also reported as never used by the highest percentages of respondents.

Finally, an interesting discrepancy appears between questions that are paired as positive and negative statements: 93.3% of respondents reported that they believed it is appropriate (or ethical) to "help clients consider ways their religious/spiritual beliefs or practices are *helpful*," but only 74.4% reported it appropriate (or ethical) to "help clients con-

TABLE 5. General Attitudes Toward Spirituality (N = 299)

Question	Strongly Agree	Agree	Neutral	Disagree	Strongly Disagree
1. Spirituality is fundamental +	65.6	26.4	5.7	2.0	0.3
2. Become more sophisticated	25.8	48.5	22.1	2.7	1.0
3. Knowledge of different faiths +	58.2	36.8	4.7	0.3	0.0
4. Religion within scope	39.1	46.5	8.0	5.0	1.3
5. Spirituality within scope +	50.8	42.8	4.3	1.7	0.3
6. Spiritual aspect empowers	20.1	45.5	24.4	8.4	1.7
7. Knowledge of beliefs +	46.2	46.8	5.7	0.7	0.7
8. Assess the positives	34.1	56.5	7.4	1.3	0.7
9. Assess the negatives	31.1	56.9	8.4	2.7	1.0
10. Religious language appropriate −	15.4	41.5	23.7	14.4	5.0
11. R/s background influential	23.7	50.8	11.7	9.4	4.3
12. Religious texts appropriate −	4.3	18.1	37.1	26.1	14.4
13. Ethical to pray with client −	14.0	46.5	22.1	13.4	4.0
14. Spiritual language appropriate	16.7	53.5	19.4	9.4	1.0
15. Share own beliefs sometimes −	6.0	54.8	17.7	15.4	6.0
16. R/s beliefs for holistic practice	23.7	52.2	15.7	7.0	1.3
17. Educ. content on r/s diversity	39.8	47.8	8.7	3.3	0.3
18. Educ. content on r/s issues	41.1	47.8	6.4	4.7	0.0

Note: R/s = Religious/spiritual; Educ. = educational; +highest agreement; − highest disagreement

sider ways their religious/spiritual beliefs or practices are *harmful.*" Similarly, 97.6% of respondents reported they believed it to be appropriate (or ethical) to help clients consider ways their religious/spiritual support systems are "*helpful,*" but only 74.3% agreed that it is appropriate (or ethical) to "help clients consider ways their religious/spiritual support systems are *harmful.*"

Analyses

Total scores were computed for the three scales created from the question sets, on general attitudes, ethical attitudes, and use of spiritual interventions (Table 8.). Correlational analyses indicate that more positive general attitudes about spirituality in practice are moderately and positively associated with greater use of spiritual interventions (r =

TABLE 6. Ethical Attitudes Toward Interventions ("Appropriateness") (N = 299)

Intervention	Appropriate	Inappropriate
1. Gather r/s information +	94.1%	5.9%
2. Recommend books	63.0%	36.7%
3. Pray privately for client	67.1%	32.9%
4. Pray with client	63.0%	36.6%
5. Use r/s language	81.6%	18.4%
6. Clarify r/s values	75.3%	24.7%
7. Recommend support groups	83.3%	13.5%
8. Refer to specialist +	94.2%	5.5%
9. Recommend journaling	75.5%	24.5%
10. Recommend forgiveness −	41.8%	58.2%
11. R/s beliefs in relation to others	81.7%	18.3%
12. Critique r/s beliefs	64.6%	35.4%
13. Assess dreams −	40.6%	59.4%
14. Consider spiritual meaning	77.7%	22.3%
15. Reflect on death	88.8%	11.2%
16. Reflect on loss +	99.3%	0.7%
17. Touch for "healing" purposes −	28.4%	62.5%
18. Help client develop rituals	70.7%	29.3%
19. Participate in client rituals −	32.6%	67.4%
20. Consider helpful beliefs	93.3%	6.7%
21. Consider harmful beliefs	74.7%	25.3%
22. R/s support helpful +	97.6%	2.4%
23. R/s support harmful	74.3%	25.7%
24. Share own beliefs	52.7%	47.3%

Note: R/s = Religious/spiritual; + highest percent of agreement; −highest percent of disagreement

0.549, $p < 0.001$) (N = 299) and that ethical attitudes (what is an "appropriate" intervention) are strongly and positively associated with the use of spiritual interventions ($r = 0.716$, $p < 0.001$) (N = 204). The general attitude and ethical attitude scales were also moderately, positively correlated ($r = 0.554$, $p < 0.001$) (N = 204). Fewer responses were available for use in computing the ethical attitude scale score (204 rather than 299), as many participants did not choose between yes or no to answer the question, "Is this an appropriate social work intervention?" but

TABLE 7. Spiritual Interventions Used (N = 299)

Question	Never	Sometimes	Often
1. Gather information +	6.0	42.8	51.2
2. Recommend books	50.8	44.8	4.3
3. Pray privately for client	33.1	43.1	23.7
4. Pray with client −	57.5	38.8	3.7
5. Use r/s language	18.1	72.2	9.7
6. Clarify r/s values	29.1	59.9	11.0
7. Recommend support group	18.4	67.2	14.4
8. Refer	13.4	66.2	20.4
9. Recommend journaling	53.5	39.5	7.0
10. Recommend forgiveness	70.9	26.1	3.0
11. R/s beliefs and others	30.1	64.5	5.4
12. Critique beliefs	49.5	46.5	4.0
13. Assess dreams −	82.6	15.7	1.7
14. Spiritual meaning	31.4	57.5	11.0
15. Reflect on death	21.1	64.2	14.7
16. Reflect on loss +	2.7	53.2	44.1
17. Touch −	75.9	16.7	7.4
18. Develop rituals	49.2	44.1	6.7
19. Participate in rituals −	79.9	19.4	0.7
20. Helpful beliefs	12.7	71.9	15.4
21. Harmful beliefs	45.5	50.5	4.0
22. Support helpful +	8.4	68.6	23.1
23. Support harmful	44.8	50.5	4.7
24. Share own beliefs	48.5	49.5	2.0

Note: R/s = Religious/spiritual; + highest percent of use; −lowest percent of use

TABLE 8. Significant Total Score Correlations

Variables	Pearson's r	Significance	N
General attitude × use of spiritual interventions	0.549	< 0.001	299
Ethical attitude × use of spiritual interventions	0.716	< 0.001	204
General attitude × ethical attitude	0.559	< 0.001	204

rather wrote in responses such as "It depends," "Sometimes," or "Each situation is unique."

A stepwise regression analysis was conducted to assess the predictive power of five variables: ethical attitude score, amount of training on spiritual issues in social work education, amount of current private spiritual activity, age, and number of clients seen per week (as an indicator of type of practice setting and/or time available for individual clients) (Table 9). In Model 1, ethical attitude was entered as the only variable, and it explained 53% of the variance in the use of spiritual interventions by gerontological social workers. The variable "ethical attitude" was derived from an ethical attitude total score response to the yes/no question, "Is this an appropriate social work intervention?" Models 2 and 3 added variables from the five listed above. In Model 4, the variables ethical attitude, private spiritual activity, number of clients, and spiritual training explain 57% of the variance. The predictor variables other than ethical attitude, therefore, account for only an additional 4% of the variance explained. Model 1 has practical significance; the results indicate that ethical attitudes explain 53% of the variance in the use of spiritual interventions. The remaining 47% of variance is explained by the other variables (4%) and by factors not measured in this study, such as the theoretical orientation of the worker or type of management of the work

TABLE 9. Model Summary of Stepwise Multiple Regression Analysis of Predictive Power of Key Variables on Use of Spiritual Interventions (N = 179)

Model	R	R Square	Adjusted R Square	Standard Error of the Estimate	Standardized Beta Values
1	0.730	0.534	0.531	5.3949	0.730 ethics
2	0.748	0.560	0.556	5.2548	0.676 ethics; 0.171 private spiritual activity
3	0.756	0.572	0.565	5.1971	0.681 ethics; 0.151 private spiritual activity; 0.111 number of clients
4	0.764	0.583	0.574	5.1434	0.656 ethics; 0.155 private spiritual activity; 0.111 number of clients; 0.109 training on spirituality in social work education

Method: Stepwise regression; Dependent variable: Intervention Total Score; Predictor variables: Model 1: Ethical Attitude Total Score; Model 2: Ethical Attitude and Private Spiritual Activity; Model 3: Ethical Attitude, Private Spiritual Activity, and Number of Clients per Week; Model 4: Ethical Attitude, Private Spiritual Activity, and Number of Clients per Week, Amount of training on spiritual issues in social work education; Excluded Variable in Models 1-4: age setting. Age is not a significant predictor of gerontological social workers' use of spiritual interventions.

Analyzing responses for correlations between personal spiritual beliefs and the use of spiritual interventions in practice produced weak, positive correlations in all areas (Table 10).

Written comments throughout the survey were themed to further clarify the participants' attitudes and behaviors on spirituality in practice. Themes mentioned most often were the importance of addressing spirituality in the context of death/dying (cited by 50.8% of respondents); loss (25.7%); psychological distress (18.6%); chronic illness (17.5%); as a coping skill (14.8%); as part of culturally competent/holistic assessment (13.1%); and as an existential issue (7.7%); and the need for professional education on spiritual issues (4.9%).

The final question in the instrument asked the respondent to share any "particularly relevant" religious or spiritual issues in their practice. Some respondents offered practice wisdom gleaned from their particular work with older adults. Regarding mental illness, one respondent suggested worker confusion: "Is the behavior psychic or psychotic?" Some noted the importance of spirituality to particular groups, such as African American women and the Jewish community. Some wrote about the use of spiritual interventions in work with youth, domestic violence, interfaith marriage, midlife issues, unfinished business, and the fear of aging as well as of dying. One respondent wrote, "My clients primarily have a diagnosis of 3rd stage Alzheimer's. They have been asked not to attend church, and many of them are neglected/abandoned by their church." One shares this thought: "Our society does not recognize death as a part of the cycle of life, making death seem like an enemy even when staying alive is hell here on earth."

Some spoke of their own development and/or concerns about spirituality in practice. One respondent simply wrote, "I lack skills"; another shared that it was "almost taboo to discuss in school, a touchy subject." Another wrote, "I know that, as a Jew, I would be horrified if the services made available to me were by, for example, fundamentalists of

TABLE 10. Personal Spirituality and the Use of Spiritual Interventions in Practice

	Spearman's rho	Significance	N
Private spiritual activity × intervention use	0.310	P < 0.001	295
Affiliation with spiritual group × intervention use	0.184	P < 0.001	296
Communal activity ×intervention use	0.217	P < 0.001	297

any religion who couldn't honor my beliefs, doubts, wishes, balance." One respondent declared, "Most literature in this area is preachy, vague, and irritating." But one respondent also shared this comment, "I seem to be more naturally integrating increased treatment focus on spiritual health the longer I do this work, and the older I get!"

DISCUSSION AND IMPLICATIONS

This research explored the spiritual attitudes and practice behaviors/interventions of gerontological social workers using an ecological theoretical framework that included a strengths perspective, normalizing both religion/spirituality and aging as components of diversity. This framework is affirmed by the results of this study, as respondents reported their attitudes that religion and spirituality are fundamental to human living and that assessing for this component is part of holistic practice. References to the need to refer, provide resources, and assist older adults in remaining connected to their spiritual community offer an ecological perspective in recognizing the importance of social involvement beyond the inner person's spiritual self. Additionally, this research considered the professional development of the social worker in regard to aging and spirituality, and results support the need for further training, for self-exploration, and for grounding in ethical decision-making for each student and professional.

The theory of social constructionism was not named, but was clearly implied in responses encouraging the gerontological social worker to "meet clients where they are," to assess more appropriately by enquiring about religious/spiritual issues, and to use interventions like life review and "hearing beyond the words." The power of religion and spirituality to increase or decrease coping skills highlights the theories of continuity, crisis intervention, and coping. Stage theories are represented in the transitions that have a spiritual component: late life wisdom and legacy, the *process* of dying, illness/disability, retirement, midlife crises, and working through family of origin issues.

The present study found significant, but weak, positive correlations between personal spiritual beliefs and activities and the use of spiritual interventions in practice. Mattison et al. (2000) found "the strongest and most consistent predictor of religious and prayer practices in work with clients is the religiosity of the worker" (2000, p. 53). In the present study, it is ethical attitudes toward spiritual interventions, much more strongly than personal spiritual activity, that predict the use of spiritual interventions by gerontological social workers. Reliance on an ethical code bodes well for gerontology and social work practice as these professionals serve older adults with ethical decision-making and professional competence, rather than relying on personal values.

In this study, the highest agreement on which specific spiritual interventions would be considered ethical ("appropriate social work interventions") included (1) reflecting on loss (99.3%), (2) considering helpful spiritual supports (97.6%), (3) referring to a specialist (94.2%), (4) gathering spiritual information (94.1%), and (5) considering helpful spiritual beliefs (93.3%). These interventions also represent the ones cited as most used by the respondents. Interventions that were reported most often as inappropriate for social work practice include participating in client rituals (67.4%), and touching for "healing" purposes (62.5%). This research also supports the position that the social work professional must assess for client spirituality, rather than expecting the client to open the discussion on this topic (94.1% agree on gathering spiritual information in assessment).

A limitation of the study is the use of an exploratory instrument that left many definitional questions unanswered for the respondent. For example, respondents asked what was meant by "touch" and "healing" in the item mentioned above. Responses, therefore, must be considered in light of differing interpretations of what certain words meant. However, even when respondents wrote their question in the margin, the tendency was still to answer the question and to complete the survey. This may be indicative of strong interest in this topic on the part of the participants.

Implications for Practice

The literature, the mandates from CSWE and NASW, and empirical research based on the opinions of practicing social workers, educators, and students clearly call for a change in the way the profession approaches spiritual issues. The religion and spirituality of the client, family, group, community, culture, or nation must be considered, as are other aspects of human diversity in any holistic assessment of client needs. Several respondents to this study wrote that it was only appropriate to discuss spirituality if and when the client raised the issue. However, studies have reported that clients often *want* professionals to initiate these conversations (Maugans & Wadland, 1991; Oyama & Koenig, 1998). Practitioners and students may need help to shift away from the idea that a client must bring up any private, and commonly considered "personal" or even "taboo," topic, rather than the worker asking questions about every aspect of life as part of holistic assessment.

At the same time, critical thinking skills must be applied to religion and spirituality, as they are to theory, practice methods, and empirical findings, in order to ensure that the unheard voices of minority groups, marginalized groups, and newly developed groups (for example, women in the military or Latino(a) political groups) are considered, as well as majority opinions. Personal and professional self-awareness and development of clear boundaries are needed as social workers interact with clients of different faith groups, or with clients who have had different experiences in the same faith tradition as the worker. The quantitative survey responses and the written comments of the present study tended to emphasize the positive effects of religion and spirituality. Critical thinking about social institutions will assist the professional in exploring for and recognizing negative, as well as positive, impacts of religious and spiritual beliefs and practices on the client or community.

Spiritual interventions can be offered as therapeutic options, just as other types of therapy are proposed when client and worker develop an intervention plan together. Indeed, if the professional does not have extensive knowledge of Native American traditions or Islam, for example, a social constructionist approach would suggest inviting the client to educate the worker in this area.

Implications for Social Work Education

Social workers, as students, faculty, and practitioners, are asking for more and better education on spiritual issues. The inclusion of material on spirituality can be accomplished in much the same way as in other areas of diversity education. Conceptualizing spirituality as a diversity component helps students to recognize this topic area as part of a truly holistic assessment, and provides a framework in which to ask assessment questions about client spirituality or meaning of life issues. Conceptualizing spirituality as a diversity component may help the classroom educator and field instructor, as well, to move beyond fears of taboo topics, personal differences and inadequacies, and insufficient preparation, toward at least opening a dialog in the classroom about spiritual beliefs. One place to begin this dialog is with self-awareness activities that helps students to explore their own spirituality, before expanding to exploration of the beliefs of others.

Of course, diversity is an enormous content area including gender, ethnicity, culture, religion/spirituality, age, sexual orientation, and disability, and there will never be enough time to cover it fully (Apple-gate & Walter, 1989; Ivry & Walter, 1992). The teaching, therefore, of transferable critical thinking skills and transferable ethical decision-making appears to be a reasonable conceptual method currently available to assist students and participants in continuing education seminars to recognize and develop their competence.

Because ethics influence gerontological social workers' use of spiritual interventions, it is critical that social work education offer sufficient ethical decision-making preparation, through content on ethical theory and delineation of ethical principles, and through the process of wrestling with ethical dilemmas under the guidance of faculty in the classroom and supervisors in the field. Personal boundary clarification, personal and professional values' clarification, and competence to choose to practice in a given area or to refer to a professional with specialized preparation in that area are elements of professional development that should be addressed in the classroom and field and as ongoing learning for the practitioner.

CONCLUSION

This research affirms the mandate that calls social workers to be holistic and non-discriminatory toward persons of diverse spiritual beliefs. It emphasizes the importance of the spiritual dimension in the client system and in the worker. It reiterates the call for more and better preparation in school on the topic of religion and spirituality. It provides baseline data on gerontological social work in the spiritual dimension. It may also serve as a voice from the front lines of social work with the old–the middle-aged, the young-old, the old, and the oldest-old–that the spiritual issues of America's older adults today are being addressed professionally, but that more and better preparation is needed.

Future research on this intersection of spirituality, aging, and social work might examine other predictive factors influencing the use of spiritual interventions with older persons. Theoretical orientation of the worker or work setting characteristics may prove to be factors in the use of spiritual interventions. An exploration might be undertaken of what it means to work in gerontology, as the worker grows older. Qualitative research would yield rich and timely information on how gerontological social workers have discerned the boundaries and ethics of using spirituality in practice as they proceeded through school and work, often with little or no training. A more clearly defined picture of the worker's personal spirituality and how that impacts on work and personal life may yield clearer answers to the correlations and interactive effects of attitudes, behaviors, personal spirituality, and the use of interventions. Further exploration of the combination of ethics and spirituality is needed, and the responses of the gerontological professionals in this study provide a beginning toward that research.

Results of this national study of gerontological social workers support the incorporation of religion and spirituality into the mainstream of practice, education, research, and policy as components of holistic assessment/intervention and diversity education. This study also supports a continuing emphasis on the ethical preparation needed to provide appropriate care to older adults and to all persons along the life span, as well as to create respectful policy and research on aging and spirituality. As the older population booms in the next generation and cultural diversity in the United States continues to increase, the sometimes hesitant steps we have taken so far toward honoring both aging and spirituality must begin to run toward that future.

REFERENCES

Ai, A. (2000). Spiritual well-being, spiritual growth, and spiritual care for the aged: A cross-faith and interdisciplinary effort. *Journal of Religious Gerontology, 11*, 2, 3-28.

Applegate, J.S., & Walter, C.A. (1989). Starting where the student is: Meeting the developmental challenge of HBSE courses. *Arete, 14*, 2, 1-11.

Atchley, R.C. (1977). *The social forces in later life* (2nd ed.). Belmont, CA: Wadsworth Publishing.

Bandura, A. (1997). *Self-efficacy: The exercise of control.* USA: W.H. Freeman and Company.

Bergin, A.E., & Jensen, J.P. (1990). Religiosity of psychotherapists: A national survey. *Psychotherapy, 27*, 1, 3-7.

Blazer, D. (1991). Spirituality and aging well. *Generations, Winter*, 61-65.

Bullis, R.K. (1996). *Spirituality in social work practice.* Taylor and Francis Publishers.

Bullis, R.K. (1993). Religious/spiritual factors in clinical social work practice: An examination of assessment, intervention, and ethics. *Dissertation Abstracts International, 30* (3), 855A.

Butler, R.N. (1963). *Why survive? Being old in America.* New York: Harper & Row, Publishers.

Canda, E.R. (1997). Does religion and spirituality have a significant place in the core HBSE curriculum? In M. Bloom & W.C. Klein (Eds.), *Controversial issues in human behavior in the social environment* (pp. 172-177, 183-4). Boston: Allyn & Bacon.

Canda, E.R. (1989). Religious content in social work education: A comparative approach. *Journal of Social Work Education, 25*, 1, 15-24.

Canda, E.R. (1988). Spirituality, religious diversity, and social work practice. *Social Casework, 69*, 238-247.

Cascio, T. (1999). Religion and spirituality: Diversity issues for the future. *Journal of Multicultural Social Work, 7*, 3/4, 129-145.

Council on Social Work Education. (2001). *Educational policies and accreditation standards*. Alexandria, VA: Author.

Council on Social Work Education/SAGE-SW. (2001). *Gerontological competencies for social work practice*. Alexandria, VA: Author.

Derezotes, D.S. (1995). Spirituality and religiosity: Neglected factors in social work practice. *Arete, 20*, 1, 1-15.

Dudley, J.R., & Helfgott, C. (1990). Exploring a place for spirituality in the social work curriculum. *Journal of Social Work Education, 3*, 287-294.

Erikson, E.H., & Erikson, J. (1986). *Vital involvement in old age*. New York: Norton.

Foley, L. (2000). Exploring the experience of spirituality in older women finding meaning in life. *Journal of Religious Gerontology, 12*, 1, 5-15.

Germain, C.B., & Gitterman, A. (1980). *The life model of social work practice*. New York: Columbia University Press.

Grinnell, R.M. (1997). *Social work research and evaluation* (5th ed.). Itasca, IL: F.E. Peacock Publishers, Incorporated.

Hillier, S., & Barrow, G.M. (1999). *Aging, the individual, and society* (7th ed.). Belmont, CA: Wadsworth Publishing Company.

Hutchison, E.D. (1999). *Dimensions of human behavior: Person and environment*. Thousand Oaks, CA: Pine Forge Press.

Ivry, P.W., & Walter, C.A. (1992). Current trends in teaching the human behavior and social environment course at the baccalaureate level. *Arete, 17*, 2, 38-50.

Jaffe, M.S. (1961). Opinions of caseworkers about religious issues in practice. *Smith College Studies in Social Work, 31*, 3, 238-256.

Kaplan, A.J., & Dziegielewski, S.F. (1999). Graduate social work students' attitudes and behaviors toward spirituality and religion: Issues for education and practice. *Social Work and Christianity, 26*, 1, 25-39.

Koenig, H.G. (1994). *Aging and God: Spiritual pathways to mental health in midlife and later years*. New York: The Haworth Press, Inc.

Loewenberg, F.M. (1988). *Religion and social work practice in contemporary American society*. New York: Columbia University Press.

Marty, M. (1980). Social service: Godly and godless. *Social Service Review, 54*, 4, 463-481.

Mattison, D., Jayaratne, S., & Croxton, T. (2000). Social workers' religiosity and its impact on religious practice behaviors. *Advances in Social Work, 1*, 1, 43-59.

Maugans, T.A., & Wadland, W.C. (1991). Religion and family medicine: A survey of physicians and patients. *The Journal of Family Practice, 32*, 2, 210-213.

Moberg, D.O. (Ed.) (2001). *Aging and spirituality: Spiritual dimensions of aging theory, research, practice, and policy*. Binghamton, NY: The Haworth Pastoral Press.

Morales, A., & Sheafor, B. (1998). *Social work: A profession of many faces* (7th ed.). Boston: Allyn & Bacon.

National Association of Social Workers. (2003). *Bereavement practice guidelines for social workers in emergency departments*. Washington, DC: Author.

National Association of Social Workers. (2001). *Standards for cultural competence*. Washington, DC: Author.

Olive, K.E. (1995). Physician religious beliefs and the physician-patient relationship: A study of devout physicians. *Southern Medical Journal, 88*, 12, 1249-1255.

Otto, R. (1917). *The idea of the holy.* London: Oxford University Press.

Oyama, O., & Koenig, H.G. (1998). Religious beliefs and practices in family medicine. *Archives of Family Medicine, 7*, 431-435.

Pargament, K.I. (1997). *The psychology of religion and coping.* New York: Guilford Press.

Quattlebaum, A.A. (2002). *A study of the use of spirituality in social work practice.* Unpublished doctoral dissertation, University of South Carolina, Columbia.

Reynolds, B. (1942, 1985). *Learning and teaching in the practice of social work* (NASW Classic Series). Silver Spring, MD: National Association of Social Workers.

Rizer, J.M., & McColley, K. (1996). Attitudes and practices regarding spirituality and religion held by graduate social work students. *Social Work and Christianity, 23*, 1, 53-64.

Rubin, A., & Babbie, E. (1997). *Research methods for social work* (3rd ed.). Pacific Grove, CA: Brooks/Cole Publishing Company.

Scovell, C. (1996). Growing old on the way to God. *Journal of Geriatric Psychiatry, 29*, 2, 145-154.

Shafranske, E.P., & Malony, H.N. (1990). Clinical psychologists' religious and spiritual orientations and their practice of psychotherapy. *Psychotherapy, 27*, 1, 72-78.

Sheridan, M.J. (2000). *The "Role of Religion and Spirituality in Practice" (RRSP) scale: Psychometric information and scoring instructions.* Unpublished manuscript, Virginia Commonwealth University, Richmond.

Sheridan, M.J. & Bullis, R.K. (1991). Practitioners' views on religion and spirituality: A qualitative study. *Spirituality and Social Work Journal, 2*, 2, 2-10.

Sheridan, M.J., Bullis, R.K., Adcock, C.R., Berlin, S.D., & Miller, P.C. (1992). Practitioners' personal and professional attitudes and behaviors toward religion and spirituality: Issues for education and practice. *Journal of Social Work Education, 28*, 2, 190-203.

Sheridan, M.J., Wilmer, C.M., & Atcheson, L. (1994). Inclusion of content on religion and spirituality in the social work curriculum: A study of faculty views. *Journal of Social Work Education, 30*, 3, 363-376.

Sherwood, D.A. (2000). Spiritual assessment as a normal part of social work practice: Power to help and power to harm. *Social Work and Christianity, 25*, 2, 80-89.

Spencer, S. (1961). What place has religion in social work education? *Social Service Review, 35*, 161-170.

Stolley, J.M., & Koenig, H.G. (1997). Religion/spirituality and health among elderly African Americans and Hispanics. *Journal of Psychosocial Nursing, 35*, 11, 32-38.

Tirrito, T., Nathanson, I., & Langer, N. (1996). *Elder practice: A multidisciplinary approach to working with older adults in the community.* Columbia, SC: University of South Carolina Press.

Tirrito, T., & Spencer-Amado, J. (2000). Older adults' willingness to use social services in places of worship. *Journal of Religious Gerontology, 11*, 2, 29-42.

Towle, C. (1954/1971). *Common human needs* (Rev. ed.). Washington, DC: National Association of Social Workers.

Vaillant, G.E. (1995). *The wisdom of the ego.* Cambridge, MA: Harvard University Press.

Weisman, D. (1997). Does religion and spirituality have a significant place in the core HBSE curriculum? In M. Bloom & W.C. Klein (Eds.), *Controversial issues in human behavior in the social environment* (pp. 177-183). Boston: Allyn & Bacon.

APPENDIX

Definitions

Theology, religious studies, and pastoral care literature offer definitions of religion and spirituality that are abstract enough to include the mysterious, but also practical enough to inform and inspire followers to service. The social sciences, however, must operationalize the theological definitions in order to generate empirical evidence. The definitions given in this article are offered to assist the reader, since the topic of religion/spirituality is both relatively new to the social sciences and often fraught with concerns about its personal nature and its "immeasurability" (Moberg, 2001).

Limitations of the Research

Limitations of the methodology of this study included instrument limitations of length (9 pages) and topic. Design limitations included the use of a predominantly unstandardized instrument. Even the standardized portion of the research instrument has only been used in a few studies (Sheridan, 2000; Quattlebaum, 2002). In addition, any methodology intending to study spirituality faces the issue of measurement validity in general as debate continues on the "measurability" of spirituality and religiosity in many disciplines (Marty, 1980; Moberg, 2001). Definitions of terms, helpful though they may be, may not be enough to address the more fundamental issue of the personal and individual nature of the spirituality of each person; many people's belief that spirituality is personal and private also may have contributed to non-response to the survey (Grinnell, 1997). The theoretical orientation of each participant in this research was not queried; rather, the research assumed participants used a generalist, ecological practice focus for gerontological social work, based on the current literature that educates and informs gerontological social workers at baccalaureate through doctoral levels (Morales & Sheafor, 1998; Tirrito, Nathanson, & Langer, 1996). Because the research assured anonymity, which is important for assuring the reliability and validity of the responses, there was no way to track non-respondents.

PRACTICE

Caregivers' Use of Spirituality in Ethical Decision-Making

Terry L. Koenig, PhD

SUMMARY. This qualitative study examined ethical dilemmas faced by female caregivers of frail elders as well as the dominant role of caregivers' spirituality in addressing these dilemmas. Dilemmas are difficult decisions that involve conflicting values, e.g., freedom versus safety. In-depth interviews were conducted with thirteen ethnically diverse caregivers recruited from a home health agency and its parent hospital. Purposive sampling was used to obtain variation among research participants. Focus group interviews of home health staff, key informant caregivers, and interviewees provided guidance for the research design, reflection on findings and development of implications. In order to deal with ethical dilemmas, all caregivers used spirituality as (1) a philosophy of life, e.g., "This is what you do when you're family," (2) an aid to decision-making, e.g., through the use of prayer; and/or, (3) a way to transcend dilemmas, e.g., "no choice is hard." Implications include the importance of care-

[Haworth co-indexing entry note]: "Caregivers' Use of Spirituality in Ethical Decision-Making." Koenig, Terry L. Co-published simultaneously in *Journal of Gerontological Social Work* (The Haworth Social Work Practice Press, an imprint of The Haworth Press, Inc.) Vol. 45, No. 1/2, 2005, pp. 155-172; and: *Religion, Spirituality, and Aging: A Social Work Perspective* (ed: Harry R. Moody) The Haworth Social Work Practice Press, an imprint of The Haworth Press, Inc., 2005, pp. 155-172. Single or multiple copies of this article are available for a fee from The Haworth Document Delivery Service [1-800-HAWORTH, 9:00 a.m. - 5:00 p.m. (EST). E-mail address: docdelivery@haworthpress.com].

giver-driven assessment, professional self-reflection, and sustained formal services for caregivers. *[Article copies available for a fee from The Haworth Document Delivery Service: 1-800-HAWORTH. E-mail address: <docdelivery@ haworthpress.com> Website: <http://www.HaworthPress.com> © 2005 by The Haworth Press, Inc. All rights reserved.]*

KEYWORDS. Ethics, caregiving, aging, religion, spiritual assessment

INTRODUCTION

Caregiver burden, defined as informal caregivers' experiences of intolerable stress or strain in caring for a frail elder, is a persistent and growing concern for practitioners, policy makers, researchers and others. Furthermore, the reduction of caregiver burden is an important outcome in the expanding body of caregiving intervention studies (Shultz, O'Brien et al., 2002). In the past decade, researchers have systematically explored the role of caregivers' spirituality or religion as an important and natural coping resource in dealing with multiple physical, emotional and social demands which contribute to this burden (Calderon & Tennstedt, 1998; Chang, Noonan, & Tennstedt, 1998; Connell & Gibson, 1997; Jones, 1995; Kaye & Robinson, 1994; Picot, Debanne, Namazi, & Wykle, 1997; Richardson & Sistler, 1999; Stolley, Buckwalter, & Koenig, 1999; Stuckey, 2001). However, little is known about how spirituality works in helping caregivers cope with the burdens and stressful situations inherent in caregiving (Chang, Noonan, & Tennstedt, 1998; Stuckey, 2001).

Finding out how spirituality is used by caregivers provides important knowledge for the development and refinement of caregiving interventions designed to reduce caregiver burden. Caregivers often use spirituality as a natural coping resource in facing the difficult decisions and demands involved in caregiving. Examining specifically how they use spirituality in decision making will inform the development and testing of these interventions.

This paper reports on findings from a qualitative study that explored female caregivers' decision-making processes in dealing with ethical dilemmas. Women as informal caregivers face a myriad of ongoing and complex conflicts and ethical dilemmas in caring for a frail elder (Bopp & Coleson, 1996). Ethical dilemmas can be distinguished from other types of conflicts. For example, a spousal caregiver may experience conflict with her adult children about which services will best help her to care for the frail elder (e.g., a bath aid or housekeeping services). She may believe she will get the greatest relief from using a bath aid, but her adult children may express strong disagreement with her about having an unfamiliar person provide this service for their father. In this example, the caregiver's decision to obtain a bath aid is potentially blocked by her adult children. The caregiver's conflict is not an ethical dilemma based on her competing values and instead represents a conflict with her adult children over service options for the frail elder.

For the purpose of this study, an ethical dilemma is defined as a conflict experienced by the caregiver in which she must make a choice "between two or more relevant, but contradictory ethical directives, or when every alternative results in an undesirable outcome for one or more persons" (Loewenberg, Dolgoff, & Harrington, 2000, p. 9). For example, one caregiver, providing care for her husband, was torn between whether or not to restrict her husband's freedom to use an electric scooter. Her husband had poor judgment and was riding the scooter in the early morning before sunrise. She was concerned that her husband would get hit by a car or that he would topple the scooter while trying to ride it in the darkness. She did not want to restrict his freedom, but she also feared for his safety. This spousal caregiver experienced an ethical dilemma between the competing values of freedom and safety. She wanted to respect her husband's freedom and yet also struggled with making sure he was safe. She used prayer and discussions with her husband to work through this ethical dilemma. Eventually, he agreed to cut back on his scooter riding at night. As in this example, all caregivers in this study used spirituality to work through and resolve ethical dilemmas involving conflicting or competing values. Using caregivers' personal narratives of decision-making processes, this paper will highlight the specific uses of spirituality in working through and resolving these difficult caregiving dilemmas.

SPIRITUALITY AND RELIGION IN CAREGIVING

In the caregiving literature, 'spirituality' and 'religion' are almost exclusively depicted as coping mechanisms for caregivers in managing associated burden and stress. Authors often do not define these terms, use them interchangeably or make few distinctions between them (Calderon & Tennstedt, 1998; Chang, Noonan, & Tennstedt, 1998; Connell & Gibson,

1997; Sistler & Richardson, 1999). Furthermore, because caregiving studies examine spirituality and religion as an overarching coping mechanism, they fail to account for the specific role religion and spirituality plays in helping caregivers make decisions about daily and often difficult dilemmas that are part of the caregiving experience.

For our purposes, spirituality is defined as the caregivers' search for meaning and purpose in providing care for the frail elder that involves both religious and nonreligious or noninstitutional expression. Religious expression is the caregivers' search for meaning and purpose through interactions with a social institution, i.e., church, synagogue, or mosque that provides community support and a continuity of traditions (Canda & Furman, 1999). Nonreligious or noninstitutional expression involves the search for meaning and purpose that emanates from sources such as positive thinking, a commitment to family or a belief in a power greater than oneself. As will be discussed in the findings, this definition of spirituality is consistent with study participants' descriptions. Caregivers expressed their spirituality, a sense of meaning and purpose in caregiving, as emanating from institutional, religious beliefs, e.g., "I just felt it [the responsibility] would be mine [because of] my vows of marriage." Caregivers also described spirituality as emanating from nonreligious sources, e.g., "This is what you do for family."

RESEARCH QUESTIONS

Through in-depth interviews with thirteen ethnically diverse caregivers, this qualitative study explored three overarching research questions: (1) What are the ethical dilemmas that female caregivers face in caring for a frail elder in the home setting? (2) What are the processes female caregivers describe in dealing with or resolving ethical dilemmas? and (3) What recommendations do female caregivers have for enhancing services to help address ethical dilemmas? All caregivers reported an important finding related to the use of spirituality in working through or resolving numerous ethical dilemmas that are part of their daily caregiving experience.

METHODOLOGY

This study used naturalistic inquiry to explore female caregiver experiences of ethical dilemmas. Naturalistic inquiry emphasizes a qualitative design in which ideas, major themes, conclusions and grounded theory emerge from analysis of the data rather than from the researcher's a priori assumptions or theories (Lincoln & Guba, 1985). Because minimal systematic research has been conducted on women's experiences of ethical dilemmas in caregiving, a qualitative design lent itself well to this exploration. The use of semi-structured interviews with open-ended questions enabled caregivers to describe detailed stories of their personal decision-making processes that incorporated a wide range of factors.[1] Although questions about spirituality were not part of the interview guide, spirituality emerged in preliminary data analysis as a dominant factor in caregivers' decision-making processes. Hence, when caregivers initiated the topic of spirituality, the researcher prompted interviewees to expound further (e.g., "Say more about how your faith helped you make this decision").

For the purpose of this study, a frail elder was defined as any person age 65 or older needing assistance from a caregiver with one or more activities of daily living such as bathing, ambulation, money management, or household chores. An informal, primary caregiver was defined as a woman who provides the major source of unpaid care in the home for a frail elder (Barer & Johnson, 1990; Montgomery, 1996). Because minimal research has been conducted on ethical dilemmas from the caregiver's viewpoint and because the majority of caregivers are women, over seventy-three percent, the researcher chose to interview only women for this study (National Alliance for Caregivers & AARP, 1997).

Participants were recruited from clients of a home health agency and its parent hospital located in the Midwest. Caregivers were selected using purposive sampling in order to obtain a broad range of perspectives concerning the research questions.[2] Home health agency staff obtained written permission from applicable caregivers to be contacted by the researcher for possible participation in this study. Caregivers who agreed to participate were mailed an introductory letter 5 to 7 days before the scheduled interview explaining the research study's purpose and procedures. Participants were encouraged to think about "hard choices" or ethical dilemmas in such areas as personal feelings about caregiving, social support from family and friends, the frail elder's resistance to the caregiver's help, the effects of outside employment or child care, the frail elder's cognitive abilities, length of time involved in caregiving, the caregiver's health, and being female and a caregiver.

The constant comparative method of qualitative data analysis as described by Lincoln and Guba (1985) was used to analyze the interviews,

observations and documents.[3] Several strategies were employed to establish trustworthiness in the study's findings, e.g., the use of a consultant
panel, member checking and focus groups. Consultant panel members,
consisting of home health staff and key caregivers, gave feedback on introductory themes and case vignettes of ethical dilemmas as a way of refining and confirming findings.[4] The researcher also conducted member
checks as to the understanding and accuracy of findings with research
participants.[5] Finally, in focus groups, members of the consultant panel
and interviewees confirmed a preliminary report of major findings and
tentative conclusions. Through the use of these strategies, interview participants were able to assert their perspectives as a way to refine and add
credibility to the findings.

FINDINGS

Demographic Characteristics

Demographic characteristics were collected on caregivers including
age, marital status, relationship to the frail elder, ethnicity, level of education, employment status and child or grandchild care status. Caregivers ranged in age from 49 to 85-years-old and included eight
spouses, two daughters, one significant other, one daughter-in-law, and
one mother.[6] Analysis indicated that no distinct subgroups of the research
participants, such as adult daughters and wives, ethnically diverse participants, and variances in education or employment distinguished caregivers' use of spirituality in dealing with or resolving ethical dilemmas.

Definitions of Spirituality

Caregivers defined their spirituality, a sense of meaning and purpose
in caregiving, as emanating from institutional, religious beliefs, e.g.,
I've been "called by God" as a Christian to care for the frail elder, "I just
ask God to take over," or I feel a sense of "duty" and "responsibility"
that flows from religious beliefs about marriage. Caregivers also described their spirituality as emanating from nonreligious sources. In describing what gives them a sense of meaning and purpose in facing
difficult decisions, caregivers stated, "You just have to do the right
thing," or "This is what you do for family," "I'm a positive thinker," and
I'm going to make decisions based on my "identity" as a caregiver.

Caregivers' Use of Spirituality

Introduction. Because this study sought to understand caregivers' decision-making processes in dealing with ethical dilemmas, findings are reported using caregiving vignettes that provide direct quotes as well as contextual factors, e.g., the caregiver's physical impairments. Central characteristics of the dilemma, e.g., personal conflict and/or conflict involving health care providers are discussed as they impinge on the caregiver's ethical decision-making. (Each caregiver is also given a pseudonym.) These particular vignettes are chosen because they highlight how caregivers use spirituality as a philosophy of life, an aid to decision making, or as a way to transcend the difficult nature of ethical dilemmas that occur internally and/or in relationships with others. Each caregiver was asked by the researcher, "Can you tell me a story about a hard choice or ethical dilemma that you faced as a caregiver?" Caregivers' responses to this question provided a rich array of caregiving narratives describing various uses of spirituality in their decision-making processes. Finally, this study will report on barriers spirituality created for some caregivers in addressing ethical dilemmas.

Characteristics of ethical dilemmas. Two central characteristics of ethical dilemmas are described by all caregivers in this study. First, an ethical dilemma always involves the personal or intrapsychic conflict of competing values for the caregiver. For example, the caregiver may be torn about whether or not to leave the frail elder at home alone (she values safety, yet also values social relationships and wants to spend time with friends). Second, although dilemmas are intrapsychic or internal conflicts, they may also involve conflicts with others: (a) conflict in close interpersonal relationships, e.g., with the frail elder or other family members and friends; and (b) conflict in relationships with agency, community, or other societal members, e.g., with health care providers or a larger entity such as a nursing facility.

Spirituality as an overall philosophy of life. Twelve caregivers referred to a philosophy of life which guided their decision-making processes in dealing with dilemmas. (One caregiver did not refer to an overall philosophy of life, but instead described her relationships with other caregivers in an informal church support group as a specific aid to her decision making in facing tough choices.) This philosophy of life, which incorporated both religious and nonreligious beliefs, gave caregivers a sense of meaning and purpose as a caregiver. For example, caregivers described the following philosophies about caregiving, "In my world, people help each other"; "Everything happens for a reason"; "You just have to rise up in this world and do what you gotta do"; "I just ask God to take over"; "I have the faith"; and, "It's what you do when you're a family." These philosophies enabled caregivers to deal with or resolve difficult dilemmas. The following narrative describes Paula's philosophy in dealing with the dilemma of whether or not to provide care for her mother. It is also a dilemma that involves conflict with Paula's sister.

Paula, an unmarried caregiver of European ethnicity, had become socially isolated and was losing out on opportunities to maintain any kind of social life. At her sister's invitation and with the promise of extra help from her sister, Paula and her mom had moved into her sister's home. However, even after confronting her sister about providing promised help, the sister refused to be involved in mom's care. Paula stated:

> I get real frustrated because I would like to just walk out of the house and do whatever I want to do. I'd like to go to a movie. I'd like to call up a friend and not have to make arrangements to have somebody take care of mother. I'd like to have the freedom that goes with not having any responsibilities. But . . . I [have] felt responsible ever since I can remember.

Paula resolved this internal and relationally-based dilemma by continuing to provide care for her mother. She found a sense of meaning and purpose as a caregiver and stated, "They [my parents] have loved and supported and cared for me all my life and it's what you do when you're a family. You take care of each other." However, Paula also indicated she would never put herself in this situation again.

Paula's overall philosophy, "It's what you do when you're a family" helped her deal with the ethical dilemma of whether or not to continue providing care for her mother. Because of her philosophy, Paula affirmatively resolved this ongoing dilemma by continually choosing to provide care for her mother. This philosophy also gave her a sense of meaning and purpose as a caregiver in facing numerous difficult dilemmas throughout the caregiving process.

Spirituality as an aid to decision making. Seven caregivers referred to the use of spirituality as a specific aid in decision making for working through intrapsychic and relationally-based ethical dilemmas. (Six caregivers had an overall philosophy of life that guided their decision making, but did not refer to specific ways in which they used their spirituality.) Some caregivers cried out to God in prayer asking for help, others fasted, obtained support from church members, read scriptures, relied on premonitions, or used positive thinking in dealing with or resolving these dilemmas. For example, Diane described her use of prayer as an aid in managing her internal and interpersonal conflict with the frail elder.

Diane, a spousal caregiver of African and Native-American ethnicity, stated that her husband, with a recent above the knee amputation, was having difficulties getting his prosthetic limb to fit comfortably and could not use it to walk long distances. From Diane's perspective, her husband had become dependent on her, didn't want to leave the house or engage in any outside activities. Her dilemma was whether or not to leave him home alone. She confronted him about his dependent, isolative behavior, which was a major departure from the many social activities they participated in as a couple before his amputation. However, her husband refused to do anything outside the home with her. Diane emphatically stated, "I'm leaving this house 'cause you just want to sit here all day . . . If you don't want to go, I'm going. I ain't [sic] staying here with you." Although Diane did not "feel good" about leaving him, she refused to isolate herself and occasionally left home alone. Diane used prayer to help her come to this decision:

> I just ask God to take over my life. You know all about me. You made me. You know what I can stand and what I can't stand, so you always said you wouldn't put no [sic] more on me than I can take. So, you know what I'm going through. That's okay, I have the faith.

A second vignette is presented to show the caregiver's use of premonitions as a spiritual aid in managing interpersonal dilemmas with health care providers. Mary, who provided care for her mother-in-law, described conflict with health care providers. The health care providers refused to give her information about her mother-in-law's health status because she was not a biological relative. Because the frail elder had moderate cognitive difficulties, she did not pass on accurate medical information to Mary. Mary respected the confidential relationship between the frail elder and health care providers, but was also concerned that she would not provide the best care for her mother-in-law without accurate medical information. She confronted the health care providers about obtaining this medical information, but to no avail. Consequently, Mary worked through this dilemma by relying on her spiritual or 'spooky' connections with others:

> My mother and I, we were spooky and I don't want to use that word to scare you, but we had kind of a connection. We could be

miles apart, both pick up the phone, it wouldn't dial, it would ring, 'Hi, mom,' and [I would] know she was on the other end. . . . My dad always called us a witch [sic].

Mary stated that she planned to use this spiritual connection with others, this ability to have premonitions of future events, to know when her mother-in-law had serious health conditions. Mary stated that even if medical staff refused to keep her informed, she would use her spiritual abilities to obtain needed medical information.

Caregivers used spirituality as a distinct decision making aid in dealing with ethical dilemmas that involved intrapsychic conflict: conflict in close, interpersonal relationships and conflict with agency or community members, e.g., health care providers. These two vignettes also highlight caregivers' unique uses of spirituality, e.g., prayer and trust in premonitions as aids in making decisions about difficult dilemmas.

Spirituality as a way to transcend difficult decisions. Three caregivers described spirituality as helping them to transcend the difficult nature of decision making. For these caregivers, no decision was hard and they seemed able to transcend difficulties in facing ethical dilemmas and in making decisions. (Ten caregivers referred to the difficult nature of ethical decision-making in providing elder care.) For our purposes, transcendent refers to the finding that these caregivers experienced no decision as hard. In the following vignette, Vera described the transcendent nature of her spiritual beliefs across many types of ethical dilemmas involving intrapsychic conflict, and conflict with a nursing facility and family members. Vera experienced no decision-making process involving ethical dilemmas as hard.

Vera, an eighty-six-year-old biracial African and Native-American caregiver, wore a Jesus lapel pin during our interview. Vera described her dilemma about whether or not to take her daughter, the frail elder, out of a nursing home and provide care for her at home. Due to Vera's own health care issues (injured hip with difficulties walking and lifting), family members discouraged her from making the decision to provide home care. Nursing facility staff did not want Vera to care for her daughter; home care meant a loss of income for the nursing home. Furthermore, in order to care for her daughter at home, Vera would have to stop handing out money to her adult children as well as stop buying her grandchildren gifts. The caregiver's money would need to be used to provide care for her daughter. By using her religious practices and beliefs, i.e., fasting, praying, reading scriptures, and talking with church members, the caregiver made the decision to provide home care for her daughter. In effect, no decision was hard because of her faith in God. "I'm just so happy and grateful that she (the care receiver) is still here with me. I just wouldn't consider nothing hard." Although the caregiver and frail elder experienced greater loneliness and social isolation because the adult children "just don't come around like they used to," these religious practices help her to hold fast to her decision to continue to care for her daughter at home.

Spirituality as a stumbling block. For all caregivers, spirituality proved to be useful in working through ethical dilemmas. However, for one caregiver, the religious expression of spirituality contributed to the presence of an ethical dilemma. Mia, a spousal caregiver of Native American and European ethnicity, had been a Sunday school teacher of a nearby church for many years. Her faith in God and relationships with church members provided a sense of meaning and purpose for living. However, when her husband became ill, she described a lack of support from the pastor and church members. Mia stated, "They don't even call and say how's [my husband] doing today?" After "a year and a half," she confronted the pastor about the lack of home visitation. The pastor responded by making one home visit. However, several months after the initial visit, no one from the church had ever returned. Now the caregiver described her current struggle to deal with her husband's new terminally ill diagnosis. Because of the church's poor track record in home visitation, Mia faced the ethical dilemma of whether or not to involve the pastor or church members in any bereavement support or funeral planning. At the time of our interview, she was angry and disappointed with the church and uncertain about how she would resolve this dilemma.

Mia's faith in God, involvement in Sunday school teaching, and social support from church members created a personal sense of meaning and purpose. However, she faced a new ethical dilemma prompted by the church's failure to provide her with spiritual support in the form of home visitation.

IMPLICATIONS

Values such as caring, dignity, safety, freedom and privacy strike at the heart of how human beings choose to live and behave in relationships. Caregiving represents the crucible of an intimate relationship in which these cherished values are tested and frequently acted upon to best meet the needs of a vulnerable elder. As demonstrated in this study, caregivers face daily, ongoing and often irresolvable ethical dilemmas or value-based conflicts in their struggle to care for a frail elder. Frequently, they use spiritual beliefs to deal with these ethical dilemmas. By encouraging "moral dialogue" or value-based discussions with caregivers, helping professionals participate in the ongoing and powerful nature of decision making that occurs in caregiving relationships. Through these value-based discussions, professionals can support and sustain caregivers in their use of spirituality and other strategies for addressing these dilemmas.

The Role of Home Health Services

Consultant panel and interview participants in this study further confirmed the importance of professional support and counseling in dealing with ethical dilemmas. Women as caregivers need people (e.g., informal support from friends or formal services such as a home health social worker) to talk with about the use of spirituality and other strategies to manage ongoing ethical dilemmas. Currently, Medicare and Medicaid policies severely limit social work and other services that can be targeted to the primary, informal caregiver. Because home-based services supported by these policies are centered on the acute needs of the frail elder, the caregivers' needs are often ignored or time limits are placed on resources for using medical social workers and others to explore and process with caregivers complex issues like ethical dilemmas. Findings from this study indicate that the role of medical social workers and other service providers could be expanded to provide this formal social support and counseling to caregivers.

Caregiver-Driven Assessment

Because many caregivers may already use spirituality as a dominant force in dealing with difficult decisions, it behooves professionals in the field of aging to be involved with caregivers in ongoing assessment and professional self-reflection as to the positive uses and barriers created by spirituality. There is a growing awareness of the importance of spiritual assessment in the aging literature and gerontological writers encourage professionals to initiate this assessment in their work with older people and caregivers. However, this spiritual assessment is typically depicted as professionally focused with little emphasis on understanding the role of spirituality from the client's perspective and for the purpose of engaging in a collaborative process with the client (Idler, 1999; Koenig, 1994; Pargament, 1999; Thibault, Ellor, & Netting, 1991).

Consistent with Canda and Furman's (1999) understanding of spiritually sensitive practice, it is this author's contention that spiritual assessment should involve a collaborative relationship in which the "client's worldview and spiritual experiences are taken seriously" (p. 188). Spiritual assessment involves a process in which professionals must suspend "disbelief in order to connect with the reality of the client" (p. 232).

Implicit in this spiritual assessment is the notion of a fiduciary relationship in which the professional has the greater responsibility for making sure no harm to the caregiver occurs in the relationship. The professional is charged with putting the caregiver's needs and interests first. Hence, in the assessment process, it is the caregiver, not the professional, who takes the lead in defining spirituality as an important component of her or his care for the frail elder. At a minimum, the professional should initiate a spiritually based assessment only when the caregiver has at least mentioned in general conversation the importance of faith, religion or spirituality.

Using an Intensive Interview

Spiritual assessment often involves the use of standardized questionnaires that require short answers or a set of options to choose from in responding to questions (MacDonald & Friedman, 2002; McSherry, Draper, & Kendrick, 2002; Pargament, 1999). In contrast, this study used an intensive interview process in which caregivers readily provided narratives of their decision-making processes and the uses of spirituality in working through these difficult decisions. An intensive interview allowed for caregivers to describe their personal understanding of spirituality.

In an intensive interview, professionals ask open-ended questions in an attempt to solicit information that allows the caregiver to initiate or lead the interview. Examples of intensive interview questions include, "Describe a hard choice (or dilemma) you faced as a caregiver?" "What are you struggling with?" "How did you work through or resolve this hard choice?" and "What helped you in dealing with this choice?" Furthermore, an intensive interview requires professionals to demonstrate basic listening and attending skills, i.e., eye-contact, paraphrasing, and the use of an uninterrupted interview environment to be able to more deeply establish a trust-based relationship. The professional's use of listening skills and open-ended questions allows for the caregiver to define important factors in her or his decision making including the use of spirituality as well as a multitude of other influential factors such as the caregiver's perceived health status and stress level, cultural and ethnic background, and financial and family support. As one research participant stated, "I didn't think you'd be interested in hearing about my faith. Doesn't this get in the way of your study?" By indicating an interest in hearing what the caregiver had to say, the interviewer encouraged the caregiver to take the lead in defining the role of spirituality and other factors in her decision making.

Self-Reflection for the Professional

Using an intensive interview guide in the aging professional's assessment process can prove difficult if the professional has limited knowledge and comfort in dealing with the personal nature of spirituality. Because researchers and practitioners alike describe the importance of spirituality for caregivers in dealing with challenging caregiving situations, professionals would better serve caregivers and frail elders by becoming more personally astute as to the uses of spirituality in daily decision making and coping processes. Engaging in self-reflection about the role of spirituality enhances the professional's comfort level and ability to explore caregivers' narratives that address the use of spirituality in decision making.

Activities that can encourage professionals' self-reflection of personal spirituality include the following: meditation and prayer; journaling about important events and feelings; physical exercise that supports mental focus and discipline such as running or yoga: and participation in a local church, synagogue or other group worship experience. Furthermore, when interviewing caregivers about the use of spirituality in dealing with difficult decisions or dilemmas, the professional is encouraged to engage in self-reflective questioning. Examples of self-reflective questions for the professional include the following: As I listen to what the caregiver is struggling with, what am I reacting to and why? As I hear the caregiver describe his or her spiritual beliefs, are they different or similar to my own? How do these similarities or differences affect my ability to work with the caregiver and the frail elder? Do I feel a need to challenge the spiritual beliefs expressed by the caregiver and/or the course of action she/he is taking? (Canda & Furman, 1999; Spano & Koenig, 2003).

CONCLUSION

In conclusion, spirituality, defined as the caregivers' search for a sense of meaning and purpose in providing care for the frail elder, is used by all caregivers in working through or resolving ethical dilemmas. The use of home health services designed to encourage moral dialogue with caregivers, as well as caregiver-driven assessment and professional self-reflection are promoted as ways to capitalize on the caregivers' use of spirituality as a strength or resource in managing these dilemmas.

Some gerontological writers indicate that the research literature is replete with descriptive caregiving studies and that we need to progress onward to the development and testing of interventions that will alleviate this stress (Schultz, O'Brien et al., 2002). However, findings from this study infer that before we can develop caregiver-based interventions (many of which are underused by caregivers), helping professionals need to know how caregivers organize and use their values to work through daily and ongoing ethical dilemmas.

This study suggests that values and the spiritual-based strategies that are often motivated by these values are important features in caregivers' decision-making. For example, if a caregiver values caring for the frail elder over self-care needs, then, she may not access interventions such as respite or adult day care. This caregiver may define caring for the frail elder as her sole responsibility and would feel tremendous guilt (emanating from her spiritual beliefs about responsibility in the marriage relationship) if she relied on structured services for assistance. Hence, she may be unable to use these structured services due to her values. It is this author's contention that professionals must enter into values-based discussions that acknowledge the importance of caregivers' spirituality in decision making before preceeding to the development and testing of interventions. In exploring and understanding caregivers' use of spirituality and values in decision making, helping professionals are in a better position to provide services that will be welcomed and accessed by caregivers.

NOTES

1. In addition to semi-structured, audio-taped interviews with the caregiver, the researcher also recorded field notes of observations immediately after completing each interview. Eleven interviews occurred in the caregiver's home or at a place chosen by the caregiver. Individual interviews with caregivers spanned one and one-half to three

hours each. Follow-up interviews, lasting fifteen to sixty minutes each, were conducted for the purpose of confirming findings.

2. Purposive sampling involved the use of selection criteria. Selection criteria were developed from studies on factors that contribute to caregiver burden or stress (Pearlin, Mullan, Semple, & Skaff, 1990; Toseland, Labrecque, Goebel, & Whitney, 1992) and included: (1) cognitive status of the frail elder (severe to no cognitive impairment); (2) perceived financial strain (severe to no strain); (3) the frail elder's resistance to the caregiver's help (severe to no resistance); (4) caregiver's employment (yes or no); and (5) the length of time the caregiver had provided care (from two weeks to over ten years). Consultant panel members, consisting of the home health agency staff and key caregivers, added the caregiver's health (excellent to poor) and the child care status (yes or no) as further selection criteria.

3. The constant comparative method involved developing tentative categories or codes for units of information. An iterative process was used to move back and forth between the raw data and tentative codes until final coding categories were developed.

4. A consultant panel was developed by the researcher in collaboration with the home health agency director and consisted of home health staff members (i.e., one physical therapist, one bachelor's level social worker, and four nurses) as well as two key caregivers who were not research participants for this study. Consultant panel members provided guidance throughout the design process, e.g., in the development of the interview guide and feedback on a preliminary report of findings.

5. For example, as each caregiving story was recounted, the researcher paraphrased the caregiver's responses to determine if a situation presented a 'hard choice' (ethical dilemma) or to clarify how a caregiver had resolved a particular dilemma. By paraphrasing caregivers, the researcher was able to check out the accuracy of her understanding of the caregivers' responses.

6. All but one caregiver described a multi-ethnic background. One caregiver was of full European ethnicity (English), nine were of mixed European ethnicity, and three of mixed European and Native-American and/or African-American ethnicity. Caregivers reported a diverse range of educational backgrounds (e.g., from the completion of junior high to the completion of a master's degree). Five caregivers were employed outside the home. Two caregivers provided care for children who lived in the home; two caregivers provided periodic care for grandchildren.

REFERENCES

Barer, B. M., & Johnson, C. J. (1990). A critique of caregiving literature. *The Gerontologist, 30*, 26-29.

Bopp, J. Jr., & Coleson, R. E. (1996). A critique of family members as proxy decision makers without the legal limits. *Issues in Law and Medicine, 12*, 3, 244. National Legal Center for the Medically Dependent and Disabled.

Calderon, V., & Tennstedt, S. L. (1998). Ethnic differences in the expression of caregiver burden: Results of a qualitative study, *Journal of Gerontological Social Work, 30*, 159-178.

Canda, E. R., & Furman, L. D. (1999). *Spiritual diversity in social work practice: The heart of helping.* New York: The Free Press.

Chang, B., Noonan, A. E., & Tennstedt, S. L. (1998). The role of religion/spirituality in coping with caregiving for disabled elders. *The Gerontologist, 38*, 463-470.

Connell, C. M., & Gibson, G. D. (1997). Racial, ethnic, and cultural differences in dementia caregiving: Review and analysis. *The Gerontologist, 37*, 355-364.

Idler, E. (1999). Values. In *Multidimensional measurement of religiousness/spirituality for use in health research: A report of the Fetzer Institute/National Institute on Aging Working Group* (pp. 25-30). Kalamazoo, MI: Fetzer Institute.

Jones, P. S. (1995). Paying respect: Care of elderly parents by Chinese and Filipino Americans, *Health Care for Women International, 16*, 385-398.

Kaye, J., & Robinson, K. M. (1994). Spirituality among caregivers. *The Journal of Nursing Scholarship, 26*, 218-221.

Koenig, H. G. (1994). *Aging and God: Spiritual pathways to mental health in midlife and later years*. New York: The Haworth Press, Inc.

Lincoln, Y. S., & Guba, E. G. (1985). *Naturalistic inquiry*. Beverly Hills: Sage.

Loewenberg, F., & Dolgoff, R., & Harrington, D. (2000). *Ethical decisions for social work practice (6th ed.)*. Itasca, IL: F. E. Peacock.

MacDonald, D. A., & Friedman, H. L. (2002). Assessment of humanistic, transpersonal and spiritual constructs: State of the science. *Journal of Humanistic Psychology, 42*, 101-125.

McSherry, W., Draper, D., & Kendrick, D. (2002). The construct validity of a rating scale designed to assess spirituality and spiritual care. *International Journal of Nursing Studies, 39*, 723-734.

Montgomery, R. J. V. (1996). The influence of social context on the caregiving experience. In *Alzheimer's disease: Cause(s), diagnosis, treatment and care.* (pp. 311-319). CRC Press.

National Alliance for Caregivers & American Association of Retired Persons (1997). *Family caregiving in the United States: Findings from a national survey.* Sponsored by the National Alliance for Caregiving, Bethesda, MD and the American Association of Retired Persons, Washington, DC.

Pargament, K. I. (1999). Meaning. In *Multidimensional measurement of religiousness/ spirituality for use in health research: A report of the Fetzer Institute National Institute on Aging Working Group* (pp. 43-56). Kalamazoo, MI: Fetzer Institute.

Pearlin, L. I., Mullan, J. T., Semple, S. J., & Skaff, M. M. (1990). Caregiving and the stress process: An overview of concepts and their measures. *The Gerontologist, 30*, 583-290.

Picot, S. J., Debanne, S. M., Namazi, K. H., & Wykle, M. L. (1997). Religiosity and perceived rewards of black and white caregivers. *The Gerontologist, 37*, 89-101.

Reed, P. G. (1994). Response to "The relationship between spiritual perspective, social support, and depression in caregiving and noncaregiving wives." *Scholarly Inquiry for Nursing Practice: An International Journal, 8*, 391-396.

Richardson, R. C., & Sistler, A. B. (1999). The well-being of elderly Black caregivers and noncaregivers: A preliminary study. *Journal of Gerontological Social Work, 31*, 109-117.

Schulz, R., O'Brien, A., Czaja, S., Ory, M., Norris, R., Martire, L. M. et al. (2002). Dementia caregiving intervention research: In search of clinical significance. *The Gerontologist, 42*, 589-602.

Spano, R. N., & Koenig, T. L. (2003). Moral dialogue: An interactional approach to ethical decision making. *Social Thought, 22,* 91-104.

Stolley, J. M., Buckwalter, K. C., & Koenig, H. G. (1999). Prayer and religious coping for caregivers of persons with Alzheimer's disease and related disorders. *American Journal of Alzheimer's Disease, 14,* 181-191.

Stuckey, J. C. (2001). Blessed assurance: The role of religion and spirituality in Alzheimer's disease caregiving and other significant life events. *Journal of Aging Studies, 15,* 69-84.

Thibault, J. M., Ellor, J. W., & Netting, F. W. (1991). A conceptual framework for assessing the spiritual functioning and fulfillment of older adults in long-term care settings. *Journal of Religious Gerontology, 7,* 29-45.

Toseland, R. W., Labrecque, M. S., Goebel, S. T., & Whitney, M. H. (1992). An evaluation of a group program for spouses of frail elderly veterans. *The Gerontologist, 32,* 382-290.

Spirituality and Social Work
in Long-Term Care

Marty Richards, MSW

SUMMARY. The spiritual aspect of care of elders in long-term care has only recently been re-affirmed. A social worker who has volunteered, worked, and consulted in nursing homes shares her perspective on the importance of the "spiritual" to nursing home social work. From the perspective of 40 years of involvement in long-term care, she offers suggestions for assessment, education of staff, and affirming rights in the religious arena. Workers are encouraged to keep hope alive for themselves as well as for those with whom they work. *[Article copies available for a fee from The Haworth Document Delivery Service: 1-800-HAWORTH. E-mail address: <docdelivery@haworthpress.com> Website: <http://www.HaworthPress.com> ©2005 by The Haworth Press, Inc. All rights reserved.]*

KEYWORDS. Spirituality, social work, long-term care, hope

Religion and spirituality are central to social work practice in long-term care settings, yet the importance of religion has not always been acknowledged. As I look back over forty years of involvement

---

With many thanks to Mary Buckley, Carter Catlett Williams, and Art Farber, special long-term care social workers, mentors, and supporters over the years.

[Haworth co-indexing entry note]: "Spirituality and Social Work in Long-Term Care." Richards, Marty. Co-published simultaneously in *Journal of Gerontological Social Work* (The Haworth Social Work Practice Press, an imprint of The Haworth Press, Inc.) Vol. 45, No. 1/2, 2005, pp. 173-183; and: *Religion, Spirituality, and Aging: A Social Work Perspective* (ed: Harry R. Moody) The Haworth Social Work Practice Press, an imprint of The Haworth Press, Inc., 2005, pp. 173-183. Single or multiple copies of this article are available for a fee from The Haworth Document Delivery Service [1-800-HAWORTH, 9:00 a.m. - 5:00 p.m. (EST). E-mail address: docdelivery@haworthpress.com].

Available online at http://www.haworthpress.com/web/JGSW
© 2005 by The Haworth Press, Inc. All rights reserved.
doi:10.1300/J083v45n01_10

with persons living in long-term care facilities as a volunteer, family member, social worker and consultant, I recognize the enduring importance of spirituality to me in my practice, yet I see that long-term care facilities have not always shared that recognition. There has always been some measure of acknowledgement of the idea that religious beliefs had relevance to life in such facilities. Indeed, religious and other not- for- profit groups for well over a century have led the way toward promoting humane care for persons with disabilities. Yet, the religious aspect of a life was often relegated to one isolated compartment of life: for example, as something to be handled by a person in a specific role as "pastor," "chaplain," or other religiously oriented ordained person who "took care of religious needs." For social work to fulfill its mission in long-term care settings, there needs to be much deeper recognition of the role of religion in the lives of facilities, residents, families, and professionals themselves.

Social workers and other staff in long-term care facilities have only recently come to a deeper understanding that care of the whole person must include care for the spirit. All staff, including social workers, must be integrally involved in spiritual aspects of long-term care. Fortunately, enhancement of spirituality is gaining more respectability in such settings. Leading the way are such groups as the Eden Alternative,[1] and the Pioneer Network,[2] nationally-known for promoting "culture change" in long-term care. Their efforts are radically changing the face of care for elders. These groups have strongly emphasized the importance of the spirit in sharing with residents, and their message has now spread across the United States and beyond.

Social work, with its modern emphasis on being a "scientific" discipline, in many ways lost its way in dealing with the "religious," let alone with the "spiritual" dimensions of life. The social work profession originated from deep roots in the Jewish and Christian traditions. The profession is now returning to its beginnings at a time when the whole field of long-term care is recognizing spirituality as a critical aspect of caring for elders and others facing disabilities. For example, the Council on Social Work Education has now recognized that religion and spirituality represent an important factor in working with people. The development of groups such as the Society for Spirituality and Social Work is an example of the growth in such interest about spirituality.

I first became aware of the religious issues ('spiritual' was not used much in those days) in long-term care facilities as an undergraduate student of sociology and social welfare at Augustana College, a small Lutheran liberal arts school in Illinois. In class work in the early 1960s, we were mission driven to serve others, so I became part of a team that visited and provided Sunday worship services. With little training we muddled our way through singing hymns and offering prayers. These residents taught us the importance of singing familiar old hymns. We quickly learned that music indeed does connect with people even when the cognitive abilities are gone. I have since come to appreciate that those residents lived a very regimented institutionalized life, and we brought something different into their day. Did we make a difference? At the very least we brought a change of pace to their lives and shared a community worship experience. This experience laid the groundwork for both my professional work as a social worker and my volunteer work in nursing homes.

Spirituality is an integrating factor in care of the whole person, and there is no aspect of care provided in nursing homes that does not have some spiritual component. This point remains true whether a person is struggling with cognitive deficits or is mentally alert. Social workers must consider all aspects of everyday life for a resident to assure that their needs are being met and to assure that they have a quality life despite facing disabilities. Basic social work tasks in long-term care include: assessment, care planning, discharge planning, counseling, finding resources, making referrals, and working with families. These aspects of the job may have spiritual implications and the social worker must be alert to them.

The spiritual affects life in long-term care facilities in many different ways. A spiritual perspective may well influence how a person deals with day-to-day physical concerns such as getting out of bed or eating a meal. In confronting daily needs, questions may arise, such as "Is my life worth living?" or "What can I now do, given that I have a disabled body?" The motivation to perform even the smallest tasks of life can raise questions of a spiritual character. Sometimes the questions are more specific, such as those that arise concerning dietary laws from a distinctive religious tradition. Sometimes the questions include a culture-bound explanation for illness, for example, "Why does God keep me alive in this condition?" Others they may feel they are being punished by a stern God, and so they may just "give up" on life.

Religious understanding about suffering can take many different forms. For example, a middle-aged woman struggling with a brain tumor and who has had two strokes can say: "I just thank the Lord that I am alive . . . others have it so much worse." This sentiment clearly reflects her religious beliefs. As a social worker, I can find myself overwhelmed with all the changes in her life caused by illness. I see a fifty-six-year-old lady struggling with so many issues and I can get discouraged. By contrast, she expresses gratitude to God for what she has. This woman's faith gives her a positive outlook on her illness.

Having a sense of meaning and purpose in life when dealing with physical and mental health problems is a major challenge. An example illustrates commonly held sentiments I have often heard from nursing home residents. A wise chaplain was listening to a bed-ridden, very frail ninety-year-old woman. She exclaimed: "I am not much good having to lay here in bed all day!" This pastor who had known that prayer was an essential part of her life, stated: "Well, Mary, you can pray and you can start by praying for my nursing home ministry." In heeding this advice, this woman discovered a purpose, something beyond herself, which gave her life meaning.

There are spiritual questions that underlie struggles faced by residents and these questions invoke "ultimate concern," such as: "Who am I?" or "What place do I have on earth now that I am a resident in a nursing home?" For persons who are or have been believers in a comforting God in the past, it can be helpful to have the assurance that there is a God, or some other Higher Being that loves and cares about them, even in their illness state. Others feel bereft because they feel God has abandoned them. Social workers can assist persons by connecting them to their spiritual advisors, enabling them to attend religious events within the facility, and by helping families to understand the importance of meaning and spiritual purpose in an elder's life.

Discovering meaning may also be tied to finding ways to be helpful to others in need. Often a long-term care resident may reach out to hold another resident's hand or to comfort a person who seems upset. Those with dementia may not know all the facts about a situation, but they may retain an acute sense of feelings and intuition for the human response that is called for in that situation. There is a great challenge to find ways for residents with dementia to sense that they still have an important place in the world. Social workers can help find ways for residents with dementia to safely meet those needs, in order that they too might have a sense of meaning in life.

Assisting elders to tell their personal stories and to leave a legacy to others can be very important in maintaining this sense of meaning. Reminiscence and life-review have long been recognized as important in later life. If social workers do not always have time to hear an elder's whole life story, they can nonetheless help the family to understand its importance. Social workers can help connect families and residents with volunteers or assist those from the faith community to listen to a life story. Social workers can listen to the bits and pieces of a narrative they pick up in the assessment process once they recognize the importance of life stories for spiritual well-being. Some practitioners have found that helping elders leave an "ethical will" as a spiritual legacy can help fulfill the important need to offer something of value to another generation, even if there is no money or material goods to be left behind. Leaving a legacy, in whatever form, can be a blessing to another generation. An ethical will can provide an occasion for life-review so that the elder and the family can come to recognize the meaning of their spiritual journey through the years.

In telling life stories, concern for needs of forgiveness and "unfinished business" will often arise. In listening in a non-judgmental way, social workers exemplify the value of acceptance. Yet, there are times when we need to refer a resident to clergy who can perform that distinctive role in a formal capacity. One case illustrates this shared responsibility between social workers and clergy. Albert P. was a blustery older man who shared with the social worker a very sad story revealing his need to ask forgiveness for his sins. Although the social worker was accepting of this gentleman, it was clear that Albert ultimately needed his priest to come in to have a private confession. The priest did come and this resident had confession and received the words of absolution, words so important in his lifelong Catholic faith. Albert was then able to get on with his time at the nursing home and confront his impending death.

Staff, including social workers, may often wonder about their own meaning and purpose as they work in long-term care settings. Those trained to use interpersonal strengths and skills often find themselves overloaded with documentation and paperwork. Burdened with such tasks it is easy enough to lose heart in our work. One way to mitigate these concerns is to spend a few moments listening to a resident's life story. Often these stories of survival, love and sheer gumption that are the fabric of persons' lives can give us hope in our own role. Residents then become our mentors; by recounting their stories, they can often work out their own purpose in life, while at the same time reminding us of our purpose. If we lose a sense of meaning and purpose in our role, how can we remain open to the spiritual needs of those we serve?

The issue of hope affects day-to-day life in so many ways. Hope is very much a factor in choices concerning death and dying for both residents and their families. Hospice reminds us that "hope changes" as people struggle with a life-threatening illness. Hope is not a blanket statement of assurance such as "Everything is going to be all right." Instead, hope is based on a realistic picture for the resident, for caregivers, and for the resident's actual situation. Farran, Herth and Popovich, in their wonderful book *Hope and Hopelessness: Critical Clinical Constructs*, stress that hope has a spiritual aspect, a rational thought aspect, a relational aspect and an experiential aspect. The spiritual aspect is rooted in values, beliefs, tradition, and faith, and the spiritual aspect reflects how residents see their life and the afterlife. A belief in an afterlife for someone who has been a strong believer in such a reality can feel either comforting or frightening. In some cases, a resident can almost look forward to dying. On the other hand, for those burdened with guilt, who have belief in heaven and hell, death can be very frightening. To a person who believes that life ends at death with no promise of an afterlife, the very thought of dying may be scary. What life-sustaining treatment such patients request and how they go into the dying process will reflect the spiritual dimension of hope.

Another aspect of hope considered is the experiential dimension where one deals with suffering and making sense out of suffering. Such questions coming out of this experiential aspect of hope can be difficult for us to hear. But over the years elders have taught me a great deal in their answers to such questions as: "Why is my loved one suffering?" or "Why is God punishing us?" We cannot receive this teaching from others unless we are open to these difficult questions in our own lives.

There is a whole school of psychology that explores the rational thought process of hope. Farran et al. argue that people have hope when they set goals, use resources, are involved in their lives in an active way, maintain control in life, and have a sense of time. This sense of hope can be compared to care planning process itself used in most long-term care settings. Thus, social workers and other staff are involved in very basic ways in keeping this sense of hope alive.

Hope as a relational process also has important implications for social workers. Relationship is the very core of much of our work, and it should be what we do well. Residents need special relationships to maintain a sense of hope. Keeping contact with their families, those in their communities of faith, and even relationships with staff are all a part of this. A very wise nurse's aide in a church-related long-term care facility spoke about her joy of working with residents in "joining them in their journey for the last part of their lives." This aide understood the relational aspect of hope that is so important for social workers, and indeed all who work in long-term care settings. A 100-year-old resident put it in a different way: "We all need someone to love us with our warts."

Questions about coping with a chronic illness, for the residents and their caregivers, will often raise spiritual concerns. Many turn to their religious beliefs to make sense out of the disabling condition which has diminished control over their lives, either for themselves or for their loved ones. For example, one spouse who daily visited a very disabled loved one told me: "I pray every day and He gives me strength to come here." Other caregivers cite the marriage vows made before God and their loved one to honor and cherish "till death do us part" as the reason for their continued involvement, despite the fact that sometimes their spouse does not even recognize them.

For others these same feelings cause guilt reactions. Siblings and adult children can feel their religious upbringing strongly as they care for their loved ones. The commandment to "Honor your Father and Mother" is a strong message in Western traditions. The value of filial piety is found in religious traditions in both East and West. Brothers and sisters can feel special responsibilities as well. One 99-year-old woman often said that "The good Lord put her on this earth to care for her baby sister." The sister at 86 is in need of a great deal of physical and emotional care. The 99-year-old, while very frail, still remains the source of emotional support for her sister.

Opportunities to worship with others, rituals for celebrating a birthday or anniversary, or ceremonies to mark the anniversary of a death or special day in one's life are all important events in long-term care. These events are occasions to respond to residents' needs for ritual. Holidays can also have rituals associated with them. However, there are times when remembering an event such as the anniversary date of a death, birthday or anniversary can create spiritual concerns for residents. Staff needs to be conscious of these special dates, and "check in" with a person in some way. Many times I have been called in to consult when someone is reported to be depressed because they are seen in their room crying. In talking to them, however, I find that the particular day is an anniversary or a birthday of a deceased loved one, and there is a need for remembering. Crying can be a part of that reminiscence. Their faith community may have a ritual to help them through such difficult times and to help with other concerns as well. At other times a specific ritual may need to be created, such as one for saying goodbye to a well-loved home or a ritual to welcome a person to the facility. Too often this need for ritual has been neglected and social workers may be the ones who raise it as an issue in care planning.

Recovering alcoholics may find the ritual of Alcoholics Anonymous meetings or participating in a Twelve-Step program to be a positive influence on their spiritual lives. Encouraging persons who are able to attend a meeting, to work with a sponsor on the twelve steps, or to find other ways of staying in touch with a sponsor may help keep this part of their spiritual lives alive.

A person's need for a ritual may come in conflict with a social worker's own belief system. Yet to respect a resident's rights the social worker has responsibility to make sure that, if possible, and as long as the resident's request does not infringe on the rights of others, the individual's needs are met. For instance, a practicing Wiccan once asked to have a Wicca ritual held at the facility. Staff at this religiously run nursing home was aghast. Yet, the social worker, using the social work principle of "starting where the person is, " found a practitioner in the Wicca tradition who came into the facility and worked with the resident. When a resident has a cultural tradition or spiritual beliefs with which the staff is not familiar, the social worker and other staff need to find out what they can from the resident and the resident's support network.

Many religious traditions have sacraments or rituals relating to healing. As these are understood for many groups today, the "healing" is not intended for some miracle to occur, but rather for a person to have healing of spirit and emotions. Social work should lead the way in assuring private time and space for healing through meeting with spiritual advisors and having rituals. This task, however, can represent a huge challenge in some facilities where every usable space is already utilized for efficiency. For example, Mary was a stroke victim who was deeply religious. She started each morning with meditation, but complained to me that her roommate woke before her and would turn on her lights, which would shine in Mary's eyes and prevent her from concentrating. My solution with her was to move Mary's bed a few feet so that the privacy curtain could be pulled, the roommate could turn the light on, and Mary could meditate. Even from such a small adaptation in the room, two persons' needs were accommodated.

Psychosocial concerns may also have spiritual components. The regulations governing long-term care facilities today stress quality of life. Social workers are very much a part of making that happen, and sharing in spiritual life is important here. At times quality of life comes down to the "quality of the moment." For example, even for the very short time a resident with dementia prays the Lord's Prayer or recites the 23rd Psalm there can be quality in that moment.

Even something as routine as discharge planning may be affected by spiritual concerns. Worry about "who is waiting at home" and whether a resident is "needed back there" can affect the motivation to return home. Having a pet at home who needs them can help residents to find meaning in life. These are examples of how residents find meaning and purpose in all the details of everyday life.

Social workers have many roles in promoting the spiritual dimension. The first task is to do a good psychosocial assessment, because spiritual and religious concerns are often tied to emotional and physical issues. Even the Minimum Data Set has seen fit to include the question about whether a person finds "strength in their faith," and to ask questions relating to how the person spends their day. A resident's daily routine may give clues to spiritual aspects of their lives. In the old days, it was simply enough to identify someone as "Protestant, Catholic, or Jewish." Today we know that the number of religious traditions is much greater. Even being a part of one of these groups has a different meaning for each person. A very basic question used by Carter Catlett Williams and Sarah Burger, well-known nursing home reformers, may lead a person to discuss their spiritual life. Williams and Burger asked simply: "What would be a good day for you?" and they found that the question could bring forth many important answers and helped to focus on the "quality of the moment."

Another role for social work is to encourage those who live in long-term care facilities to be mentors to staff so that they can understand their personal view on the importance of spirituality. By carefully assessing and listening to what a resident and those who care about him or her say about what is meaningful in their lives, we can begin to get a window on their world of the spirit. Words are not totally adequate to explain spiritual feelings, but they are one way that such feelings become accessible to others. Knowing what connection to a particular religious group means to a person is important. There are also those who would not connect with any tradition who are deeply spiritual as well. Those with dementia may go back to the religious practices of their youth when their short-term memory fails. This might explain why a Unitarian shows up at Mass. We have to be open to looking not only at the NOW in residents' spiritual lives, but also at the THEN. Each person is unique and expression of spiritual views is a part of their personhood.

Social workers are important advocates for residents' spiritual concerns. To be effective in that role, a good assessment remains crucial. Advocacy based on what is known about a person occurs in the care planning process. An illustration of this happened in my practice some years ago. John was a very quiet man whose only activity was attending the weekly Friday mass. But John's bath day was also Friday, and because of scheduling needs, the facility was having difficulty adjusting the time. The social worker had to advocate for a change in bath time in order for John's quality of life and spiritual well-being to be affirmed. It seemed like such a simple thing to do, but it took some convincing before a change actually took place. Staff in a facility are usually tuned in to what is important to a person and are flexible to help meet the resident needs. But advocacy for spiritual well-being is still necessary, as this example shows. Advocating for a person's spiritual needs may also include making sure that objects with religious meaning which they may have in their room (Koran, prayer book, cross or other objects) are treated with respect by all.

Social workers can educate other staff about the importance of the spirit in long-term care. Sometimes social workers act in conjunction with other staff such as a chaplain or recreational therapist and sometimes they act alone. It can be useful to ask staff to think about what is important in their own spiritual life or to consider how their concerns would be honored in the nursing home. Asking these questions often helps people understand why religious services are held or why persons need privacy to interact with their spiritual advisor. Even emphasizing the importance of calling residents by a name that they chose (often covered in resident rights workshops) can have a spiritual dimension. If I am a person with a name that I prefer, then I am special person with worth and dignity.

Modeling for other staff the sense of "being present " with a resident, in the way discussed by theologian Henri Nouwen, is probably the single most important role for social services. Really "hearing" what residents are saying for even the few minutes you are present is a gift to them. What they share is a gift to you. Even the words used to describe the resident to others can convey this important quality of "being present."

Social workers need to keep their own spirits alive in the work that they do and to encourage other staff as well. They may be required to address spiritual questions in their own lives as they face issues of living and dying in their daily work. As a family member using long-term care services, I became aware of my own personal perspectives which in some way had a different emotional quality than did my professional ideas. This was an important part of my growth.

Social work practice in long-term care require all of us to sustain our sense of hope. It calls us to remember basic social work principles of starting where the person is, knowing the individual, and building on people's strengths. One poignant example of this point is the case of Anne, who taught me an important lesson that has stayed with me through the years. Struggling with dementia, Anne would often spend her days fidgeting with her sweater and exploring the nursing home. Her loving son came every night to visit her and they often would share finger food at a nearby McDonalds. One night after he had left, I saw her and asked: "Who was that?" She replied: "I don't know, but I know he was a kind man." Ultimately what Anne taught me is that all we can offer another is to share our heart with them. And indeed I believe that is the soul of social work practice, and the source of hope for all staff who share the life of residents of long term-care facilities. We need to be open to this movement of the heart and the spirit in our own lives and in the lives of those we are entrusted to serve.

NOTES

1. Bill Thomas, MD, founder of the Eden Alternative, has done ground-breaking work on humanizing long term care through the use of plants and animals. The website of the Eden Alternative (www.edenalt.com) contains information. Workshops are held on a regular basis to train persons to carry out the work.

2. The Pioneer Network has a website with educational links: www.PioneerNetwork.net. The Pioneer Network also publishes a newsletter, and sponsors conferences to enhance the work of culture change work in long-term care.

Geriatric Care Management:
Spiritual Challenges

Leonie Nowitz, MSW

SUMMARY. Geriatric care managers face a complex task of helping families negotiate challenges of caring for frail elders and meeting everyday practical needs. At the same time care managers can respond to clients and families with acknowledgment of the spiritual dimension of caregiving. By being fully present to the suffering of families and elders, care managers can experience their own spiritual growth and can offer help to others at the same time. *[Article copies available for a fee from The Haworth Document Delivery Service: 1-800-HAWORTH. E-mail address: <docdelivery@haworthpress.com> Website: <http://www.HaworthPress.com> © 2005 by The Haworth Press, Inc. All rights reserved.]*

KEYWORDS. Spirituality, caregiving, dementia, geriatric care manager

Like the elderly clients they serve, geriatric care managers operate within a web of illness, fear, guilt, loss and a variety of negative stereotypes and modern cultural assumptions. Even the label "geriatric care manager" is a rather clinical term. On first reflection, it may reaffirm the commonly held regret that care for the elderly in modern times is discharged to strangers and institutions rather than by loving relatives who

[Haworth co-indexing entry note]: "Geriatric Care Management: Spiritual Challenges." Nowitz, Leonie. Co-published simultaneously in *Journal of Gerontological Social Work* (The Haworth Social Work Practice Press, an imprint of The Haworth Press, Inc.) Vol. 45, No. 1/2, 2005, pp. 185-201; and: *Religion, Spirituality, and Aging: A Social Work Perspective* (ed: Harry R. Moody) The Haworth Social Work Practice Press, an imprint of The Haworth Press, Inc., 2005, pp. 185-201. Single or multiple copies of this article are available for a fee from The Haworth Document Delivery Service [1-800-HAWORTH, 9:00 a.m. - 5:00 p.m. (EST). E-mail address: docdelivery@haworthpress.com].

grant older people the respect they deserve and earned as done in previous eras.

In fact, the geriatric case manager, a relatively new phenomenon, is a moral, practical and potentially spiritual response to new realities: people living longer, a more mobile society, and a more complex web of available services and institutions (medical, legal, and social) that are not easily understood by the average person and his or her family. With longer life expectancies, adult children, relatives, and spouses are responsible for pro- viding care while in the midst of their own middle or older age.

It is also a helpful response to another fact of contemporary life: namely, the intricate family relationships that are often so weighed down by history and habit. Role reversals, in which the elderly parent is now dependent on others, can be a source of tension. While not minimizing the positive impact of a caregiver who is also family, the availability of a neutral source and supportive professional can do much to guide the family members in their growth, their attitude and actions. By the time a parent is in crisis and in need of care, the objectivity and vision of the professional care manager who has traversed this path with many families can be helpful to all in facing the tasks of caregiving and care receiving.

Geriatric care managers usually enter into the lives of their clients and kin at a point of crisis when older members of the family are in ill health and need care. The shift to a life of illness and disability has an impact not only on the older person, but also on the entire family system. Family caregivers must accept changes and rally to care for their elders in whatever ways are possible for them. Family members' roles are in flux. The situation demands an ongoing commitment of time, energy and finances in caring for the sick relative. Uncertainty about the future and the emotional impact on everyone concerned creates stress for all.

It is a painful process for everyone, as the older person's illness may herald death. On the other hand, family and friends may be living at a distance or are physically unavailable on a regular basis because of the demands of work or young children. Unresolved issues and practical considerations of time, money or energy will limit what is possible for even well intentioned relatives to give.

In most circumstances, people need information about the many resources available for their relative. Often, the older person's community is diminished due to illness, relocation of friends and family and death of close family members. Among the tasks for the geriatric care manager is to help everyone in the family face these challenges. This includes finding the resources they need to manage in the present time and to plan for future care. The care manager enables families to do what is possible. The care manager also validates the paths that need to be taken and provides emotional and concrete support in accomplishing the care plan and finding the necessary personnel. The geriatric care manager provides both practical and emotional support and is available to hear the struggles of all members of the family. Finally, the geriatric care manager provides comfort and may offer an opportunity for relatives to resolve familial issues and find meaning in the care-giving and care-receiving process.

The geriatric care manager, by providing practical services and reassurance to clients and families, can be a positive agent of comfort and relief of stress and uncertainty and it is here that the spiritual dimension becomes important. The spiritual challenge is to help older people and their families find meaning and value in their situation of illness, multiple losses and need for care giving. When the care manager also nurtures the spiritual possibilities in these situations, there is potential not just for relief or sharing burdens, but also for positive growth and transcendence for everyone involved in the condition of care-giving.

SPIRITUAL CHALLENGES FOR THE CARE MANAGER

The work of a geriatric care manager offers an opportunity to look at our own questions regarding life's true meaning. Among the many professional and personal gifts of this work, is that in doing this work, the care manager can experience growth along with clients and families. As witness to suffering, the care manager encounters the challenge of reflecting on the meaning of the suffering endured by our clients and asking how one can grow through this process.

To respond fully to this challenge, the care manager needs to ask very personal questions: What makes us get into this work as professional caregivers? What is our story, our vision and our journey about? How does the work affect our own life choices? Inasmuch as this work provides the opportunity to witness each person's journey, it also presents an opportunity to be transformed by the work itself and to look at our own values in a deeper way. Our work encourages being open to the spiritual traditions and values of our clients, which become a mirror in which we can see ourselves.

Rabbi Dayle Friedman, former director of chaplaincy services at Philadelphia Geriatric Center, wrote "I have heard people wonder how much would change if they could live their lives backward, knowing at life's beginning the lessons gleaned at its end. I often ponder how greatly all of our lives would be enriched if we were able to take in not just *Pirkei Avot* [Wisdom of the Fathers] and other classic texts of our tradition, but . . . the wisdom of the *bubbes and zaydes* [grandmothers and grandfathers]. Their lessons for living are myriad" (Friedman, 1997).

Friedman's comment reminds us that the work of care management can be mind-expanding and open us to other parts of ourselves as we ask the deepest existential questions: Can we find value in the pain and loss at life's end? If we could live our lives over again, would we want to do things differently? Can we learn from the experience to embrace values we would like to nurture in ourselves? The work of geriatric care management encourages us to open our hearts to our clients and we need to consider practices that encourage this process and focus on those qualities to cultivate in our work.

But we may wonder: can this approach be applied to clients with dementia? In fact, there are gifts in working with clients with dementia who offer unexpected possibilities:

1. *Relationships.* What people with limitations can teach us is to rethink our lives regarding what's really important: for example, connections with each other. As cognitive powers decline, the relational aspects of our lives can gain importance, as Connie Goldman's argues in her book on the hidden rewards of caregiving (Goldman, 2002).
2. *Living in the Present Moment.* Clients with dementia can remind us to slow down and be present. Slowing down opens us to empathy for the way the mind works with dementia. Circular and repetitive thinking can be appreciated as almost meditative.
3. *Giving and Receiving.* Watching a nursing aide slowly feed a client helps us remain present to the acts of giving and receiving,
4. *Cultivating Spiritual Qualities.* We sometimes witness qualities in clients, family or caregivers that we would like to cultivate in ourselves, such as being present, loving, caring, valuing, listening, and helping to feel understood. This witnessing can uplift the spirit by one's presence, meaningful activities and acts of faith.
5. *Being.* The work of witnessing encourages a shift to a perspective that cultivates *being* rather than *doing:* i.e., seeing a higher power or a larger view of the human situation. If we receive these gifts, we ask, in a deeper way, what are the possibilities in healing with our clients?

6. *Spiritual Growth.* Our work can encourage the mind to be more focused, flexible, responsive, open and trusting, and can allow us to be more receptive to the spiritual. These qualities can be encouraged by cultivating within ourselves an attitude of reverence, respectfulness, humility, supportiveness, warmth, and calmness.

As we think of the gifts of spiritual growth in caregiving and care management, we must also acknowledge our limits. It is not always easy to access or reach deep into ourselves in the ways just mentioned. Questions come up about suffering and coping with limited resources. If we are honest, we may ask ourselves: How would I cope with debilitating disease? Could I maintain a sense of equanimity in the midst of suffering?

It is often painful to witness the situations of our clients. We want to "make things better" so we find it easier to focus on the doing as opposed to the being. We may think: "I'd never want to live in a nursing home" and unwittingly transmit that attitude to a client who could actually need and benefit by moving to a facility.

Most of us share the fear of being old, alone and vulnerable. In her 1994 book, tellingly titled *Fear of Fifty*, author Erica Jong observed, "At the beginning of the journey, a baby has a loving mother thumbing through volumes of Dr. Spock for clues and cues. But in the seventh age of woman, there is no loving mother [long since dead], no designated caretaker, no books. We make this backward journey all alone."

This painful, pessimistic passage highlights the void that is filled by the geriatric care manager. The passage illuminates the gift that a skilled care manager can bring to clients and families–ultimately to all of us–in those later, more vulnerable years. As care managers, our work provides an opportunity to strengthen values about caregiving. We can provide comfort, create caring communities, help resolve issues for family members and older clients, and in the process bring healing and family connections. We can extend our commitment to seeking value and purpose in the midst of loss. Our work also provides opportunities to look at the way we touch each other. We may feel like agents of God in creating community and caring for each other.

The profession of geriatric care management also unfolds in a wider social context. A critical challenge today is to redefine society's negative view of aging and of older people. We must struggle with the values that are promoted by our 'hyper-cognitive' society (Post, 1995), and negativity about age that, to some extent, we have all internalized. (For example, even at meetings of professional geriatric care managers, we often talk about how 'young' we look.) Against this background, the care manager must be able to reframe aspects of aging, illness, and brokenness in an affirming way. While not denying the impact of loss, health, function, finances, and family, a spiritual perspective can emphasize the values of wisdom and experience and help reveal ways in which people find meaning in life in the midst of their struggles. The geriatric care manager can help people focus on what really matters in life.

At its best the work of geriatric care management offers an opportunity to create caring environments. Through receptivity, we cultivate more positive responses among both professionals and homecare workers, who are themselves caring and responsive to our clients. Many homecare workers feel they are doing "God's work" and the most devoted workers accept a client's limitations and focus on strengths.

Who do we chose as caregivers? Someone who is caring, valuing and responsive to a client's pain and disability; someone who can love the patient, the work, the service; someone who can nurture the strengths within an aging and ill individual; someone who can understand the client's needs when he/she is barely able to communicate; and someone who embraces wholeness, and can nurture the soul.

Psychologist James Hillman has noted that finding meaning in our lives is not accomplished by looking "out there." It is actually the opposite. We need to look within our hearts to discover what we truly love. Just as the oak tree is present in the acorn, so is each soul encoded for a particular destiny (Hillman, 1997).

In our work with our clients, we need to listen to their inner spirit and help them focus on their strengths. This shift in perspective is a challenge in the face of disability. Focus on the positive does not mean denying the losses sustained by each person; it does not diminish the importance of listening to our clients' grief for what has been lost. The task is to help clients redefine themselves in the face of loss. The geriatric care manager needs to look for strengths in the past and present of each person, and to help each client to construct meaning.

This challenge may be even greater when the client in cognitively impaired. Listening to a client's history from family and friends, looking around a house or apartment, can give a sense of what gave meaning and comfort. It may then become possible to finding sources of meaning by walking in nature, in prayer, listening to music, or whatever appeals to the client as a ways of becoming more connected to what gives meaning in life. It can also be helpful to counteract older people's negative views of themselves by sharing what remains worthy about them, their inner resources of courage, wisdom, humor, or ways of seeing the world. Our clients have many gifts and we need to articulate them in the presence of loss and pain.

One of the major challenges is how we as professionals view our own work. Do we see ourselves as helpers? As healers to older people and their families in facing the last part of life with all that it brings? Spiritual care means care that encompasses the person as a whole and responds to what is meaningful in that person's life. Listening to their stories; sharing what we know about them with them; acknowledging them; seeing to it that each client is valued as an individual–these are the responses that help clients experience themselves and their journey as understood (Dunn, personal communication).

The following case illustrates ways of responding to the spiritual challenge of older people through the compassionate presence of a geriatric care manager:

> *Eighty-year-old EG, a woman who was a former alcoholic lived a very unhappy life and now suffered from dementia. The care manager arranged for her to receive twenty-four hour Medicaid homecare. EG lived in a tiny apartment and found it difficult to have caretakers around the clock in her home. After sharing bitter feelings about her life during bi-monthly visits by the care manager for a few years, the client showed a shift in attitude and feelings. She began to appreciate her caregivers and now welcomes the care manager's visits. EG shared her view on life with the care manager which included her belief in Buddhist practices; when the care manager responded to a comment she made about God, the care manager enquired further. EG shared her thoughts about God's presence in her life as a support and companion. EG saw this phase of her life as the opportunity to "roll with the punches" and not fear death.*

As we seek new possibilities and potential for our clients, we can experience our own growth as well. We need to consider our view of the older person and his or her family. In doing this work, questions arise about how lives are lived, and what the future may hold for our clients and ourselves. We need to think about how we view brokenness, sadness and pain. Our clients often call for an end to the suffering and to the blow of living life with reduced capacity and in need of so much care. Acceptance of brokenness in a positive light is part of many spiritual traditions. Most religious traditions view frailty and loss as meaningful, valuable parts of life. Ralph Waldo Emerson said that "there is a crack in everything God has made." It has been said that as we age, the cracks begin to show. Are they just about darkness and brokenness? Or are they also a place for the light of the spirit to stream through?

Betty Friedan, author of books on feminism and aging, admitted, "Originally, I wasn't interested in the subject of age. I had the same dreary view of age as anybody in America, the same absolute denial. . . . But once I began on that large path that led me to break through an even more pernicious, pervasive mystique–the mystique of age only as a decline from youth" (Friedan, 1993, 1994).

One of our challenges is to be able to see the values of the spiritual dimension in the midst of the suffering. Sometimes it is difficult to witness, but usually, there is someone within the system of care who approaches the suffering with a spiritual dimension. For example, one caregiver remarked: "This work helps me be strong in my faith. I pray for God to give me the strength and courage to know how to handle this situation. If you don't have God's love, you can't handle the care. It's challenging." Another commented: "The challenge of caring for Ms. J. is spiritually uplifting. Every week I look forward to working with Ms. J. It helps me grow stronger in my faith." Yet another caregiver observed, "when I play religious music, she sits with her eyes open and is very quiet. You're learning in the process. . . ."

If we are able to view illness and suffering as an opportunity for growth and connection, we can be present to everyone in the family system and not overreact to the issues before us. One of the obstacles we face in talking about religious or spiritual issues is that we may have been advised not to discuss these topics early in our professional training. The GCM needs to be comfortable with his/her spirituality and to be open and aware of the major religions that will influence clients so that they can be understood completely. In concrete terms, this means helping clients access spiritual resources or supports that may have been meaningful to them earlier in their lives. It can also mean helping them come to terms with their faith or lack of faith. Facing up to these issues can be one of the most challenging and yet most rewarding aspects of our work.

Geriatric care managers need to know where they are on their own spiritual path and how to engage with clients who have similar or different viewpoints on these matters. It is important not to try to convert the client to a perspective that the care manager believes would be of benefit, but instead to be respectful of where the client is. In psychological terms, this means care managers need to note possible counter-transference reactions. Cultivating empathy means taking seriously a remark by Kierkegaard: "Men are objective toward others and subjective toward themselves. The task of religion is to reverse this."

By cultivating our own spiritual perspective, we can strive to find the right approach so that we can value the person beyond the limitations of illness and beyond the limitations of our own subjectivity. This task is ultimately what leads to transcendence.

"It's about transcendence," says Teresa Dieringer, certified care manager with Caregiver Support Network, "the ability to connect with someone or something outside of yourself. Most people assume that people with dementia can't transcend, when in fact they do it all the time." Hearing a hymn, or smelling incense burned at Mass may be the sensory key that unlocks a memory of God's love and the comfort of a time when the world was less foggy, more hospitable. So it is important for caregivers to provide these experiences, Dieringer says. Finding hymns, scriptures, and prayers often make a person less agitated.

It is sometimes hard to know if an intervention is having a positive impact, yet the most important fact may simply be the ministry of presence, letting clients know they are not alone. Priest, Rabbi, care manager, family member, friend, and home care workers can fill this role. Stephen Sapp states, "If we are to continue to value people with dementia as children of God, we must treat them as if they are still able to experience a relationship to God and therefore God's love. Who are we to say that God cannot continue to speak to even the most severely demented person if God so chooses?" (Sapp, 1987).

Elbert Cole, founder of the Shepherds Centers movement and caregiver during his wife's years of dementia, wrote that "People with Alzheimer's Disease are still people with the same needs of all people. They need to know that they are loved, to feel good about themselves, to be respected, to feel secure, to be included, to celebrate the joy of life, to be needed, and to have the approval of others who are important to them and to be stimulated in body, mind and spirit." The challenge is to enable people with dementia to be heard–especially with regard to their spirituality. We may reflect on the essence of the person who cannot communicate. How can one call forth what was and is still there?

SPIRITUAL CHALLENGES IN WORKING WITH THE FAMILY SYSTEM

Focus on the spiritual aspects of caregiving can be difficult during a health crisis when we need to access the physical resources as quickly as possible. It is hard to be contemplative at such times. Our task is to carve time to talk with family and client to listen to their pain and perspective, while being active in caregiving aspect. Listening to everyone's perspective, and being open to the possibilities in the situation, creates the opportunity for understanding client's and family view of the world.

The care manager can facilitate healing by:

- Accepting each person's pain in the situation
- Seeing the gifts that are there
- Being able to make a connection with each person
- Doing vs. Being–trying to be present to each person
- Bringing our essence to the situation
- Bringing a heart space as well as administrative and clinical perspective
- Being receptive to the challenges faced by each person in the situation

Families are often confused or overwhelmed by the extent of their tasks as caregivers. The geriatric care manager can serve as their guide to help them fulfill the tasks physically, emotionally, financially and spiritually. The care manager can assist them to see a parent's journey and their own journey by being present to them. The care manager should expect that for some people, it will be frightening and all too natural to see their elders as if they are seeing their future selves. Some will shrink back and want to avoid the situation. Our challenge is to help adult children to be present to the pain of change.

One way to do this is to be present to them and hear their own pain. We need to help adult children get a vision of their parent's journey, to appreciate what gave and currently gives their parent's life meaning, to understand how the parent copes with suffering. By helping adult children reflect, we provide support in facing what is difficult for them to bear. Witnessing the change in a parent is painful. Our role as geriatric care managers is to be a calm presence who is witnessing their story, and this is not an easy thing to do. We must listen to unresolved issues, grief, and anger–and help family members work it through.

We can also help families be open to new ways of relating to each other–rather than continuing with destructive patterns. We are helping families in pain by helping them practically to live with situation at hand and spiritually, to help transform their experiences of loss. We can help families work through their meaning of illness and change in relationship with parents. We can review unresolved conflicts and suggest possibilities of transformation. We can encourage the family members to honor both their own needs and those of their parents. We can explore what they are able or are in a position to give without resentment.

Accomplishing this kind of growth is a time consuming process and can evolve over years. Sometimes family members have spiritual breakthroughs and are able to be present to their parent's wishes and needs. Sometimes families struggle with less success. Some clients are not able to move beyond pain and anger. It is challenging to be present in such a situation, but care managers need to be patient. We can only move to protect the older person if the actions of their family members could jeopardize their health and safety.

As agents of psychological growth, care managers face the question: How can we use ourselves as a healing source? One answer is by helping clients to experience caregiving itself as meaningful, as part of a spiritual journey. The spiritual journey of caregiving provides an opportunity for personal growth and spiritual possibilities (McLeod, 1999). Caregiving need not be seen simply an obligation or doing good for someone else. This deeper perspective is what Ram Dass has labeled "Fierce Grace" (Dass, 2000).

What is called for here is to recognize the sanctity of service. But we must also acknowledge that, while some family members can go beyond their limits, not everyone can do it. If the relationship between a parent and family member had not been good, the geriatric care manager needs to be empathetic to family member's situation. The care manager must listen to their pain and struggles with the parent without judgment. The care manager then becomes a sounding board, reflecting past hurts and current demands for care. The care manager can value an adult child's perspective and enable them to make moves to provide care for a parents' care, either directly or using the professional care managers' services to do so.

Another possibility is helping the adult child gain a new perspective of their parents through an exploration of the parent's own life story and struggles. This exploration can allow the possibility for empathy for the parent's situation in life, their dilemmas and ways of dealing with their lives. Listening for themes in a parent's story and helping adult children accept their parents' shortcomings may facilitate a broader perspective for the adult child and allow for healing of the relationship before the parent dies, thus providing the opportunity for change and growth.

"The joy of passing on wisdom to younger people not only seeds the future, but crowns an elder's life with worth and nobility,"said Rabbi Zalman Schachter-Shalomi, leader of the Jewish renewal movement (Schachter, 1997).

The following case is an example of a client who was emotionally absent to her daughter:

> *While reviewing mother's life, the daughter shared the family story of loss. Her grandfather was murdered in Europe while being an advocate for people's rights. His daughter, her mother, came to the U.S. and brought the rest of the family. She worked as a maid, and eventually became a union representative voicing the concerns of the workers to management.*
>
> *At the time the daughter engaged the geriatric care manager, the mother was writing her memoirs of her late father. Despite visual deficits, and encroaching memory disorder, she was refusing care at home. While listening to the daughter's emotional pain about her mother's limited nurturing to her in earlier years, the GCM encouraged the daughter to share her thoughts about her mother's life and she shared how she admired her mother who was quite heroic in bringing the family from Europe and providing for them. The GCM also engaged the mother to consider caregivers for an acceptable amount of time, and helped the mother get the care she needed. The daughter subsequently was able to bring her mother to her home for the holidays and took care of her mother herself despite her family and work responsibilities. She clearly wanted to provide the care.*
>
> *As her mother's care needs increased, the mother reluctantly accepted more care. When she suffered a severe stroke, the daughter honored her wishes by not taking her to the hospital and she moved into her mother's home to take care of her for the last week of her life. Though difficult, it seemed important to her to do.*
>
> *A week after the stroke, the daughter called to tell the care manager that her mother had died the previous night. The daughter said the experience had been perfect; it was beautiful to be alone with her mother. She had gone out with friends for dinner and came home relaxed. She sat on the floor and spoke to her mother.*

I told her gently that she was dying, that she had been sick since Monday and now it was Friday. I talked about all her accomplishments, how everyone admired her, including her homecare workers. I told her I loved her and that I knew how much she loved me. It was an exquisite moment. I went on to say that I knew she didn't believe in heaven, but suggested that if it were possible that there is a heaven, then perhaps mother could meet and continue her discussions with Roger (a family friend) in heaven.

Mrs. N was very deaf, very ill, and cognitively impaired and her daughter was not sure she had heard her. But Mrs. N smiled, took a few breaths, and then stopped breathing. The geriatric care manager said it was wonderful that the daughter could be so present to her mother. The daughter said that she did not feel guilty but perfectly at peace.

Mrs. N's daughter initially had difficulty providing care for her mother because her mother resisted it. With support and encouragement of the geriatric care manager, she was able to help her mother come to accept the help she needed. Despite her sadness at her mother's earlier emotional unavailability, which she talked about with the care manager, the daughter was able to consistently care for her mother or use the geriatric care manager's resources when she was not able to do so.

She was able to help her mother when she was dying, by her physical and emotional presence, and acknowledged her mother's life's gifts, enabling her mother to leave her life with good feelings about herself and her daughter and with hope for the future. The care manager's support and acknowledgement of the daughter's feelings throughout the difficult care taking period, and the provision of appropriate home care workers, may have eased this process.

The daughter was able to rise above her ambivalent feelings and provide care and nurturing to her mother in a loving manner. The geriatric care manager witnessed the daughter's inner resources and strength and supported all she did for her mother. By being present to the family member's struggles and providing emotional support and concrete assistance, care managers can help their cli-

ents find healing possibilities, not only for the parent, but themselves and their families.[1]

Many of our clients find caregiving to be challenging, but many are also able to articulate the positive aspects of caregiving. Some say it gives them a sense of being useful, and of finding out what is really important in life. Others say it extends their compassion to all those who need and give care. Some families are stuck because they've had challenging relationships throughout their entire lives. Some people can accept a parent's limitations and provide care to parent by following their morale dictates of providing care to the old and vulnerable. Others hire geriatric care managers because the challenge of caregiving is too difficult for them. In these latter instances, it is important for the care manager not to move too fast in an effort to provide healing.

The appropriate response is staying with each side and listening to pain of the children, even though it is sometimes difficult to do. The care manager must be prepared for those times when a family member's anger is so great that it will play out in behavior or in their taking positions that sabotage care. The care manager must also prepare for those instances when adult children are either emotionally unavailable or displacing their disappointments of the family relationship on the geriatric care manager.

The spiritual approach helped Patti Davis perceive the ongoing mutuality between family members and the Alzheimer's patient, in her case, that of her father, former President Ronald Reagan. Speaking of her reconciliation with her mother and her father's longevity in spite of his illness, Davis observed, "I think it's the tenacity of his soul that he just isn't ready to leave his reunited family." As for the holidays, she maintains, "I'm not sure if my father still understands Christmas, but I'm sure he understands giving" (quoted in *The NY Times*, 1999). For Patti Davis, the ability to give and receive still exists. "When we are in the presence of someone who is leaving this world, we have the opportunity to grow," she observed (source: *The Tri-City Herald*, October 8, 2000).

SPIRITUAL CHALLENGES IN CARING FOR THE DYING

In working with clients who are dying, we need to be comfortable in their presence and support family members during this process. This can be a very meaningful time for saying goodbyes and for sharing the gifts given and received over time. The most important task is for the practitioner to take time to listen as the client seeks, finds and creates the meaning of their last days. Remembering events during his or her life, taking the opportunity to reconcile with family members and friends, or finding ways to forgive oneself, can all be a gift to both patient and practitioner.

The geriatric care manager need not do it all alone. Referral to a chaplain or spiritual counselor should be initiated well before a person is dying if the client is open to this. The role of the care manager at this stage is to open the door and let the client proceed. Jane Thibault has offered profound insights on how to open discussions of remembering, reconciliation, reassessing and reunion (Thibault, 1993). Some tasks that help clients find meaning in the very last stage of life include:

- Accepting their life as it has been lived
- Working toward reconciliation of past hurts
- Developing appreciation for the pain and joy of the present moment
- Finding hope for what may come

Some people will have difficulty in talking about their spiritual issues so it is important to attend to behavioral cues such as agitation, complaints, apathy, depression, isolation, anxiety and respond in ways that comfort the client, i.e., singing to them a favorite song/hymn, telling a story about them. Our work provides opportunities to look at the way we care for clients and bring healing to everyone in the system including ourselves. Our work is challenging inasmuch as it is both demanding on a practical level as well as emotionally charged. Geriatric care managers can be pulled by family members or older ill clients as our own unresolved psychological issues come to the surface.

In conclusion, I offer here some suggestions for specific spiritual practices for geriatric care managers:

1. *Being Centered in the Midst of the Storm.* It is important for the care manager to have compassion for their client's fears, and for the care manager to remain as centered as possible. Geriatric care managers need to find a way to retain equanimity, to do what needs to be done, to hear all sides in the situation in order to be able to consider a care plan that is responsive to everyone's needs.

2. *Emotional Support.* It is important for the care manager to release the pain of clients and ourselves with clinical supervision, therapy, or

communication with a friend or partner. The care manager needs to be aware of his/her own reactivity.

3. *The Witness.* What practices does the geriatric care manager need to cultivate to remain centered, to be "the Witness," and not be over-reactive to challenging situations?

4. *Spiritual Practices.* These include prayer and meditation; seeking environments that provide healing, such as nature, music, or muse-ums; reading books of spiritual inspiration; writing poetry, produc-ing works of art, or other creative ventures; physical exercise; taking periods of respite for rebalancing oneself and contemplating one's own gifts; thinking about small actions to encourage a posi-tive response; and being a blessing to others and noticing the reci-procity in clients.

The spiritual challenges we face are not one-sided because we can experience spiritual responses from clients and their caregivers. I re-member well a client's daughter, Ms. G, who was responding to her fa-ther Harry's decreasing cognitive capacity. She summed up her re-sponse to him in these words: "You are the essence of Harry. That's what I get: little fleeting moments of the essence of Harry. It's a differ-ent way of seeing the world and I take it as a gift."[1] As we begin to see all the fleeting moments of our lives as a gift, we will find the deepest re-sponse to the spiritual challenge of geriatric care management.

NOTE

1. Example cited in article by Leonie Nowitz, "Incorporation a Spiritual Perspec-tive into Geriatric Care Management," Cress, Cathy, *Handbook of Geriatric Care Man-agement*, Jones and Bartlett, Boston.

REFERENCES

Dass, R. (2000). *Still Here: Embracing Aging, Changing, Dying*, Riverhead Books.
Dunn, Rev. D., Ecumenical Chaplain at Alma Street Centre, Fremantle, Western Aus-tralia, personal communication.
Friedan, B. (1993). Quote from interview with Brian Lamb on C-SPAN *Booknotes*, November 28.
Friedan, B. (1994). *The fountain of age*, Simon & Schuster.
Friedman, D. (1997). *Journal of the Central Conference of American Rabbis*, Summer.

Goldman, C. (2002). *The gifts of caregiving: Stories of hardship, hope, and healing,* Fairview Press.

Hillman, J. (1997). *The soul's code,* Warner Books.

Jong, E. (1994). *Fear of Fifty: A midlife memoir,* Harper-Collins.

McLeod, B. (1999). *Caregiving: The spiritual journey of love, loss, and renewal,* John Wiley.

Post, S. (1995). *The moral challenge of Alzheimer disease,* Johns Hopkins University Press.

Sapp, S. (1987). *Full of years: Aging and the elderly in the bible and today,* Abingdon Press.

Schachter-Shalomi, Z., and Miller, R. (1997). *From age-ing to sage-ing,* Time Warner.

Thibault, J. (1993). *A deepening love affair: The gift of God in later life,* Upper Room Books.

Postcards to God:
Exploring Spiritual Expression
Among Disabled Older Adults

Mark Brennan, PhD
Sarah B. Laditka, PhD
Amy Cohen, MFA

SUMMARY. *Postcards to God* was a creative method to allow individuals to express their spirituality. The purpose of this study was to examine the validity of this innovative method. At a skilled nursing facility in a geriatric residence, 19 older disabled workshop participants created collage and message "Postcards to God," and completed a brief survey. Postcard content and construction were coded and analyzed using qualitative methods around self-reports along two attitudinal dimensions: (a) making a postcard to God, and (b) level of religiousness. Spiritual and religious dimensions were related to postcard thematic content. Postcards were used

The authors thank the Gurwin Jewish Geriatric Center and staff, Commack, NY for their cooperation with the workshop described in this study.

The pilot workshop that formed the basis of this project was supported, in part, by a grant to Amy Cohen, MFA, from the New York State Council on the Arts Suffolk Decentralization Grant administered through the Huntington Arts Council.

Portions of this article were presented at the Annual Conference of the State Society on Aging of New York, October 10-12, 2001, Albany, NY, and at the Annual Scientific Meetings of the Gerontological Society of America, November 15-18, 2001, Chicago, IL.

[Haworth co-indexing entry note]: "*Postcards to God*: Exploring Spiritual Expression Among Disabled Older Adults." Brennan, Mark, Sarah B. Laditka, and Amy Cohen. Co-published simultaneously in *Journal of Gerontological Social Work* (The Haworth Social Work Practice Press, an imprint of The Haworth Press, Inc.) Vol. 45, No. 1/2, 2005, pp. 203-222; and: *Religion, Spirituality, and Aging: A Social Work Perspective* (ed: Harry R. Moody) The Haworth Social Work Practice Press, an imprint of The Haworth Press, Inc., 2005, pp. 203-222. Single or multiple copies of this article are available for a fee from The Haworth Document Delivery Service [1-800-HAWORTH, 9:00 a.m. - 5:00 p.m. (EST). E-mail address: docdelivery@haworthpress.com].

for expressions of spirituality and prayer across all levels of self-reported religiousness. The *Postcards* project seems like a useful way to facilitate spiritual expression. If validated in further study, this method may prove a useful way to promote spiritual expression in a variety of older and frail populations. *[Article copies available for a fee from The Haworth Document Delivery Service: 1-800-HAWORTH. E-mail address: <docdelivery@haworthpress.com> Website: <http://www.HaworthPress.com>*

KEYWORDS. Qualitative analysis, spirituality, spiritual expression

The present study presents a creative workshop model that facilitates spiritual expression, namely, *Postcards to God*. Frail, older people participated in this workshop where they were invited to create postcards to God as a way to express their spirituality. Most participants used their postcards as a vehicle for prayer. We examined the content of the way in which participants expressed their spirituality using a thematic analysis of the postcards created in the workshop, along with survey responses obtained during the workshop regarding levels of religiousness and how participants felt about making a postcard to God. Results suggest the *Postcards* workshop may be a useful form of spiritual expression alone or in conjunction with other methods.

DEFINING THE "SPIRITUAL" IN SPIRITUAL EXPRESSION

As noted by Miller and Thoresen (2003), the notion of spirituality has varied, and the connection between spirituality and religion has been hotly debated. While many people consider spirituality and religiousness to be distinct, albeit, overlapping constructs, there is a lack of consensus on the precise relationship between them (Hill & Pargament, 2003; McFadden et al., 2003; Miller & Thoresen; Moberg, 2002; Pargament, 1997). Our operational definition of spirituality focuses on a sense of purpose and meaning in life, a sense of inner-connectedness or integration, reliance on personal resources, and the ability to transcend one's immediate experience (Chandler, Holden, & Kolander, 1992; Hill & Pargament, 2003; Lindgren & Coursey, 1995; Miller & Thoresen, 2003; Pargament, 1997). Spirituality may or may not be expressed through religiousness, which is the adherence to specific creeds, doctrines, and beliefs associated with particular denominations or sects. By its nature, religiousness represents a social aspect of spirituality and for many provides the bridge between one's inner spiritual world and the larger community. Thus, spiritual expression may involve private and/or idiosyncratic expressions of one's connection to the sacred, or more easily recognizable symbolism when it is expressed through the religious forms and rituals.

SPIRITUAL WELL-BEING AMONG OLDER ADULTS

There is a growing interest in the connections between religion and spirituality and physical and psychological health, particularly for older people (McFadden, Brennan, & Patrick, 2003; Miller & Thoresen, 2003). The most recent development in the gerontological literature has been the notion of Positive Spirituality enunciated by Crowther and colleagues (Crowther, Parker, Achenbaum, Larimore, & Koenig, 2002). Positive Spirituality is defined as ". . . a developing and internalized personal relation with the sacred or transcendent that is not bound by race, ethnicity, economics, or class and promotes the wellness and welfare of self and others" (Crowther et al., p. 614). Crowther and colleagues have advocated for the incorporation of Positive Spirituality into the model of successful aging developed by Rowe and Kahn (1998). Including the spiritual dimension in the model of successful aging is especially important as the vast majority of older adults report a spiritual or religious component to their lives (Koenig & Brooks, 2002).

Spirituality and Physical Health. The move to incorporate Positive Spirituality in the "Successful Aging" model stems, in part, from the burgeoning literature that has uncovered positive associations between spirituality and physical and mental health (Crowther et al., 2002; Powell, Shahabi, & Thoresen, 2003; Seeman, Dubin, & Seeman, 2003). In terms of physical health outcomes, while many studies have reported positive associations between this aspect of well-being and spirituality, methodological limitations have made this association less clear-cut (Powell et al., 2003; Seeman et al., 2003; Sloan, Bagiella, & Powell, 1999). Part of the problem may be that spirituality has only indirect effects on physical health, for example, influencing lifestyle choices (e.g., tobacco use) and practices that in turn relate to one's physical health (Crowther et al., 2002).

Spirituality and Psychological Well-Being. Older adults face multiple challenges in later life, ranging from health problems, to losses of significant others, changes in social roles, and so forth, so spiritual coping with such life events may be even more germane to the psychological well-being of older adults. There have been numerous studies that have examined spiritual and religious coping (see Pargament, 1997). Spiritual coping with life events has been formulated as the process through which our spiritual and religious beliefs lend meaning to life's challenges (Brennan, in press; Crowther et al., 2002; Ferraro & Koch, 1994; Hettler & Cohen, 1998; Pargament, 1997) and help to ameliorate or mitigate feelings of suffering and loss. In addition, core values in many spiritual traditions, such as the emphasis on a relationship with the transcendent and with others along with self-respect and humility, may be beneficial in coping with adverse life circumstances, such as illness, disability and loss (Crowther et al., 2002). While, as Pargament notes, spiritual coping does not always lead to positive psychological outcomes, generally research in this area has found a positive relationship between spiritual coping and adjustment to life events.

SPIRITUALITY IN LONG-TERM CARE SETTINGS

There has been growing attention to the issue of quality-of-life among recipients of formal and informal long-term care services. Older adults typically enter into formal long-term care arrangements due to physical illness, frailty, and other circumstances that no longer permit continued independent living in community settings. Many older adults would choose death over a permanent nursing home placement (Kane, 2001). Thus, in addition to coping with the challenges that necessitated receipt of long-term services, these older adults are also facing issues of loss of independence and, in the case of nursing home placement, a change in residence from community to facility. Thus, spiritual well-being may be particularly important to these older adults who are facing multiple challenges due to life circumstances and can utilize this personal resource to bolster themselves in light of such conditions (Friedman, 1995; Simmons, 1998).

Spiritual well-being is considered integral to quality of life in long-term care. According to Kane (2001), one of the challenges to life quality for these older adults is being able to perceive that they are engaged in meaningful activities and the need for vital relationships with others. Spiritual well-being is closely related to both of these life quality aspects in that one's spirituality can lend meaning to life and reinforces our relationships with others (Crowther et al., 2002; Durkin, 1992).

Thus, fostering spiritual well-being has been identified as an important facet in both quality-of-care and quality-of-life in institutional long-term care settings (Hicks, 1999; Kane, 2001).

ENHANCING SPIRITUAL WELL-BEING THROUGH SPIRITUAL EXPRESSION

There are numerous ways to help promote spiritual well-being among older adults in long-term care settings beyond the chaplaincies and pastoral care departments are found in many nursing homes (Friedman, 1995). One way is to provide residents with opportunities for spiritual activities and expression. Such activities not only promote connections between residents, but help to connect the older person to their spiritual roots in the community and promote spiritual well-being. These activities may be private or shared, and include religious rituals, prayer, and other types of traditional activities.

Forms of Spiritual Expression. Spiritual expression is not limited to traditional activities, or conventional modes of religious behavior. For example, spirituality among older residents of long-term care facilities can be enhanced through occupational therapy, as the therapist enables and empowers the individual to engage in meaningful activities (Howard & Howard, 1997). Spirituality may also be articulated through the arts (Anandarajah & Hight, 2001). To illustrate, Palmer (1995) postulates that spirituality is an integral experiential component of music, citing transcendental states engendered by music, religion, and art. Silverman (1997) discusses poetry therapy as a vehicle for getting in touch with inner spiritual feelings as well as religious and spiritual values. In addition, art therapy has been used as a means of both addressing religious and spiritual concerns (Koepfer, 2000), as well as a way of facilitating spiritual recovery from substance abuse (Feen-Calligan, 1995). Furthermore, there is an extensive literature on the connection between Native American art and spirituality (e.g., Herring, 1997; Pakes, 1987).

The Content of Spiritual Expression. Just as spirituality may be expressed in many different ways, the content of such expression is also extremely variable. For example, Hawks (1994) describes spiritual expression on the personal level through attributes of trust, honesty, integrity, altruism, compassion, service, and interpersonal relationships. Spirituality may be expressed through one's conception of the "Higher Power" which may portray God as beneficent, the source of good fortune, a source of assistance for material things or in times of hardships, and as an omniscient and all-powerful deity (Barusch, 2002). Spiritual expression often involves prayer, especially in situations of distress requiring adaptation (Dunn & Horgas, 2000; Maltby, Lewis, & Day, 1999). Prayer is often targeted at one's health or that of a significant other, money and finances, general societal problems, protection from danger or bad luck, and alleviation of guilt (Casey, 1938; Patrick, Barnes, & Ash, 2002). When spirituality is expressed through artistic symbolism, it may be either realistic or abstract (Wyly, 1990). Material symbols through which spirituality is expressed may involve traditional religious symbols (e.g., Star of David, Crucifix) or naturalistic forms (e.g., fire, heavenly bodies, animals, water, etc.; White, 1926). Thus, given the wide variety of forms and content of spiritual expression, opportunities for such expression may be satisfied both through traditional means (e.g., religious service attendance, other rituals) and nontraditional ways as well (e.g., art).

POSTCARDS TO GOD

Postcards to God was developed as an intergenerational workshop to explore the connections between spirituality and artistic expression. The *Postcards* project was a workshop in which participants created a communication to God using blank postcards and a variety of art supplies and collage materials. One of these workshops, which is the focus of the present study, was conducted with disabled older adults at a geriatric care facility. This method allowed participants to explore spirituality expression through a highly accessible form of artistic composition. Participants were free to express themselves both within and outside of traditional ideas of spirituality. Analogous to the concept that "a picture is worth a thousand words," the postcards are rich in visual content as well as text messages. The workshop presented here embodied the principles of Positive Spirituality (Crowther et al., 2002) in that it provided participants with a vehicle for spiritual expression in a group setting.

We are not aware of any literature that has addressed spiritual expression and the content of spiritual expression using this type of artistic mode of expression. Ours is an exploratory study of a small sample of older adults. We present a creative form of spiritual expression, postcards to God. We examined the content the postcards for the association between participants' spiritual expression as evidenced by their postcards and two survey items, namely, their level of religiousness and how they felt about making a postcard to God using qualitative analysis. We suggest the *Postcards* method is an innovative way to allow people to express their spirituality.

METHOD

Participants

A convenience sample of 19 physically disabled, frail, older adults was used for this study. The sample was comprised of individuals residing in a skilled nursing facility in a geriatric care facility in Commack, New York. Although physically disabled, participants for this workshop were not cognitively impaired. On average, participants were 83 years of age, with approximately three-quarters age 75 years or more (see Table 1). Of the 19 participants, 18 were female, and 18 of the 19 participants reported their religious affiliation as Jewish. Only one participant was nonwhite (results not shown). Participants were relatively well educated for this older cohort, with nearly 80% reporting that they had completed high school or some college. Somewhat surprising given the frail nature of the sample, nearly half (47%) reported their health as "good" or "very good" (see Table 1).

Procedures

After obtaining permission to hold the workshop as a residence sponsored event, the third author (A.C.), a studio artist, met with the director of the creative arts therapy program at the geriatric care facility to discuss the purpose of the project. The third author (hereafter referred to as the facilitator) conducted the two-hour workshop. Participation was voluntary and informed consent was obtained in writing from all participants. At the beginning of the workshop, the facilitator explained that the purpose of the workshop was to provide an opportunity to explore a personal definition of spirituality by making a "postcard to God."

Using examples of her own psychologically oriented collage artwork, the facilitator instructed participants on some simple collage techniques. She invited participants to create a postcard to God. The facilitator asked participants to consider their communications from a spiritual point of view, "What would you say to God if you had a chance? If words fail you, there are always pictures." The facilitator acknowledged that some people in the group might not believe in God,

TABLE 1. Demographic and Attitudinal Characteristics of Sample

Variables	n	%
Age Group		
Ages 56-74	5	26.0
Ages 75-89	7	38.0
Ages 90-96	7	38.0
Female gender	18	94.7
Education		
Less than High School	4	21.1
High School	8	42.1
Some College	6	31.6
College	1	5.3
Health Status		
Poor	2	10.5
Fair	8	42.1
Good	7	36.8
Very Good	2	10.5
How making art made you feel		
Frustrated	4	21.1
Anxious	2	10.5
Calm	2	10.5
Satisfied	10	52.6
Refused	1	5.3
How making postcard to God made you feel		
Frustrated	2	10.5
Anxious	2	10.5
Calm	4	21.1
Satisfied	10	52.6
Mixed feelings	1	5.3
How religious are you?		
Uncertain	3	15.8
A little	4	21.1
A moderate amount	10	52.6
A lot	2	10.5
Do you believe in God? (Yes)	17	89.5

Note. Total n = 19. Average Age = 82.5, SD = 12.0.

suggesting, "If you don't believe in God, shouldn't you tell someone? Who should you tell, and how would you tell them?"

Participants were then provided with blank postcards (10.5 × 15.25 cm), and a large assortment of collage materials consisting of hundreds of old magazines, patterned paper, sheet music, stickers, scores of rubber stamps, dozens of plain and colored markers, paste, and scissors. Most participants completed their postcards independently. In several instances in which the handwriting of the participant was unsteady, they were assisted by a nursing aide who wrote a short message on the participant's postcard. One participant who was visually impaired supervised a nursing aide in the design and construction of her postcard.

All participants completed at least one postcard. Three participants completed two postcards. The facilitator made a black and white photocopy of each postcard during the workshop. In addition to black and white photocopies, color copies were made of several of the postcards. After the postcards were completed, the facilitator provided postage stamps and the cards were collected and mailed to God, in care of the address of the workshop location. The facilitator explained that part of belief is taking risks and letting go. Thus the experience would not be complete, the facilitator emphasized, without sending the postcards out into the world. Immediately after the workshop, all participants completed a brief survey. When the postcards arrived by mail back at the facility, they were informally displayed for the residents and staff. The workshop participants and their families were encouraged to keep the postcards. Several original postcards, which were not picked up by participants, were returned to the facilitator.

Measures

A brief survey distributed at the end of the workshop collected the following demographic information: age, sex, race, self-rated health, religious affiliation, and level of education. In addition, participants were asked to indicate "How religious do you consider yourself to be?" Responses to this item were; "a lot," "a moderate amount," "a little," and "uncertain." Participants were also asked to indicate whether they believed in God, selecting from "yes," "no," and "undecided." One other attitudinal item asked, "How making a postcard to God in this workshop made you feel?" Responses to the latter question were "satisfied," "calm," "anxious," or "frustrated." The survey also included one open-ended question asking the participant to "Describe in a sentence or two how making the postcard to God made you feel." All participants completed a survey. The 22 collage and message postcards and responses to this survey comprised the qualitative and quantitative data for this study, respectively.

Design and Analysis

This study used a qualitative design in which the "Grounded Theory" approach (Glaser & Strauss, 1967) was used to code postcard content and construction. That is, codes were developed from a review of pictorial elements and text messages rather than constructing codes *a priori.* For qualitative analyses of the relation between the two survey items and postcard content, conceptual matrices were constructed in which such content was organized by the various item response categories to facilitate the detection of themes and patterns in the data (see Miles & Huberman, 1994).

Postcards were scanned into computerized bitmap files, and then imported into a qualitative image and text analysis program, Atlas/ti for Windows (Muhr, 1997). Two raters (M.B. and S.B.L.) coded all text and images in detail using standardized criteria. The criteria were to be comprehensive in coding all text and images, and to clearly distinguish among themes. For example, we distinguished between six types of prayers observed in the postcards (e.g., prayer for happiness for others, prayer for happiness for self, prayer for wealth for self) as well as a separate code for general prayer. Raters worked independently to code the postcards. Raters coded the postcard text and images without knowledge of, or reference to, the self-report attitudinal items used in subsequent analysis (see discussion below). We used Kappa statistics to determine the comparability of coding between the raters or interrater agreement. The Kappa for the two raters was excellent at .93 (95% CI = .93 1.00). Interrater agreement for the initial coding was 96%. After both raters completed the coding, any areas of disagreement were discussed with the third author. Unanimous agreement for all codes was reached. A codebook was constructed which provided a definition, brief description, and one or two examples for each code (see Table 2 for a list of codes). Using the codebook, the raters independently re-examined all of the postcards to ensure consistency of coding and comprehensiveness. Unanimous agreement was reached in all instances.

Second-order qualitative data analysis was performed by constructing conceptual matrices along two dimensions: (1) how making a postcard to God made you feel; and (2) how religious you consider yourself, to be (see Miles & Huberman, 1994). A set of summary matrices compiled individual level responses for the two self-report items, indicating counts of similar codes under each response category. The third author reviewed the summary matrices independently of the two other raters. All differences were resolved through discussion. Unanimous agreement was reached in all instances.

TABLE 2. Postcards to God Content Codes

1. Abstract beauty	19. Love or affection toward others
2. Acknowledgment of God's omnipotence	20. Money, wealth
3. All-powerful God	21. Music
4. Animals/fish/insects	22. Nature or natural beauty
5. Baseball	23. Prayer
6. Blessing, good fortune	24. Prayer for better health for self
7. Diversity/many faces of humanity	25. Prayer for general assistance for self
8. Faith and trust in God	26. Prayer for happiness for others
9. Food/sustenance	27. Prayer for happiness for self
10. God's ability is limited	28. Prayer for strength
11. Gratitude toward God	29. Prayer for wealth for self
12. Gratitude toward others	30. Provide help or assistance to God
13. Greeting and salutations	31. Provide help or assistance to others
14. Happiness, enjoyment, "life is good"	32. Questioning the nature of God
15. Heaven on earth	33. Self-reflection
16. Holiday (vacation)	34. Sexuality
17. Human beauty	35. Youth and exuberance
18. Love or affection toward God	

RESULTS

Self-Report Attitudinal Items

In response to how making the postcard to God made you feel, 53% reported it made them feel satisfied, 21% said it made them feel calm, while about one-in-ten reported it made them feel either frustrated or anxious (11% and 11%, respectively) (see Table 1). A majority of participants indicated they were either moderately (53%) or very (11%) religious. One-in-five (21%) felt they were "a little" religious and 16% said they were uncertain about their level of religiousness. Thus, our sample consisted of a relatively secular group of older adults in terms of their level of formal religiousness.

Qualitative Analyses of Postcard Content and Construction

Themes observed during the coding of the postcard content were suggestive of a broader spiritual dimension rather than a reflection of underlying religiousness (i.e., adherence to a particular theology or creed). An inspection of the codes developed (see Table 2) revealed themes around nature, connections to other humans and a Higher Power, and the ability to transcend limitations which are consonant with definitions of spirituality (e.g., Howden, 1992). There was a noted absence of religious symbolism, which was somewhat surprising given the homogeneity of religious affiliation in the present sample. In terms of postcard construction, some postcards were conventional, that is, pictorial elements on one side and text on the other. Other postcards showed greater flexibility in artistic expression, consisting of mixtures of text and pictures on the same side of the postcards.

In the following sections, the qualitative results of postcard content and construction along the two self-report dimensions described above are presented. For each dimension, we first provide a summary of the results, followed by a description using two case examples. These cases illustrate representative postcard themes among participants with similar responses to the self-report items, and show how themes varied among participants in different response groups based on the attitudinal items (i.e., satisfied or calm versus anxious or frustrated).

How Making a Postcard to God Made You Feel

Several recurring themes emerged along this dimension. Participants who reported that making a postcard to God made them feel satisfied or calm expressed gratitude to both God and other people. These themes were not found among people who reported that making a postcard to God made them feel anxious or frustrated. Postcards of participants who were satisfied or calm portrayed themes of food, sustenance and abundance. These themes are consistent with belief in a God who meets their needs and more. These themes were not found in the anxious and frustrated groups.

In addition, those who felt anxiety and frustration about making a postcard to God included prayers for material happiness; this theme may suggest an underlying sense of deprivation among these participants. Individuals who reported feeling "satisfied" may have been comfortable in expressions of love and affection for God. In contrast, "anxious" respondents expressed love for other people instead. The latter finding may indicate people who reported feeling anxious were uncomfortable in expressing love to God directly and used other people as a proxy for these feelings. Several content themes were present among all groups including abstract beauty, animals, and music. Prayers for better health also cut across groups, and likely reflected the frail health of the sample. No patterns in the use of pictorial elements or text in terms of postcard construction were apparent in relation to how making a postcard to God made participants feel.

Case Example One. Mrs. S., 74-years-old, reported her health as being "good," and had two years of college education. Mrs. S. reported that making a postcard to God made her feel "satisfied." The pictorial elements of her postcard portrayed the theme of food, sustenance, and abundance (see Figure 1). The theme of "sustenance and abundance" was representative of postcards of the participants in the "satisfied" and "calm" groups for this self-report item. Her postcard text (not shown) expressed gratitude as follows: "Dear God, thank you for Florida. The closest place to paradise! Love, Mrs. S." In response to the open-ended question about how making the postcard to God made her feel, Mrs. S. wrote, "I felt happy," reinforcing the themes of abundance, gratitude and love portrayed in her postcard.

Case Example Two. Mrs. B. responded that making a postcard to God made her feel "anxious." Mrs. B. was 86-years-old and reported her health as being "good." She reported having completed six months of teachers training. Themes portrayed in her postcard were consistent with others who felt anxious or frustrated about making a postcard to God. Mrs. B. expressed love and concern for other people; the text of her postcard read, "Make Julia and Susan happy. Forget about me; after all your time is precious!" The pictorial elements of her postcard included abstract beauty and music. When describing how making the postcard to God made her feel in the open-ended item, Mrs. B. wrote, "It would only help in the scheme of life." Mrs. B., like others in the anxious or frustrated groups, expressed both love for other people and uncertainty about the availability of God to meet her needs.

Level of Religiousness

Participants who were very religious expressed the theme of the omnipotent, all-knowing God. In contrast, those who were "uncertain" referenced God as being all-powerful. Themes of a bountiful, blessed world, where life is good were expressed by those responding they were at least "a little" religious, but not among participants who were "uncer-

FIGURE 1. Postcard from Case Example 1 (making postcard to God made her feel satisfied) with pictorial elements of food portraying "sustenance and abundance."

tain." Participants who were "a little" religious expressed love and affection for God; interestingly, this was not seen in those who were at least "moderately" religious. Participants who felt they were "very" or "moderately" religious may have considered love for God as a given and did not need to use the postcard message for that purpose. Persons saying they were "a little" religious expressed the notion of serving God directly. In contrast, those who were "moderately" religious expressed themes of service to others. This may have reflected a more mature stance toward their religion. Participants who were "uncertain" about their degree of religiousness expressed love or concern for other people, but not directly for God. Postcard construction in terms of pictures and text was not related to levels of religiousness.

Case Example Three. Mrs. R. had a high school education, was 71-years-old and reported her health as "fair." She felt that she was "a little" religious. Her postcard expressed the notion of serving God directly and contained a mixture of text and pictorial elements on the same side of the postcard. The pictures portrayed sustenance, consisting of a loaf of bread and a bowl of pasta. Her message reads: "Dear God, If you are hungery [sic] I would love to make some of my stuffed cabbage for you. It would be my mitvah [sic] & pride. My love to you and yours." In response to the open-ended question on how making the postcard to God made her feel, she wrote, "I feel like a kid writing to Santa Claus. I hope He will answer me."

Case Example Four. Mrs. K. also had a high school education and felt that she was "moderately" religious. Mrs. K. was 96-years-old and reported her health as being very good "all my life." The pictorial elements of her postcard (see Figure 2) portrayed themes of a blessed and bountiful world. This was represented by images of hands clasped in prayer and food/sustenance, respectively. The text on her postcard reads: "Dear God, Thank you for all my blessings." In response to the open-ended question, Mrs. K. wrote, "It made me feel better about myself and that I was able to thank God for the help that I received."

DISCUSSION

Our study presented an innovative method of spiritual expression, *Postcards to God*. The spiritual and religious dimensions (i.e., feelings about making a postcard to God and levels of religiousness, respectively) were related to the content of the postcard. For example, participants who considered themselves more religious expressed themes of a bountiful and blessed world. These themes were not present among those who reported they were "uncertain" about their level of religiousness. Postcards of participants who responded that making a postcard to God made them feel satisfied or calm portrayed themes of food, sustenance, and abundance, which were not present in those who were anxious or frustrated with this activity. Overall, the postcards methods appeared to be a useful way of promoting the expression of spirituality among our small group of frail older adults.

Validity of Postcard Content

Examination of the contents included by participants in their *Postcards to God* suggest that this workshop is a valid means of spiritual ex-

FIGURE 2. Postcard from Case Example 4 (moderately religious) expressing gratitude for a bountiful and blessed world through text and images of food and hands clasped in prayer.

Dear G-d,
Thank you for all
my blessings.

pression regardless of level of traditional religiousness. For example, older adult participants used the postcards as vehicles for prayer regardless of their levels of level of religiousness. As noted previously, prayer is often used as a form of spiritual coping in times of stress or uncertainty (e.g., Dunn & Horgas, 2000; Maltby et al., 1999). The objects of prayer in this sample were also consistent with other research, namely, praying for the health of oneself or others, praying for money and happiness, etc. (Casey, 1938; Hicks et al., 2002). The symbolic messages portrayed on the postcards was also consistent with prior work, for example, taking on both abstract and realistic forms (Wyly, 1990), or involving naturalistic forms of animals and nature (White, 1926). These results also underscore the connection between spirituality and artistic activity that are abundant in the literature (e.g., Anandarajah & Hight, 2001; Koepfer, 2000; Silverman, 1997) and were also apparent in the *Postcards* workshop.

Research Implications

The postcards method, which relied on a process that allowed participants to express their spiritual nature by hand-crafting their own expressions of spirituality (i.e., the postcards) in a creative, largely unstructured way, complements and extends previous work. It should be noted, however, that our sample size was small, and homogeneous in terms of gender, race, religious affiliation, and physical and cognitive ability. Further studies can address these limitations by including more diverse groups. Based on our experience, the process reported here could be adapted for use among diverse groups in terms of age, race, and religious background.

It should also be noted that some view the process of allowing individuals to express their feelings about spirituality as a personal resource is, in and of itself, an intervention (Hodge, 2001). Quoting Laird (1994, in Hodge, 2001), Hodge notes that feelings and stories about spirituality ". . . shape our evolving construction of reality . . . and our ability to lead successful lives" (p. 209). The *Postcards* workshop was not designed as an intervention. It may be useful for future research to explore the intervention aspects of the *Postcards to God* workshop, for example, by including pre- and post-intervention assessments of participants' spiritual and/or psychological well-being.

Practice Implications

There has been increasing concern about addressing the spiritual well-being of individuals, including older adults, in a variety of settings (Berggren-Thomas & Griggs, 1995; Chandler, Holden, & Kolander, 1992; Seaward, 1992; Hicks, 1999; Leetun, 1996; Witmer & Sweeney, 1992). All participants in the current study were highly engaged in the project and the mood of the workshop was upbeat and positive. Furthermore, most workshop participants expressed how much they enjoyed the activity of making a postcard to God. The overwhelmingly positive reception of this workshop on the part of these participants emphasizes the importance of providing opportunities for spiritual expression in long-term care settings. In addition, experience with the workshop participants, as well as the results of the qualitative analysis suggest that the *Postcards to God* method may be successful as a way to promote spiritual expression in a variety of other older adult populations including frail, disabled older people from a variety of cultural and religious backgrounds. We encourage researchers to further explore the validity of this approach in other populations, as well as to examine the effectiveness of this method as an intervention to improve psychological well-being.

REFERENCES

Anandarajah, G., & Hight, E. (2001). Spirituality and medical practice: Using the HOPE questionnaire as a practical tool for spiritual assessment. *American Family Physician, 63* (1), 81-89.

Barusch, A. S. (1999). Religion, adversity, and age: Religious experiences of low-income elderly women. *Journal of Sociology & Social Welfare, 26* (1), 125-142.

Berggren-Thomas, P., & Griggs, M. J. (1995). Spirituality in aging: Spiritual need or spiritual journey? *Journal of Gerontological Nursing, 21*(3), 5-10.

Brennan, M. (in press). Spirituality and religiousness predict adaptation to vision loss in middle-age and older adults. *International Journal for the Psychology of Religion.*

Casey, R. P. (1938). The psychoanalytic study of religion. *Journal of Abnormal & Social Psychology, 33,* 437-452.

Chandler, C. K., Holden, J. M., & Kolander, C. A. (1992). Counseling for spiritual wellness: Theory and practice. *Journal of Counseling & Development, 71,* 168-174.

Crowther, M. R., Parker, M. W., Achenbaum, W. A., Larimore, W. L., & Koenig, H. W. (2002). Rowe and Kahn's model of successful aging revisited: Positive spirituality–The forgotten factor. *The Gerontologist, 42* (5), 613-620.

Dunn, K. S., & Horgas, A. L. (2000). The prevalence of prayer as a spiritual self-care modality. *Journal of Holistic Nursing, 18*(4), 337-351.

Durkin, M. B. (1992). A community of caring. Patients in a rehabilitation unit experience holistic healing through a spiritual support group. *Health Progress, 73* (8), 48-53.

Feen-Calligan, H. (1995). The use of art therapy in treatment programs to promote spiritual recovery from addiction. *Art Therapy: Journal of the American Art Therapists Association, 12* (1), 46-50.

Ferraro, K. F., & Koch, J. R. (1994). Religion and health among black and white adults: Examining social support and consolation. *Journal for the Scientific Study of Religion, 33,* 362-380.

Friedman, D. A. (1995). Spiritual challenges of nursing home life. In M. A. Kimble, S. H. McFadden, J. W. Ellor, and J. J. Seeber (Eds.), *Aging, spirituality, and religion* (pp. 362-373). Minneapolis, MN: Fortress Press.

Glaser, B., & Strauss, A. (1967). *The discovery of grounded theory.* Chicago: Aldine.

Hawks, S. (1994). Spiritual health: Definition and theory. *Wellness Perspectives, 10,* 3-11.

Herring, R. D. (1997). The creative arts: An avenue to wellness among Native American Indians. *Journal of Humanistic Education & Development, 36* (2), 105-113.

Hettler, T. R., & Cohen, L. H. (1998). Intrinsic religiousness as a stress-moderator for adult Protestant churchgoers. *Journal of Community Psychology, 26* (6), 597-609.

Hicks, T. J. Jr. (1999). Spirituality and the elderly: Nursing implications with nursing home residents. *Geriatric Nursing, 20* (3), 144-146.

Hill, P. C., & Pargament, K. I. (2003). Advances in the conceptualization and measurement of religion and spirituality. *American Psychologist, 58* (1), 64-74.

Hodge, D. R. (2001). Spiritual assessment: A review of major qualitative methods and a new framework for assessing spirituality. *Social Work, 46* (3), 203-214.

Howard, B. S., & Howard, J. R. (1997). Occupation as spiritual activity. *American Journal of Occupational Therapy, 51*(3), 181-185.

Howden, J. (1992). *Development and psychometric characteristics of the Spirituality Assessment Scale.* Unpublished doctoral dissertation. Texas Women's University.

Kane, R. A. (2001). Long-term care and a good quality of life: Bringing them closer together. *The Gerontologist, 41* (3), 293-304.

Koenig, H. G., & Brooks, R. G. (2002). Religion, health, and aging: Implications for practice and public policy. *Public Policy and Aging Report, 12* (4), 13-19.

Koepfer, S. R. (2000). Drawing on the spirit: Embracing spirituality in pediatrics and pediatric art therapy. *Art Therapy: Journal of the American Art Therapy Association, 17* (3), 188-194.

Leetun, M. C. (1996). Wellness spirituality in the older adult. Assessment and intervention protocol. *Nurse Practitioner, 60* (8), 65-70.

Lindgren, K. N., & Coursey, R. D. (1995). Spirituality and serious mental illness: A two-part study. *Psychosocial Rehabilitation Journal, 18,* 93-107.

Maltby, J. L., Lewis, C. A., & Day, L. (1999). Religious orientation and psychological well-being: The role of the frequency of personal prayer. *British Journal of Health Psychology, 4*(4), 363-378.

McFadden, S. H., Brennan, M., & Patrick, J. H. (2003). Charting a course for the 21st Century studies of late life religiousness and spirituality. In S. H. McFadden, M. Brennan, and J. H. Patrick (Eds.), *New directions in the study of late life religiousness and spirituality.* Binghamton, NY: The Haworth Press, Inc.

Miles, M. B., & Huberman, A. M. (1994). *Qualitative data analysis: An expanded sourcebook* (2nd ed.) (pp. 8-141). Thousand Oaks, CA: Sage.

Miller, W. R., & Thoresen, C. E. (2003). Spirituality, religion, and health: An emerging research field. *American Psychologist, 58* (1), 24-35.

Moberg, D. O. (2002). Assessing and measuring spirituality: Confronting the dilemmas of universal and particular evaluative criteria. *Journal of Adult Development, 9* (1), 47-60.

Muhr, T. (1997). *Atlas/ti for Windows. Visual qualitative data analysis, management, & model building.* [computer software]. Berlin: Scientific Software Development.

Pakes, F. (1987). Traditional Plains Indian art and the contemporary Indian student. *Canadian Journal of Native Education, 14* (1), 1-14.

Palmer, A. J. (1995). Music education and spirituality: A philosophical exploration. *Philosophy of Music Education, 3* (2), 91-106.

Pargament, K. I. (1997). *The psychology of religion and coping*. New York: Guilford Press.

Patrick, J. H., Barnes, K. A., & Ash, T. W. (2002, November). *The frequency and content of prayer: Age and gender differences*. Poster session presented at the 55th annual scientific meeting of the Gerontological Society of America, Boston, MA.

Powell, L. H., Shahabi, L., & Thoresen, C. E. (2003). Religion and spirituality: Linkages to physical health. *American Psychologist, 58* (1), 36-52.

Seaward, B. (1992). A spiritual well-being program at the United States Postal Service headquarters. *Wellness Perspectives, 8,* 16-28.

Seeman, T. E., Dubin, L. F., & Seeman, M. (2003). Religiosity/spirituality and health: A critical review of the evidence for biological pathways. *American Psychologist, 58*(1), 53-63.

Silverman, H. L. (1997). The meaning of poetry therapy as art and science: Its essence, religious quality, and spiritual values. *Journal of Poetry Therapy, 11,* (1), 49-52.

Simmons, H. C. (1998). Spirituality and community in the last stage of life. *Journal of Gerontological Social Work, 29* (2/3), 73-91.

Sloan, R. P., Bagiella, E., & Powell, T. (1999). Religion, spirituality, and medicine. *The Lancet, 353,* 664-667.

White, L. A. (1926). An anthropological approach to the emotional factors of religion. *Journal of Philosophy, 23,* 546-554.

Witmer, J. M., & Sweeney, T. J. (1992). A holistic model for wellness and prevention over the life-span. *Journal of Counseling & Development, 71* 140-148.

Creating Sacred Scenarios:
Opportunities for New Rituals
and Sacred Aging

Richard Address, DMin

SUMMARY. Population studies within all communities have confirmed the rise of what has been referred to as a revolution in longevity. With the first wave of the baby boom generation about to join the existing over sixty-five generations, new life stages and experiences are being created in ways that will challenge religious communities. An important aspect of this revolution will be the opportunity to create new religious rituals that will respond to and reflect these new life stages and experiences. This growing multi-generational cohort will increasingly seek that their religious communities respond to their changing life experiences in ways that infuse their lives with meaning. *[Article copies available for a fee from The Haworth Document Delivery Service: 1-800-HAWORTH. E-mail address: <docdelivery@haworthpress.com> Website: <http://www.HaworthPress.com> © 2005 by The Haworth Press, Inc. All rights reserved.]*

KEYWORDS. Longevity, religion, rituals, sexuality, intimacy, caregiving, dementia

---

[Haworth co-indexing entry note]: "Creating Sacred Scenarios: Opportunities for New Rituals and Sacred Aging." Address, Richard. Co-published simultaneously in *Journal of Gerontological Social Work* (The Haworth Social Work Practice Press, an imprint of The Haworth Press, Inc.) Vol. 45, No. 1/2, 2005, pp. 223-232; and: *Religion, Spirituality, and Aging: A Social Work Perspective* (ed: Harry R. Moody) The Haworth Social Work Practice Press, an imprint of The Haworth Press, Inc., 2005, pp. 223-232. Single or multiple copies of this article are available for a fee from The Haworth Document Delivery Service [1-800-HAWORTH, 9:00 a.m. - 5:00 p.m. (EST). E-mail address: docdelivery@haworthpress.com].

For a large part of the life span, religious tradition provides opportunities to mark special moments with long established rituals related to the life cycle. From birth until death, these moments allow for the possibilities of sanctifying relationships, events and transitions within a context of specific prayers, ceremonies, and acts. The revolution in longevity that is now emerging, presents to religious traditions new possibilities to capture life-transitioning events within a sacred context. There are few rituals created by contemporary religious traditions that have been designed to speak to the changes and challenges that are now part of the aging process. Being responsive in this area may go a long way in forging meaningful spiritual linkages to the expanding older adult community in every major religious community. Failure to develop these responses may swell the numbers of individuals who choose to absent themselves from religious communal life if they feel that the community does not speak to their life styles, needs and search for meaning.

Rituals help link an individual to a moment, a community and something beyond the self. Rituals reinforce the fact that a person exists within a certain context and history, and that by celebrating or recognizing an event in one's life in a formal way, that event, and thus the person, takes on additional meaning and definition. This relational aspect of ritual is key to the power of ritual creation. It is especially important as we age, when the need for a relationship-oriented life is even greater.

Aging involves understanding loss, on the one hand, and the celebration of new aspects of consciousness on the other hand. There is a sense of personal liberation in each of these transitions that can be enhanced and indeed, made sacred, by placing them in the context of religious rituals. The extension in life span and the reality that much of that longevity can be healthy and productive reminds us of the value of seeking to create moments of sacred possibilities for this longevity revolution. Rituals can connect us to our traditions, reinforce the value of community, provide meaning for what is being commemorated and most importantly, celebrate the necessity and power of being in relationships with other people and the transcendent meaning of our own existence.

This latter dimension of ritual opens the door to a discussion of the issue of transformation. Many view transformation as one of the key elements in religious ritual. Ritual allows for the individual to transition from one phase of life to another, often liberating that individual for change. The longevity revolution is now providing opportunities to aid in this process of personal and cultural transformation by creating new rituals that respond to life styles and life cycles more diverse than in previous generations. Driver notes this when he wrote: "rituals not only can change, or help to change, a situation but they themselves are subject to change in the course of time. In other words, rituals belong to human history. Ritual process belongs to historical process. It is not some kind of detached thing remote from the events that it influences. Agents of transformation, rituals are themselves transformed by the histories to which they belong."[1]

The demographics of aging are now fertile field for ritual creation. W. A. Achenbaum wrote of this reality several years ago when he noted that: "In recent years, clergy and lay people have developed rituals and customs expressly designed to draw attention to the distinctive features of being old. Demographics often are the primary engine driving this 'invention of tradition.' Few once lived past seventy-five. Now the median age of most U.S, religious bodies approaches or exceeds forty-five. Clergy are ministering to more and more older people in aging congregations . . . More innovative are calls for some 'official' recognition of changes in (self)-identity . . . Even more daunting is the challenge of finding ways to acknowledge the shedding of earlier roles in life as a natural, theologically grounded response to the finitude of life." [2]

The demographic engine is driving new possibilities within the Jewish community. Recent analyses of the previous decade of population studies conducted within the Jewish community of the United States echo Achenbaum's words. The median age of the Jewish community is approaching the mid-forties; the community is close to twenty percent over the age of 65 with those over 75 representing one of the largest growth areas. With the aging of the baby boom generation on the near horizon, we can anticipate the Jewish older adult population to swell. Slowly, the possibilities for new age-based ritual creation are developing. A recent collection of essays and reflections by Susan Berrin contains an entire section on new rituals the have been recently developed. Rituals that celebrate aging and education, life cycle changes in women and the welcoming of new residents into assisted living and life care residences point to the importance and relevance of linking new life transitions to new religious based rituals.[3]

An important aspect of this new ritual development is that much of it stems from the life experiences of people and not just programs that emanate from clergy or denominational officials. Over the past few years, as part of the development of its project on Sacred Aging, the Union for Reform Judaism's Department of Jewish Family Concerns has sponsored workshops for older adults specifically devoted to ritual creation. The results of those sessions have been challenging and inspiring. Over two hundred participants in these workshops suggested a wide variety of new rituals, prayers, and ceremonies. One of the challenges inherent in these discussions was the tension between creating a ritual that would be public and part of a community's tradition and the creation of more personal or private rituals. This represents a challenge for religious communities in the coming decades. How can we maintain the connection between ritual and community and a sense of the transcendent while creating, or being open to the creation of newer, personal rituals and prayers that focus on the individual? Does a ritual speak to me in the context of a greater "other," or does it speak to me only in order to meet my need, at a particular moment in my life? This tension reflects the rise in the development of private or personal religious practices that seems to be reflective of the current society.[4] One such personal ritual request evolved from a congregant who, one year after his wife's death, approached his rabbi to write and lead a small private ceremony in the sanctuary that would mark the moment that the congregant would remove his wedding ring. This would be a private ceremony, shared between the family rabbi, the surviving spouse and other family and friends. The rabbi did write such a ceremony.

Many of the suggestions in the ritual creation discussions reflected this more personal and private need. Obviously, a large number of requests centered on issues related to grandchildren and family. Likewise, significant numbers of suggestions looked at the acceptance of the gradual losses associated with aging. People sought ways to make meaningful their losses of mobility, activity and independence, usually from a life affirming perspective. Optimism and love of life; even as it ebbed, was a constant factor. Likewise, a sense of time passing and a rising desire for a sense of meaning and purpose was in constant evidence.

It is important here to remember that in every religious tradition there already exist prayers and meditations that could be, and often are, re-interpreted and then applied to many of these concerns. Congregations are often remiss in not teaching the richness of their own tradition to their own people to allow them opportunities for spiritual support. For example, many workshop attendees asked that their synagogue and or denomination create prayers and rituals that thanked God for their successful surgery or good diagnosis or their emergence from serious illness. What many did not know, and were pleased to discover, is that such blessings already existed. Within Jewish tradition, the *birkat gomel* gives thanks to God for successful completion of a dangerous journey or survival of a dangerous situation is one such traditional blessing, which is being reinterpreted. The rise in special healing services and ceremonies in many religious communities speaks to the need to place the sickness-healing dyad within a sacred context.

The fact of our growing longevity, the impact of medical technology to aid that longevity and the decline of community that is reflective of much of contemporary society has produced a powerful need for rituals, ceremonies and prayers that celebrate and enhance personal relationships and intimacy. In the new life styles and life stages that the longevity revolution is creating, this desire for intimacy–that is, close personal relationships that speak to the essence of the individuals involved–has become a driving force in the creation of new ritual possibilities. Three examples reflect the dynamic changes now presenting themselves to religious communities. These examples, which look at issues of care giving, cohabitation and end of life concerns, are present in every congregation regardless of the religious community. I frame them here in the context of the Jewish community as it is in this community that I live my life.

HONORING THE CARE-GIVER

We have, in our current society, created a new life stage: that of caregiver. Taking care of loved one is not new. Indeed, the commandment to honor one's parents forms a basis for society itself. Yet, I would submit to you, that the nature of the care-giving process has changed. Gone are extended families and close knit neighborhoods where shared time and respite care were part of a community and family's fabric. Medical technology, mobility, dual career families, single parent families, and economic constraints have combined to create new challenges for care-givers. Families usually have a "designated care-giver" who, more often than not, is female. We all know people who are that primary caregiver who live great distances from the loved one being cared for despite the fact that a sibling may be closer. Care giving is not something that one usually volunteers for. How many people choose to devote untold years to rearranging schedules, family time, personal and financial resources in order to become the care-giver. This new life stage is usually entered into in a moment, with a phone call or an event that transforms both the caregiver and the family member. In addition, the "trend to older" that many communities are witnessing has trend what some called the "sandwich generation" into what some now refer to as the "club sandwich generation." In other words, multi-generational care giving is no longer a rarity in any of our communities. Repeatedly studies on this issue remind us of the stresses and strains placed upon the family systems that enter this new stage.

We are aware of the positive spiritual and psychological changes that do take place in the care-giving mode. Despite this, however, often the designated caregiver toils in isolation. There are, after all, things that are reserved for the intimacy of the parent-child relationship that must be honored. Moments of great personal transformation take place at these times. Roles are reversed and new perspectives on life and love are often understood. Care giving is a life stage that can last, thanks to medical technology, for years. We do it because that is what human beings do, and in doing so we honor the Commandment and help set an example of proper behavior for the next generation.

In Hebrew, there is a three-letter root: *shin, mem, resh* (*shamahr*) which carries the meaning of guardian, or to take care. In a significant book on bioethics, the late Dr. Benjamin Freedman developed a concept of the *shomer* or caregiver. Implicit in this concept, and essential to the contemporary activity of care giving, is the idea that care giving is a two-fold enterprise. One takes care of a loved one and is also duty bound, within the framework of Jewish tradition, to care for one's self, for one's own health (physical and mental) must be protected in order to be in a position to care for another.[5]

The longevity revolution has created an explosion in care giving and given rise to the new life stage of caregiver. In light of that, it is suggested that congregations take a Sabbath at some time during the year to honor and celebrate those who are *shomrim* (care-givers). This is a unique opportunity for a congregation to publicly honor and thank those members, and by extension their families, who are engaged in this sacred work. It is a community honoring the often private work of caring. It is an opportunity to create new prayers, establish a community ritual of care giving and in doing so, teach a valuable lesson to all generations that in honoring the Commandment to honor and respect parents, we honor ourselves, our God, and our community. Ideally, the congregation celebrates this new category of life transition, for, as anyone who has or is care-giving will tell you, this is a life stage that can be both transitional and transformative. This idea to create a Sabbath to Honor the care-giver responds to the realities of what many in a congregation are living through and provides, by means of ritual, prayer, and ceremony, an opportunity to connect with a tradition, see the art of care-giving within a sacred context and bring honor and meaning to the relationships that are being strengthened.

COHABITATION WITHOUT MARRIAGE

A second example of an opportunity to create new rituals based on changing life styles is presented by the number of older adults who choose to be together without benefit of a formal marriage ceremony. As we live longer, these circumstances may increase. The situation is familiar to many of us: the widow or widower, the divorced man or woman who meets someone special and, for a wide variety of reasons, choose to be together but not be legally married. They come to their clergy person and ask for a blessing that will sanctify their being together. There is no issue of children. There is an issue of intimacy as one ages, the security of a caring partner and the need to thank God that two people have found each other and to ask for peace and comfort in the years that may be granted. The question: should the clergy, or the denomination, develop such a prayer or ritual that sanctifies this "union"?

Many clergy have not embraced this idea. They argue as representatives of a tradition that such ceremonies should be within a formal marriage. Some have argued that to participate in such a ceremony would see them as participating in some sort of fraud as such unions may deny legal rights to the partner or families if such a union were to be within a formal marriage. Some have mentioned that it presents a dangerous precedent in that if blessing grandmother and her boyfriend is fine with the rabbi, then why not a blessing for the twenty-something graduate students who choose to live together?

The reality, however, is that these type of living arrangements are no longer unfamiliar to all of us. I would suggest that much of the way we look at the need for these new rituals be framed within the context of the individuals themselves and viewed through the filter of a human need for intimacy and relationships. Genesis 2:18 is correct when it reminds us that it is not good that we go through life alone. The extended life spans that are now emerging will allow for more of these type situations. Shall we just ignore them? Or, shall we see in many of these relationships unique opportunities to develop something sacred and special to many people who choose to come to their faith community and have this new relationship blessed. No, it is not a marriage, and that must be part of the evolution of the ceremony. Yes, it is a blessing of thanks that people have found each other and a hope that they may find peace and security in the years ahead.

The scientific community has already recognized the benefits of extended social and personal relationships in fostering health and well-being. In a way, the development of such rituals and blessings to honor these "senior unions" may also assist the congregation in being a center for healthy aging.

In the end, the openness to the development of such unions allows for the continuing evolution of faith communities to the new realities presented by the dynamic changes in life spans and life styles.

INTIMACY, ALZHEIMER'S, AND DEMENTIA

The third suggestion for new rituals and ceremonies is, perhaps, the most difficult. It stems from the increasing challenges that are presented in dealing with the issue of a loved one institutionalized with Alzheimer's or dementia. The scenario may be familiar to some. It is the well spouse who comes to the clergyperson to seek counsel. They have met someone, that someone provides a sense of comfort and intimacy, not necessarily sexual in nature. There is no talk of abandoning the spouse who is ill, yet, there is the argument that, given the nature and duration of the illness, should not the well spouse be freed to find someone with whom they can share life and find support? There are people now who are living such arrangements. The psychological and spiritual tolls may be burdensome. Can they find some sense of comfort and caring within their faith community? Do those faith communities have to now reexamine new contexts and life situations and perhaps evolve new responses? Or, should such situations remain private and personal?

The suggestion here is that congregations and denominational groups need to think about teaching how people can negotiate these situations. Surely every faith tradition has points of view, texts, and teachings that may be instructive. These texts and teaching may need to be reinterpreted in light of the changes in life situations that the longevity of congregants will and are experiencing. This may be very difficult for some traditions. Yet, it also may be liberating in that the discussions can shed light on how meaningful to people a tradition can be and what guidance can be gleaned from sacred texts. At the very least, to develop discussions around such scenarios as these within the congregational setting needs to take place so as to educate congregants to what their faith says and to open the dialogue between people on the possibilities that they may choose.

We already see the value of this in terms of making sacred decisions at the end of life and teaching people about advance medical directives, health care proxy forms and specific rituals and traditions that religions have developed to guide decision making a the end of life. The issues of prolonged hospitalization in light of Alzheimer's, dementia or persistent vegetative states, also calls on religious bodies to look at what blessings, rituals and perhaps formal ceremonies can be developed to ease and guide people through this tragic and difficult path.

A psychologist in California has developed one such tool for personal and perhaps congregation-based education. In the April 1999 Parent Care Advisor newsletter, Dr. William F. Fitzgerald writes of the need for older couples to draft an agreement "that addresses their conduct within marriage if one partner becomes incapacitated." Fitzgerald's "Open Letter to My Spouse" recognizes the love and commitment the partners have for each other. The letter states that the partners are taking time to "advise" the other of the beliefs and wishes regarding what would happen if one "should be alive in body but significantly compromised mentally and/or physically." There is a recognition that the other partner will be "faced with a double burden: the stress of caring for me and the absence of my emotional, physical, and intellectual support." In such a situation, the partner expresses the understanding that there may be a need for additional support. There then appears the following sentence. "Please find someone you like who will be available to provide the emotional, intellectual and physical support and companionship that I then cannot provide to you."

Fitzgerald's document concludes with the recognition that some may find this document unusual or even controversial. He reinforces the mutuality of the document and the issue in his concluding paragraph which reads: "If you decide that I am emotionally, physically, and/or intellectually unavailable to you, please know that I urge you to find support in the form of a companion who can help you through this difficult time. Let other people think what they may. My concern is for your welfare and the ability to cope. Please take care of yourself, knowing this is what I want for you."[6]

Should such discussions regarding what couples may wish to do be held within the confines of religious bodies? Should such discussions lead to the development of documents, prayers, or rituals that attempt to anticipate these tragic circumstances and, in doing so, provide guidance for individuals from within their specific faith? We do so for end of life situations. Should we not begin to do the same for the growing number of families and individuals caught in the web and wilderness of another new life stage?

The revolution in longevity is now presenting religious institutions with unprecedented opportunities for creative and dynamic responses. As the next decades evolve and the aging population grows, the need for meaning and purpose in new life stages will only increase. People will turn to their faith communities to provide that meaning and purpose. How we meet that challenge will determine, in large measure, the nature and impact of religion in the aging society of the future.

NOTES

1. *The Magic of Ritual.* Tom F. Driver. Harper. San Francisco, CA, 1991. p. 184.

2. "Age Based Jewish and Christian Rituals." W. A. Achenbaum. *Handbook of Aging Spirituality and Religion.* Vol. 1. Kimble, McFadden, Ellor, and Seebor, Eds. Augsberg Fortress Press. Minneapolis, MN, 1995. pp. 213, 214.

3. *A Heart of Wisdom.* Susan Berrin. Jewish Lights. Woodstock, VT, 1997.

4. Discussions on the increase in personalized religious expression and the impact of that trend on contemporary religious life is a theme discussed in such recent works as: *Habits of the Heart.* Robert N. Bellah. University of California Press. Berkeley, CA, 1985, 1996; *A Generation of Seekers.* Wade, Clarke, Roof. Harper-Collins. New York, 1993; *Bridging Divided Worlds.* Carroll and Roof. Jossey-Bass. San Francisco, CA, 2002; *Bowling Alone.* Robert Putnam. Simon Schuster. New York, 2000; *The Jew Within.* Cohen and Eisen. Indiana Univ. Press. Bloomington, IN, 2000; *The Transformation of American Religion.* Alan Wolfe. Free Press. New York, 2003.

5. *Duty and Healing.* Benjamin Freedman. Routledge Press. New York, 1999.

6. *Parent Care Advisor* . LRP Publications. Horsham, PA (April, 1999), p. 9.

Culture Change in Long-Term Care: Educating the Next Generation

Dwight Roth, MSW

SUMMARY. Long-term care facilities for frail elders are usually based upon the medical model, which is focused primarily on the biological functioning of these elders. The medical model allows for little choice on the part of the residents of these facilities. By way of contrast, culture change is a new approach to long-term care. This model of care seeks to meet a wide variety of needs for the elders and aims to expand their choices. This article presents the observations of college students responding to interactions with frail elders and looks at the implications of culture change for young adult college students. *[Article copies available for a fee from The Haworth Document Delivery Service: 1-800-HAWORTH. E-mail address: <docdelivery@haworthpress.com> Website: <http://www. HaworthPress.com> © 2005 by The Haworth Press, Inc. All rights reserved.]*

KEYWORDS. Culture change, frail elders, young adult college students, joy and woe

It's no big deal when you can't remember someone's name as long as you remember their story.

–a resident of Schowalter Villa nursing facility

[Haworth co-indexing entry note]: "Culture Change in Long-Term Care: Educating the Next Generation." Roth, Dwight. Co-published simultaneously in *Journal of Gerontological Social Work* (The Haworth Social Work Practice Press, an imprint of The Haworth Press, Inc.) Vol. 45, No. 1/2, 2005, pp. 233- 248; and: *Religion, Spirituality, and Aging: A Social Work Perspective* (ed: Harry R. Moody) The Haworth Social Work Practice Press, an imprint of The Haworth Press, Inc., 2005, pp. 233-248. Single or multiple copies of this article are available for a fee from The Haworth Document Delivery Service [1-800-HAWORTH, 9:00 a.m. - 5:00 p.m. (EST). E-mail address: docdelivery@haworthpress.com].

Available online at http://www.haworthpress.com/web/JGSW
© 2005 by The Haworth Press, Inc. All rights reserved.
doi:10.1300/J083v45n01_14

Woe says: Hence, go! But joy wants all eternity, wants deep, profound eternity.

–Friedrich Nietzsche

While change has always been part of the human story, we live in an era of unique revolutionary change. Part of that change is the demographics of aging–the growing number of older adults seen in both absolute numbers and as a percentage of the population. Conversely, one constant throughout the ages is the reality of joy and woe. This article focuses upon joy and woe among frail elders as perceived by young adult college students. These student perceptions grew out of their interaction with elders in a long-term care facility, Showalter Villa, whose philosophy of care is based in culture change The article concludes with a look at the importance of education of young college students–the next generation–regarding the significance of culture change in long term care settings.

CULTURE CHANGE AT THE SCHOWALTER VILLA LONG-TERM CARE FACILITY

Culture change is a movement in the United States and other countries in terms of how we improve care for frail elders in institutional settings. It is a departure from the traditional medical model for elder care that tends to focus on physical or biological needs of residents. Culture change, sometimes described as *person-centered care* (Culture Change Now, 2003), seeks to care for residents in a holistic manner–meeting as many needs of residents as possible. Moreover, it seeks to expand the choices which residents have in their daily lives. It encourages the elders' learning and developing new relationships with people from a variety of age groups. It promotes quality of life and quality of care. Culture change may be of importance, too, as a factor in cost saving measures and in anticipation of the aging of Baby Boom generation (Bell & Troxel, 2003; Holburn & Vietze, 2002).

Perhaps the most widely known approach to culture change is The Eden Alternative™ (2003), created in 1991 by Dr. William Thomas and Judy Meyers-Thomas. The Eden Alternative, in the words of its founders, seeks to do away with three negative aspects of long-term care facilities: loneliness, helplessness, and boredom. The Eden Alternative is a community-centered approach committed to "creating a Human Habitat where life revolves around close and continuing contact with plants, animals and children. It is these relationships that provide the young and old alike with a pathway to a life worth living." This approach aims to provide a place of positive elder living where pills and therapies often have little success (For details, E-mail: <contact@edenalto.com>).

Culture change, as an approach to long-term care, has importance as well when we think about the role of religion in the care of frail elders.

· based in meaningful religion goes against a "theology that seeks to accustom (people) to a good conscience in the face of suffering and guilt" (Marcuse, 1955:6). More specifically such religion challenges individuals from the larger society to act upon the words of Jesus in Matthew (25:34-40), where Jesus speaks of a time when the Son of Man will come in glory for the last Judgment. In the Gospel Jesus says the King will speak these words to the blessed:

> *34* Then the King will say to those on His right. 'Come, you who are blessed of My Father, inherit the kingdom prepared for you from the foundation of the world.

> *35* For I was hungry, and you gave Me *something* to eat; I was thirsty and you gave me drink; I was a stranger, and you invited Me in;

> *36* naked and you clothed Me; I was sick, and you visited Me; I was in prison, and you came to Me.'

> *37* "The righteous will answer Him, saying, 'Lord when did we see You see hungry, and feed You, or thirsty, and give You drink?

> *38* "And when did we see You a stranger, and invite You in, or naked, and clothed You?

> *39* 'And when did we see You sick, or in prison, and come to You?'

> *40* 'And the King will answer and say to them, 'Truly I say to you, to the extent that you did it to one of these brothers of Mine, *even* the least *of them*, you did it to Me.'

Within the Schowalter Villa Retirement Community, located in the town of Hesston, Kansas, there is a nursing facility that seeks to respond to frail elders who are among "the least of these" mentioned by the words of the Gospel. The purpose of effective culture change is fully consistent with the mission statement of the Villa to "provide optimal quality of life and quality of care to enrich those we serve in a Christian not-for-profit retirement community." The high quality of the Villa's work with frail elders is reflected in its being one of only three Kansas nursing homes to be recognized in 2003 by the Kansas Department on Aging for accomplishments in four domains of culture change. These domains include Resident Control, Staff Empowerment, Home Environment, and Community Involvement. This recognition is part of a program to promote high quality services and progressive models of care in Kansas long-term care facilities. The program, PEAK, stands for Promoting Excellent Alternatives in Kansas and is more fully described at: http://www.ksu.edu/peak

The Perspective of the Villa–Student Volunteers Interacting with Frail Elders

A significant part of culture change at Schowalter Villa is the involvement of Hesston College students. Located 500 yards from each other, the College and the Villa are both affiliated with the Mennonite Church, a Christian denomination whose theology emphasizes pacifism and service to humanity. Villa staff appreciate the help of students and the attention given to residents. Residents in turn appreciate students in terms of new relationships formed and the energy provided by youth. As a result of being with young adults, memories of the elders' own youth are triggered and reflection is stimulated. This encourages reminiscence that is an important part of life review in the last stage of life. Students benefit from understanding the wisdom and experiences of residents as well as gaining appreciation of the impact of aging and of declining health. Students bring a great deal of energy and compassion to their volunteer work and residents benefit enormously.

Along being a part of a various Villa activities the student role is simply that of being a presence among the residents. Students bring ideas and energy from the "outside community" into the nursing home. This interaction provides a vital balance to the rhythm of life in an institution. A move into an institution often necessitates routines allowing the most people to be served at the same time. Students, just by coming, break up that routine cycle. Life in most nursing homes does not represent the range of life in the wider community. Students help the nursing home to look and feel more like the community which the resident moved from.

At the beginning of each college term, Showalter Villa staff provide an orientation for the students who will be involved with Villa elders during that term. This orientation includes clear expectations of what is required from the student volunteers. For example, a brief training is given so students are able to assist with feeding residents who need help. The Villa also provides students with weekly and monthly calendars of scheduled activities so students can see if there are events in which they would like to participate. Students are encouraged to create activities that benefit either small or large groups.

The Academic Perspective–Students and Frail Elders

This engagement of students with frail elders is part of a strategic design within the Sociology Department at Hesston College where students enrolled in sociology classes are encouraged to interact with frail elders at the Villa. Between the beginning of fall term 2002 and the end of fall term 2003 over one hundred students were involved directly in culture change at the Villa. This number represents about twelve percent of the student body at Hesston–a significant scale of impact at the College. Student volunteers typically serve one to two hours each week throughout the semester . The remainder of this article reports on the experience of students in two different classes, *Cultural Anthropology* and *Marriage and the Family*, where students were reflecting upon the joy and woe of elders with whom they interacted during the fall term of 2003.

Students in *Cultural Anthropology* and *Marriage and the Family* have a choice of volunteering at the Villa or responding to videos related to course themes. When volunteering at the Villa, *Cultural Anthropology* students generally tend to develop a more positive view of the culture of frailty in old age. This shift in attitude is intended to promote an understanding of cultural relativity and a reduction of ethnocentrism. In their weekly reports, students write a 300 word, mini-ethnography based on observing various aspects of Villa culture. The academic assignment allows students to see the significance of culture change in long-term care.

In the *Marriage and the Family* class, students sometimes observe the extended family dynamics that arise when frail elders are placed in a nursing home. In this process, students may reflect what they might do when their own parents become frail elders. Schowalter Villa's emphasis on person-centered care endeavors to provide a home-like atmosphere and students make a contribution in this regard. Students and elders often develop a relationship similar to a grandchild-grandparent relationship. When the students recognize that they are part of significant culture change in long care facilities they are more concerned with the individual elder.

In view of the religious orientation of Hesston College the involvement of students at the Villa is inspired by service based in the name of Christ. The intent is one of mutual service involving both youth and age. There is a hope students will grow spiritually in seeing the frail elders as spiritual exemplars. It is assumed in the connection between the College and the nursing home, the experience of culture change will disclose to students ". . . the strong face of aging, the face that is hidden from us in our own secular, contragerontic society" (Guttman 1994:221).

YOUNG ADULTS, FRAIL ELDERS, AND A SENSE OF TIME

Eugene Bianchi (1986:54) reminds us that the different age groups, much like the idea of the complementary opposites yin and yang, contain each other in symbolic ways:

> In the depths of our psyches live an assortment of child images: the pouting, demanding, spoiled, or hurt child, the spontaneous, resilient youth who is ever leaping beyond the confines of linear history to probe the transcendent and eternal. We also carry within ourselves the senex, the wise old (person), awakening in us by our experience as elders, as well as by own immersion into the historical process of aging (which can provide wisdom or meanness of heart).

Despite their differences, the two age groups, youth and age, need one another. Youth needs the wisdom of older adults. Elders need the energy, vision, and excitement of young people.

Cole and Winkler (1997:5) remind us of the enduring necessity of living within limits, especially the limits of time. "Time–invisible, intangible, yet inexorable–is perhaps the most mysterious limit of all. Aging is about living in time. Born into the world as a certain historical moment, descended to pass out of it at a later, uncertain moment, we are creatures who change significantly over a lifetime."

This passage of time brings with it loss and gain, integrity and despair, joy and woe. As a rule, it is the older people, because of their longevity, who experience these conditions in the most profound way. It is perhaps because of their age that elders are more likely to understand the "vulnerability of the moment." It is often elders who experience the deepest levels of joy and woe. In discussing the concept of time Abraham J. Heschel writes (1985:42):

> Time is perpetual, perpetual novelty. Every moment is a new arrival a new bestowal. Just to be is a blessing, just to be is holy. The moment is a marvel; it is in evading it that boredom begins that ends in despair.
>
> Old age has the vicious tendency of depriving a person of the present. The aged thinks of himself as belonging to the past. But it is precisely openness to the present that he must strive for.
>
> He who lives with a sense of the Presence knows that to grow older does not mean to lose time but rather to gain time. And, he knows in all his deeds, the chief task of man is to sanctify time. All it takes to sanctify time is God, a soul, a moment. And the three are always there.

The relationship between Villa elders and Hesston students is often one of enchantment, a communion of spirit, a celebration of precious time together.

JOY AND WOE

It may seem that joy and woe are categorical and opposed to each other. Yet these profound human feelings often contain each other. This dialectical relationship of joy and sorrow is seen in literature from around the world and across the span of human existence. While joy and woe is felt by people of all ages, the focus here is that of frail elders as perceived by the college students. Joy and transcendence often come from experiencing what Rudolph Otto calls the *mysterium tremendum*: that is, realization of the nature of the awe inspiring mystery of life. The intuition is a kind of grace, something given to us miraculously. Green and Sharman-Burke (2000:255) write, "Grace, although the term is Christian, is something not limited to Christianity: it is a mysterious inner release that arises from within and makes sense not only of our goodness, but of our evil as well."

While this grace is available to any age group, elders are more likely to be open to this experience. Long life and a closer proximity to death intensify this sense of the *mysterium tremendum* of the universe. Joseph Campbell in *The Power of Myth* (1990) refers to this as the state of transcendence–going beyond the limits of the finite ego. In the elders' experience of woe and joy, and in students' comments about these feelings, one is reminded of Hammarskjold's (1972:xii) reflection: "But at some moment I did answer *Yes* to Someone–or Something–and from that hour I was certain that existence is meaningful and that, therefore, my life, in self-surrender had a goal." In person-centered care there is hope that elders can find meaning in whatever state they may exist. This sense of meaning is not a material goal that so dominates the western, postmodern mind; rather it is a discovery of meaning interwoven of joy and woe and in closeness to death. Paraphrasing Greene and Sharman-Burke (2000:255), it may be that we find our way to joy through the agency of our woe.

STUDENTS REFLECT ON JOY AND WOE IN INTERACTION WITH FRAIL ELDERS AT SCHOWALTER VILLA

Reflections by students placed in Schowalter Villa often turn out to be, implicitly or explicitly, reflections about stories told to them by elders. These stories represent elders as "*homo narrans*–humankind as storyteller, implying that culture in general–specific cultures, and the fabric of meaning that constitutes any single human existence–is the 'story' we tell about ourselves" (Turner, 1978:xv).

In expressing joy and woe, the elders perhaps are sometimes engaging in what have been called definitional ceremonies. As described by Barbara Myerhoff (1978:185), definitional ceremonies ". . . allow people to reiterate their collective and personal identities, to arouse . . . emotion and energy," which give the elder a sense of being and identity. These interactions might also be said to be informal rites of passage that elders unwittingly create. Rites of passage are ceremonies that mark the change in status from one life's position to another. Such transitional events appear to be critical to the well-being of a person. Yet in postmodern society there is lack of such ceremonies, and that lack is one reason why living in a nursing home is so difficult. The move from independent, autonomous living to life in a nursing home may be the most difficult move elders have to experience. This move needs definitional ceremony but it is extremely rare for nursing homes to provide such a ritual. Perhaps the stories told by the elders are a type of self-healing for the profound loss they experience upon entering a long-term care facility. Moreover, Myerhoff (1978:222) writes

> Reminiscence is no mere escapist desire to live in the past, as some claim; rather it should be regarded as a major developmental task for (elders), resulting In the integration that will allow them to age well and die well. The discovery of personal counterpart of myth-making . . .

STUDENTS REFLECT ON JOY AND WOE IN INTERACTION WITH FRAIL ELDERS AT SCHOWALTER VILLA

The following quotes in italics are culled from weekly reports written by *Cultural Anthropology* and *Marriage and the Family* students throughout the fall term 2003. Fictitious names of students are in regular print; fictitious names noting the elders are in *italics*.

Julie: *I sense a sort of melancholy mood from many of the residents that I think is derived from the loss of friends, family, and husbands as their generation ages and completes the cycle of life. Especially at a nursing home, where the culture is made up of solely one age group or generation, the atmosphere of death and deterioration is only heightened because of the loss of contact from a diverse group of people, made up of all ages.*

However, many of the residents I have helped have a sense of fulfillment, especially when talking about their families. They find joy in their life's contribution to society and the legacy they maybe leaving through their children. They seem content with the lives they have led and the accomplishments they have achieved, and often reminisce. This week, as I talked to one of the women, she discovered she knew my family. This helped her to reminisce and talk about her own family. She was pleased to make connections, and see the constancy of life, even through the years and the various generations. I think that many of the residents find joy in the gift of life and in reminiscing about their own lives, sharing with one another.

Joel: *I could see the sadness in him as he told me about the loss of his wife. He didn't like that he couldn't get to places that he wanted to anymore and that he had to have someone wheel him around in a wheelchair. His happiness seemed to come from God. He said that he was happy when he could do the little things and could make peoples' day better even when they just came to see him. It helps him see the next day and keep him from being depressed. It is interesting how believing in a God can help people out and give them comfort beyond the normal monotonous day of life for them. This man was a good example of a happy man that could be happy in the middle of the Villa even with all the sadness of not being able to walk. God gives him strength to keep hope until he dies.*

Pat: *My final interaction today was with one lady occurred as she was eating dinner. She was in a wheelchair and had both legs amputated. She just seemed to have one of those peaceful faces that is approachable. I sat down and asked her how her day was going. To my surprise she was as sweet as could be. I had to think of myself in that position and how disgusted I might be. The way she acted was really inspiring to me.*

Sara: *Sorrow, pain, and woe seem to be the traditional image of the typical elderly person. While working at the Schowalter Villa, I have experienced these generalizations, but I have also seen much joy. While working around the elderly people at the Villa, I watched carefully for actions that would suggest sorrow and joy. On the surface, I was only able to find sorrow and pain. James, a man that sits at the same table as the man I feed, was a minister before his retirement. During his ministry he could bring people to the Lord, now he can not bring a fork to his mouth. I am not sure if James sees this as a sorrow, but I feel sorrow for him when I see this.*

June: *As I was contemplating how to strike up a significant conversation, one of the dear women turned and asked me, 'Honey, did you ever think an old person's home could be like THIS?' I fumbled my way through a shabby, 'Oh, I had no idea.' It was a great revelation to hear this woman talk about how she enjoys the activities, informality, and sense of family at the Villa. She chuckled when she said that it's no big deal when you can't remember some-one's name, as long as you remember their story and care about them. This was a joy to her. At the same time, a bittersweet feeling had a home in her speech, as we have also discussed how said it is to leave behind precious homes, recipes, freedoms, and abilities.*

Personally, my greatest joy in serving at the Villa is realizing my own smallness, yet ability to make an impact. This happens when I see that my presence is not crucial to the operations there, but by doing my work with joy, I am serving people. Truly, I am the one best served. I leave with a feeling that, though my day with my peers may be so-so and I am not the most beautiful or popular student, there is a part of me that is deeper and longer lasting than those things.

Lehla: *Today I volunteered for the activity of nail painting. I came to learn about the feelings of the residents as much as I did the manicure. I came across this lady who has been staying at the Villa for the last ten years. She has two children and she said they never come to visit her. When I asked her more about them she said she does not want to talk about it. She was sad. And then, in order to cheer her, I told her a funny joke.*

In Nepal too, where I am from, some families have abandoned old people but since the government of Nepal does not have proper old residential houses they go to the temples and become "Yogis" (holy people). While they can stay at the temple for shelter, they have to beg for their food.

CULTURE CHANGE: EDUCATING THE NEXT GENERATION

While there are a variety of practice models for culture change in long-term care there are few pedagogical models in higher education which are designed to help students grow from their experiences with this distinctive approach to care for frail elders. Creating such an educational design fits well into the changes that are developing in higher education in general. As Grauerholz, McKenzie, and Momero (1999: 594) write:

> Perhaps more than at any previous period in the academy's history, the pedagogical challenges, and the possibilities and means for meeting these, are tremendous. . . . we must recognize the exciting opportunity before us: we are in a position to reshape our own futures and those of our students in significant ways.

Education in on-site culture change demands something different from the traditional practicum or field experience in gerontology. Such experiences have tended to be, like most of formal education, *instruction centered* and not *learning centered*. The formal educational paradigm sees the classroom instructor or field supervisor as providing the content and direction of the educational experience whether it is academic content or field based. The learning paradigm suggests that faculty are primary designers (not directors) of learning in *conjunction* with students. In the learning paradigm, as presented by Barr and Tagg (1999), faculty work with students in teams. In the case of culture change this team involves staff and residents of long-term care facilities. Staff and college faculty work with students to give them *choices* about what their activities include, as documented in this article.

The Soul of Education by Kessler (2001) is a text that has been used in developing the Hesston-Villa culture change learning paradigm. Although the text does not explicitly focus on person-centered care involving students and elders, key themes have proved helpful in small group discussions of youth and elders, including: yearning for deep connection; longing for silence and solitude; the search for meaning; hunger for joy; the creative drive; and the urge for transcendence. When used strategically, this text allows elders and youth to function simultaneously as *teachers* and *learners* working along with college faculty and Villa staff.

Unlimited Love: Compassion, Service, and Altruism by Post (2003) is another text that is not aimed specifically at older adult education yet is useful in developing a pedagogy of learning in person-centered care. Post writes that in compassionate education "a new self–is released from the old self." This idea of the new self fits well the Latin root of the word education–*educare*, which means to "lead-out." In education at its best, a new person is led-out from the former self. This transformative experience can be a powerful one for youth and elders inasmuch as both at points in the journey of life where the search for self-identity is especially critical. While youth is struggling with the issue of intimacy and isolation elders are struggling with issues of ego-integrity and despair (Erikson 1983). Person-centered care can help frail elders respond in a positive way to a negative self concept. Frail elders in this process find "reasons to grow old–meaning in later life" (Manheimer, 1999-2000:5).

Person-centered pedagogy, borrowing from the words of Leader (1999-2000:40) ". . . views the process of aging as a profound curriculum for the soul that is capable of enhancing both inward contemplation and service to others." When engaged in person-centered care in long-term care, youth may develop a greater degree of intimacy and a sense of self-efficacy–the belief that a person can make a positive difference in their own life and in the lives of others. Moreover in person-centered education youth have the opportunity of learning from elders–a key learning in the development of the next generation.

This vision is expressed in the words of Carol Thiezsen (2003), Director of Volunteers at Schowalter Villa, who identifies the importance of educating the next generation in culture change:

> These interactions between Hesston students and Villa elders set the stage for contributions and exchanges for the future. Young adults college students are business owners, community leaders and service providers of the future. Those students involved in culture change who receive a positive experience are probably more likely to become involved in a nursing home at a later date. This may be through business donations if he or she should be become a business owner or manager. Or it may be by wanting their children to experience intergenerational opportunities with older adults. They may come with their toddlers and/or encourage them as teenagers to be involved in school or civic organizations. There's always the possibility of stirring their career goals to work in a long-term care facility. This small project of students and elders has potentially far-reaching ramifications for choices and behaviors not only as the students age but also as their parents age and they are faced with long-term care decisions. By exposing the students to positive experiences with older adults, hopefully negative stereotypes of "old" are changed to a positive understanding of aging.

Even more broadly, we can hope that the experience of work in long-term care can help students think about their own future and their own spiritual development over the life-course. On this point, C. G. Jung observed that western society does not prepare people for growing old. More specifically, Jung writes (1987:17):

Our religions were always such schools in the past (where youth was prepared for age) but how many people regard them as such today? How many of us older ones have been brought up in such a school and really were prepared for the second half of life, for old age, death, and eternity?

Perhaps engaging young adults in the work of culture change in long-term care and in an active learning paradigm can prove to be a corrective for this lack of attention to preparation for old age noted by Jung.

CONCLUSIONS

This article has focused upon the involvement of young adult students at Hesston College with frail elders at Schowalter Villa in the process of culture change. The experience to date has been that both age groups benefit. Given the dramatic demographic aging of America it is important that coming generations become more aware of these benefits and become involved with elders in this new approach to long-term care. Most importantly perhaps is the lesson that frail elders have to teach the non-frail of any age. This lesson is well expressed in an article by Wendy Lustbader entitled "Thoughts on the Meaning of Frailty" (1999-2000:24). Lustbader tells of the Sufi idea that two veils separate humans from the divine–health and security. As people enter and live in long-term care facilities they are in the process of losing both of these traits. In spiritual terms they are more likely to experience the divine. The frail elders–"the least of these"–can teach eternal realities. Their experience with woe can become a path toward infinite joy, toward knowing the divine. In the words of William Blake (2003):

And when this we rightly know.
Joy and woe are woven fine.
A clothing for the fire divine.
Under every grief and pine
Runs a joy with silken twine.

NOTE

In coming semesters plans are to quantitatively measure the effects on college students who are involved in culture change at Schowalter Villa. The research will use a pre-test and a post-test based upon the Bandura Self-Efficacy Paradigm. The Perceived Competence and Functioning Inventory (PCFI) will be used in this process. The PCFI measurements include role competence, self-competence, and relational cognition (Bandura 1997). The research hypothesis will be that the students and elders will increase in their sense of self-efficacy based in their intergenerational interaction.

REFERENCES

Bandura, A. (1997). *Self-efficacy: The exercise of control*. New York: W.H. Freeman Company.

Barr, R.B., and Tagg, J. (1999). From teaching to learning: A new paradigm for undergraduate education. (pp. 564-581). *The social worlds of higher education: Handbook for teaching in a new century*. (Eds.) B.A. Pescosolido and R. Aminzade, Thousand Oaks, CA: Pine Forge Press.

Bell, V., and Troxel, D. (2003). Ten ways to change the culture of long-term care in the U.S. (p. 13). *Aging Today: The bi-monthly Newspaper of the American Society on Aging*. XXIV(1).

Bianchi, E. (1986). *Aging as a Spiritual Journey*. New York: Crossroads Publishing.

Blake, W. (2003). "Auguries of Innocence." http://www.online-literature.com/blake/ 612/

Campbell, J. (1990). *The Power of Myth*. New York: Doubleday.

Cole, T.R., and Winkler, M.G. (Eds.) (1994). *The oxford book of aging: Reflections on the journey of life*. New York: Oxford University Press.

Culture Change Now. (2003). http://www.culturechangenow.com/people/ Milwaukee: Action Pact, Inc. E-mail: brendan@actionpact.com

Eden Alternative (2003). *http://www.edenalt.com/* Sherburne, NY. E-mail: contact@ denalt.com

Erikson, E. (1983). *The life cycle completed*. New York: Norton.

Grauerholz, E., McKenzie, B., and Momero, M. (1999). Beyond these walls: Teaching within and outside the expanded classroom–Boundaries in the 21st century. (pp. 582-600). *The social worlds of higher education: Handbook for teaching in a new century*. (Eds.) B.A. Pescosolido and R. Aminzade, Thousand Oaks, CA: Pine Forge Press.

Greene, L., and Sharman-Burke, J. (2000). *The mystic journey: The meaning of myth as a guide for life*. New York: Simon and Schuster.

Guttman, D. (1994). *Reclaimed powers: Towards a new psychology of men and women in later life*. New York: Basic books.

Hammarsskjold, D. (1972). *Markings*. New York: Alfred A. Knopf.

Heschel, A.J. (1985). The older person and the family in perspective (pp. 35-44). *Aging and the human spirit: A Reader in religion and gerontology*. (Eds.) C. LeFevre and P. LeFevre. Chicago: Exploration Press.

Holburn, S., and Vietze, P.M. (2002). *Person-centered planning: Research, practice, and future directions*. Baltimore: Paul H. Brooks Publishing.

Jung, C.G. (1987). *The portable jung*. New York: Penguin Books.

Kessler, R. (2000). *The soul of education: Helping students find connection, compassion, and character at school*. Alexandria, VA: The Association for Supervision and Curriculum.

Leader, D. (1999-2000). Aging into the spirit: From traditional wisdom to innovative programs and communities: A quarrel with the 'successful aging' model. *Generations: Journal of the American Society on Aging* (pp. 36-41). XXIII (4).

Lustbader, W. (1999-2000). Thoughts on the meaning of frailty. *Generations: Journal of the American Society on Aging*. (pp. 21-24). XXIII (4).

Manheimer, R. (Eds.) (1999-2000). Introduction: Is it practical to search for meaning? *Generations: Journal of the American Society on Aging*. (pp. 5-7). XXIII(4).

Marcuse, H. (1955). *Eros and civilization*. New York: Vintage Books.

Matthew 25:31-46. (1973). *New American standard bible*. LaHabra, CA: The Lockman Foundation.

Myerhoff, B. (1978). *Number our days*. New York: Simon and Schuster.

Otto, R. (1963). *The idea of the holy*. New York: Oxford University Press.

PEAK. (2003). *Promoting excellent alternatives in Kansas. http://www.ksu.edu/peak*

Post, S.G. (2002). *Unlimited love: Altruism, compassion, and service*. Radnor, PA: Templeton Foundation Press.

Theiszen, C. (2003). Volunteer coordinator. Interview at Schowalter Villa Retirement Community. October 15. Hesston, KS.

Turner, V. (1978). Introduction, xiii-xvii. In B. Myerhoff's *Number our Days*. New York: Simon and Schuster.

Autobiography as a Spiritual Practice

John-Raphael Staude, PhD

SUMMARY. In this article autobiography is defined as "a dialogue of the self with itself in the present about the past for the sake of self-understanding." Spirituality involves connectedness to oneself, others, nature and to a larger meaning. It is associated with creativity, play, wisdom, faith, and a sense of oneness. Writing and reflecting on one's autobiography enhances spiritual growth and can be therapeutic, freeing people from outlived roles and self-imposed images. After discussing the history of spiritual autobiography as a genre, the author compares and contrasts four approaches to autobiography: the structured life review, the guided autobiography, the intensive journal workbook, and autobiographical work in twelve-step programs. For those who work with older persons these techniques should prove very useful. *[Article copies available for a fee from The Haworth Document Delivery Service: 1-800-HAWORTH. E-mail address: <docdelivery@haworthpress.com> Website: <http://www.HaworthPress.com> © 2005 by The Haworth Press, Inc. All rights reserved.]*

[Haworth co-indexing entry note]: "Autobiography as a Spiritual Practice." Staude, John-Raphael. Co-published simultaneously in *Journal of Gerontological Social Work* (The Haworth Social Work Practice Press, an imprint of The Haworth Press, Inc.) Vol. 45, No. 3, 2005, pp. 249-269; and: *Religion, Spirituality, and Aging: A Social Work Perspective* (ed: Harry R. Moody) The Haworth Social Work Practice Press, an imprint of The Haworth Press, Inc., 2005, pp. 249-269. Single or multiple copies of this article are available for a fee from The Haworth Document Delivery Service [1-800-HAWORTH, 9:00 a.m. - 5:00 p.m. (EST). E-mail address: docdelivery@haworthpress.com].

Available online at http://www.haworthpress.com/web/JGSW
doi:10.1300/J083v45n03_01

KEYWORDS. Autobiographical consciousness, guided autobiography, spiritual autobiography, confession, creativity, family histories, life-review, memoir, memory, spirituality, spiritual disciplines, story-telling, wisdom

I became a great question to myself.

–Saint Augustine

INTRODUCTION

In this article I will discuss the writing of and reflection upon our life stories as a tool for spiritual growth and healing of unfinished life issues for older adults. As an adult educator and counselor, I have frequently invited individuals and groups to explore and share their life stories for the sake of personal growth and self-understanding. I have also taught autobiography and memoir writing classes for seniors. In most cases I have found that my students and clients became fascinated with the process of life story writing, and they seemed to learn a lot about themselves and others from these exercises. Although it was not therapy as such, it was therapeutic, for it often freed people from unresolved conflicts in the past and from outlived roles and self-imposed images they had been trapped in for too long. Reflecting on their autobiography after it was written often brought people an appreciation of their own inner wisdom, which revealed itself in their stories.

Here is an example: One sixty-nine-year-old woman who had had a difficult childhood wrote that earlier in her life she had felt as if she was a passive observer "on a river being carried away by the stream without being able to control it and carried away from both pleasant and unpleasant things." After reflection on her life story she wrote that "Today I feel like the river. I feel that I'm part of the flow that contains both the pleasant and the unpleasant things." Now she feels that she "participates in a wider circle, in humanity."

Spiritual autobiography is a history and interpretation of a person's life written by the person who experienced it, considered in relation to its spiritual foundations. In other words, it is our life story viewed from a spiritual perspective. I find this approach has been particularly helpful and successful with older adults who often have a spiritual perspective for finding meaning in their lives (Birren and Hedland, 1987; Birren and Birren, 1996; McFadden, 2000a; Randall and Kenyon, 2001; Sulmasy, 2002) and want to bring it into their writing.

In my writing classes with older adults I define spirituality very broadly as the personal experience of connectedness and relationship to something transcendent, however that may be construed. Spirit in its many manifestations–love, art, music, poetry, nature–is all around us, everywhere. I find that everyone has a spiritual history–a history of their personal relationship with spirit or soul–even if they have not thought of it in these terms before (Atchley, 2000; Casey, 1991; Moody, 1997; Moore, 2002; Sulmasy, 2002). An easy way to access this history is to make a list of significant moments, I call them "stepping stones," following Progoff (1975), in one's spiritual and creative life. For example, aside from experiences in a designated sacred place like a church, one might recall an experience of feeling the divine Presence in a sunset, or witnessing a beautiful wedding ceremony, or attending a glorious uplifting presentation of Mozart's *Magic Flute*, Handel's *Messiah* or Beethoven's *Ninth Symphony*, and feeling deeply moved. Alternatively, one might have felt a sense of the sublime in Nature when watching the night sky or the churning wild waters of the ocean crashing on the rocks in the moonlight, or flying above the luminous clouds in a supersonic jumbo jet airliner.

WHAT IS AUTOBIOGRAPHY?

Before launching into a deeper discussion of teaching spiritual autobiography writing to older adults, however, I want to consider some aspects of teaching general autobiography writing of which spiritual autobiography is a subgenre. A theme that almost always comes up in my autobiography classes with older adults is recollections of family members, particularly parents and grandparents. Some people bring in pictures of their ancestors and actually commit themselves to writing a detailed and extensive biography of their mother or father as a person whose memory they want to pass on to their children and their children's children. Sometimes they feel it is more important for them to write about that deceased parent than it is to write about themselves. There seems to be a deeply felt almost instinctive need to connect with our ancestors and to situate ourselves as an essential link across the generations with a sense of mission to bear witness to those who come after us in the great chain of time. If our goal in writing self-narratives is to get to know ourselves and our roots, what better starting point could there be than to examine the crucible of our family's history and to recall and record the deeds of our ancestors?

Genealogy is of great interest, too. It is understandable that as we grow older and become more like them we identify more and more with the old ones, the grandfathers and the great-grandmothers in our family history. As Hillman (1999) pointed out, we cannot extend our lives into the future, but we can expand backwards into times before we were born and beyond the immediate historical past even into archaic times. As psychotherapist Mandy Aftel (1996) points out, autobiography can be liberating. It gives us a chance to set things right, to tell our side of the story, and hopefully to forgive perceived and remembered injustices inflicted upon us, or at least to make peace with the past. The work is cumulative. Those writing with a spiritual perspective claim to recognize the hand of a Higher Power at work in their lives and through their autobiographical work may recognize a greater meaning in their lives than they were aware of before.

For many older adults, especially those in institutional settings, events of daily life often damage feelings of identity and self-worth. Writing one's autobiography can reinforce the belief that one's life is meaningful. The revitalization of power and a feeling of meaning in life that comes from autobiographical reflection can be very satisfying. Through writing about and reflecting upon their life stories, and discussing them in groups, older adults can be helped to come to terms with their lives, to overcome a passive victim perspective, and to meet future changes with increased confidence and competence (Aftel, 1996; Randall and Kenyon, 2001).

Autobiographical consciousness is prospective as much as it is retrospective. The self of the autobiographer exists as something unfinished, full of potentiality, always overflowing the actuality. Autobiography is a dialogue of the self with itself in the present about the past for the purpose of self-understanding. "Since there is no one true description of the past there is no one 'true text' " (Charmé, 1984) and "anyone can reel off multiple autobiographies of his own life" (Bruner, 1990).

We all practice the craft of autobiography every day in our inner conversations about the meaning of our experiences and those conversations, no matter what language or metaphors we use, are fundamentally philosophical and theological by their very nature in that they are concerned with meaning and values. So although only some of us actually set about writing down the results of these autobiographical reflections and ruminations and perhaps publish them for others to read, we are all autobiographers. Few of us, however, give much attention to the prevailing culturally and gender-determined forms and tropes through which we see, interpret, and report ourselves to ourselves (Conway, 1998).

As Kenyon and Randall (1997) point out, an autobiography imposes structure on a lived life. Whereas entries in a journal may freely take whatever form the spirit prescribes, events and experiences recounted in an autobiography are bound by the discipline of temporality, the ordinance of time. An autobiography like any extended narrative must be plotted and have a beginning, a middle and an end. This simple requirement forces a premature closure on our still unfolding experience. Related to the closure issue is the pressure to construct a happy ending for ourselves, which may lead us to portray the present as one in which we have arrived in some way, have found some solutions to the long standing issues of our life or at least have summoned the courage to commit ourselves to write. There is even pressure to get outside our own death and preview the shape of our life in the future before we have completely lived it.

According to Nan Phifer, a teacher of spiritual autobiography writing, who has written an excellent introductory manual on the subject, "the work of writing an autobiography is the work of finding out who you really are. Writing an autobiography takes you on a journey into the roots of your own life that may reveal to you aspects of yourself you didn't even know existed. It involves the reconstruction of the *movement of your life*–or part of your life–in the actual circumstances in which it was lived. Its *center of interest is your soul, not the outside world;* yet the outside world must appear so that the authorial personality can find its particular shape in give and take with it" (Phifer, 2002).

"Autobiography is not just a *reconstruction* of the past but an *interpretation*," says Roy Pascal. "It is a *judgment on the past within the framework of the present. . . .* Autobiography is an interplay, a collusion, between past and present; its significance is indeed more the revelation of the present situation than the uncovering of the past. . . . In autobiography the *spiritual identity* of the personality is sought as it is *expressed in its concrete experienced reality*" (Pascal, 1985).

Why do older people write autobiographies? People write autobiographies to recollect the past and preserve that memory for future generations. For example, in her eighties, like many another grandmother, my mother wrote and dedicated her memoirs to me, "that knowing from whence he came, he may better carry the torch I hand him while passing it on to his sons." Writing an autobiography may be motivated by a desire for reunion, integration, or construction of a unit self, to replace the longed for unattainable lost security and union with mother, recollected from our earliest moments of consciousness.

There are other motives for autobiography. One may wish to provide understanding of the meaning of what seemed to be an emotionally powerful and important experience in one's life, such as participation in a war. Or, through writing about one's life one may attain emotional release, catharsis, or self-healing, freeing oneself from a painful or inadequately integrated past experience, such as the loss of a loved one, as did James Agee, C.S. Lewis, and Simone de Beauvoir in their memoirs of "a death in the family."

Autobiographers may write to teach, advise, convert or warn others, particularly the next generation, or they may be engaged in a process of self-justification or self-confirmation, seeking to influence themselves and their future through understanding and highlighting aspects of their past in a positive way (Gaustad, 1999; Conway, 1998; Murdock, 2003).

AUTOBIOGRAPHY AND HISTORY

Our life stories take place within a historical context, in a particular society in a particular place and time, yet few of us take this into account when we write or tell our life stories. However, by privatizing our stories we diminish our understanding of the larger structures and forces that shaped us, our choices and our decisions, and even the myths and metaphors which we use to tell our stories.

"All autobiography is personal history," says cultural historian Carl Schorske of Princeton University. [It is] "a narrative construction that involves both remembering and forgetting, evoking some parts of one's past and repressing others. Yet most autobiographers define their past on a narrow band of personal experience, with little reference to the wider world. Through ever-renewed encounters with the shifting elements in the stream of history one can come to know oneself in the present, and also acquire an altered understanding of what one has been in the past. In autobiography, to *think with history* helps to establish a certain distance from oneself by seeing it as both shaped by the structures and conflicts of society, and as responding creatively to their pressures. Thus if I reflect in my life story the larger developments of the society, I also reflect (as knowing subject) on that particular historical consciousness, its formation and changes, that my personal encounters with my time elicited as modes of coming to terms with it, whether by resistance or adaptation" (Schorske, 1998).

And the distinguished historian of American religious experience, Edward Gaustad, tells us that "Memory is always fallible, and history is always partial. Yet these two weak reeds do lean upon each other, do inevitably depend on each other. Memory provides the initial impetus for history, while history becomes a reinforcement, possibly even a validation of memory. Like wounded warriors, the two support each other as they make their way toward a brighter light" (Gaustad, 1999).

At the same time it must be pointed out that to write an autobiography successfully one must be able to distance oneself from the tyranny of historical facts, and be able to conceive of one's life metaphorically searching for underlying motifs and patterns. Furthermore, to fully benefit from reading autobiographies one must free oneself from excessive concern with the accuracy of the works as historical documents, in order to savor the quality of the central personality revealing itself at the core of the life being recalled and recounted.

Jung's *Memories, Dreams, and Reflections* (1961) is a good example of this rule. It is filled with small historical inaccuracies, and even gaps in the biographical narrative, but he was not concerned to tell the history of his times or his involvement with them. Intent on communicating the wisdom he had accumulated over his long life, he dictated a spiritual autobiography, an account of his encounters with his guiding spirit and with his demons and of the works that emerged out of his psycho-spiritual alchemical endeavors. Reading this book more than any of his other works one feels his genius at work and his living presence on the page though he is long gone.

Jung spoke of the development of one's self as a vocation or calling. The same might be said about autobiography. Whether it is consciously thought of as "spiritual" or not, there is a call within human beings that leads us towards discovering and "disclosing a life story that is progressively bigger and better, and more embracing of our actual existence." Kenyon and Randall (1997) have identified this as the "autobiographical imperative" and with Mary Catherine Bateson the process of responding to it "composing our lives" (Bateson, 1989).

WHAT IS SPIRITUALITY?

Before moving into further discussion of spiritual autobiography let us briefly consider the nature of spirituality. We said above that spiritual autobiography is a self-narrative considered in relation to its spiritual foundations or with what is our "ultimate concern." Atchley (2002) defines spirituality or *ultimate concern* as "an inner region of human awareness within which people experience the sacred as a higher power, whether this be called the Absolute, Allah, Buddha, Yahweh, the Tao, Christ or Krishna Consciousness, Nature, or God."[1] One might include Christ Consciousness and the Holy Spirit in this category as well.

Spirituality is a transformational process through which the different aspects of life are integrated (physical, emotional, occupational, intellectual, and relational). It involves a connectedness to oneself, others, nature, and to a larger meaning or Presence. It is strongly associated with creativity, play, love, forgiveness, compassion, trust, reverence, wisdom, faith and a sense of oneness.

Some level of spiritual awareness is present in the life of each person. Whether one's need for meaning is met within a formal religious structure, or outside religion altogether, a person's search for meaning seems to be fundamentally and universally human. Many people express their spirituality in religious practice. Others express it in their relationships with nature, the arts, philosophy, or relationships with friends and family.

One can argue that the term "spiritual" must be differentiated from religious and that spiritual need not refer to God. According to Reker (2003) for example, there are three components to a spiritual experience: inner-connectedness, human compassion, and connectedness with nature. Some writers like Sulmasy view religion as a subcategory of the spiritual rather than the reverse. I agree with Pargament that spirituality should not be separated from the concept of the sacred for "what is it that makes the categories 'meaning in life' or 'interconnectedness' spiritual unless they are somehow sacralized? Invoking the label *spiritual* adds luster and legitimacy to any number of values and practices, but the label may ultimately lose meaning and power when it is separated from its sacred core" (Pargament, 1997).

Of course, people have written spiritual autobiographies without reference to God, but historically in the Western spiritual tradition at least, most have been accounts of a person's very personal relationship to the sacred, which they have usually identified with God.

A BRIEF HISTORY OF SPIRITUAL AUTOBIOGRAPHY

When in the history of Western civilization did attention begin to turn to examining one's inner life? It is already evident in the papyri of ancient Egypt in a dialogue of a man with his soul and in the Hebrew Bible in the stories of Abraham, Moses, Joseph, and Solomon, and in the Psalms of David, in which David examined his conscience and confessed his sins to God (Mandelker and Powers, 1999).

With the philosophical autobiographies of Socrates and Marcus Aurelius we can witness their quest for truth and understanding, see how they were engaged in self-examination, and how they made an active effort to resolve their moral and spiritual conflicts. As all autobiographers have done since, these men engaged in moments of self-assessment and reflection, stepping outside the flow of experience to ascribe meaning and give shape to the past.

Although the foundations for the modern form of spiritual autobiography were established by Saint Paul in the New Testament, undoubtedly the most significant figure in the evolution of spiritual autobiography was Saint Augustine (354-430), whose *Confessions* influenced every autobiographer from Dante, Petrarch, Saint Theresa, and Saint Ignatius to modern religious autobiographers such as Dorothy Day, Bede Griffiths, Thomas Merton, and C. S. Lewis.

In his *Confessions*, Augustine utilized the old trope of the epic quest, but here it is internalized; the goal of the quest is not external (such as the Golden Fleece of the Argonauts) nor even the goal of coming home (Ulysses). The goal of Augustine's *itinererium mentis* is to be found within his own heart. But this was a very difficult quest to achieve because Augustine found he was an enigma to himself. How could the mind hope to contain the mystery of God? "The house of my soul is too narrow for thee," he wrote. But then "I do not myself grasp all that I am," he realized and he became amazed at the discovery of the depths and heights of his own soul (*Confessions*, Bk. 10).

Long before Dante's *Divine Comedy*, Augustine traced a mental pilgrimage from sin through conversion and repentance to beatitude. He recounted how God rescued him from his wayward life and false beliefs. Augustine recorded both the most significant moments in his interactions with God, such as his conversion, and the mystical experience he shared with his mother, and the anxiety and guilt he felt about his sinfulness, particularly his addiction to sex. But despite all his ups and downs the reader detects Augustine's amazement that God graciously rescued him from his errant ideas and self-destructive behaviors. Nevertheless, despite the moments of ecstasy and his mystical visions, one senses in the text that his existential anxiety never left him, and his all too human vulnerability makes him accessible to us and his book a model of courageous honesty and forthright self-disclosure.

Following the example of Augustine, the basic plot structure of most classic spiritual autobiographies contains four parts: (1) a description of the individual's life before spiritual awakening; (2) an account of the events leading up to the individual's encounter with God; (3) a description of the actual encounter with God and the impact of this event on the narrator; and (4) a celebration of the new life following this event. There are few surprises or changes in this basic story line even in modern revisitations.

Although the classic spiritual autobiography was called a *Confession*, this was–and is–often not so much a confession as a type of testimonial intended to sway the reader to the author's way of belief. Recounting one's spiritual autobiographies has sometimes been described as "first person evangelization." The idea of providing witness reappeared in the term "personal testimony" introduced by the American puritans. Yet the personal testimony is more than a conversion narrative, as it continues to relate the spiritual progress and growth of the confessor as a proof of God's power and love.

Contemporary spiritual autobiographies, such as Dag Hammarskjöld's *Markings*, Kathleen Norris's *Dakota: A Spiritual Geography*, and Annie Dillard's *An American Childhood*, often have a *secular* starting point and are no longer based on a conventionally religious worldview. Curiously, this perspective brings them closer to their antecedents in antiquity, such as those by Saints Paul and Augustine and others who sought God while living in a pagan world. The works of Day, Merton, Lewis, and other modern spiritual autobiographies indicate how the shadow of God persists even in a faithless world.

CHRISTIAN SPIRITUALITY AUTOBIOGRAPHIES

According to Richard Peace, a well-known Christian author of a manual on the subject, "a spiritual autobiography is the story of God's interaction in our lives. It chronicles out pilgrimage as we seek to follow God" (Peace, 1998). According to Mandelker and Powers (1999), editors of an anthology of spiritual writings, "unlike sister genres–travelogues and family memoirs–spiritual autobiographies focus on events and experiences that shape the *inner* person in relation to God. The authors of spiritual autobiographies concentrate on examining their interior experiences in order to discover coherence, structure, and meaning in the shape of an individual life."

From a Christian point of view, according to Peace, writing a spiritual autobiography is a way of attempting to bridge the gap between the natural and the spiritual worlds and of becoming sensitized to the hidden work of God in our lives–and in the process becoming a whole person. From this perspective, writing a spiritual autobiography can be called a *spiritual discipline* or practice because it teaches us a new way of seeing God, ourselves, our world, and our relationship with God and of appreciating God's action in our lives.

Perhaps the main reason to write and reflect on our spiritual autobiographies, Christian writers from Augustine to C. S. Lewis (1956), Merton (1948), Moore (2002), and Peace (1998) tell us, is so that we will grow as followers of our Lord, who embodies our spiritual ideal of Christian adulthood. It is a matter of discernment of God's action in our lives. First we develop skill in noticing God and His grace at work in our lives. Second, by seeing our stories as a whole, we may come to understand at a new level God's intentions for us (Peace, 1998).

Most Christians believe that everyone has a God-designated role to play in the world, though each role is different. This is where faith is important, says the Christian autobiographer. We can only understand our particular role fully when we see our lives in the context of divine love. Then we can see how the pieces fit together and discern how seemingly unrelated elements, past and present, have combined to prepare us for our various works. From this theological perspective, as we review our lives we may come to see that God has been present and active in our lives from the beginning. Through working on our life stories we may gain a growing sense of being sheltered in the loving arms of God. In understanding the meaning of our past, we may understand better the meaning of the present, and glimpse something of what the future might hold. Knowing our past, and willingly accepting the consequences of decisions we have made, helps us in our decisions about the future. Sensing the meaning of our lives, we can then make choices that are consistent with that meaning (Peace, 1998; Moore, 2002).

AUTOBIOGRAPHY AND PSYCHOLOGY

According to McFadden (2000b), from a psychological perspective we can say that writing a spiritual autobiography presents adults with an opportunity to reflect upon formative experiences across the life span that have contributed to their current religious and spiritual orientations. By engaging in this process, older adults often realize the sources of many of their beliefs and feelings about religious institutions, creeds, persons, and experiences.

The past is never dead. In fact, it is always changing in the light of the present. We live in an ever changing world, past, present and future. In any life, in light of present experiences, there can be moments of self-assessment and reflection when a person may step outside the flow of immediate experience and ascribe new meanings (Kenyon, 2000) and attend to memories that now appear to have a new life of their own (Murdock, 2003). In looking back over our lives we try to pick out the connecting threads, to see themes and patterns of as Henry James put it "the figure in the carpet."

THE STRUCTURED LIFE REVIEW [2]

Psychiatrist and gerontologist Robert Butler developed the concept of the Life Review in the early 1960s and put it to therapeutic use with individuals. He describes the life review process as one "characterized by the progressive return to consciousness of past experiences and particularly the resurgence of unresolved conflicts that can be looked at again and reintegrated. If the reintegration is successful it can give new significance and meaning to one's life" (Butler, 1963). He asserted both the significance and the universality of life review among all people as they age and, particularly, as they become more aware of their own mortality. The significance of life review lies in its relationship to the completion of the life cycle of the person. The goal, Butler said, is integration of the personality. Over the course of a structured review of a person's life, if all goes well, the subject will find meaning and value in his or her life as it has been lived. People who have used the method of life-review with older adults have reported remarkable results.

Haight and Webster (1995) have compiled a protocol of fifty six suggested standard questions that have been drawn from years of experience conducting structured life reviews. Here is a sample of some of the Life Review questions that one might use to bring up autobiographical material particularly relevant for a spiritual autobiography: (1) What is the first thing you remember about your life? (2) Did someone close to you die when you were growing up? (3) On the whole, what kind of life do you think you had? (4) Did you give and receive love well? (5) Did you use your gifts in a way that you feel benefited others as well as yourself? (6) Can you now see positive outcomes or blessings in some events that at the time they happened appeared to be wholly negative?

(7) If you could live your life over again, what would you change, if anything?

Since Butler's initial article appeared, some questions have been raised as to whether this process of reminiscence is really universal among older people. Critics have argued that life review does not appear to be a universal process, that it does not appear to be precipitated by approaching death, that there is no evidence linking it with age or approaching death, and that there appears to be no discernable pattern with regard to life review and life satisfaction.

According to Webster and Young (1988), a life review must cover the entire lifespan and must contain (a) recall, (b) integration, and (c) evaluation. Burnside (1996) observed that life review is not merely a perfunctory reliving of the past. It has to have a purpose and that purpose must be the discovery of meaning, and the achievement of integrity. We might also call it cohesiveness (Kaufman, 1986; Kenyon, 2000; McFadden, 2000a).

THE GUIDED AUTOBIOGRAPHY METHOD[3]

Another psychologically based technique for generating autobiographical reflection is the Guided Autobiography method developed by James Birren. "Guided autobiography is a method of obtaining histories of lives organized according to major themes that are commonly experienced" (Birren and Birren, 1996). This involves story telling and story listening in a non-judgmental atmosphere of mutual respect with no master narrative in mind. Each guided autobiography session begins with a group activity in which the leader discusses with the participants a particular theory of human development or examines different aspects of the story metaphor. In the second part of each session the participants are introduced to a selected theme for the day by means of sensitizing a particular part of their life stories. They are encouraged to address this theme in their own unique way and may use literature, poetry and metaphors to do so.

While Birren recognizes that the role of religion and spirituality is often very significant in the lives of older adults, it is generally not singled out as a special theme except when used with groups for whom the spiritual component is an essential aspect of their worldview. The first theme is about finding a metaphor to characterize one's life as a whole whether a branching tree or some other image. A search for this metaphor is also raised in the first session of Progoff's Intensive Journal

Work, to be discussed below. Other themes include telling the story of our life work or career, health, lovers and significant others in our lives, our view of money, of death and dying, and our dreams and aspirations, including exploring how we find meaning in our lives.

The themes must be flexible and reflect the interests and backgrounds represented in the group. Having been introduced to the theme, persons spend the remainder of the session in personal reflection on that theme. As part of this process they write two pages on how that theme relates to their lives. This written part of their life story forms the basis for discussion in small groups during the following session.

Attesting to the adaptive nature of autobiographical writing and reflection, Birren and Deutchman found the following outcomes:

- Sense of increased personal power and importance;
- Recognition of past adaptive strategies and application to current needs and problems;
- Reconciliation with the past and resolution of past resentments and negative feelings;
- Resurgence of interest in past activities or hobbies;
- Development of friendships with other group members;
- Greater sense of meaning in life;
- Ability to face the nearing end of life with a feeling that one has contributed to the world.

According to Birren, Guided Autobiography is an excellent instrument for "entering the internal world of the individual" and "it has been further posited that it provides unique insights into issues of spiritual development and the role of religion and maturation." While scholars in theology and letters have looked at confessional literature, it is only recently that psychology and the social sciences have recognized that many older persons interpret their lives in religious or spiritual terms (Birren and Birren, 1996). The healing that comes from being part of a guided autobiography group has particular value at specific phases of the lifespan. For example, retirement or moving into a smaller home as one grows older is an advantageous time to review one's life, as new plans or alternative possibilities for the future may be explored. Also, following difficult life events such as the loss of a job or a spouse, health changes or financial reversals are appropriate times to re-examine one's life history in order to see more clearly one's strengths and weaknesses and from this knowledge base to make plans for the future (Birren and Birren, 1996).

THE INTENSIVE JOURNAL WORKBOOK [4]

Another psychologically based method of autobiographical work was developed by a Jungian psychologist, Ira Progoff. Although the primary instrument is called an "intensive journal," actually it is a structured workbook divided into a number of broad categories including: the daily log, or diary; the period log, which we use to understand the period in our lives we are now in; and dialogues with persons, such as parents and significant others, works and projects, our relationship with society, and dialogues with our bodies. The next section Progoff calls *The Depth Dimension*. In it are included *dreams and dreamwork*, active imagination or what he calls *twilight imagery*, and a *dialogue with our inner wisdom*. *The Lifetime Dimension* includes a *life history log, stepping-stones, intersections* and *NOW: The Open Moment*. Finally there is what Progoff calls *the Meaning Dimension*, which includes meditations, mantras, and explorations of peak experiences.

According to Progoff, this workbook provides "an integrated system of writing exercises for accessing your feelings and experiences in an organized way." Through writing in sections of this cross-referenced workbook issues that may have been difficult to describe become tangible and accessible. It is claimed by Progoff that in the workbook a person approaches his or her life themes from several perspectives, overcomes obstacles and resistances, and gains inner awareness of underlying patterns and meanings in one's life (Progoff, 1975).

One can learn how to use the Intensive Journal through reading Progoff's manual *At a Journal Workshop* (1975), but it is preferable to attend a workshop in which one can learn and practice the tools and techniques. These introductory workshops take place around the country in groups, often large groups. But the groups are not interactive as Birren's groups are. Here everyone works in silence and participants are not required to read from their writing if they do not wish to. According to Progoff "Growth takes place in a person by working at a deep inner level in a sustained atmosphere of silence. It is the inner process of subjective experience that draws a person's life together so that it can find its direction and eventually reach its meaning."

The first session begins with the *Period Log* and reflection on the period in our lives in which we find ourselves at the present time. Participants are asked to draw a line horizontally across the page and to indicate significant moments in their lives on this line. The present moment is then singled out and expanded into another line so that one can become aware that this present period has a beginning, a middle, and an end, just as our whole life does. We are then asked to reflect on how and when the period we are now in began and where we are in it now and to imagine how it might unfold henceforth. We are then asked to find an image to characterize it.

The spiritual autobiography aspect of the workbook can come up anywhere, as in recording the stepping stones in our spiritual life, which is what I do with my students. It may also emerge in an inner wisdom dialogue. Spiritual contemplation is stimulated by the inspiring guided "process meditation" used to introduce each section before writing begins. These guided meditations are used by the leader to get people into the mood to reflect and write at a deep level. The meditations provide a means of entering the realm of quietness in which inner experiences can take place. By creating a contemplative atmosphere, they provide a neutral starting point from which we can gain access to our depths. Once meditation carries us to the quiet place in the depths of ourselves, it frees us to follow our own rhythms of inner experience. We can then explore the symbolic and spiritual aspects of our lives. Images and feelings rise up to us from our depths. Exploring intuitions, direct perceptions and sensations of all kinds, we approach our inner lives, including our diverse spiritual experiences past and present, enabling us to discover deep fundamental truths about our lives.

Whereas the Guided Autobiography technique systematically explores the whole life, past, present, and future, the Intensive Journal technique focuses more on the present. It is more like a series of snapshots indicating how we feel and think at the moment about people, events, and circumstances in our past present and future. The purpose of the exercises is to tune us in to our intuitive knowledge about our lives. Once the basic technique for writing in the different parts of the journal/workbook is learned it is recommended that it should be continued on a regular basis as a spiritual practice.

AUTOBIOGRAPHY AND TWELVE-STEP PROGRAMS[5]

Another approach to spiritual autobiography is offered by twelve-step programs that derive from the program of *spiritual* recovery outlined in the "Big Book" of Alcoholics Anonymous and the AA "Twelve by Twelve" which offers inspiring reflections on working each of the steps and the traditions of Alcoholics Anonymous. In working step four, one is asked to make a fearlessly honest moral inventory of one's life, which is not unlike some of the work that may go into writing one's spiritual autobiography. But even before that, in working the first three steps, in acknowledging one's powerlessness over one's addictions and turning one's life and will over to the care of God, one is doing spiritual autobiography work. Step ten requires one to continue the work begun in step four by making a daily moral inventory and assessment of one's spiritual health. And steps eleven and twelve move from the past into the future, asking us to continue improving our conscious contact with God and to practice the spiritual principles of the program in all of our affairs.

Many older adults are or have been participants in twelve-step recovery groups, and these sometimes form the basis of their spirituality. If they have worked the steps, particularly step four, then their experience in step work can provide a launching pad for them to become engaged in autobiographical writing and reflection from a spiritual perspective.

CONCLUSION

Autobiography represents a form of creativity that emerges more strongly in later life than at any other time in the life cycle for obvious reasons. With age, both one's store of information and one's perspective on life has grown, and most people want to pass on a legacy of wisdom based on their lived experience. Life story writing is particularly useful for older adults who have to reconcile past values and goals with present realities just as they had to do in previous periods of transition such as making a job change, leaving a marriage or entering retirement. Life story writing is most salient when future opportunities for altering the life course are perceived as limited. Renewed confidence in one's capacity to adapt, along with increased understanding of one's personal agendas, can form the basis for successful future choices. The writing and sharing of one's life story leads to a stronger sense of identity about who and what one is at every stage in life (Aftel, 1996; Cohen, 2001; Kotre, 1999).

The autobiographical process can be health promoting and even therapeutic (Aftel, 1996; Cohen, 2000). Sometimes it is only when we tell our whole story that we are able to connect the dots to gain a meaningful view of ourselves and our lives. In the process of taking stock of our lives–the disappointments and joys, failures, and accomplishments–we make a journey toward self-knowledge, understanding and acceptance. Beginning with perhaps only an elusive sense of meaning, continued exploration of our life stories can enable us to understand ourselves more fully and appreciate our experience and contribution to life in the broadest sense.

Autobiography writing can prompt memories of events and experiences that have remained hidden for many years. Therefore, life story writing from a spiritual perspective can also help people reformulate meanings of past events that may now have potential spiritual significance for them but which may not have been recognized as spiritual when they occurred.

In this article I have attempted to indicate the utility of autobiographical writing as a tool for spiritual growth and healthy emotional adjustment for older adults. I emphasized the importance of approaching the life stories from a spiritual perspective in order to reach to the essential forces and patterns in our lives. Autobiographical writing was seen to be both satisfying and healing for older adults. Several techniques of gathering and working with autobiographical data were discussed: life review, guided autobiography groups, the intensive journal technique, and twelve-step work. For those who work with older persons, these techniques should prove very useful. I want to close with a poem from a 60-year-old retired woman, Molly Srode (2003).

Reflection

I walk along this one familiar road
Memories lie scattered at my feet
all precious now, all with gifts to give.
What I once discarded, passing this way before
I pick up again and in the light of the years now passed
I see a vein of gold running through its center.

NOTES

1. In *the Varieties of Religious Experience* William James defined spiritual as follows: "The feelings, acts, and experiences of individual men in their solitude, so far as they apprehend themselves to stand in relation to whatever they may consider the divine."

2. The best source for all matters related to reminiscence and life review is still Barbara Haight and Jeffrey Webster's *The Art and Science of Reminiscing: Theory, Research, Methods, and Applications* (1995). Complete protocols and instructions for administering the structured life review are given there. A more recent version of their work appears in Webster and Haight's *Critical Advances in Reminiscence Work: From Theory to Application* (Springer, 2002).

3. James Birren and Kathryn Cochran have written a very simple and user-friendly guide entitled *Telling the Stories of Life through Guided Autobiography Groups* (2001).

A useful earlier guide by Birren and Deutchman is entitled *Guiding Autobiography Groups for Older Adults* (1991).

4. In 1975 Ira Progoff published a manual/guide book on how to use the Intensive Journal. This title, *At A Journal Workshop*, is still in print and can be ordered along with tapes and other instructional materials on the web from http://www.intensivejournal.org/

5. The handbook for all things related to twelve step programs is the *Big Book of Alcoholics Anonymous* and *Twelve Steps and Twelve Traditions*.

REFERENCES

Aftel, M. (1996). *The story of your life: Becoming the author of your experience.* New York: Simon and Schuster.

Atchley, R. (2000). "Spirituality" in *Handbook of the humanities and aging*, Cole, T.R., Kastenbaum, R., and Ray, R.E. (Eds.) 2nd ed. New York: Springer Publishing Company.

Atkinson, R. (1995). *The gift of stories. practical and spiritual applications of autobiography, life stories, and personal mythmaking.* Westport, CT: Bergin and Garvey.

Augustine, Saint (1999). *The Confessions.* Trans. by Edward Pusey. New York: Modern Library.

Bateson, M.C. (1989). *Composing a life.* New York: Atlantic Monthly Press.

Bianchi, E. (1995). *Aging as a spiritual journey.* New York: Crossroad.

Birren, J.E., and Deutchman, D.E. (1991). *Guiding autobiography groups for older adults.* Baltimore, MD: The Johns Hopkins University Press.

Birren, J.E., and Hedland, B. (1987). "Contribution of autobiography to Developmental Psychology" in N. Eisenberg (Ed.) *Contemporary topics in developmental psychology.* New York: John Wiley and Sons.

Birren, J.E., and Birren, B.A. (1996). "Autobiography: Exploring the Self and Encouraging Development" in *Aging and biography. explorations in adult development*, J. E. Birren, G. M. Kenyon, J.-E. Ruth, J. J.F. Schroots, & T. Svensson (Eds.). New York: Springer Publishing Company.

Burnside, I. (1996). "Life review and reminiscence in nursing practice" in *Aging and biography: Explorations in adult development*, J.E. Birren, G. M. Kenyon, J.-E. Ruth, Johannes J.F. Schroots, T. S. (Eds.). New York: Springer Publishing Company.

Butler, R. (1963). "The life-review: An Interpretation of reminiscence in the aged." *Psychiatry*, 26, 63-76.

Bruner, J. (1990). *Acts of Meaning.* Cambridge, MA: Harvard University Press.

Casey, E. (1991). *Spirit and soul. Essays in philosophical psychology.* Dallas, TX: Spring Publications.

Charmé, S. (1984). *Meaning and myth in the study of lives. A sartrean perspective.* Philadelphia: University of Pennsylvania Press.

Cohen, G. (2000). *The creative age: Awakening human potential in the second half of life.* New York: Avon Books.

Cole, T. R., Kastenbaum, R. and Ray, R. E. (Eds.) (2000). *Handbook of the Humanities and Aging (2nd ed.).* Springer Publishing Company.

Conway, J. K. (1998). *When memory speaks: Reflections on autobiography.* New York: Alfred A. Knopf.

Gaustad, E. S. (1999). *Memoirs of the spirit. American religious autobiography from Jonathan Edwards to Maya Angelou.* Grand Rapids, MI: William B. Eerdmans Publishing Company.

Haight, B. and J. Webster (Eds.) (1995). *The art and science of reminiscing: Theory, Research, methods, and applications.* Washington, DC: Taylor and Francis.

Heilbrun, C. (1997). *The last gift of time: Life beyond sixty.* New York: Ballantine.

Hillman, J. (1999). *The Force of character and the lasting life.* New York: Random House.

James, W. (1906). *The varieties of religious experience.* London: Longmans Green.

Jung, C.G. (1961). *Memories, dreams, reflections*, recorded and edited by Aniela Jaffé, translated by Richard and Clara Winston. New York: Random House.

Kaufman, S. R. (1986). *The Ageless self: Sources of meaning in late life.* New York: New American Library.

Kenyon, G. (2000). "Philosophical foundations of existential meaning" in *Exploring existential meaning: Optimizing human development across the life span.* G. T. Reker and K. Chamberlain (Eds.). Sage Publications.

Kenyon, G. M. and Randall, W. L. (1997). *Restorying our lives: Personal growth through autobiographical reflection.* Westport, CT: Praeger.

Kenyon, G. Clark, P., and de Vries, B. (Eds.) (2001). *Narrative Gerontology: Theory, Research, and Practice.* Springer Publishing Company.

Kotre, J. (1999). *Make it count: How to generate a legacy that gives meaning to your life.* New York: The Free Press

Lewis, C.S. (1956). *Surprised by joy: The shape of my early life.* New York: Harcourt Brace Javonovich.

Mandelker, A. and Powers E. (Eds.). (1999). *Pilgrim souls: A collection of spiritual autobiographies.* New York: Simon and Schuster.

McAdams, D (1993). *Stories we live by: Personal myths and the making of the self.* New York: William Morrow.

McFadden, S. H. (2000). "Religion and meaning in late life" in *Exploring existential meaning: Optimizing human development across the life span.* G. T. Reker and K. Chamberlain (Eds.). Sage Publications.

McFadden, S. H. (2000). "The spiritual autobiography." Unpublished ms.

Merton, T. (1948). *The seven story mountain.* New York: Harcourt Brace Javonovich.

Moody, H.R. (1997). *The five stages of the soul: Charting the spiritual passages that shape our lives.* New York: Anchor Books.

Moore, T. (2002). *The soul's religion: Cultivating a profoundly spiritual way of life.* New York: Harper Collins.

Murdock, M. (2003). *Unreliable truth: On memoir and memory.* New York: Seal Press.

Osis, M. and Stout, L. (2001). "Using narrative therapy with older adults" in *Narrative gerontology: Theory, research, and practice.* G. Kenyon, P. Clark, and B. de Vries (Eds.). Springer Publishing Company.

Pargament, K. I. (1997). *The psychology of religion and coping: Theory, research, practice.* New York: The Guilford Press.

Pascal, R. (1985). *Design and truth in autobiography.* New York: Garland Publishing.

Peace, R. (1998). *Spiritual autobiography. Discovering and sharing your spiritual story.* Colorado Springs. CO: NavPress.

Phifer, N. (2002). *Memoirs of the soul. Writing your spiritual autobiography.* Cincinnati, OH: Walking Stick Press.

Progoff, I. (1975). *At a journal workshop.* New York: Dialogue House.

Rainer, T. (1997). *Your life as story: Discovering the "new autobiography" and writing memoir as literature.* New York: Tarcher Putnam.

Randall, W. L. (2001). "Storied worlds: Acquiring a narrative perspective on aging, identity, and everyday life." In *Narrative gerontology: Theory, research, and practice.* Kenyon, G., Clark, P., and de Vries, B. (Eds.). Springer Publishing Company.

· Randall, W., and Kenyon, G. (2001). *Ordinary wisdom: Biographical aging and the journey of life.* Westport, CT: Praeger.

Reker, G. (2003). "Restoring, maintaining. and enhancing meaning and purpose in life through autobiographical methods." Paper at the GSA Pre-conference workshop, *"Exploring Mature Lives: Autobiographical Steps toward Wisdom."*

Schorske, C. (1998). *Thinking with history. Explorations in the passage to modernism.* Princeton: Princeton University Press.

Shaw, M. (2001). "A history of guided autobiography" in *Narrative gerontology: Theory, research, and practice.* G. Kenyon, P. Clark and B. de Vries (Eds.). Springer Publishing Company.

Srode, M. (2003). *Creating a spiritual retirement: A guide to the unseen possibilities in our lives.* Woodstock, VT: Skylight Paths Publishing.

Stone, R. (1996). *The healing art of storytelling: A sacred journey of personal discovery.* New York: Hyperion.

Sulmasy, D. P. (2002). A biosocial-spiritual model for the care of patients at the end of life. *The Gerontologist,* Vol. 42. Special Issue III.

Tornstam, L. (1999). "Late life transcendence: A new developmental perspective on aging" in *Religion, belief, and spirituality in late life.* L. E. Thomas and S. A. Eisenhandler (Eds.). Springer Publishing Company.

Webster, J.D., and Young, R.A. (1988). Process variables of the life review: Counseling implications. *International Journal of Aging & Human Development,* 26 (4), 191-194.

Webster, J. D. (2001). "The future of the past: Continuing challenges for reminiscence research." In: *Narrative Gerontology: Theory, Research, and Practice.* G. Kenyon, P. Clark, and B. de Vries (Eds.). Springer Publishing Company.

Dreams for the Second Half of Life

Harry R. Moody, PhD

SUMMARY. Dreams in midlife and old age can reveal a process of spiritual growth described by Tornstam as gerotranscencence. This same process of inner growth has also been described in theoretical terms as self-actualization (Maslow), ego-integrity (Erikson), and individuation (Jung). The process is illustrated through dream symbols of transpersonal development, displaying the duality of self-fulfillment and self- transcendence. In lifespan development terms this process can be studied in detail in the autobiography of Helen Luke. The interpretation of dreams has importance for what has recently come to be known as "Conscious Aging." *[Article copies available for a fee from The Haworth Document Delivery Service: 1-800-HAWORTH. E-mail address: <docdelivery@haworthpress.com> Website: <http://www.HaworthPress.com> © 2005 by The Haworth Press, Inc. All rights reserved.]*

KEYWORDS. Dreaming, gerotranscendence, individuation, conscious aging, ego-integrity, self-actualization

And Jacob dreamed that there was a ladder reaching from the earth up to heaven. And the angels of the Lord were ascending and descending on it. The Lord stood above the ladder and said, 'The land on which you lie I will give to you and your descendants, and

[Haworth co-indexing entry note]: "Dreams for the Second Half of Life." Moody, Harry R. Co-published simultaneously in *Journal of Gerontological Social Work* (The Haworth Social Work Practice Press, an imprint of The Haworth Press, Inc.) Vol. 45, No. 3, 2005, pp. 271-292; and: *Religion, Spirituality, and Aging: A Social Work Perspective* (ed: Harry R. Moody) The Haworth Social Work Practice Press, an imprint of The Haworth Press, Inc., 2005, pp. 271-292. Single or multiple copies of this article are available for a fee from The Haworth Document Delivery Service [1-800-HAWORTH, 9:00 a.m. - 5:00 p.m. (EST). E-mail address: docdelivery@haworthpress.com].

Available online at http://www.haworthpress.com/web/JGSW
© 2005 by The Haworth Press, Inc. All rights reserved.
doi:10.1300/J083v45n03_02

by your descendants shall all the families of the earth bless themselves. Behold, I am with you, and will keep you wherever you go.'
(Genesis 28: 1-22)

The dream of Jacob and its image of Jacob's ladder is perhaps the
oldest dream recorded in the Judaeo-Christian tradition, but it is far
from the only dream of spiritual significance (Kelsey, 1974; Savary,
1984; Sanford, 1989). Indeed, dreams have played a crucial role in the
spiritual life of virtually every culture on the face of the earth, from pre-
historic times on, with the single exception of our own modern culture
(Bulkeley, 1995). Sigmund Freud inaugurated the modern interest in
dreams with his landmark book, *The Interpretation of Dreams* (1899).
Yet today interest in the meaning of dreams seems minimal among the intellectual elite, where dreams are routinely dismissed as random events,
as purely private phenomena or as something best explained by neuro-
physiology. Within gerontology there has been virtually no interest at all
in late-life dreams, despite the enormous importance of sleep and dreaming for positive mental health.

In this brief space, attention is given to one aspect of dreams in later
life: namely, the role of dreams in revealing the process of spiritual
growth in the second half of life. This process of growth has been theoretically conceptualized in helpful ways by Lars Tornstam (Tornstam,
1997, 1999), who has described it as "gerotranscendence," which
Tornstam defines as "a shift in meta perspective, from a materialistic
and rational view of the world to a more cosmic and transcendent one,
normally accompanied by an increase in life satisfaction" (See: *http://
www.soc.uu.se/research/gerontology/gerotrans.html*).

INDIVIDUALISM AND THE SPIRITUAL SEARCH

"Spirituality" is sometimes understood as a process of detachment or
diminishing the sense of individual self. But we may find it more helpful to begin by thinking of spiritual growth in terms of what Carl Jung
called *individuation* (Edinger, 1992) Individuation is a complex, many-
sided psychological process, but for our purposes we can define it as a
drive toward becoming more authentic, more wholly oneself (Hillman,
2000). Jung understood individuation, in its broadest terms, to be the ultimate psychological goal for the second half of life. Defined in this way,
individuation evidently has a kinship with concepts such as self-actualization (Maslow) or ego-integrity (Erikson). Later life can be a period where

we come to acquire a deeper sense of distinct and unique identity, a feeling well conveyed by the following recurrent dream of a woman in her late sixties.

Finishing the House

Gretchen D., recently retired, reported the following recurrent dream:

> Over a period of years I had dreams in which I was living in my house. At the beginning I was living in the basement, and the house was in a dilapidated condition. In later dreams the house was always in an unfinished state. There were exposed beams instead of floor boards; wiring was dangling; water didn't come out of faucets in the bathroom. More recently, the house has become finished. Furniture is now in place and the house is now much taller.

This recurrent dream invokes the image of a house, a common symbol of the self. We live in this self, just as we live in our own house, yet the structure of the self remains unfinished. In earlier dreams Gretchen was living "in the basement" of the house: that is, in a lower part of herself, while the rest of her identity "was in a dilapidated condition." In these recurrent dreams the self "was always in an unfinished state," represented by the exposed beams and dangling wiring, faucets that didn't work, and so on. By the time of retirement, Gretchen's self–her sense of ego-integrity–had grown more solid: "The house has become finished." This sense of wholeness and completion is symbolized by the fact that her house now finally has furniture and "is now much taller." Gretchen's dream is a beautiful image of late-life self-actualization and individuation.

The process of individuation in later life will often entail encountering the "Shadow" or unacknowledged elements in ourselves, as in the following dream of Hal White, rector of an Episcopal church, who was 60-years-old.

A New Church

> I was in a house that had multiple levels, staircases, and rooms. The walls and ceilings kept moving into new configurations. I was attempting to pick up a few things in the house and go to another place. I was having a difficult time deciding on the things I wanted to take. There was a small child, a toddler, in a pink outfit that kept clinging to my leg so that it was difficult for me to go. Also I kept

looking for what it was I was to take with me and couldn't find it. The other thing that happened was that I was not able to control a bowel movement, so I had this stuff in my pants. I was attempting to get to the bathroom, and at the same time I was frustrated because I needed to get to this other place, the first church I served thirty-two years ago. It had a new building attached to the old one in a geographical location near to the original. (Montague Ullman and Claire Limmer, *The Variety of Dream Experience*, 1999)

Trying to "become the person we were meant to be" means acknowledging child-like elements in ourselves, things we can't control, as the dreamer here cannot control his bowel movement. This forgotten child in us keeps clinging to us, like the child who clings to the dreamer's leg, even as we are trying to move on with our lives. This dream invokes a feeling of life-review, as the dreamer tries to return to the first church he had served many decades ago. Going forward and going backward are part of the same movement toward construction of the self.

One difficulty with Erikson's ideal of ego-integrity is that it implies a condition of finality or self-completion. Transpersonal psychology would offer a different perspective (Wilber, 2000) more open to ego-transcendence. Indeed, the second half of life can be a period of psychological and spiritual search: for example, seeking to reconcile orthodox religion and individuation, as in the following dream of a 58-year-old actress long involved in Buddhism.

An Apple a Day

In the dream the dreamer has left her Buddhist Temple, where she worked on security, making change for people, and so on. She was driving down the road on Long Island, passing many fruit stands. She stopped to get a big red apple for herself, but the fruit vendor, who reported not feeling well, said he didn't have change for a dollar, so she was unable to get an apple. The dreamer continued on her way, aiming to undertake an important Buddhist ritual, "enshrinement," which involves bringing a gift offering, sometimes fruit, in worship around a sacred object of cosmic significance. The dreamer then stopped at two different doctor's offices to ask them for an apple, but received only a thermometer.

On the road again, she came to a crossroads where three roads went in different directions. She chose the middle path, slightly to the left, which was a new highway, never used before. She asked advice from two nameless passengers in the car but they could offer no help. The whole trip was taking longer than expected and she realized she would not get back to the Temple at the appointed time.

This dreamer reported having had many dreams about her Buddhist Temple, which had become a major focus in her life. In commenting on the dream she mentioned thinking about the old saying "An apple a day keeps the doctor away."

The dream is centered around images of searching and seeking. The fruit vendor, the doctors, and all the figures in the dream all symbolize a search for healing and wholeness. At the outset the dreamer has left the Temple, as if leaving the framework of external religion for a personal journey, here represented by a car trip. Instead of orthodox ritual ("enshrinement"), which involves giving fruit as a gift, the dreamer wants the apple for herself. But the fruit vendor, strangely, cannot make change, ironically the same task she herself routinely performs in her official role at the Temple. The dreamer then turns toward healing figures, doctors, who also prove to be in no position to provide fruit. Instead the healers offer only an instrument to detect illness (the thermometer). The apple itself might have made her healthy and not in need of cure by a physician.

In the next scene in the dream, the dreamer is back on the road again, now at a crossroads in her life. The three roads represent possible paths to some nameless destination. Buddhists are often advised to seek safety in the "triple refuge" (Buddha, Dharma, Sangha): that is, the teacher, the law and the spiritual community. But these three constitute the refuge of external religion. The triple is paradoxical for a religion of Enlightenment in which the seeker is advised, in Buddha's words, to "Be a light unto yourself": that is, find your own way, the "pathless path" of true Enlightenment. At the crossroads, the dreamer here follows the middle road, like the Buddhist Middle Way. But this "pathless path" is precisely a new highway, a road that has never been traveled before.

The genuine spiritual path involves what Suzuki Roshi called "beginner's mind" or an encounter with something utterly unprecedented (Suzuki, 1972). The older seeker must go beyond "crystallized intelligence" or life experience in favor of another kind of wisdom. The dreamer can therefore get no guidance from the external community (Sangha), symbolized here by other passengers in the vehicle. Indeed,

Buddhism itself is divided into the "lesser vehicle" (Hinayana) and the "greater vehicle" (Mahayana). Driving her own vehicle in this dream, the dreamer has come a long way from the ritual act of enshrinement or search for nourishment (an apple) or healing (the doctors). The dreamer finally understands that she cannot return to the Temple, to conventional religion, within the appointed time. The message of the dream is this journey toward personal Enlightenment will take longer than expected and will take her down a new road toward an unknown destination.

The "Apple a Day" dream presents for us a critical question for gerotranscendence in relationship to orthodox religious traditions: how to reconcile individuation with the beliefs of tradition in order to achieve a "mature spirituality?" These issues arise in the following dream of a 57-year-old woman, Lynn H., long involved in Christian spiritual circles.

Light of the World

> I am in a large rustic hall in a conference center set up like a dining hall with long tables parallel to each other in three rows. There is a small group gathered around a table in the back. I am a participant and the leader is a young woman. There are about eight of us. One is a young man with an excellent singing voice. I have brought candles in a large paper bag. We use a fat red one at our table.
>
> At one point we're talking about scriptures and I mention a favorite in Corinthians 3:16. We talk about what part of the body we are. I realize the man is the voice and I also realize I am to be the hands. I have been taking notes for the group.
>
> An older black woman enters in a professional dress–she is the appointed leader and is late. She has found out that I am the priest's wife and a speaker in my own right, and says I should be doing the teaching. With no ambivalence, I say I'm there to learn, but offer her a tall, thin, golden-blown candle to be set in a glass holder. We have trouble lighting it and she helps. It feels like mutual acceptance. I awaken and think: I am *not* the head, the voice, the mouth, even the heart. I am the hands, and am willing to be so. A new thing. I notice I also bring the light. This feels good.

This dream begins in a location outside of ordinary life–in a "large rustic hall" at a conference center, where a spiritual retreat might take place. The dreamer describes herself as only "a participant" in the group meeting there. She finds herself not in the center of the meeting area but in the back of the room, in a small group led by "a young woman," who may be a younger version of the dreamer herself. The dreamer brings candles to this table and later realizes that she has brought the light, which "feels good."

What sort of light is this? In the New Testament Jesus says of himself "I am the Light of the World." But, equally, "Ye are all children of light, and children of the day. . . therefore let us not sleep, but let us watch and be sober." What the New Testament calls "watching" denotes a state of wakefulness or higher consciousness, which can be linked to gero-transcendence: "The light of the body is the eye; if therefore thine eye be single thy whole body shall be full of light." In the gnostic *Gospel of Thomas*, the disciples ask Jesus to show them where he abides, and he answers: "Within a man of light there is light, and he lights the whole world. When he does not shine, he is in darkness" (*Gospel of Thomas*, #24, Meyer, 1992).

In this dream, a small group of spiritual seekers is discussing Scripture, where they juxtapose two verses from the Gospel of John and First Corinthians, the famous passage associated with the mystical body of Christ. It turns out that figures in the dream actually represent different parts of the body, as the group recognizes. The "young man with an excellent singing voice" represents the voice, while the dreamer herself represents the hands. In fact, all the time she has been "taking notes for the group," recording their deliberations just as this dream records her inner spiritual life unfolding.

Next there appears an "older Black woman" who turns out to be "the appointed leader." At first the leader of the group was a young woman, presumably Caucasian (like the dreamer). But now the "appointed leader," arriving late, is no longer young but old; no longer white but Black.

The numinous Black woman, of course, is also the dreamer, but now depicted as "the Other," an unknown figure who insists that the dreamer is not to remain only "a participant" in this spiritual study group. In fact, the new leader says that the dreamer is actually "the priest's wife" and "a leader in her own right" who should be doing the teaching. The dreamer resists this call ("with no ambivalence"), saying she is only there to learn, not to teach. Yet in the dream she is the one who brings the candles, who brings the light into the world, and the new leader helps her to light a candle.

At this point we come to the core of some of the deepest currents in Christian tradition. Believers are to be a "Light unto the nations," and they are not to "hide their light under a bushel." Yet "He who is first, shall be last" and Scripture repeatedly warns that the way to new life comes from dying to the old self. How are these contradictions to be reconciled?

The figure of the Black woman, the genuine appointed leader, is "the stone that the builders rejected" which has now become the foundation for the whole structure, a new transpersonal sense of self to be built in later life. Yet we have trouble building this new self, just the dreamer has trouble lighting the candle or acknowledging her own leadership role. We need help with illumination, as the dreamer does when the appointed leader helps to light the candle, resulting in a feeling of "mutual acceptance."

The "Light of the World" dream highlights the Christian path to individuation and gerotranscendence. The dreamer herself reconciles all contradictions in a powerful feeling that emerges at the end of the dream: "I am *not* the head, the voice, the mouth, even the heart. I am the hands, and am willing to be so." This "willing to be so" conveys the truth of genuine humility and servanthood: "Those who are last shall be first." At the same time the dreamer will not resist the new life and power rising up in her in this dream: she is, after all, "the priest's wife" and "a speaker in my own right." Now, at the end of the dream, she notices "I also bring the light" and this feels good. The dream is an abiding message of faith or "assurance in things unseen." All figures in this dream are the dreamer herself, and all are, in the end, united. Head and voice, heart and hands, all belong to the Mystical Body of Christ, "the Light of the world."

The following dream also reflects dynamic movement within the psyche in the spiritual search.

Up and Down the Magic Mountain

The dreamer, Bill R., is a 57-year-old executive long interested in Eastern religions:

> I dreamed I was going up a huge mountain, very dangerous but also strangely attractive to me. There were trails that winding around the mountain, many with sheer cliffs next to the road. I was in a mini-bus going up the mountain with several people familiar to me but whose names I couldn't remember. I recognized the driver of the mini-bus and wanted to warn him of danger as we ap-

proached a crossroads. He was dressed in a leather jacket zipped up completely.

> The driver took a path that brought us to the edge, then we started going over in a free fall off the cliff. Next we were all in some kind of lodge or house, evidently injured from the fall. Everyone, including me, had bandages on, but I wasn't in bad shape. We were grateful that the driver had prevented a disaster and someone inquired about him: Did he have long hair and a tail? Someone unzipped his leather jacket and reported that he did indeed. The driver was Hanuman [the Hindu monkey god].

In religious traditions the world over we often come upon the symbol of the holy mountain as a representation of the spiritual path. Sometimes the holy mountain is identified with a specific geographic location: Mount Sinai, Mount Fuji, Mount Olympus, and so on. In the Indian Tantric tradition, the holy mountain is Mount Meru, the *axis mundi*–the central pillar of the cosmos. The ascent of the outer mountain is actually a symbolic statement about the inner spiritual journey, as Rene Daumal describes it in his allegorical tale *Mount Analog* (Daumal, 1986).

In Bill's dream, the spiritual search is symbolized by the ascent up a holy mountain, "very dangerous but also strangely attractive" to the dreamer. His fellow passengers are known to him, yet he cannot remember their names. The trip up the mountain, in a mini-bus, is perilous and Bill remains dependent on the unusual bus driver. Then the worst happens: the bus veers off the cliff. Everyone survives but the identity of the bus driver remains obscure. It turns out that, beneath his covering, this driver is none other than the Hindu monkey god, Hanuman, a powerful image of salvation in the Hindu tradition. This dream is a reminder that the spiritual path in later life is fraught with difficulty and danger. The seeker, the one who aims to ascend the holy mountain, is dependent on a guide but vulnerable just the same. Bill's dream underscores the importance of guidance in the spiritual Search in order for the perilous Struggle to be successful (Moody, 1997).

I myself had a dream of similar import (at age 58), a dream that underscores the tension between individuation and the spiritual search.

Story Board

> I dreamed I was at a party, actually was the host of the party, at my house. It was not my real house but a large, rambling country man-

sion. The guests were people from my professional field: one a very superficial woman, another a man of deep spiritual interests. We were all seated around a bar and I asked a woman if she had ever been to my house before. She had not, hadn't even known this was my home.

We all started examining this board game–actually, not a game but a graphic model of a life story. The 'story-line' ran around the top of the board as a long line. I noticed the line was intersected at points by names: 'Claudio Naranjo' was one. Someone asked me what these intersections meant, and I explained that they showed the silsila (chain of spiritual teachers).

Next I began examining another life story board, this time in the form of a labyrinth. I was fascinated by it and traced the line to an end point where the board had a little trap door that opened, revealing darkness below. At that moment the owner of the story board came by and abruptly took possession of it. I realized that the board belonged to this man. I knew him but couldn't remember his name. He folded up the story board like a portable chess set and then proceeded to walk away, down the stairs, into the basement of the house.

This dream begins in the dreamer's own house, yet it is somehow not his house but a "large, rambling country mansion." We begin the spiritual journey in a place where we are not truly "at home." In everyday existence, the self we fashion to operate in the world is represented here by the artificial social atmosphere of a party. The superficial woman and the man of deep spiritual interest are two sides of the dreamer himself. The woman, ironically, hadn't even known that this house, this self, was the actual residence of the dreamer, which of course it is not. The dreamer is at home yet not at home.

The next image in the dream is a numinous symbol of the human life-course: a "story board" representing life in graphical terms as an arc or a line, as we see in iconographic images of the life course from the Middle Ages and the Renaissance (Cole, 1992). This secular representation of life is interrupted or intersected at points by elements that point toward a spiritual search: i.e., a Sufi term silsila, or spiritual lineage.

But there are two story boards in this dream. The first is the arc of the life-course, while the spiritual search itself, the drive toward gerotranscendence, is represented by the second story board. The second board is designed in the form of a labyrinth, like the great labyrinth in Chartres Cathedral replicated in Grace Cathedral in San Francisco and in many other sites as well. The labyrinth is an image of movement toward the center of ourselves, a movement through concentric circles (Artress, 1996). Ultimately, in this dream the path of the labyrinth culminates in a little trap door opening into darkness. At just that moment, a mysterious figure, the "owner of the story board," comes along. Significantly, the dreamer recognizes him but cannot not remember his name. This numinous figure is a Divine Power, one who is the owner of the board representing the life story. We already recognize this higher element within us, yet we cannot express that knowledge in words, just as the dreamer cannot remember the name of the numinous figure. Finally, the owner picks up the board, takes it away and disappears through another door down into darkness, into an unknown space.

The story board dream reveals the way in which individuation (ego integrity) and gerotranscendence (ego transcendence) are both allied and opposed to one another. There are two story boards here: one the arc of life, the second the labyrinth that moves like a concentric circle toward the center. Psychological and spiritual growth moves through this same duality: I must become more myself yet I must also go beyond myself, even become "nobody," as Emily Dickinson writes:

> I'm nobody.
> Who are you?
> Are you nobody, too?

SYMBOLS OF TRANSCENDENCE

Gerotranscendence ultimately involves a degree of freedom from previous roles, attachments, and the sense of one's identity achieved in adulthood. This transcendence is akin to the "Cloud of Unknowing" described by the medieval mystics (Progoff, 1989).

The transpersonal dimension of freedom is sometimes symbolized by the flight of a bird, as in the Sufi poet Attar's allegorical treatment, *The Conference of the Birds* (Attar, 1984). Here are two dreams from women in their seventies that invoke the image of the bird as a symbol of gerotranscendence.

Bird Dreams

These two dreams are from Elizabeth, a widow in her late seventies:

> I find an exhausted little white bird. I hold it gently in my two hands and wonder if I can keep it alive.

> I am driving a car, being shown the right way to go by a low-flying bird that flies just ahead of me. There is a highway on my right and an abyss on my left.

This is the dream of Nanette, in her late seventies:

> I am in a room in a house, probably the dining room. There are several white doves fluttering against the window, with light coming through it. I am very careful not to open the door. I am very concerned that they shouldn't go out of the house. They should stay. I feel very happy. I love it. (Garfield, 1991, pp. 334, 343)

The little white bird in Elizabeth's dream conveys a sense of vulnerability and preciousness on the spiritual path. The bird is a creature that can fly free, can be released from earth and go upward into the heavens. There is an element in us like the bird that wants to be free but is easily exhausted. Even if we have this attachment to a higher power in our youth, it is easy to lose that attachment, to become disillusioned, even hopeless. The dreamer here cherishes the little bird but also wonders if she can keep the bird alive.

In the second dream, the bird is a symbol of spiritual guidance. Elizabeth is driving a car: an image of the ego in charge of one's life, the locus of control or sense of autonomy so prized in our culture. Like the Holy Spirit that comes down in the form of a dove, this low-flying bird guides the dreamer through peril.

In Nanette's dream she is in a house, not necessarily at home. The birds are fluttering around, seeking for the light, just as the spiritual seeker seeks divine illumination. But the dreamer wants to keep these birds in the house; she is concerned that they must not fly away, but should stay close to her. The feeling tone at the end of the dream is very positive.

Another image of light is apparent in the following dream, reported by Marie-Louise von Franz (1987).

Light in the Tunnel

> I found myself once again in the darkness, in the inside of a spiral-shaped tunnel. At the far end of the tunnel, which was very narrow, I saw a bright light. Then someone began to talk to me. Someone was there in the darkness. He began by explaining to me the meaning of my life. Every question which anyone could possibly ask was answered for me. Then the voice ordered her to return to life, for her time had not yet come.

This powerful dream constitutes a moment of Breakthrough, one of the stages of the soul in the process of spiritual growth coming after Search and Struggle (Moody, 1997). The imagery is similar to what is reported in Near Death Experiences, where survivors commonly report a light at the end of a long tunnel of darkness (Ring, 1985). In this dream, the dreamer has a deep insight: "Every question which anyone could possibly ask was answered for me." Yet this Breakthrough is to be followed by a Return to everyday life "for her time had not yet come."

In her study, Von Franz includes only dreams that actually occurred soon before death. Other dreams from the second half could be regarded as a reminder to the dreamer of *momento mori* or what the alchemist Gerhard Dorn calls a window of light, *fenestra aeternitatis* ("window into eternity") (p. 146).

Von Franz quotes Jung's comment: "The spectacle of old age would be unendurable did we not know that our psyche reaches into a region held captive neither by change in time nor by limitation of place. In that form of being our birth is a death and our death a birth. The scales of the whole hang balanced" (Jung, 1992, p. 569).

Gerotranscendence involves a different sense of time, or of eternity beyond the span of an individual life. This intuition sometimes expressed as a feeling of the unreality of time, as in the following dream.

Golden Light

The dreamer is a 74-year-old woman long involved in a spiritual path:

> In my dream I was in a circle of golden light, and in that circle I knew that time was not real, not in the least. As I was waking up I began to move away from that golden radiance and as I gradually woke up I began to move back into time.

This altered sense of time here is important for gerontologists to appreciate. The literature on life-review has emphasized the importance of reconciliation of past and present (Webster and Haight, 2002). Life-review can be triggered by thoughts of impending death, as illustrated by the powerful dream sequence in Ingmar Bergmann's film "Wild Strawberries," where the protagonist, Dr. Borg, reviews his life and struggles with unresolved issues from the past (Erikson, 1978). Here again we see the tension between reconciliation or affirmation, on the one hand, and transcendence or detachment, on the other: ego-integrity versus ego-transcendence.

The movement toward of gerotranscendence–"I knew that time was not real"–is not always understood in verbally self-conscious terms. Sometimes it is symbolized in a purely iconic vision, as in the following dream.

Center of the Cross

This is the dream of an eighty-year-old woman, shortly before her own death:

> She saw a cross; at the center stood a radiating sapphire. She knew in the dream she was experiencing a moment of heavenly existence. (Elrod, p. 171)

The process of gerotranscendence leads to a very different perspective on what one's "real life" has actually been. This altered perspective is beautifully conveyed in the following dream of Carl Jung, at age 69, a dream rich with religious imagery.

Yogi's Dream

> I was walking along a little road through a hilly landscape; the sun was shining and I had a wide view in all directions. Then I came to a small wayside chapel. The door was ajar, and I went in. To my surprise there was no image of the Virgin on the altar, and no crucifix either, but only a wonderful flower arrangement. But then I saw that on the floor in front of the altar, facing me, sat a yogi–in lotus posture, in deep meditation. When I looked at him more closely, I realized that he had my face. I started in profound fright, and awoke with the thought: 'Aha, so he is the one who is meditat-

ing me. He has a dream, and I am it.' I knew that when he awakened, I would no longer be.' (Jung, 1989, p. 323)

Jung's dream left him with an ambiguous sense of reality. The Yogi represents a kind of cosmic double and evokes the question: who is real? This ambiguity is conveyed in the story of the Chinese Chuang Tzu, who awoke from a dream one day and wondered, "Am I a man dreaming I am a butterfly, or a butterfly dreaming I am a man?" He goes on: "When one is changing, how does one know that a change is taking place? When one is not changing, how does one know that a change hasn't already occurred? Maybe you and I are still in a dream and have not yet changed . . . Be content with what is happening and forget about change; then you can enter into the oneness of the mystery of heaven" (Chuang Tzu, 1974, p. 136).

The mystery of heaven is what an altered sense of consciousness may convey to us, and the same sense is sometimes conveyed through dreams in the condition known as lucid dreaming. The following dream is a moment of Breakthrough accompanied by a clear direction to move to the stage of Return, or integration of transpersonal consciousness back into everyday life.

The Way of Surrender

> I enter a church and know that I am expected to speak. The congregation is singing hymn #33 from a red hymnal. While they go through the usual preliminary exercises, I decide to go outside to gather myself. I am worried and afraid because I don't know what I will say. I sit down on the grass and suddenly come up with a topic which feels right–'The Way of Surrender.'

> At this point I look up in the eastern sky and see a large orb of white light many times the size of the moon. I realize that I'm dreaming. I yell out in joy knowing it is coming for me. As soon as I do, the Light withdraws into the sky as if it is awaiting a more appropriate response on my part. I know that I must turn my eyes away and trust. As I do, the Light descends. As it approaches, a woman's voice says, 'You've done well reflecting this Light within yourself. But now it must be turned outward.'

> The air becomes charged and the ground is brilliantly lit. The top of my head begins to prickle and be warmed by the Light. I awaken. (LaBerge, 1991, p. 292)

Just like a near-death experience, this dream conveys the message that it is not yet time for the dreamer to escape the bonds of ordinary existence: instead, [the Light] must be turned outward, when we awaken to the demands of ordinary consciousness. The stage of Breakthrough is followed by Return.

HELEN LUKE: JOURNEY INTO SIMPLICITY

We may summarize this discussion of gerotranscendence in late-life dreams by looking at a powerful series of dreams recorded by the late Helen Luke, noted therapist and author of a remarkable autobiography through dreams, *Such Stuff as Dreams Are Made On* (Luke, 2001).

We begin with one of Helen Luke's dreams, recorded at age 73, a dream which conveys the challenge of individuation in the second half of life.

Seeing Clearly

> In my dream I had lost my spectacles, and first my friend Jane offered to lend me a pair of hers but I could see nothing through them. Then my friend Else offered hers and, though I could have seen enough to read through them, they were otherwise no use to me. Then I realized that I had my own glasses all the time but had been looking through them upside down. As soon as I turned them the right way up, I could see perfectly well. (p. 140)

Moving into old age, the dreamer struggles with the dynamics of individuation, with the need to stand on one's own feet, see with one's own eyes. In this dream, Helen Luke cannot see without her spectacles. But it is no use borrowing other people's glasses: Jane's glasses give no help and Else's glasses are only partially useful. Finally, the dreamer realizes "I had my own glasses all the time" but she had been looking through them upside down. Once turned rightside up, her vision is perfect.

This image is a wonderful illustration of the psychological situation that persists as long as we try to imitate other people, which is the product of what we commonly call "socialization." This process of internalizing social imperatives may even include spiritual beliefs that we borrow from others but do not make genuinely our own. In later life, such "borrowed beliefs," like borrowed glasses, are likely to prove useless and so we become disillusioned: hence, Erikson's duality of ego-integrity versus despair. The solution is to see things through our own eyes, of course demanding some help (spectacles) but help uniquely crafted for our distinctive vision. Seeing through our own glasses is a perfect symbol of individuation.

We began with Gretchen's dream of an unfinished house and the process of self-completion in later life. Helen Luke, too, offers several dreams that also invoke the image of a house. Here is one at age 78, recorded in her journal.

Country House

> In my dream I was standing outside a country house on a bright, sunny day. It was empty and had been completely repainted–a creamy white, inside and out. The doors stood wide. Someone who was showing it to me suggested I go over it. I said, 'I don't need to do that. I remember it very clearly, every room in it.'
>
> Then I remembered that this house (which was a small Georgian type, very gracious) was joined at the back to a much older, dark building; a corridor from the white house's upper story led to a series of rooms, also on two stories, almost like a warren–perhaps stables underneath. It was dark, Tudor-feeling–oak beams, etc. I thought to myself, 'I used to know those dark rooms too,' but I could not remember them so clearly as the 'white' house in the front, and I wondered if I should go through the latter and explore again those other rooms behind it. I seemed to know they were all clean and empty too, the whole place, front and back, awaiting a new tenant. (p. 206)

Is this house her own house, her own self? The dreamer doesn't say, but she remains detached from the house, a house that is both old and new, empty and repainted. She has been invited to go into the house again, but she doesn't need to do that. For Helen Luke, the process of life-review is complete: "I remember it very clearly, every room in it."

Yet the dream suggests that the work of gerotranscendence is not yet complete. The house, the self, is joined "at the back" "to a much older, dark building." Like the dark trap door in the labyrinth story board, this dark building is somehow familiar to the dreamer. Like the owner of the story board, this part of ourselves is both known and unknown. The clean and empty house is "awaiting a new tenant," who is the dreamer herself in a new condition.

Helen Luke lived to age 94 and recorded her dreams during the years when she joined the ranks of the "old-old." The following dream, also of a house, occurred at age 84.

A Burning House

> I dreamed of a house in which I was living, with other people living in other rooms of it. There was a fire in adjacent property and the firemen were at work, but it began to look as though our house was threatened. I was talking to a fireman and he asked whose house it was. I suddenly realized that it was not a place I had rented temporarily but my *own* house. I said so clearly, yet at the same time felt a kind of clarity and release, as though if it burned down no one but myself would be the loser, and it didn't matter to me much. There was no sense of danger to anyone's life in the dream, only to possessions. (p. 247)

The house in which the dreamer was living represents the self, finished or unfinished, which is the life she has lived into advanced old age. This period of life will involve losses and a measure of physical decline, here symbolized by the fire that destroys an adjacent property. By age 84, it begins to look as if her own life is threatened.

Helen Luke's dream conveys a powerful intuition of both life-affirmation and detachment. She suddenly realizes that this life she has been living is not something "rented temporarily" but her *own* real life, now threatened with destruction in old age. Yet this intimation of mortality is not depressing. The dreamer clearly realizes her condition, there is no denial here. Yet at the same time she feels "a kind of clarity and release." Loss of the house of her life, including all the "possessions" of accomplishments and memories, is somehow no longer threatening.

A final dream, one year later, offers an unforgettable symbol of gerotranscendence.

In the Eye of the Storm

> I was standing in a sphere, colorless, empty, and moving slowly and calmly from side to side. I was holding out my cupped hand, into which a succession of small spheres, each representing my

next task or the next small necessity of my life, was gently put by an unseen giver hidden in the storm clouds surrounding the eye, the calm center. This center space itself moved, as I moved within it, with the movement of the clouds or unseen forces around it–the eye of the storm. (249)

The sphere represents totality and perfection, the unity of the self and of the Divine beyond words ("colorless, empty"), as the medieval mystic Nicholas of Cusa puts it in describing God as "a circle whose circumference is nowhere and whose center is everywhere." The dreamer is here embraced in a perfect sphere and she herself receives in her cupped hand a series of small spheres, symbols of all the multiple tasks of life. The unspoken message is that the life-course itself is contained and guided by a divine "unseen giver." Later life, even amid a storm of losses, moves onward, like the dreamer in this center space. At the calm still point of the circle, in the eye of a storm, the dreamer is embraced by a Cloud of Unknowing.

CONCLUSION: COMING HOME

The dreams of later life can be a rich source of guidance and inspiration. As we move from individuation and ego-integrity toward full gerotranscendence, dreamwork can be part of a path of "Conscious Aging" (Schacter-Shalomi, 1995; Ram Dass, 2000; Moody, 2002). I conclude here with a dream published many years ago by the great contemporary spiritual writer Thomas Merton, who lived only to his mid-fifties but left behind a legacy of writings that are part of a growing ecumenical sensibility enriching to seekers from all spiritual traditions.

In the dream, Merton is invited to a party, just as I found myself at a party in the "Story Board" dream. The setting of the party then gives way to a journey by water, like the night journey of the hero described by Joseph Campbell (Campbell, 1972). But the vessel cannot carry the dreamer, so he must strike out on his own and plunge into the water, as each of us must do along the path of individuation. Finally, the dreamer is given a vision of the Divine Child, symbol of transcendence and homecoming at the end of the dream of life.

Divine Child

I am invited to a party. The people are dressed in fine new clothes walking about by the waterfront of a small fishing village of old stone houses. The gay, light dresses of the women contrast with the dark stones of the houses. I am invited to the party with them, and suddenly they are all gone, and the party is much farther away than I thought it would be. I must get there in a boat. I am all alone; the boat is at the quay.

A man of the town says that for five dollars I can get across on a yacht. I have five dollars, more than five dollars, hundreds of dollars and also francs. He takes me to the yacht, but it is not a yacht. It is a workaday fishing schooner, which I prefer. But it does not move; we try in many ways to make it move, and it seems to have moved a little. But then I know that I must strike out and swim.

And I am swimming ahead in the beautiful magic water of the bay. From the clear depths of the water comes a wonderful life to which I am not entitled, a life and a power which I both love and fear. I know that by diving down into the water I can find wonders and joy, but that it is not for me to dive down. Rather I must go to the other side, and I am indeed swimming to the other side. The other side is there. The end of the swim. The house is on the shore. The wide summer house which I am reaching with the strength that came to me from the water. The water is great and vast beneath me as I come toward the shore. And I have arrived. I am out of the water. I know now all that I must do in the summer house. I know that I must first play with this dog who comes running from one of the halls.

I know the Child will come, and He comes. The Child comes and smiles. It is the smile of a Great One, hidden. He gives me, in simplicity, two pieces of buttered white bread, the ritual and hieratic meal given to all who come to stay. (Merton, 1968, pp. 29-30)

The dream ends on a note of celebration: the ritual meal, communion or wedding feast, is a time of homecoming, made perfect by the gesture of simplicity, just as Helen Luke has described old age itself as a "journey into simplicity" (Luke, 1988). As the Shaker hymn puts it, "'Tis a gift to be simple, 'Tis a gift to be free, 'Tis a gift to come down where you ought to be.'" The dreams of the second half of life can be such gifts to guide us on the journey toward simplicity.

REFERENCES

Artress, L. (1996). *Walking a Sacred path: Rediscovering the labyrinth as a spiritual tool*. Riverhead Books.

Attar, F. (1984). *Conference of the birds*. Penguin, 1984.

Bulkeley, K. (1995). *Spiritual dreaming: A cross-cultural and historical journey*. NY: Paulist Press.

Campbell, J. (1972). *The hero with a thousand faces*. Princeton University Press.

Chuang, T. (1974). *The inner chapters*. Trans. G.-F. Feng and J. English. NY: Random House.

Cole, T. (1992). *The journey of life: A cultural history of aging in America*. Cambridge University Press.

Dass, R. (2000). *Still here: Embracing aging, changing, dying*. Riverhead Books.

Daumal, R. (1986). *Mount analog*. Shambhala.

Edinger, E. F. (1992). *Ego and archetype*. Shambhala.

Elrod, D. *Psychodynamics of the dying process* (cited by von Franz, op cit, p. 134).

Erikson, E. (1978). "Reflections on Dr. Borg's Life Cycle," in *Adulthood*. (Ed.) E. H. Erikson. New York: W. W. Norton.

Garfield, P. (1991). *Women's bodies, women's dreams*. Ballantine Books.

Hillman, J. (2000). *The force of character: And the lasting life*. Ballantine.

Jung, C. (1989). *Memories, dreams, reflections*. Recorded and edited by A. Jaffe, translated by R. and C. Winston, Vintage Books.

Jung, C. G. (1992). *Letters Volume 1*. Selected and edited by Gerhard Adler in collaboration with Aniela Jaffé. Translated by R. F. C. Hull. Princeton University Press.

Kelsey, M. T. (1974). *God, dreams, and revelation: A Christian interpretation of dreams*. Augsburg.

LaBerge, S., and Rheingold, H. (1991). *Exploring the world of lucid dreaming*. Ballantine Books.

Luke, H. (2001). *Such stuff as dreams are made on: The autobiography and journals of Helen M. Luke*. Harmony/Bell Tower.

Luke, H. (1988). *Old age: Journey into simplicity*. McGraw-Hill.

Merton, T. (1968). *Conjectures of a guilty bystander*. Image Books.

Meyer, M. (1992). *Gospel of Thomas: The hidden sayings of Jesus*. Harper-San Francisco.

Moody, H., and Carroll, D. (1997). *The five stages of the soul: Charting the spiritual passages that shape our lives*. New York: Doubleday.

Moody, H. R. (2002). "Conscious aging: A strategy for positive development in later life" in J. Ronch and J. Goldfield (Eds.), *Mental Wellness in Aging: Strength-based Approaches*. Health Professions Press.

Progoff, I. (1989). *The Cloud of unknowing*. Delta.

Ring, K. (1985). *Heading toward omega: In search of the meaning of the near-death experience*. Quill.

Sanford, J. (1984). *Dreams: God's forgotten language*. Harper San Francisco.

Savary, L. et al. (1984). *Dreams and spiritual growth: A Christian way of dreamwork*. NY: Paulist Press.

Suzuki, S. (1972). *Zen mind, beginner's mind.* Weatherhill.

Tornstam, L. (1997). Gerotranscendence: The contemplative dimension of aging. *Journal of Aging Studies.* 11:2 (Summer), 143-154.

Tornstam, L. (2000). Transcendence in later life. *Generations.* 23:4 (Winter, 1999-2000), 10-14.

Ullman, M., and Limmer, C. (1999). *The variety of dream experience: Expanding our ways of working with dreams.* State University of New York Press.

Ullman, M., and Limmer, C. (Eds.) (1999). *The Variety of Dream Experience.* 2nd ed. SUNY Press.

Von Franz, M.-L. (1987). *On dreams and death: A Jungian interpretation.* Trans. Emmanuel Xipolitas Kennedy and Vernon Brooks. Boston: Shambhala.

Webster, J. D., and Haight, B. (2002). *Critical Advances in Reminiscence Work.* Springer.

Wilber, K. (2000). *Integral psychology: Consciousness, spirit, psychology, therapy.* Shambhala.

Zalman, S.-S. and Miller, R. (1997). *From age-ing to sage-ing.* Time Warner.

A Pastoral Understanding
of Positive Aging

Samuel R. Seicol, DD, MAHL

SUMMARY. Positive aging may be more dependent on spiritual well-being than physical capacity. Understanding the spiritual perspective derives from the dichotomy between the "perceptual" and the "spiritual" realms of human awareness. Awareness of spiritual process in relationship to positive aging may also offer counseling additional challenges and opportunities, including: a balanced perspective on life issues, a sense of humor, counter-factual thinking, internal strengths and resources for growing through life losses and crises, and compensation skills that focus on current capacity and chosen pathways rather than dwelling on lost abilities. *[Article copies available for a fee from The Haworth Document Delivery Service: 1-800-HAWORTH. E-mail address: <docdelivery@ haworthpress.com> Website: <http://www.HaworthPress.com> © 2005 by The Haworth Press, Inc. All rights reserved.]*

KEYWORDS. Positive aging, spirituality, well-being, pastoral counseling, life perspective, aging

---

[Haworth co-indexing entry note]: "A Pastoral Understanding of Positive Aging." Seicol, Samuel R. Co-published simultaneously in *Journal of Gerontological Social Work* (The Haworth Social Work Practice Press, an imprint of The Haworth Press, Inc.) Vol. 45, No. 3, 2005, pp. 293-300; and: *Religion, Spirituality, and Aging: A Social Work Perspective* (ed: Harry R. Moody) The Haworth Social Work Practice Press, an imprint of The Haworth Press, Inc., 2005, pp. 293 300. Single or multiple copies of this article are available for a fee from The Haworth Document Delivery Service [1-800-HAWORTH, 9:00 a.m. - 5:00 p.m. (EST). E-mail address: docdelivery@haworthpress.com].

Available online at http://www.haworthpress.com/web/JGSW
© 2005 by The Haworth Press, Inc. All rights reserved.
doi:10.1300/J083v45n03_03

DEFINING SPIRITUALITY

Spiritual well-being is one of the most difficult concepts to define, yet it is one of the most essentials aspects in understanding and supporting healthy positive aging.[1] Having worked as a Geriatric Chaplain for the past 20 years, I have been privileged to learn from older adult "life pioneers" ranging in age from early 70s to 113. Among them I have found the most spiritually healthy people even as they struggled with multiple losses and personal decrements of aging. Reflecting on the life lessons from these elder mentors, I have developed a conceptual framework of spiritual well-being that undergirds many counseling techniques useful in practice with older adults.

Positive aging is related more to attitude toward life than it is to capabilities and capacity. This point was reinforced to me on many occasions over the course of my ministry in long-term care facilities. One of the most frequent questions I heard is, "Why is this happening to me (or why is God doing this to me)?" The most effective answer is neither theological–defending or defining God's ways–nor empirical–discussing the antecedents to the disease. Rather, the most effective approach is spiritual–challenging and sharing in the possibility to create meaning and purpose within the confines of current opportunities.

OVERVIEW

Understanding the issues of positive aging from a spiritual perspective is a doubly confounding task. On the one hand, positive aging is ultimately based on a subjective and individual perspective. A loss or setback that is perceived as insurmountable or a major obstacle to well-being and life satisfaction in one person may be inconsequential or quite resolvable in another. On the other, deriving a universally acceptable and complete definition of spirituality is, by its very nature, impossible. With these caveats in mind, however, it is far from futile to attempt to create a working philosophy of spiritual well-being as a tool for therapeutic intervention in enhancing an individual's perception and attitude toward "positive" aging.

From the standpoint of defining approaches to human awareness and comprehension, we begin with a basic dichotomy. There is the "perceptual" world, which consists of all that is objective, knowable, measurable, definable, and quantifiable. The counterpart to this is the "spiritual" world, which is subjective, intuitive (at best), illusive, inaccessible to full measurement and definition, and unquantifiable. In many older languages the word for "spirit" is the same as the word for "air," "wind," or "breath." The term denotes an unseeable and unmeasurable aspect of the world. Just as the "air" could be known by its influence, so also can a working philosophy of the realm of the spiritual be developed by assessing its influence on–and through analogy with–the perceptual realm.

In the arena of the perceptual there are three interdependent dimensions of height, width, and depth. An object must be seen in all three in order to be fully perceived. When one dimension is missing or distorted, as in a two-dimensional rendition, optical illusions are possible. These create perceptions that are false and counter to reality. By analogy the domain of the spiritual may be viewed as consisting of three discrete but fully interdependent dimensions of meaning, value, and purpose.[2] These three dimensions also relate to the human capacity for temporal awareness: i.e., past, present, and future. In a philosophy of spirituality there is a correlation between the three-fold framework of meaning, value, and purpose and the temporal structure of past, present, and future. This underlying philosophy of spirituality as discussed in this paper has practical value for spiritual and pastoral counseling.[3]

MEANING

Victor Frankl–in response to the theologies of suffering being developed in the latter part of the 20th century–stated emphatically, "Suffering is inherently meaningless!"[4] Through this statement he wished to convey his view that there is no intrinsic or externally derivable meaning in an individual's suffering. Rather, there is the inherent challenge to the individual to create a personal sense of meaning out of the event or incident causing the suffering. In spiritual terms Frankl's point can be extended to the understanding that "life is inherently meaningless" with the same challenge and opportunity. Thus, the language of meaning is the language of personal identity and spiritual rootedness. Meaning derives from actions by and accomplishments of an individual. What a person has done and how the perception of self has developed in the past defines the dimension of meaning in life. While this sense of meaning is ultimately individually chosen (and, indeed, always open to personal revision and redefinition), we cannot ignore that there are also external definitions of meaning (e.g., societal views and values) that may be internalized and accepted as a part of one's self image.

PURPOSE

The second dimension of human spirituality is purpose. Where meaning is linked to the past and derives from self-perceptions of accomplishments, purpose is fundamentally future oriented. Purpose can be viewed in terms of goals, hopes, and plans. External expectations by others or society may also have as much influence on the internalized sense of purpose as they exert on our sense of meaning. From the standpoint of the spiritual self, however, meaning and purpose are mutable and internally chosen dimensions which vary from person to person and from time to time within a single person.

VALUE

Value, the final dimension of the spiritual self–unlike meaning and purpose–is constant at all times and equal for all people. Value, in spiritual terms, is not related to values. Values are actually a part of the perceptual world and are generally reflective of the dimensions of meaning and purpose. Spiritual value is the intrinsic quantity of human beingness. Each person is born, lives, and dies as a person with a unique but universally equal value. The perception of the value of an individual, both internally and externally, may vary according to circumstance and situation; the actual value never increases or decreases. The perception of varied value comes from the distortion of seeing meaning and purpose as the operative dimensions. Consider the commonly known Moller-Franz optical illusion (Figure 1). The perceptual distortion, in which the eyes focus more on the directions of ends "M" and "P," leads to the illusion that line "V_1" is longer than line "V_2." Experience, on the other hand, teaches that the two lines are equal in length. This, by analogy, illustrates a "spiritual illusion" where ends "M" and "P" represent meaning and purpose and line "V" is the intrinsic human value.

SPIRITUAL RESOURCES FOR POSITIVE AGING

There are many implications for applying this philosophy of spirituality to counseling and supportive practice. A few of the more salient uses will be discussed here. The first intervention that presents itself derives from the analogy of the spiritual illusion. Consider that a person's sense of meaning and purpose (or the vision of opportunities for creat-

FIGURE 1

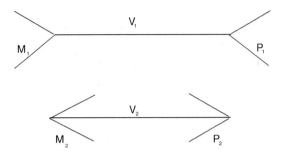

ing such) may become limited or restricted (as through the decrements often associated with aging). The internally realized or the externally imposed view of the value of the individual may be seen as line "V_2." A spiritually based intervention to enhance the sense of personal value, rather than working directly on the issues of self-worth and value, would focus on assisting (or challenging) the individual to create new meanings and purposes with the available resources. Positive aging thus becomes a spiritually based attitudinal process that is available to any person at any age. Some of the oldest and frailest residents in nursing homes appear to have a more hope-filled and positive outlook on their life than do younger elders with fewer losses. These elder "life pioneers" have discovered personal resources that help them either to see past the "illusion" or to choose to see the opportunities for meaning and purpose as moving their lives from line "V_2" to line "V_1."

FULL OR EMPTY

While common wisdom states that the optimistic view of the "glass as half-full" is preferable to the pessimistic view as "half empty," positive aging may involve rejecting both views in order to find a more functional third alternative. This point was best expressed to me some 15 years ago by a 90-year-old, wheelchair-bound nursing home resident. In a group discussion, S., when asked to share on which better represented her approach to life, replied, "Neither! I prefer to see the cup as twice as big as it needs to be. Full reminds me of what I no longer can do and empty says things will get worse. I simply pour my current capacities into a cup of the right size and I will always know that my life's cup will always 'runneth over.' "

JUST LUCKY

Another implication for practice in this philosophy of spirituality is the reminder that choice is always an option. Aging may force many losses on an individual, but there is always an opportunity to create meaning and purpose to choose one's personal focus and attitude. Aging can provide resources of strengths developed out of overcoming prior adversities. These strengths may then be applied to muster spiritual wellsprings for the current concern or crisis. Aging can also teach perspectives of patience and reflection that lead to the ability to imagine and restructure the experience in the light of alternatives. There is research that demonstrates that people who consider themselves lucky in life (and therefore are more likely to adopt a vision of positive attitudes) are not inherently luckier. Rather they have developed coping skills that are referred to as "counter-factual."[5] Frail elders who have survived, and often thrived, also demonstrate this attitude as a learned coping mechanism.

CONCLUSION

Understanding personal spirituality as a three-dimensional interrelationship of meaning, value, and purpose provides a framework for enhanced counseling interventions. This framework involves several components: (1) listening for cues to a person's earlier meaning creation; (2) adaptive skills for encountering life-transitions and crises; (3) strengthening desires for fulfillment of purpose; and (4) opportunities for compensatory responses to current life situations. All can be affective means for developing therapeutic interventions to validate and foster the individual's own spiritual well-being. One final example illustrates a common statement I have heard from failing frail elders: "I have lived long enough!" they might say, and then add: "Why can't I just go to sleep and not wake up?" Building on spiritual relational approaches, I often respond along the lines of, "I will share in your prayer! But, in the meantime, until God grants your wish, what will you do when you wake up in the morning?" I have seen 98-year-olds revitalize and rejoin communal and family life following such discussions and validation.

Thus, utilizing an awareness of spiritual process can be an effective way to support and foster attitudes that lead to an enhanced sense of positive aging. Spiritual and pastoral counseling can challenge individuals to develop coping mechanisms that include: a balanced perspective on life issues, a sense of humor, counter-factual thinking, internal strengths and resources for growing through life losses and crises, and compensation skills that focus on current capacity and chosen pathways rather than dwelling on lost abilities. Positive aging involves the learned ability to see spiritual illusions as a distorted perception and to respond accordingly.[6]

NOTES

1. Spiritual well-being was first formally defined in 1971. Further research and developments in the mid 1980s into the 90s led to a search for more useful broad based definitions. One example of this process can be found in *Aging and Spirituality: Newsletter of ASA's Forum on Religion, Spirituality, & Aging.* Vol IX, No. 1 (Spring,1997).

2. Use of the language of meaning, value, and purpose is based on Victor Frankl's definition of the fundamental human condition in terms of a "will to meaning." The application and expansion of the condition of the search to create meaning into the areas of purpose and value are derived from the author's experience in pastoral counseling with frail elders, coupled with attendance at lectures by and personal discussions with Dr. Frankl at the 35th Annual Meeting of the American Society on Aging (ASA) in Washington, D.C. March 18-21, 1989. A bibliography can be found in: Frankl, V.E., *Man's Search for Meaning.* Washington Square Press, Inc., New York, 1965. Additional discussions can be found in the works of Mel Kimble, a student of Victor Frankl. See especially Melvin Kimble, *Viktor Frankl's Contribution to Spirituality and Aging,* New York: The Haworth Press, Inc., 2000.

3. There is an additional aspect of human spirituality which is external and relational. The three basic dimensions of meaning/value/purpose are still the fundamental system but the spiritual expression develops in the affirmation and acceptance of the self in and by others. The philosophy of relational spirituality, based on the "I and Thou" as presented by Martin Buber, is beyond the scope of this current paper. The full text is available in a translation by Walter Kaufmann: Buber, M., *I and Thou,* New York: Charles Scribner's and Sons, 1970.

4. Presented at the Keynote Address and in various workshops and sessions during the ASA 35th Annual Meeting.

5. A full discussion of the luck factor and some interesting interventions can be found in: Wiseman, R., "The Luck Factor," *Skeptical Inquirer,* May/June 2003, Vol. 27 No. 3, pages 26-30.

6. For additional resources helpful in developing the framework described in this article see Melvin A. Kimble and Susan H. McFadden (Eds.), *Aging, Spirituality, and Religion: A Handbook*, Volume 2, Minneapolis: Fortress Press, 2003; Julie Barton, Marita Grudzen, and Ron Zielske, *Vital Connections in Long-term Care: Spiritual Resources for Staff and Residents*, Baltimore: Health Professions Press, 2003; and Koenig Harold and Andrew Weaver, *Pastoral Care of Older Adults: Creative Pastoral Care and Counseling*, Fortress Press, 1998.

Land of Forgetfulness:
Dementia Care as Spiritual Formation

Wayne A. Ewing, PhD

SUMMARY. The personal circumstances of dementia caregiving are sometimes experienced as so severely demanding as to be overwhelming. While sustenance within, and recovery from these experiences are increasingly addressed in helpful ways from psychological, emotional, and practical life planning frames of reference, we are still learning how to speak with one another about the spiritual dimensions of this peculiar journey. From a spiritual perspective, the caregiver initially, and frequently perpetually, finds her/himself in a state of spiritual exhaustion. Oddly enough, there are ample resources at hand to address this existential state with wisdom and grace, allowing for the possibility that the caregiver might move from spiritual weariness to enhanced spiritual formation. *[Article copies available for a fee from The Haworth Document Delivery Service: 1-800-HAWORTH. E-mail address: <docdelivery@ haworthpress.com> Website: <http://www.HaworthPress.com> © 2005 by The Haworth Press, Inc. All rights reserved.]*

KEYWORDS. Spirituality, aging, religion, dementia care, spiritual formation, mysticism, spiritual growth

---

[Haworth co-indexing entry note]: "Land of Forgetfulness: Dementia Care as Spiritual Formation." Ewing, Wayne A. Co-published simultaneously in *Journal of Gerontological Social Work* (The Haworth Social Work Practice Press, an imprint of The Haworth Press, Inc.) Vol. 45, No. 3, 2005, pp. 301-311; and: *Religion, Spirituality, and Aging: A Social Work Perspective* (ed: Harry R. Moody) The Haworth Social Work Practice Press, an imprint of The Haworth Press, Inc., 2005, pp. 301-311. Single or multiple copies of this article are available for a fee from The Haworth Document Delivery Service [1-800-HAWORTH, 9:00 a.m. - 5:00 p.m. (EST). E-mail address: docdelivery@haworthpress.com].

Available online at http://www.haworthpress.com/web/JGSW
doi:10.1300/J083v45n03_04

Are your wonders known in the darkness,
or your saving help in the land of forgetfulness?

–Psalm 88:12

I am not alone among the 19 million dementia caregivers who have come to the realization that nothing in the ordinary circumstances of our lives prepared us for the journey we undertook with our Beloved. In my situation, immediately upon the time of the diagnosis my spouse received at age 55–probable early onset dementia, Alzheimer's type–I realized that the ordinary skills in which I had acquired some modicum of training, education, experience and even wisdom, were not going to be of much aid for the path upon which we were directed. Of course there was some relevance in the habits of life I had assimilated as clergy, educator, pastoral counselor, spouse, lover, and parent. But relevance and succor are not always companions, and in my case they were not.

I quickly learned that there were resources at hand for me and my Beloved to usher us gently into the journey: material from the local Alzheimer's chapter, the counsel of caring medical personnel, the shared experience within a family support group. Over the handful of years from the time of increased attention to the rigors of dementia care to the time of my Beloved's diagnosis, there had been a rather rapid accumulation of wisdom focused on caregiver needs. A vast gamut of human experience was gathered up in that material. Physical matters–from the arrangement of the kitchen to the assessment of one's own physical limitations–were addressed. Cognitive concerns–from the new knowledge required regarding medications, research, the progression of the dementia and its stages to a recognition of legal matters now suddenly in the forefront of our relationship–were among the affairs introduced to us. Emotional aspects of the experience–from guilt and anger to sorrow and laughter–were projected. Social and familial issues–from the rigors of preparing for an outing to the idiosyncratic nature of one's family–were weighed with careful commentary. Ethical and moral dilemmas–from end of life preparations to the new place of "truth" in my relationship to my Beloved–were spelled out, evaluated and given guidelines.

In sum, a kind of attentiveness never asked of me before was emerging in my daily life. I began to recognize that on this walk through the garden, no flower would remain untrampled; every aspect of our lives would be touched by this passage. While I did my most to bring myself into some sense of harmony with the Land of Forgetfulness journey and its strange, unbidden newness, I increasingly struggled with a jarring realization that all this language *about* dementia caregiving was adding to my anxiety and sense of inadequacy. I found myself casting about for some kind of language *of* caregiving. I was very much wanting to find some way to express the numbness and shock of the journey in a manner that provided actual nurturing and sustenance.

What I was becoming familiar with were added activities, suggestions for tending to these new responsibilities, and programs for successful discharge of these accountabilities. I was surrounded with the counsel of Doing, while I experienced needfulness in Being. The closest I can come to describing this experience is simply to note that I–like others in these circumstances–was looking at an infinitely expanding horizon of expectations. There was no pause button, and certainly no stop button, on the relentless dailiness of caregiving. Even respite care, graciously provided by agencies, friends, and family, did not address the dynamic Aeschylus so eloquently described millennia ago:

> Pain that will not forget,
> Falls, drop by drop,
> Upon my heart . . .

While I did find solace from time to time for my tired mind and my aching body, the soulful dimension of my experience was bereft of reference points and direction. I refer to this as "soulful" out of the primary sense that I was engaged in the impossible in something much larger than myself. And, of course, the impossible was unfolding as the possible, and that which was larger than I was not the disease, but the circle of caregiving itself. Here I was, in the company of millions, and yet quite alone, facing an infinitely demanding circumstance with an extraordinarily finite resource: myself. That is the feel of spiritual weariness; that was my front door to the house of soulful need in dementia caregiving.

While there was no continuum of experience that informed me how I might proceed in this aspect of the journey, there did appear a moment of transformation. I have since learned that many of us have these moments; I have cherished every caregiver's story of such moments. This is mine.

About six months or so into our journey with dementia, while we were still learning our way through the fog, my mother called one evening, as was her weekly practice. My mother, at 80, was vibrant, witty, the life of the party at the retirement village where she and my father resided. This call, though, was somber, and I sensed something was troubled. "Wayne," she finally and quietly confided, "today I was diagnosed with an inoperable, cancerous brain tumor. I have about three months to live." And so it was. During those 90 days, my Beloved and I were able to travel from Colorado to Pennsylvania on several occasions to be with my parents in their new encounter.

On one of those visits I accompanied my mother to her treatment at a nearby radiation clinic. She looked dreadful. Slumped in her wheel-chair, she was uncharacteristically in disarray, gloomy and gray as the rain swept day. In one of those moments in which my tongue was fat, my brain empty, my heart a lump of black ice, I knelt down by her, put on a smiley face, and said, "Hey, Mom, how are ya' doin'!" My mother seized that moment to introduce me to caregiving. She sat bolt upright, arranged the few wisps of hair she had, straightened her sweater and skirt, and said as loudly as she could–so that I, all the folks in the waiting room, the nurses in white behind the glass-windowed counter, and if they were lucky, the robed technicians and physicians deep in the bowels of the clinic, might hear–"Son, I'm terrific. And I'm not afraid. I'm only going where God has gone before."

I got it. As an only child, I had been close to my mother all my life, and she had certainly come to be familiar with me. She knew her stupid son had just asked a very stupid question. And I knew that my mother was telling me something she didn't "believe." She was way beyond belief. She was in the realm of sure and certain knowing, and celebrated in that public moment a straightforward report on what it is like to live in the fire.

I learned the language I was seeking from her: the language intuitive knowers use to speak of the impossibly possible, the language of those who grasp that which is larger than we, enveloping us in Presence. In short, I recognized in that moment that the language *of* caregiving is the language of the Abrahamic mystical traditions. What my mother had so intimately revealed to me also included an invitation: a welcoming to holy ground, a gentle beckoning to step into the sacred space we know as suffering and death. What changed for me was perception. And, of course, when perception changes, so does reality.

My reality now became an arena where the unknown was not simply a source of fear and terror. Now I entered the unknown as the place where the sustaining of spirit could take place. The process took some time, and I worked with the luxury of time still given me. I, unlike my Beloved, was still able to move between the past, via memory, and the future, via imagination. I was not locked in the interminable present of dementia, Alzheimer's type.

And so I did. Looking backwards, I was able to redo the awful dread I had experienced at the time of diagnosis. I recalled the frame of reference of the late medieval English mystical treatise, *The Cloud of Unknowing*. Unknowing is not so much an object to be feared, these meditations on holiness contend, as it is a state to be yearned for, a desirable place where all that has in fact hindered relevant knowing falls away. It seemed to me that this perspective was ever so much more useful for dementia caregiving than the view that I had chosen to take on: this is a dark and dreary shadowland, where every turn is into an alien place. Rather, I could choose, as this old spiritual counsel advocated, to see the unknown lying before us as filled with promise and hope, with love, power, and intimacy.

Gradually, I began to play with the topsy-turvy world of dementia and dementia care as if it included all the proper directional signals, not the erroneous ones I and others have been schooled to perceive as the mark of the disease and its progressive journey. So my perceived future began to take on a different hue as well. Rather than expecting for myself and my Beloved an increasingly desperate and demanding environment of feelings and actions, I was free to construe our journey as one that would hold immense gifts and wonders.

One of the earlier gifts I chose to receive involved the simple reversal of the way in which all we well-intentioned people perceive the relationship between the caregiver and the Beloved to change. How often I had heard from friends, "Oh, it must be so sad for you that Ann no longer knows you or recognizes you . . . " Well of course I was sad. Yet along with the source of that sadness was the growing awareness that in my passage in the Beloved's eyes from familiar partner and lover to total stranger, I was also experiencing a dimension of trust and intimacy previously untapped in our long relationship.

When my Beloved repeatedly said to me, "I don't know who you are, but I know you are my friend," I was each time transported to a realm of such loving acceptance that I wept–not always in grief, and often in joy. Not even the mystic's language of love–Bernard of Clairvaux on *The Song of Songs* would come to mind and heart–could really wrap itself around this stunning instance of truly "unconditional" loving. To be loved in this raw, unmediated way would lift me from the mundane of the task at hand and take me to a space where my spirit was soulfully refreshed.

Mystics speak of "spiritual gifts," and this sense of totally giving trust in immediate love is one of them. There are many others. Among them is a reworking of the sense of time I noted just a few sentences ago, a sense that my Beloved was "locked" in an unending present. Yet this appearance of being captive to lost sensibilities can also be construed as a unique ability to celebrate every given moment as refreshingly new–a posture advocated within the mystical traditions, where awareness counts for all.

Rumi, a Sufi mystic from within Islam, and a near contemporary of *The Cloud of Unknowing*, has put it this way:

> Notice how each particle moves.
> Notice how everyone has just arrived here from a journey.
> Notice how each wants a different food . . .
> Look at this cup that can hold the ocean.

Accompanying my Beloved through the ravages of disorientation in time, where the links between past and future progressively go missing, I was introduced to the beauty Rumi refers to here as a persistent present.

For example, when I walked with my Beloved on our daily strolls through the pine forest near our mountain home, she would pause to look at a variety of small wonders catching her attention–the bloom of a columbine, a spider's web cast between lichen covered rocks, a cluster of button cacti. And then, over and over again, she would say, "See! See! See how beautiful this is!" What I might have taken for the sing-song repetitiveness of an Alzheimer's consciousness stuck in the groove of an unyielding moment, I could choose to receive as the giftedness of single moments. There really was no urgency to move on to the next thing, the next point in time; this was a unique, holy moment, filled with the awe of the present.

The more attentive I became to the Beloved, the more I began to recognize the odd shape of awareness she enjoyed, in comparison to my own. The perspective she was revealing rather consistently was actually in harmony with the repertoire of attitudes and behavior recommended by the spiritual elders of the Abrahamic religions. I gave myself a kind of mental exercise, and then more or less converted it to an ordered discipline of learning, I began to cluster my awareness of the possibilities of spiritual growth within dementia caregiving around the well-known list of behaviors provided by the national Alzheimer's Association, and widely available through every local chapter: *Is it Alzheimer's? Ten Warning Signs.*

I began to challenge myself, and others as the occasion presented itself, to imagine that this pamphlet or hand out sheet had absolutely no reference to Alzheimer's disease. Supposing it were headed "Ten Steps

in Spiritual Formation," or "Enhancing and Nurturing Spiritual Life"–
what might our response be? In that setting, things like "memory loss"
and "difficulty performing familiar tasks," and "problems with language" take on an entirely different cast. There is simply an uncanny
correlation between the popular symptomatic description of dementia,
Alzheimer's type, and the counsel towards spiritual growth advocated
by the mystics of the Abrahamic religions.

St. John of the Cross has described the "sum of all perfection" as
"oblivion of the world," a state within which "memory loss" might be
the merest of beginning, faltering steps towards nurturing spiritual life.
He is one of the many who encourage us to detach from the ordinary, in
order to experience meaning from another direction:

> I entered I knew not where,
> and remained without knowing,
> there transcending all knowledge.
> It is God's mercy that leaves us
> without any understanding,
> there transcending all knowledge.

And St. Paul, though not constantly writing from an ecstatic consciousness, nonetheless puts his own mystical experiences within the
grasp of ordinary experience: "Be transformed by the renewing of your
mind." And "problems with language?" Mother Teresa gathers up millennia of spiritual wisdom in her simple statement, "God is the friend of
silence," as does the Seraphim of Sarov, in noting that "No spiritual exercise is as good as that of silence."

But perhaps the most demanding of our attention is the weight given
"disorientation of time and place" in the observation of the Beloved's
journey into and through dementia. In the context of spiritual wisdom,
this very perception is sought and promoted above all else. Meister
Eckhart summarizes the thrust of this particular tradition in Abrahamic
spirituality in stating, "I am as certain as I live, and as God lives, that the
soul who knows God knows God above time and place." It is ordinary,
and not pathological, to seek deliverance from "time and place" in order
to advance one's spiritual state.

These same peculiar connections can be made throughout these
handy referents to the likely characteristics of dementia, Alzheimer's
type. "Poor or decreased judgment" has its corollary in the spiritual
counsel, across all religions actually, to abandon judgment of all kinds.

"Problems with abstract thinking" is a mark, in the spiritual traditions, of advance in dissolving thinking into quietude. "Misplacing things" would be a happy sign of increasing abilities to forsake attachment to things and possessions.

"Changes in mood or behavior" are absolutely required by these spiritual elders, were one, in the phrase of Nicolas of Cusa, "to enter into the garden of delights," where spiritual wisdom flowers. "Changes in personality" are also expected of the journey in spiritual growth, as noted, again by Nicolas of Cusa: "But, O my God, the Absolute and Eternal One, it is beyond the present and the past that you exist and utter speech . . . I behold you, O Lord my God, in a kind of mental trance, for if my sight is not sated with seeing, nor my ear with hearing, then much less is my intellect with understanding." "Loss of initiative," the tenth and final "sign" of possible Alzheimer's disease, is a primary condition in spiritual enhancement, and again Meister Eckhart makes the appeal precisely and concisely: "To know ourselves, to be installed in God, this is not hard–seeing that God must be working in us; for it is Godly work: we must acquiesce and make no resistance; we are passive while allowing the Holy to act in us."

In other words, at every turn in our recognition of the distinctive journey the Beloved is embarked on in dementia, there is a spiritual counterpoint that makes of this same dynamic a way station in spiritual development. I do not make of that parallelism, however, any kind of observation about the spiritual status or state of the beloved; that is not for me to know. The relevance for dementia caregiving lies elsewhere; it lies with us. That is, should I choose not to view the Beloved as a black hole into which every vestige of personality is sinking, but rather as an angel of light who presents an occasion for reflection on the sensibility of my own posturing in the world, then I do know this: that I am lifted up, that I am refreshed for the likelihood that I stand in the embrace of the Holy, and not abandoned to the darkness of the land of forgetfulness.

And I can come, with some relief, to the remainder of the passage from Aeschylus:

> Pain that cannot forget
> falls drop by drop
> upon the heart . . .

And in our sleep,
against our will,
comes wisdom
from the aweful
grace of God.

A COMMENT ON RESOURCES

This article, as well as my decade long reflection on the spiritual dimensions of dementia caregiving, can be construed as a commentary on, perhaps even an exegesis of, two passages. The first is quoted at the head of the article, from the Psalmist's inquiry of the Holy One in Psalm 88: Is there "saving help in the land of forgetfulness?" that "land" being an ordinary Hebrew reference to Gehenna, the place of the dead. The second is an extraordinary passage from Sherwin Nuland's 1994 book, *How We Die* (New York, A. Knopf), where he writes (p. 105):

> [Alzheimer's disease is] one of those cataclysms that seems designed specifically to test the human spirit . . . If there is wisdom to be found, it must be in the knowledge that human beings are capable of the kind of love and loyalty that transcends not only the physical debasement but even the spiritual weariness of the years of sorrow.

The sentiment represented in these ancient and rather recent sentences capture the dilemma I think I address. A considerably growing body of literature, as I suggest in the article, addresses the interplay of spirituality, religion and aging (e.g., cf. the quarterly newsletter, *Aging and Spirituality*, published by the American Society on Aging Forum on Religion, Spirituality, and Aging [www.asaging.com]), yet little of it to date specifically focuses on those who accompany the Beloved in both body and soul through the journey of dementia in its varied forms, Alzheimer's type being only the most familiar.

In order, the mystic literature on which I draw in this article includes *The Classics of Western Spirituality*, 1981 edition of *The Cloud of Unknowing* (New York, Paulist Press), and the Cistercian Fathers series 1970 edition of *The Works of Bernard of Clairvaux*, Volume I, where his sermons on *The Song of Songs* are translated. The quote from Rumi is taken from his poem "Special Plates," in Coleman Barks and John

Moyne's 1995 collection of his poetry, *The Essential Rumi* (San Francisco, Harper Collins). I use the translation of St. John of the Cross provided by Ken Krabbenhoft in his masterfully crafted 1999 bi-lingual collection, *The Poems of St. John of the Cross*, illustrated by Ferris Cook (New York, Harcourt Brace).

The references to Mother Teresa and the Seraphim of Serov are but two of the hundreds of sources so wonderfully gathered up in Frederic and Mary Ann Brussat's 1996 anthology, *Spiritual Literacy: Reading the Sacred in Everyday Life* (New York, Scribner). I have found this collection a treasure trove of invaluable references to ancient and contemporary spiritual and mystic commentary.

I draw my references to Meister Eckhart from Ursala Fleming's provocative 1988 edition of some of his writing in the collection bearing his name and the sub-title *The Man from Whom God Nothing Hid* (Springfield, Templegate). Nicolas of Cusa I draw on from an older (1928) translation of *The Vision of God* republished in 1960 with an introduction by the inestimable Evelyn Underhill (New York, Frederick Ungar).

The Aeschylus quotation I saw some time ago in a small magazine of poetry and narrative now no longer available; it was featured in a story of a woman in recovery from the death of her young son–she carries this passage with her on a laminated card, and refers to it incessantly. Dr. Sophie Mills, a friend and colleague at the University of North Carolina, Asheville who chairs the Classics Department helped me trace the words to their original context: *Agememnon*, l. 176 ff.

The literature of caregivers and persons in the early stages of dementia, Alzheimer's type is growing as well. While not necessarily focused on the spirituality I here pursue, they are as varied as the well known work of England's John Bayley on his passage with his spouse, the eminent philosopher and critic Iris Murdoch: *Elegy for Iris* (New York, St. Martin's, 1998) and the lesser known account by Thomas DeBaggio's in *Losing My Mind* (New York, Free Press, 2002). I suggest my own book, *Tears in God's Bottle: Reflections on Alzheimer's Caregiving* (Evansville, 1st Books) as a quiet notation on the way one caregiver finds his way through this demanding territory in the company of Biblical reference points.

One of the earlier booklets to take on the specific connection between faith and Alzheimer's was the 1995 *You are one of us: Successful Clergy/Church Connections to Alzheimer's Families*, authored by Lisa Gwyther and published by the Duke University Medical Center. More recently published collections which I find helpful and sometimes inspirational include Julia Barton, Maria Grudzen, and Ron Zielske's *Vital*

Connections in Long-Term Care: Spiritual Resources for Staff and Residents (Baltimore, Health Professions Press, 2003) and the absolutely delightful *In Their Hearts: Inspirational Alzheimer's Stories*, written by a personal friend, Mary Margaret Britton Yearwood, who here recounts some of her experiences in ministry as chaplain in dementia settings (Victoria, Canada, Trafford, 2002).

Readers are undoubtedly aware of helpful, focused material I do not mention here. The author would love to hear from you as we collaborate in constructing an existential answer to the Psalmist!

Caregiving and Our Inner Elder:
Insights from a Spiritual Master

Richard Griffin, MDiv

SUMMARY. Dutch Priest Henri Nouwen, who died in 1996, has a large following of devoted readers. Though not formally a gerontologist, he wrote one small book, *Aging: The Fulfillment of Life*, full of remarkable insights into the meaning of growing old. Two approaches to caring for older people have special resonance. First, a person must appropriate his or her own aging, coming to grips with one's aging self. Secondly, one must allow the old person to enter into one's own life. Incorporating these two principles into service of elders gives it a spiritual value that goes beyond merely routine contact. *[Article copies available for a fee from The Haworth Document Delivery Service: 1-800-HAWORTH. E-mail address: <docdelivery@haworthpress.com> Website: <http://www.HaworthPress.com> © 2005 by The Haworth Press, Inc. All rights reserved.]*

KEYWORDS. Self-appropriation, spiritual rationale, kinship, the aging self, caring

Henri J. M. Nouwen was a Catholic priest whose ministry of writing and speaking touched the hearts of many searchers after a deeper spiritual life. Though Dutch by birth and upbringing, he spent most of his

[Haworth co-indexing entry note]: "Caregiving and Our Inner Elder: Insights from a Spiritual Master." Griffin, Richard. Co-published simultaneously in *Journal of Gerontological Social Work* (The Haworth Social Work Practice Press, an imprint of The Haworth Press, Inc.) Vol. 45, No. 3, 2005, pp. 313-317; and: *Religion, Spirituality, and Aging: A Social Work Perspective* (ed: Harry R. Moody) The Haworth Social Work Practice Press, an imprint of The Haworth Press, Inc., 2005, pp. 313-317. Single or multiple copies of this article are available for a fee from The Haworth Document Delivery Service [1-800-HAWORTH, 9:00 a.m. - 5:00 p.m. (EST). E-mail address: docdelivery@haworthpress.com].

Available online at http://www.haworthpress.com/web/JGSW
© 2005 by The Haworth Press, Inc. All rights reserved.
doi:10.1300/J083v45n03_05

adult years in the United States where he received some of his training in psychology. As a teacher at Notre Dame and in the divinity schools of both Yale and Harvard, he exercised a transformative influence on the lives of his students. Widespread speaking engagements plus his more than thirty books broadened that influence much further and these writings continue to speak to many people.

A community of close friends and associates continues to make known the work of this dynamic spiritual leader. Toronto, where he spent his last years living at Daybreak, a residence for people with developmental disabilities, has become the center of studies about him and other activities connected with his life and work. The web site http://Nouwen.net carries information about his life and activities that both keep his memory fresh and explore further his spiritual legacy.

Henri Nouwen's Personal Journey. Since his death in 1997, Henri Nouwen has become a cult figure for many people in North America and for some in other parts of the world. Through his writings and teaching, this Dutch priest has left a spiritual legacy that has moved many to a more reflective and prayerful life. They have found inspiration in a man who was charismatic in his ability to present spirituality clearly and with deeply personal resonance. Those who heard him speak look back with gratitude for having had the opportunity to listen to this master of the spoken and written word.

Henri Nouwen also had a gift for personal relationships. Not without some exaggeration perhaps, he was said to have had ten thousand personal friends, people who continue to cherish his memory now. Those many thousands more who knew him only in his writings find there a dynamic spiritual presence that keeps them reading his works.

I count myself among the mythic ten thousand who can claim friendship with Henri. During the period when he was teaching at Harvard Divinity School, I had significant contact with him, as I had previously before he came to Cambridge. Opportunities to converse with him meant much to me and I relished my meetings with him, meetings that included at least one meal in my home. His writings helped fill in the larger picture of his soul and ministry, especially the published material that came late in his life. These latter works ultimately revealed another Henri, one whom I had never known intimately. In these writings, especially in his journals, he emerges as a man who had to struggle with personal issues too tortuous to resolve. In fact, this spiritual master seems never to have known much peace of soul.

This revelation of a person troubled in spirit and always restless in the world has endeared Henri Nouwen even more to his legions of devotees.

Though so successful along a variety of fronts, he frequently doubted the value of his own work. He was also terribly restless, moving from one job to another with surprising frequency, always picking up and leaving and never settling down. The Netherlands, the United States, Notre Dame, Yale, Harvard, Peru, upstate New York, and finally Toronto–all served as his home. In Toronto, he became spiritual advisor at Daybreak, one of the Arche communities established by Jean Vanier. Here he found at least a measure of peace (not without a severe crisis of depression) and planned to settle down there. But he never could follow through on that plan because he was surprised by death in 1996 at age 64.

Nouwen's Insights on Aging. When I once told Henri of my esteem for his slim volume *Aging: The Fulfillment of Life* (written with Walter Gaffney), he disavowed knowing much of anything about the subject. However, my familiarity with this work of some 150 pages (many of them devoted to photos) was sufficient to refute the author's claim. I still hold *Aging* as my favorite piece of writing on the subject of growing older. Written when Henri was only 42, it shows remarkable grasp of the later life that he was never to experience himself. As I come closer to the realm of old age and deal with many other people older than I, my appreciation for it grows.

This book first appeared in 1974, then was published in an Image Book edition and has continued to remain in print. In this article I deliberately neglect what part Henri's co-author Walter Gaffney may have had in the writing of the book. Whatever Gaffney's spiritual doctrine may be, it is clearly compatible with Henri Nouwen's.

Of particular importance are Nouwen's insights into the caregiving given to older people by those younger than they. On this subject he offers a deeply spiritual approach that I find invaluable and almost unique. At first sight, his point of view can seem easily accessible, almost obvious. I have discovered from experience, however, that many social workers and other professionals in the field of providing care have difficulty grasping it. They tend to think they already know and practice this approach even though the comments of those served frequently suggest otherwise.

Wendy Lustbader, for example, has explored the dilemmas of dependency in her book *Counting on Kindness* (Free Press, 1991), where she observes that caregivers often have difficulty grasping the situation of people they care for because they start from a different position: The one who gives help is more powerful than the one who receives it. The sheer acknowledgment of this inequality is a relief to those who have to occupy the inferior position (p. 34). Overcoming such distance is a challenge for caregivers. But some do indeed fulfill those ideals, incorporating, in Lustbader's words, the highest qualities of mercy in their work.

At the same time, they may not be aware of a deeper spiritual rationale behind their work. It can prove useful for them also to reflect upon the ideals explained in *Aging* and to reexamine their ways of relating to elder clients. Such an approach may make a difference, enough to add much value to their work. They can even come, perhaps, to a greater appreciation of their profession as a vocation and derive greater satisfaction from it.

The Spiritual Rationale of Service. What Henri Nouwen suggests is that ultimately you cannot serve old people as they need, if you have not appropriated yourself as an aging person. And furthermore, you must allow the receiver of services to enter into your own life.

Of course, without doing these two things you can still take care of an older person decently and efficiently. No one is going to give you bad marks for lack of the inner spiritual dimension in your work. However, your service will fall short of the ideal and probably will not reach into the other person's soul. Nor will you profit from it spiritually as you could do by following Nouwen's insights.

Care for the elderly, writes Nouwen, means, first of all, to make ourselves available to the experience of becoming old. This first principle suggests an effort to break through the illusion that we will always be the same. Those bursting with good health and buoyant spirits most often find it difficult to believe they will ever be old and infirm. They are swayed by a culture that prizes youth and youthful exuberance above all and successfully tries to hide the realities that characterize the later years. Thus we not only tend to deny the real existence of old men and women living in their closed rooms and nursing homes, but also the old man or woman who is slowly awakening in our own center.

Appropriation of ourselves as aging establishes a deep kinship between us and those we serve. Aging becomes a common denominator, a shared gift that brings us together as members of one human family. We see the elder as our future self, and we reach out, not to a member of a race apart, but rather to another one of us. Then the compassion we show takes on a profoundly human quality that dignifies us as well as the person we serve.

This spiritual attitude undermines the subtle superiority that elderly people not infrequently experience at the hands of those who attend to their needs. Instead, one learns to deal with elders, not as children but as mature adults. It does away with artificially cheery greetings in words such as, "And how are we this morning, Mrs. Smith?" Instead this spirituality works to establish a basic equality that flows from a recognition that server and served belong to the same human family with similar needs either now or in the future.

This approach allows us to drop defenses that so often cause alienation. It unveils the true nature of the mechanisms that put people off. As Nouwen says, it is no secret that many of our suggestions, advice, admonitions, and good words are often offered in order to keep distance rather than to allow closeness. When we are primarily concerned with giving old people something to do, offering them entertainment and distractions, we might avoid the painful realization that most people do not want to be distracted but heard, not entertained but sustained.

Providing help for others can thus prove a smokescreen obscuring what is really needed. As Nouwen emphasizes, although old people need a lot of very practical help, more significant to them is someone who offers his or her own aging self as the source of their care. When we have allowed an old man or woman to come alive in the center of our own experience, when we have recognized him or her in our own aging self, we might then be able to paint our self-portrait in a way that can be healing to those in distress.

Closely related to the need for self-appropriation is the willingness to allow the elders we serve to enter into our life. As Nouwen puts the challenge, how to allow the elderly to enter into the center of our own lives, how to create the space where they can be heard and listened to from within with careful attention. Instead, those who minister to elders are tempted to neglect what those receiving care have to give them.

Nouwen makes a point of explaining this mistake: Quite often our concern to preach, teach, or cure prevents us from perceiving and receiving what those we care for have to offer. Here he seems to envision religious ministry but the lesson applies to caregivers of any sort.

In only a few short pages, Henri Nouwen has provided the elements of a spirituality that, when applied, has the potential to place gerontological service on a different level. I feel grateful to this charismatic and much valued friend and priest who has left behind a legacy of understanding and wisdom that can inspire those committed to serving others. Aging as the fulfillment of life can seem utopian when you have to deal with physical decline and disintegration. By putting service to older people in a context of both self-appropriation and a mutual exchange of gifts, we elevate it to an activity profoundly human and spiritual.

Living with Elder Wisdom

Eugene Bianchi, PhD

SUMMARY. This study is based on interview research with over a hundred creative elders. Their spirituality is explored through their life experiences as re-interpreted in later years. Spirituality is often expressed in "non-religious" language. They speak of inner empowerments: cultivating self-esteem, harvesting memories, transformative turning points, life-long learning, themes of humor and gratitude, and encountering mortality. They also explore outward empowerments: developing new purposes, welcoming possibilities, fostering more freedom, cultivating family and friends, forming intentional communities, and taking on larger social causes re peace, justice and ecology. This elder spirituality manifests important changes in their earlier views of religion. *[Article copies available for a fee from The Haworth Document Delivery Service: 1-800-HAWORTH. E-mail address: <docdelivery@ haworthpress.com> Website: <http://www.HaworthPress.com> © 2005 by The Haworth Press, Inc. All rights reserved.]*

KEYWORDS. Spirituality of aging, psychology in later life, religion and older people, self-actualization in elderhood, creative eldering

---

This article first appeared in *The Way: A British Journal of Spirituality* (Vol. 36, No. 2, April, 1996, pp. 93-102) and is reprinted by permission of the author. Further reflections on ideas in this article are more fully elaborated in E. Bianchi, *Elder Wisdom: Crafting Your Own Elderhood* (Crossroad, 1994).

[Haworth co-indexing entry note]: "Living with Elder Wisdom." Bianchi, Eugene. Co-published simultaneously in *Journal of Gerontological Social Work* (The Haworth Social Work Practice Press, an imprint of The Haworth Press, Inc.) Vol. 45, No. 3, 2005, pp. 319-329; and: *Religion, Spirituality, and Aging: A Social Work Perspective* (ed: Harry R. Moody) The Haworth Social Work Practice Press, an imprint of The Haworth Press, Inc., 2005, pp. 319-329. Single or multiple copies of this article are available for a fee from The Haworth Document Delivery Service [1-800-HAWORTH, 9:00 a.m. - 5:00 p.m. (EST). E-mail address: docdelivery@ haworthpress.com].

Available online at http://www.haworthpress.com/web/JGSW
doi:10.1300/J083v45n03_06

I would like to reflect on points of spiritual wisdom for ageing that I discovered in researching the lives of a hundred creative elders in the United States. The people in the study were a cross-section of men and women, averaging seventy-seven years of age, from different religious, ethnic and professional backgrounds. My intention was to explore the concrete experiences of older persons as they negotiated the ups and downs of life from early childhood to their later years. I wanted the themes for the study to come out of their real experiences rather than be imposed from abstract concepts of how we "should" age. I also was hoping to find models for creative ageing whose lives could stand against the negative stereotypes that too often accompany the old. Maggie Kuhn, the founder of the Gray Panther movement, characterized these negative images by saying that the old were erroneously viewed as mindless, useless and sexless. In her mind, a culture driven toward productivity and profit tended to reduce the old to dependent "wrinkled babies." The aim of my project about ageing spirituality was to present a truer image of the potentials for elderhood.

The importance of developing a spirituality for ageing is underscored by the demographics of many nations where populations are graying in ever increasing numbers. In the United States and elsewhere we are being challenged to develop a whole new phase of life that I call elderhood. In the past, life expectancy for the majority of the population would not have extended much beyond sixty. Today by contrast, millions of people can expect to have twenty-five or more years after retirement. For example, ninety-five percent of persons over sixty today in developed nations are in relatively good health. What are they going to do with the rest of their lives? We are on the cusp of a great cultural challenge: how to shape this new period of elderhood in ways that are beneficial to individuals and communities. Christianity and other religions have just begun to address the vocation of elderhood in modern society.

Before we discuss themes for wise ageing, I want to relate spirituality and storytelling, since my study was based on life-review narratives. Learning to investigate one's life history, its problems and promise, becomes a springboard for shaping one's elderhood. The work of retrieving one's past calls for both revision and insight. Revision involves a reinterpretation of past events. These are always subject to new meaning in light of one's current experiences. This reinventing of our stories, this seeing of old patterns in novel ways, means "remythologizing" one's life, building on the past for the sake of the present. The polarity of past and present can be worked on in a variety of ways, including personal journal work, autobiographical groups and other therapeutic modes.

A number of advantages accrue to elders in the storytelling process. There is the possibility of healing memories that, when suppressed or ignored, can lead to rigidity and bitterness. Some other benefits of storytelling among elders are: overcoming isolation by group work, becoming freer to share with others, finding new friends and confidants, and cultivating a sense of community. In the narrative process elders recognize the skills and accomplishments from their past that can be helpful for the future. Storytelling can also aid us to become unstuck from repeating stifling "life tapes." It can teach us the art of empathetic listening.

But what does storytelling have to do with spirituality? All religious traditions sprang from the dreadful and wonderful stories of human existence. Written and oral religious narratives grip us in mind and emotion; they draw us to new thresholds of spiritual transformation. Religions are more significantly immersed in stories than in theological abstractions. The very telling of our stories, especially when we share vulnerabilities, is a spiritual act, a quest for personal meaning at deeper levels. The word "spirituality" derives from "spirit," that longing in us for wider understanding and richer experience which are hallmarks of religiousness. It is important to engender a contemplative environment in storytelling groups; this can be fostered by music and meditation.

The following themes drawn from the stories of creative elders are not expressed in traditional theological language for the most part. I will attempt to make some connections to religious heritages when appropriate, but I hold that the topics discussed are intrinsically religious. To the eyes of faith, life itself, especially in its deeper experiences, is sacred. For the most part, the elders who spoke with me were talking about their spiritual journeys in what we call secular language. It is important to decipher the spiritual meaning in words that are not immediately religious-sounding.

INNER EMPOWERMENT FOR ELDERHOOD

1. Creative elders are able to move beyond negative cultural stereotypes of being old by cultivating their inner resources. There is no one way of tapping into the talents and skills developed over a lifetime, qualities that have become part of one's core personality. But an example may illustrate. An elderly actor noted the importance of keeping one's imagination and emotions alive in late life. Not only did he exemplify this by continuing to perform, but during our interview, his wife

and daughter were rehearsing a play in an adjacent room. The aesthetic and imaginative dimensions of all the arts are akin to the spiritual because they express the deeper longings of the soul for beauty and meaning. We may not sufficiently appreciate how valuable for healthy eldering is participation in art, music, film, crafts, gardening, and many other aesthetic ways of experiencing the beauty and tragedy of life.

Another aspect of cultivating inner resources among creative elders is their ability to discover within a serene self-esteem. They seem less driven by outward norms of personal worth. They speak about having greater self-confidence than when they were younger; they are at ease with a more authentic self. This quality appears to stem from an ability to put aside false expectations of how thing ought to be for them. They have moved beyond embitterment over past disappointments and resentment over a less than ideal present. Reducing false expectations is a core element toward enlightenment in Buddhism, as well as in Christianity's call to simplify and purify one's life. This serene self-esteem is also related to living a less fear-motivated life. I was impressed by the one-hundred-and-six-year-old woman who told me that she faces life with little or no personal fear: "When I wake up each day," she said, "I look at the trees, say a little prayer and I put away fear; the doctors say I'm very peaceful and self-confident." Moving from a fear-driven to a love-motivated life is a goal of both contemporary therapy and all religious traditions.

2. Another mode of cultivating inner resources among enlightened elders is the harvesting of memories. Reminiscences that merely stay in the past, as it were, are not as useful as those that can be explored for the sake of the present and future. In many ways my whole project with elders was a mining of memories. Often these stories of the past entailed hardship and suffering. For example, an elder black woman talked about scenes of racial discrimination towards her share-cropper family in the South. She explained how long it took her to overcome negative feelings towards whites as she went on to become a respected educator. There were many stories of hard beginnings. An American Indian elder described a dramatic journey from alienation and alcoholism to his present state as an altruistic and healing leader in his community.

Built into these tales is a clear spiritual "metanoia" or change of heart. To get a clearer picture of such personal transformation, I inquired into special turning points in life. The variety of such transitional moments was itself fascinating. They could include meeting a particular marriage partner, encountering an illness, or more dramatic episodes such as leaving the priesthood or experiencing a difficult divorce. A striking ex-

.ample of a spiritual turning point was recounted by President Jimmy Carter. A low point in his life came with his first failed attempt to be governor of Georgia. In this traumatic time, his evangelist sister urged him to let go of his ego in order to let God lead him in new ways. Carter remembers this event as a key turning point in his life.

3. Two themes that manifest themselves in the inward development of elders are humor and gratitude. The ability to laugh with and at oneself characterizes these people. Humor and playfulness may be neglected as religious virtues, which tend to be associated with seriousness. An older woman, who became a lay spiritual director in late life, talked about her semi-professional involvements as a clown. She contrasted these experiences to the dire soberness of her early Calvinist upbringing. Moreover, she pointed out how these ventures in playfulness coincided with her new images of God as compassionate, in contrast to those of stern judge learned in childhood. An octogenarian Catholic social justice advocate referred to his wife who used to tell him that he would never grow up. He took this as a partial compliment meaning that his inner child was still alive. Laughter is one of the most distinctive human traits; it can be an act of faith in the face of death and of the tragic events that surround a long life. Humor can protect us from becoming stuck in resentments, and it thus opens us to living with gratitude. A Jewish scholar-rabbi in his nineties told me that he was responsible for the care of a very disabled wife. Yet when this man looked back at a long career, he said: "I am awash in a sea of gratitude." This ability to be thankful, even in pain and loss, is eminently religious, when we recall that Christian eucharist is a thanksgiving prayer inherited from the Hebrew tradition.

4. Another trait for inner empowerment that I found in these elders was a commitment to learning, to keeping their minds alive. Some did this by taking courses, others by reading and discussing, still others through travel-learning adventures with the Elderhostel movement. The medieval Christian tradition at its best saw a close link between the love of learning and the quest to know God. As the mystics of that period tell us, such learning was intimately joined to knowledge and appreciation of nature. Study of Torah in Judaism was so highly regarded that it may explain in part the remarkable contributions that Jews have made to learning and education in the modern world. Maintaining a vibrant mind through education may also be related to preserving relatively good health into later life. Research into longevity is increasingly showing the salutary effects of a lively mind with balanced emotions on physical well-being. Learning among elders is extending itself to the

body-mind relationship. It is significant that modern theology and natural science have focused on the interpenetration of spirit and matter. An example of this is the current development of ecological spirituality in various traditions.

5. Encountering one's own mortality is a crucial aspect of spiritual growth; in elderhood this takes on special ramifications because of particular losses and the proximity of death. The elders I studied have in a sense rehearsed their confrontation with death by dealing with "small deaths" on physical and emotional levels. Some of these people have debilitating chronic diseases; others have experienced heart attacks, strokes, and cancer. I noted a remarkable resiliency among them, an ability to learn from their setbacks and face the future with hope. This is not a pollyannish attitude. These elders know the anxieties and suffering of their physical deficiencies. They also know the "little deaths" of an emotional nature such as unresolved alienation from their children or the long sicknesses and deaths of loved ones. I was somewhat surprised that these elders almost universally did not fear their own deaths. They were concerned about the dying process with its potential loss of mental and physical control, but they did not fear death itself. This was true for those who believed in an afterlife and those who did not. Perhaps a reason for this equanimity about death can be attributed to the achievement of a certain integration of life meaning and experience, that is, a deepening of personal spirituality. Fear and anxiety about death are probably not relieved by mere beliefs, religious or naturalistic. There may be a kind of acceptance of death that is a result of living out the qualities or traits manifested by these elders. Some even saw their deaths as a positive culmination of life. A West Coast woman is not only preparing a liturgy for her funeral; she also wants her friends to have a party after her death to celebrate her life. Our ways of grappling with death go to the core of spirituality. The awareness of our death-proneness is a central element of religious traditions from the cross and the *memento mori* of Christianity to escaping the wheel of birth and death in Buddhism.

OUTWARD EMPOWERMENT FOR ELDERHOOD

Creative elders oppose the ageing stereotype of withdrawal from social involvements. They refuse to be consigned to the periphery of life by the images of being "over the hill" or being "out to pasture." They want to balance the inward aspects of spirituality with its outward responsibilities. The moment of contemplation or enlightenment impels one toward compassion and service as part of the rhythm or polarity of spiritual withdrawal for the sake of re-entry into the world's needs. The following are some themes for outward empowerment revealed by the elders in my study.

1. To develop purposes in elderhood was an often repeated motif for wise ageing. Our culture propagates the image of elders floating blissfully on "golden pond" or of playing leisurely on the outskirts of society, away from its central responsibilities. Such stereotypes render the old as passive and dependent. Another statement from Maggie Kuhn stands against such withdrawal visions: "My aches and pains are less important than my agenda." As I was interviewing this frail lady in her late eighties, one of her younger assistants (Kuhn lived in an intergenerational household) interrupted us to have her review a telegram she was sending to then President Bush on a social issue. To develop purposes or social goals can also be done in quieter ways. An elder in San Francisco, partially blinded by small strokes, finds her purposes in visiting grammar school children to talk about being older; she also campaigns to keep local libraries open when they are threatened by budget-cutting politicians. Another woman in her late eighties has become an ecumenical lay minister in her retirement community. Still another elder continued her human rights activities almost to the day of her death. In pursuing social purposes these elders were frequently responding to a sense of vocation from their Christian or Jewish heritages. They understood that one's religious calling does not end with retirement from a job.

2. Creative elders seem especially able to welcome possibilities, be they gentle or difficult opportunities. An evangelical minister in the Midwest found himself responsible for his wife who suffered from a debilitating muscular disease. As he cared for her and wheeled her chair in public, he went through an inner spiritual transformation that he recorded in a book that inspired others in similar circumstances. An elderly black woman in California was disappointed some years ago with the poor educational opportunities for her own children. To address this situation, she began a rather famous alternative school for children. Upon retirement, a navy admiral started the Center for Defense Information in Washington to act as an independent source of information on political/military activities. He accessed possibilities, building on his military career. He also carried with him a striking change of heart from military patriot to advocate for nonviolence. These examples underline the spiritual lesson of reading the signs of the times in one's own life

and allowing the Spirit to lead one from given circumstances toward further opportunities.

3. Another theme among creative elders is the ability to foster freedom in their lives. Instead of viewing the last phase of life as a restricting of freedom, they look upon it as a period of greater freedom from past problems and for new expression. The freedom from relates more to inward development discussed above, as elders move beyond their bondage to past addictions and to old mental scripts. Freedom for has an outward thrust, as when elders find themselves freer to speak out on issues, overcoming their fears and inhibitions. A classic example of such elder freedom to speak out is the case of a well-known nun who signed a statement in *The New York Times* calling for dialogue among Catholics on abortion. Her action got her in trouble with the Vatican, but she told me that she was no longer afraid to express her conscientious convictions. She discovered in late life a sense of freedom to speak out to what she saw as a closed clerical patriarchy determining important moral issues. In the words of Tillie Olsen, a highly respected writer, such elders were overcoming silences imposed by self, family and cultural milieu. They were taking the risks of freedom in prophetic ways.

4. As elders reach outward, family and friendship assume important roles. When I asked two elderly women who had achieved significant notoriety in their professions what was their most important achievement, both pointed to their families. They spoke of sustaining relationships with their adult children and of their own mentoring roles in the wider family of their students and associates. Later life can be an occasion for healing rifts that occurred in earlier family relations. Others spoke of the role of grandparenting in their families. Although family remains a vital unit for elders, sometimes friendships beyond family members can be even more important. Some older people have lost most family members or they live at a distance from family or they have become alienated from their own kin. For example, studies in recent years document a shocking amount of elder abuse: physical, psychological and financial within families. In such cases, friends can be much more supportive than personal family. The theme of cultivating friendships in later life was very important in my study. This is especially vital for men who tend to make work such a supreme life goal, and who narrow themselves to emotional dependence on a spouse.

5. A number of creative elders have expanded friendship and service through intentional communities. The latter are relatively small groups of people who meet regularly for social and service-oriented goals; sometimes there is a directly religious aspect to these groups. One ex-

ample is a group of women in Chicago who meet in the home of an elderly member to dine, socialize, worship, and plan their involvements for the benefit of shelters for abused women and ministry to women in prisons. The elder host spoke of how meaningful the group is to her, because it fosters an awareness of feminist issues, helps her find a vibrant small community for worship and gives her a sense of valuable outreach in the world. This woman also noted that this intentional community has become more important to her spiritually than routine parish involvement. Another example is a Jesuit Priest in his eighties who works as part of a small social justice advocacy community; the friendships with men and women and the group's enlivening purposes greatly enhance his old age. An older resigned priest in California has formed a mostly Hispanic intentional community that performs home liturgies, offers mutual support to participants, and does outreach services in the region. These intentional communities are particularly significant in our era of isolated elders amid a mass culture driven by commercialism that denigrates close human groupings. Intentional communities may be contemporary ways of reviving traditions pioneered by western religious orders and Buddhist *sanghas*.

6. Many creative elders work against cultural expectations by embracing great human causes. They see their elder vocations as calling for the application of skills and talents to leaving the world better for future generations. We have already mentioned President Carter, who has used his position since losing the White House to resolve international conflicts and contribute to major health improvements in Third World Nations. Carter speaks freely about his motivations connected to gospel values in his Baptist heritage. Eugene Odum, who is referred to as the father of modern ecological studies in academic circles, sees his role in retirement to be that of a preacher of environmental responsibility, as he shifts his writing and speaking style to reach a wider audience. In a similar way, Thomas Berry, the Octogenarian Catholic "Geologist," maintains that a principal task for elders as mentors for future generations is to take up ecological causes. As an old man, Berry has been an inspiring leader for many younger thinkers who are revising or "remythologizing" Christianity in ecological directions. In speaking with these men, I realized how deeply great causes for humanity and for the earth had permeated their spirituality, and I also believe that the heartfelt pursuit of such causes profoundly enriches their later years. I have mentioned some well known names above, but many lesser known elders in my study have attached themselves to causes great and small, far and near.

In concluding these reflections on elder wisdom, I would like to discuss an overall theme of developing a personal spirituality in later life. As I said above, all of the themes elaborated are dimensions of elder spirituality. But I also asked these elders about specific religious traditions in which they were formed. It became clear that these elders are crafting their own spirituality as they age. This means that they are willing to say "yes" and "no" to teachings received from their traditions. I did not find a "cookie-cutter" religiosity in these persons, contrary to the notion that the old simply repeat patterns learned in their churches and synagogues. This point is emphasized in a remark by a late-life woman playwright: "I wish no one had told me about Jesus until I was sixty." The exaggerated comment sums up her personal religious journey from a rule-bound Catholicism of childhood to a more flexible spirituality which seeks wisdom wherever it can be found.

Another aspect of shaping a personal spirituality in elderhood was how images of God or of the divine changed for these older persons over the years. In general, these divine images moved from those of a severe or at least sober father figure with fixed regulations and sanctions mediated through religious institutions to a compassionate entity or spirit that is increasingly shrouded in mystery. It may be that a fuller experience of life with its beauty and its tragedy brings such elderly persons to a more compassionate vision towards the world. Such experience may attune them to the compassionate divine. These elders also report that they have become more tolerant of diversity and ambiguity in religious expressions. When they speak of a greater appreciation of mystery, this does not mean that humans are unable to communicate with God. Rather, it seems to indicate the need for a more contemplative style in relating to the transcendent.

Some elders spoke of the importance of opening contemplative spaces in life, especially from midlife onward. It seems to me that they were calling for a greater place for mysticism in the lives of religious institutions. It is particularly unfortunate that Christian churches neglect the cultivation of contemplative and mystical traditions, western and eastern, for both laity and clergy. These institutions seem satisfied with participation in religious services such as mass or sermon-oriented worship. But Catholic and Protestant churches do not teach people how to meditate, how to use silence contemplatively. Services are filled with sound and motion. They do not help the faithful to develop a meditative life able to experience the spiritual presence of mystery, whether it be called God or Tao. Our typical Christian religiosity of observance and performance is very inadequate for the second half of life which calls for a personalized deepening of spirituality. If our churches focused on educating for deeper prayer, meditation, and contemplation, they would equip people to form their own spirituality, a religiousness that in the last seasons of life would help elders weave the strands of their years into an integrated tapestry.

Index

Achenbaum, W. A., 225
Acts of Meaning (Bruner), 267n
Addams, J., 52,65n
Address, R., 6,223
Adversity, spirituality, 208
Aeschylus, 303,308
African-Americans
   caregiving, 73
   congregations, 106
   religious coping, 51
   social work, 51
   spirituality, 31
   well-being, 17
Aftel, M., 252,265,267n
After Heaven: Spirituality in America
   Since the 1950s (Wuthnow),
   103m
Afterlife, belief in, 30
Agee, J., 254
Aging
   Australia, 17
   caregiving, 155,313
   cohort studies, 41-49
   conscious, 289
   coping theory, 17,135
   dementia care, 301-311
   demographics, 225
   devotional groups, 91
   diversity, 134
   Duke longitudinal study, 19,38n
   elder wisdom, 328
   ethical decisions, 155
   fear of, 189
   feminism, 192
   future research, 28,150
   impressions, 7
   knowledge and practice, 1-9

   life review model, 134
   long-term care, 173-183
   methodology, 29,89,100n
   paradox, 3
   phenomenology, 133
   positive, 108
   prayer and health, 19-21
   religion, 1,15,85
   research, 11,15
   rituals, 223-232
   sacred scenarios, 223-232
   secrets, 15
   self-appropriation, 316
   social work, 4,22,86,173
   spirituality, 85,96,155,173,301,313
   stereotypes, 324
   successful, 32
   theory, 133-136
   transcendence, 97
   triangulation research, 30
   United States, 106
   vital and successful, 7
   see also Older adult
Aging and Biography: Explorations in
   Adult Development (Birren),
   267n
Aging and God: Spiritual Pathways to
   Mental Health in Midlife and
   Later Years (Koenig), 152n
Aging and Spirituality (ASA), 309
Aging and Spirituality (Moberg),
   23,38n
Aging and the Religious Dimension
   (Thomas and Eisenhandler).
   10n
Aging as a Spiritual Journey (Bianchi),
   9n

   331

BOOK ORDER FORM!

Order a copy of this book with this form or online at:
http://www.HaworthPress.com/store/product.asp?sku=5674

Religion, Spirituality, and Aging
A Social Work Perspective

_____ in softbound at $39.95 ISBN-13: 978-0-7890-2499-2 / ISBN-10: 0-7890-2499-3.
_____ in hardbound at $69.95 ISBN-13: 978-0-7890-2498-5 / ISBN-10: 0-7890-2498-5.

COST OF BOOKS _____

POSTAGE & HANDLING _____
US: $4.00 for first book & $1.50
for each additional book
Outside US: $5.00 for first book
& $2.00 for each additional book.

SUBTOTAL _____

In Canada: add 7% GST. _____

STATE TAX _____

CA, IL, IN, MN, NJ, NY, OH, PA & SD residents
please add appropriate local sales tax.

FINAL TOTAL _____

If paying in Canadian funds, convert
using the current exchange rate,
UNESCO coupons welcome.

❑ BILL ME LATER:
Bill-me option is good on US/Canada/
Mexico orders only; not good to jobbers,
wholesalers, or subscription agencies.

❑ Signature _____

❑ Payment Enclosed: $ _____

❑ PLEASE CHARGE TO MY CREDIT CARD:
❑ Visa ❑ MasterCard ❑ AmEx ❑ Discover
❑ Diner's Club ❑ Eurocard ❑ JCB

Account # _____

Exp Date _____

Signature _____
(Prices in US dollars and subject to change without notice.)

PLEASE PRINT ALL INFORMATION OR ATTACH YOUR BUSINESS CARD

Name	
Address	
City	State/Province	Zip/Postal Code
Country	
Tel	Fax
E-Mail	

May we use your e-mail address for confirmations and other types of information? ❑ Yes ❑ No We appreciate receiving
your e-mail address. Haworth would like to e-mail special discount offers to you, as a preferred customer.
We will never share, rent, or exchange your e-mail address. We regard such actions as an invasion of your privacy.

Order from your **local bookstore** or directly from
The Haworth Press, Inc. 10 Alice Street, Binghamton, New York 13904-1580 • USA
Call our toll-free number (1-800-429-6784) / Outside US/Canada: (607) 722-5857
Fax: 1-800-895-0582 / Outside US/Canada: (607) 771-0012
E-mail your order to us: orders@HaworthPress.com

For orders outside US and Canada, you may wish to order through your local
sales representative, distributor, or bookseller.
For information, see http://HaworthPress.com/distributors

(Discounts are available for individual orders in US and Canada only, not booksellers/distributors.)

Please photocopy this form for your personal use.
www.HaworthPress.com

BOF05